HOW MUCH DO YOU REALLY KNOW ABOUT THE FOOD YOU EAT?

What you don't know *can* hurt you! Here's the book that lets you eat your favorite foods and count fat grams too! If you're watching your fat intake you'll find the information you need in the guide that helps you save your health and your shape.

THE CORINNE T. NETZER FAT GRAM COUNTER

THE
CORINNE T. NETZER
FAT GRAM COUNTER

Revised Edition
(formerly *The Fat Content of Food*)

Corinne T. Netzer

A DELL BOOK

Published by
Dell Publishing
a division of
Bantam Doubleday Dell Publishing Group, Inc.
1540 Broadway
New York, New York 10036

ISBN: 0-440-20740-1

Printed in the United States of America

Published simultaneously in Canada

May 1992

10 9 8 7 6 5 4

RAD

THE
CORINNE T. NETZER
FAT GRAM COUNTER

The Fat Content of Food

Fat is not funny—not eating it and not being it. The "jolly" fat man is one big lie: he's laughing in order to keep from crying.

I am not a scientist but a concerned dieter. In this book I'm going to tell you, in the simplest and most direct way I know, why you should cut down on your fat intake and how you can lose weight by doing it.

THE SURGEON GENERAL'S REPORT

In the most far-reaching report on nutrition and health ever prepared by the government, reduction of fat intake was identified as the number-one dietary priority in the country.

The Surgeon General stated, "If you are among the two out of three Americans who do not smoke or drink excessively, your choice of diet can influence your long-term health prospects more than any other action you might take." He went on to say: "Of greatest concern is our excessive intake of dietary fat and its relationship to risk for chronic diseases."

The Surgeon General's report strongly recommends that the consumption of both saturated and unsaturated fats be reduced in the average American's diet.

How do these fats differ? There is a chemical distinction in the structure of each fat molecule; specifically, in the number of hydrogen atoms. When the fat is carrying as many hydrogen atoms as it can hold, it is considered *saturated* with hydrogen. When the fat contains room for more hydrogen, it is called *unsaturated*. Unsaturated fats are further divided into *mono*unsaturated and *poly*unsaturated.

Although there are exceptions, animal fats are generally more saturated than vegetable fats. Another general rule is that saturated fats are usually solid at room temperature, while unsaturated fats are usually liquid at room temperature. Fats can be made more solid by adding hydrogen. That's the difference between soft and stick margarine: the hard stick has had hydrogen added in a process called *hydrogenation*. Although there are exceptions, the more hydrogen added to a fat or oil, the more saturated and firm it becomes.

THE TROUBLE WITH FAT

I doubt if there is a dieter in the United States who isn't aware of the fact that studies indicate saturated fats contribute to cardiovascular disease, particularly heart attacks and stroke. We have been bombarded with the idea that polyunsaturates are "heart-healthful" and saturates (especially animal fats, which contain cholesterol) are unhealthful. Consequently there has been a distinct decline in our consumption of red meats and eggs and an increase in the use of polyunsaturated oils. This is fine as far as it goes—but it doesn't go far enough.

Heart disease is not the only problem to be concerned about when you're eating fat. High-fat diets of *both* saturated and unsaturated fats have been tied to cancer. Studies have linked "fatty" eating to colon/rectal cancers. Former President Reagan's doctors advised him to change his diet to one lower in fat and higher in fiber to reduce his risk of developing a second colon cancer. And there is mounting evidence from international studies that too much fat in the diet leads to increased risk of breast and prostate cancers.

No one knows for certain if fat starts cancer or if it accelerates already existing cancer, but there is a definite link.

Contrary to the studies on heart disease, which point a finger at saturated fats, research indicates that unsaturated fats seem to increase cancer risk even more than saturated fats. (Fish oils may be the rare exception to the rule. Preliminary work indicates a possibility that fish oil may be helpful in lowering the risk of cardiovascular disease and cancer. But these studies are in an early stage and are by no means conclusive.)

Since high-fat diets of both kinds of fat have been linked to disease, the Surgeon General suggests—and most heart and cancer experts agree—that it's best to reduce the amount of *all* fat in the diet.

FAT AND DIETING

Ounce for ounce, spoon for spoon, fat contains more calories than carbohydrates or protein. A gram of fat contains nine calories, while a gram of protein or carbohydrate has only four. Do you think a tablespoon of sugar is fattening? Just compare it to a tablespoon of butter or margarine. The sugar has about 40 calories, the fat a whopping 100! Consider this: An ounce of *any* fat is more fattening than an ounce of pasta or potato—or anything!

So, not only is fat unhealthful, fat is fattening!

The government suggests that since we now eat too much fat, we should reduce our fat to 30 percent of our caloric intake. This means that no more than 30 percent of our calories should come from fat. Such diet gurus as the late Nathan Pritikin suggest a 5 to 10 percent intake. I have found that you can lose weight, feel good, and still not feel denied with an intake of 20 percent fat in relation to total calories.

How do you know how much fat you are having? Simple. This book is a fat-gram counter, and everything you eat is listed with its gram count. Add up the grams of fat that you consume each day and multiply this amount by nine (the number of calories in a fat gram) and you know how many calories of fat you've had.

THE 22-GRAM SOLUTION
(CTN's Low-Fat Weight-Loss Diet)

This diet is designed for you to lose weight while lowering your fat intake. The 22-Gram Solution works for me, it works for all of my friends who have tried it—and it should work for you. The principles are easy to remember and, with a little willpower, very easy to follow. Remember, not only will you be thinner—you'll be eating more healthfully.

This plan is based on a daily intake of 1000 calories, which, for most people, allows maximum weight loss without sacrificing nutrition.

You may have 1000 calories per day. If you don't already own a calorie counter, I suggest you buy one so that you can plan your meals in advance and know, without question, how many calories you're consuming.

Limit yourself to no more than 22.2 total fat grams per day. Use this book to look up each and every thing you eat and drink. You may be below 22.2 grams—in fact, that is to be encouraged—but *never* more than that amount. You may choose your own foods as long as you stay within the limit.

Have at least 1 serving of fruit and 1 serving of vegetables every day. One of the main points of low-fat dieting is to encourage intake of food with complex carbohydrates and fiber. Actually, you'll find yourself willingly adding more fruit and vegetables to your diet because they're low in fat and help you stay within your gram goal. You'll find you're *automatically* eating more nutritiously as well as losing those pounds because you'll be limiting fatty foods.

One of the reasons this diet works so well is the hunger factor. Remember, fat has nine calories a gram while carbohydrates and protein have only four, so when you cut down on fats, you can actually eat more food, be more "filled," and not have that hungry feeling.

Vary the kinds of food you eat. It is not healthful to eat the same exact thing every day. The body needs different kinds of nutrients that can come only from different kinds of foods.

If you don't vary your diet, you won't stay on it, because it will become tiresome. My friend Joy, who had never, *ever,* been able to stick to a diet regimen, was successful with the 22-Gram Solution. She was able to choose from a multitude of foods, and she didn't get bored eating the same cottage cheese and carrot sticks every day. She made a game out of making up her menus—and it worked!

I have found that if you don't vary your choices, the body eventually becomes accustomed to a sameness of input, and after a while, no matter how strict you are, the body "plateaus" (it's happened to all of us on diets) and adjusts to the input, and you stop losing weight.

The beauty of this diet is that the options are yours as long as you stick to the 1000 calories, 22.2 fat grams per day.

Walk half an hour every day (unless you're on a doctor-regulated exercise program). If you already walk, good. If you don't, start. A half hour a day is not a lot to devote to fitness, and walking is not so strenuous that you can find an excuse not to do it. Walk briskly and continuously. Walk to work, walk around the block, walk to lunch, walk around the house if it's raining—but walk. It's good for your diet and it's "heart healthy." And if you're so busy a person that you can't find half an hour in the day, then take two brisk 15-minute tours. Try it, you'll feel better.

The 22-Gram Solution Diet Tips:

• Cut *all* visible fat off meat and poultry.
• Fry nothing (it uses too much oil or fat). Bake, broil, or boil foods, or use nonstick pans.
• Poach fish. Fish has few calories and contains those oils that may be good for you.
• On salads, use lemon with herbs and spices added—it may not taste as good as oil but you will get used to it and it's good for you.
• Steam vegetables and use herbs and spices instead of butter or margarine to "spike" them. Experiment—go to the

store and buy some spices you've never tried before and use them to top your veggies.

• When eating in a restaurant, inquire how things are prepared before you order. If a sauce is included, tell the waiter to leave it off or put it on the side. Restaurants are accustomed to dieters and no longer get upset at such requests.

• Limit your alcohol intake. No, there's no fat here, but it's highly caloric without being nutritious. The same is true of most sweets.

• Finally, consult your doctor before going on this or any other diet.

HOW TO USE THIS BOOK

This book is alphabetized, so there's no index. Simply look up the food you are interested in and you will find its fat-gram content.

Look up everything you eat in a day, add up the fat grams and you will get your total. Again, plan your menus in advance so that the total won't come as an awful surprise after the fact.

If you are following the 22-Gram Solution, you will not go over 22.2 total fat grams per day. However, if losing weight is not your goal, or if you do not want to go below the government-recommended 30 percent of fat in your diet, there is a simple formula for figuring out how many fat grams you should have. Take 30 percent of the calories you consume per day and divide by nine (the number of calories in a fat gram). For instance, if you have 1500 calories per day, 30 percent of 1500 is 450, and 450 divided by nine is 50—and that should be your maximum fat-gram intake.

If your goal is 20 percent fat in your diet, take 20 percent of your caloric intake and divide by nine. If your caloric intake is 1500, 20 percent is 300, which divided by nine is 33.3

No matter what your desired fat percentage is, the equation remains the same—percentage of calories divided by nine. That is how you find your maximum intake permitted, and that is the number you should not go over. And when you use this counter you won't.

MAXIMUM DAILY GRAMS

The following chart, based on a fat intake of 30 percent, has been compiled so that you may quickly see your maximum daily allowable fat. Find the figure closest to your daily caloric intake, and do not go over the corresponding fat grams indicated.

MAXIMUM DAILY FAT INTAKE

Average calories	Maximum fat grams
1000	33.3
1100	36.6
1200	40.0
1300	43.3
1400	46.6
1500	50.0
1600	53.3
1700	56.6
1800	60.0
1900	63.3
2000	66.6
2100	70.0
2200	73.3
2300	76.6
2400	80.0
2500	83.3
2600	86.6
2700	90.0
2800	93.3
2900	96.6
3000	100.0

SOURCES OF DATA

The information contained in this book is based on data obtained from the United States Department of Agriculture and the various producers and processors of brand-name foods.

It contains the most complete and up-to-date fat-gram material ever compiled in book form, and I have included saturated fat counts in all instances where they are obtainable. It is, I feel, easy to use, because you will find all the information you need listed in sensible, common household measures.

As we go to press, this book has the most accurate data available. However, food companies do sometimes change their recipes. If need be, these changes will be dealt with in future editions. In the interim, should a food you're particularly fond of suddenly sport a label reading "new" or "improved," you may wish to write directly to the manufacturer to see if there has been a change in fat content.

Good luck and good dieting!

C.T.N.

Abbreviations and Symbols

approx.	approximately
diam.	diameter
fl.	fluid
gms.	grams
"	inch
lb.	pound
<	less than
*	Prepared according to basic package directions
m.q.	measurable quantity
n.a.	not available
(0)	may contain trace amount
oz.	ounce
pkg.	package
pkt.	packet
qt.	quart
tbsp.	tablespoon
tr.	trace
tsp.	teaspoon
w/	with

food and measure	total fat (gms.)	saturated fat (gms.)
Abalone, raw, meat only, 4 oz.	.9	.2
Acapulco dip *(Ortega),* 1 oz.	0	0
Acerola, trimmed, 1/2 cup	.1	(0)
Acerola juice, fresh, 6 fl. oz.	.5	(0)
Ale, see "Beer, ale, and malt liquor"		
Alfalfa seeds *(Arrowhead Mills),* 1 cup . . .	1.0	n.a.
Alfalfa sprouts, raw, 1/2 cup	.1	< .1
Alfredo sauce:		
canned *(Progresso* Authentic Pasta Sauces), 1/2 cup	30.0	19.0

Alfredo sauce, continued

refrigerated *(Contadina Fresh)*, 6 oz. . . .	53.0	n.a.
mix *(French's Pasta Toss)*, 2 tsp. dry . . .	2.0	n.a.
mix *(Lawry's* Pasta Alfredo), 1 pkg. . . .	13.3	n.a.
Allspice, ground, 1 tsp.	.2	.1
Almond:		
dried, 1 oz., 24 whole kernels.	14.8	1.4
dried, all varieties *(Planters)*, 1 oz.	15.0	2.0
dry roasted, 1 oz.	14.7	1.4
oil roasted, 1 oz., 22 whole kernels	16.4	1.6
toasted, 1 oz.	14.4	1.4
Almond butter:		
raw *(Hain* Natural), 2 tbsp.	18.0	2.0
blanched, toasted *(Hain)*, 2 tbsp.	19.0	2.0
honey and cinnamon, 1 tbsp.	8.4	.8
Almond meal, partially defatted, 1 oz. . . .	5.2	.5
Almond paste, 1 oz.	7.2	.7
Amaranth, boiled, drained, 1/2 cup	.1	< .1
Amaranth, whole grain, 1 cup	12.7	3.2
Amaranth dinner, canned, w/garden vegetables *(Health Valley Fast Menu)*, 7.5 oz. . . .	3.0	n.a.
Amaranth seed *(Arrowhead Mills)*, 2 oz. . . .	3.0	n.a.
Anchovy, canned, in oil, 5 medium, .7 oz.	1.9	.4
Anise seed, 1 tsp.	.3	n.a.
Apple:		
fresh, w/skin, 1 medium, 2 3/4" diam. . . .	.5	.1
fresh, peeled, sliced, 1/2 cup	.2	< .1
canned, sliced, sweetened, unheated, 1/2 cup	.5	.1
dried, sulfured, uncooked, 1/2 cup	.1	< .1
Apple, escalloped, frozen *(Stouffer's)*, 4 oz.	2.0	n.a.
Apple, glazed, frozen, in raspberry sauce *(The Budget Gourmet* Side Dish), 5 oz.	3.0	n.a.
Apple butter, all varieties *(Smuckers)*, 1 tbsp.	0	0
Apple cobbler:		
deep dish *(Awrey's)*, 1/8 pie	14.0	3.0
frozen *(Pet-Ritz)*, 1/6 pkg.	9.0	n.a.
frozen *(Stilwell)*, 4 oz.	4.0	n.a.

Apple crisp, frozen *(Weight Watchers),*
3.5 oz. . . . . 5.0   < 1.0
Apple danish, 1 piece, except as noted:
  (Awrey's Miniature), 1.7 oz. 8.0   2.0
  (Awrey's Round), 2.75 oz. 14.0   3.0
  (Awrey's Square), 3 oz. 8.0   2.0
  fried *(Hostess Breakfast Bake Shop)* . . . 22.0   10.0
  frozen *(Pepperidge Farm)* . . . . 8.0   n.a.
  frozen *(Sara Lee* Individual), 1.3 oz. . . . 6.0   n.a.
  frozen *(Sara Lee Free & Light),* 1/8 pkg. 0   0
  frozen, twist *(Sara Lee),* 1/8 pkg. . . . . . 10.0   n.a.
Apple drink or juice, all blends, 6 fl. oz. . . < .1   (0)
Apple dumpling, frozen *(Pepperidge Farm),*
3 oz. . . . . 13.0   n.a.
Apple fritter, frozen *(Mrs. Paul's),* 2 pieces 9.0   n.a.
Apple sticks, frozen, breaded *(Farm Rich),*
4 oz. . . . . 8.0   n.a.
Apple turnover:
  frozen *(Pepperidge Farm),* 1 piece . . . . 17.0   n.a.
  refrigerated *(Pillsbury),* 1 piece 8.0   2.0
Applesauce, canned, all blends . . . . <.5   (0)
Apricot:
  fresh, 3 medium, about 12 per lb. 4   < .1
  fresh, halves, 1/2 cup 3   < .1
  canned or frozen (all brands), 1/2 cup . . < .3   < .1
  dried, sulfured, cooked, 1/2 cup 2   < .1
Apricot nectar, canned, 6 fl. oz. 2   tr.
Arby's:
  sandwiches, 1 serving:
    beef 'n cheddar, 7 oz. 26.8   7.6
    chicken breast, 6.5 oz. 25.0   5.1
    ham 'n cheese, 5.5 oz. 13.7   4.7
    roast beef, regular, 5.2 oz. 14.8   7.3
    roast beef, super, 8.3 oz. 22.1   8.5
    roast chicken club, 8.3 oz. 33.0   8.0
    turkey deluxe, 7 oz. 16.6   4.1
  french fries, 2.5 oz. 13.2   3.0
  potato cakes, 3 oz. 12.0   2.2
  shake, Jamocha, 11.5 oz. 10.5   2.5
Arrowhead, fresh, 1 medium corm,
2 5/8″ diam. . . . . < .1   (0)

Arrowroot, powdered *(Tone's)*, 1 tsp. 0   0
Arthur Treacher's:

chicken, 2 patties, 4.8 oz.	21.6	3.5
chicken sandwich, 5.5 oz.	19.2	2.8
chips, 4 oz.	13.2	2.3
cod tail shape, bake 'n broil, 5 oz.	14.2	n.a.
coleslaw, 3 oz.	8.2	1.1
fish, 2 pieces, 5.2 oz.	19.8	2.8
fish sandwich, 5.5 oz.	24.0	4.2
Krunch Pup, 2-oz. piece	14.8	3.7
Lemon Luv, 3-oz. piece	13.9	2.2
shrimp, 7 pieces, 4.1 oz.	24.4	3.3

Artichoke, globe:

fresh, raw or boiled, 1 medium, 11.3 oz.	.2	< .1
fresh, hearts, boiled, drained, 1/2 cup . . .	.1	< .1
hearts, canned, marinated *(S&W)*, 3.5 oz.	26.0	n.a.
hearts, frozen, boiled, drained, 4 oz. . . .	.6	.1

Artichoke, Jerusalem, see "Jerusalem
artichoke"
Arugula *(Frieda* of California), 1 oz. . . . . < .1   (0)
Asparagus:

fresh, raw, cuts and spears, 1/2 cup	.2	< .1
fresh, boiled, drained, 4 medium spears	.2	< .1
fresh, boiled, drained, cuts and spears,		
1/2 cup	.3	.1
canned or frozen (all brands), 1/2 cup . .	< .4	.1

Asparagus pilaf, frozen *(Green Giant*
Microwave Garden Gourmet), 1 pkg. . . 4.0   2.0
Au jus gravy:

canned *(Franco-American)*, 2 oz.	0	0
canned *(Heinz* HomeStyle), 2 oz. or		
1/4 cup	1.0	n.a.
mix* *(French's)*, 1/4 cup	0	0
mix* *(Lawry's)*, 1 cup	1.6	n.a.
mix* *(McCormick/Schilling)*, 1/4 cup . . .	.3	(0)

Avocado, fresh:

California, 1 medium, 8 oz.	30.0	4.5
California, pureed, 1/2 cup	19.9	3.0
Florida, 1 medium, 1 lb.	27.0	5.3
Florida, pureed, 1/2 cup	10.2	2.0

Avocado dip *(Kraft)*, 2 tbsp. 4.0   2.0

B

food and measure	total fat (gms.)	saturated fat (gms.)
Bacon, cooked:		
3 slices, 20 slices per lb.	9.4	3.3
(Oscar Mayer), 1 slice	2.8	1.2
(Oscar Mayer Center Cut), 1 slice	1.8	.8
(Oscar Mayer Thick Sliced, 1 lb.), 1 slice	4.8	1.9
Bacon, Canadian-style:		
unheated, 1-oz. slice	2.0	.6
grilled, 2 slices, 6 per 6-oz. pkg.	3.9	1.3
(Hormel Sliced), 1 oz.	2.0	n.a.
(Light & Lean), 2 slices	1.0	n.a.

Bacon, Canadian-style, continued
(Oscar Mayer), .8-oz. slice	1.0	.3
Bacon, substitute, cooked:		
beef *(JM)*, 2 slices	7.0	n.a.
beef *(Sizzlean)*, 2 strips	5.0	n.a.
pork *(Sizzlean)*, 2 strips	8.0	n.a.
pork, brown sugar–cured *(Sizzlean)*,		
2 strips	9.0	n.a.
turkey *(Louis Rich)*, 1 slice	2.4	.7
"Bacon," vegetarian, frozen:		
(Morningstar Farms Breakfast Strips),		
3 strips	6.0	1.0
(Worthington Stripples), 4 strips	9.0	1.0
Bacon bits, real or imitation:		
(Bac*Os), 2 tsp.	1.0	n.a.
(Hormel), 1 tbsp.	2.0	n.a.
(Libby's Bacon Crumbles), 1 tbsp.	1.0	n.a.
(McCormick/Schilling Bac'N Pieces),		
1/4 tsp.	.1	(0)
(Oscar Mayer), 1/4 oz.	1.0	.3
Bacon and horseradish dip:		
(Breakstone's/Sealtest), 2 tbsp.	6.0	3.0
(Kraft/Kraft Premium), 2 tbsp.	5.0	3.0
Bacon and onion dip:		
(Breakstone's Gourmet), 2 tbsp.	6.0	3.0
(Kraft Premium), 2 tbsp.	5.0	3.0
Bagel, frozen, 1 piece:		
all varieties:		
(Lender's Bagelettes), .9 oz.	< 1.0	n.a.
except oat bran and soft *(Lender's)*	1.0	n.a.
except cinnamon raisin and egg *(Sara*		
Lee), 2.5 oz.	1.0	n.a.
plain, garlic, or onion *(Lender's Big'n*		
Crusty)	1.0	n.a.
plain *(Sara Lee)*, 3.1 oz.	1.0	n.a.
cinnamon'n raisin *(Lender's Big'n Crusty)*	2.0	n.a.
cinnamon raisin *(Sara Lee)*, 2.5 oz.	2.0	n.a.
cinnamon raisin, egg, or sesame seed		
(Sara Lee), 3.1 oz.	2.0	n.a.
egg *(Lender's Big'n Crusty)*	2.0	n.a.
egg *(Sara Lee)*, 2.5 oz.	2.0	n.a.

oat bran *(Lender's)*	2.0	n.a.
onion or poppy seed *(Sara Lee)*, 3.1 oz.	1.0	n.a.
soft *(Lender's)*	3.0	n.a.
Baked beans, see "Beans, baked"		
Baking powder or soda, all varieties	0	0
Balsam pear, leafy tips or pods, boiled,		
1/2 cup	.1	(0)
Bamboo shoots:		
fresh, raw, sliced, 1/2 cup	.2	.1
fresh, boiled, drained, sliced, 1/2 cup	.1	< .1
canned, drained, 1/8" slices, 1/2 cup	.3	.1
canned *(La Choy)*, 1.5 oz.	.2	n.a.
Banana (see also "Plantain"):		
fresh, 1 medium, 83/4" × 113/32"	.6	< .1
fresh, mashed, 1/2 cup	.5	< .1
Banana, red, fresh, 1 medium, 71/4" long	.3	n.a.
Banana nectar *(Libby's)*, 6 fl. oz.	0	0
Barbecue loaf *(Oscar Mayer)*, 1-oz. slice	2.3	1.0
Barbecue sauce:		
(Hunt Original), 1 tbsp.	0	0
all varieties:		
(Enrico's), 1 tbsp.	1.0	n.a.
(Kraft Thick'N Spicy), 2 tbsp.	1.0	0
(Heinz/Heinz Thick and Rich), 1 tbsp.	< .2	(0)
(Maull's), 1 tbsp.	< 1.0	n.a.
(Ott's), 1 tbsp.	.1	n.a.
except garlic *(Kraft)*, 2 tbsp.	1.0	0
Cajun style *(Golden Dipt)*, 1 fl. oz.	8.0	1.0
Dijon and honey *(Lawry's)*, 1/4 cup	1.2	n.a.
garlic *(Kraft)*, 2 tbsp.	0	0
honey *(Hain)*, 1 tbsp.	1.0	n.a.
mild or smoky *(French's Cattleman's)*,		
1 tbsp.	0	0
w/orange juice *(Lawry's* California Grill),		
1/4 cup	.7	n.a.
Oriental *(La Choy)*, 1 tbsp.	< .1	tr.
sloppy Joe w/beef *(Libby's)*, 1/3 cup	7.0	n.a.
Barley, pearled:		
raw, 1 cup	2.3	.9
cooked, 1 cup	.7	.1
Basil, dried, ground, 1 tsp.	.1	(0)

Baskin-Robbins, 1 regular scoop, except as
noted:

ice, daiquiri	0	0
ice cream:		
almond fudge, *Jamoca*	14.0	n.a.
chocolate, regular or *World Class* . . .	14.0	n.a.
chocolate chip	15.0	n.a.
chocolate raspberry truffle,		
International Creams	17.0	n.a.
pralines'n cream	14.0	n.a.
rocky road	14.0	n.a.
strawberry	10.0	n.a.
vanilla	14.0	n.a.
vanilla, French	18.0	n.a.
sherbet, rainbow	2.0	n.a.
sorbet, raspberry, red	0	0
sugar cone, 1 cone	1.0	n.a.
waffle cone, 1 cone	2.0	n.a.
Bass (see also "Sea bass"), meat only:		
freshwater, raw, 4 oz.	4.2	.9
striped, raw, 4 oz.	2.6	.6
Batter mix *(Golden Dipt),* 1 oz.	0	0
Bay leaf, dried, crumbled, 1 tsp.	< .1	tr.
Bean curd, see "Tofu"		
Bean dip, hot or Mexican *(Hain),* 4 tbsp.	1.0	n.a.
Bean mix* (see also specific listings):		
Cajun, and sauce *(Lipton),* 1/2 cup	3.0	n.a.
chicken, and sauce *(Lipton),* 1/2 cup . . .	4.0	n.a.
Bean salad, canned, 1/2 cup:		
four bean *(Joan of Arc/Read)*	1.0	n.a.
green bean, German-style *(Joan of Arc/ Read)*	3.5	n.a.
three bean *(Green Giant)*	< 1.0	0
three bean *(Joan of Arc/Read)*	0	0
Bean sprouts:		
kidney, mature seeds, raw, 1/2 cup	.5	.1
kidney, mature seeds, boiled, drained, 4 oz.	.7	.1
mung, raw, boiled, or stir-fried, 1/2 cup	.1	< .1
mung, canned, drained, 1/2 cup	< .1	< .1
navy, mature seeds, raw, 1/2 cup	.4	< .1

navy, mature seeds, boiled, drained, 4 oz.	.9	.1
pinto, mature seeds, raw, 1 oz.	.3	< .1
pinto, mature seeds, boiled, drained, 4 oz.	.4	< .1
soy, mature seeds, raw, 1/2 cup	2.3	.3
soy, mature seeds, steamed, 1/2 cup	2.1	.2
canned, drained *(La Choy)*, 2 oz.	.1	(0)
Beans, adzuki:		
boiled, 4 oz. or 1/2 cup	.1	tr.
canned, sweetened, 4 oz. or 1/2 cup	< .1	(0)
Beans, baked, canned (see also specific		
listings):		
(Allens), 1/2 cup	6.0	n.a.
(Allens Vegetarian), 1/2 cup	1.0	n.a.
(B&M Hot N Spicy/Vegetarian), 8 oz.	3.0	n.a.
(Campbell's Home Style), 8 oz.	4.0	n.a.
(Campbell's Vegetarian), 7.75 oz.	1.0	n.a.
(Grandma Brown's), 1 cup	3.0	n.a.
(Grandma Brown's Saucepan), 1 cup	4.8	n.a.
(S&W Brick Oven), 1/2 cup	2.0	n.a.
(Van Camp's), 1 cup	2.0	n.a.
(Van Camp's Deluxe), 1 cup	4.0	n.a.
(Van Camp's Vegetarian Style), 1 cup	.6	n.a.
barbecue *(B&M)*, 8 oz.	6.0	n.a.
barbecue *(Campbell's)*, 77/8 oz.	4.0	n.a.
w/beef, 1/2 cup	4.6	2.3
Boston *(Health Valley)*, 4 oz.	1.0	n.a.
brown sugar *(Van Camp's)*, 1 cup	5.1	n.a.
w/franks, 1/2 cup	8.4	3.0
w/franks *(Van Camp's Beanee Weenee)*,		
1 cup	15.4	5.0
honey *(B&M)*, 8 oz.	2.0	n.a.
hot chili *(Campbell's)*, 7.75 oz.	4.0	n.a.
maple *(B&M/Friends)*, 8 oz.	2.0	1.0
w/miso *(Health Valley* Vegetarian), 4 oz.	1.0	n.a.
in molasses and brown sugar sauce		
(Campbell's Old Fashioned), 8 oz.	3.0	n.a.
pea *(B&M)*, 8 oz.	6.0	n.a.
pea, small *(Friends)*, 8 oz.	4.0	3.0
plain or vegetarian, 1/2 cup	.6	.1
w/pork, 1/2 cup	2.0	.8
w/pork *(Hormel Micro-Cup)*, 7.5 oz. . . .	5.0	n.a.

Beans, baked, canned, continued

w/pork *(Hunt's)*, 4 oz.	1.0	n.a.
w/pork *(S&W)*, 1/2 cup	2.0	n.a.
w/pork *(Van Camp's)*, 1 cup	1.9	1.0
w/pork, all varieties *(Allens)*, 1/2 cup	1.0	n.a.
w/pork, in sweet sauce, 1/2 cup	1.8	.7
w/pork, in tomato sauce, 1/2 cup	1.3	.5
w/pork, in tomato sauce *(Campbell's)*, 8 oz.	3.0	n.a.
w/pork, in tomato sauce *(Green Giant)*, 1/2 cup	1.0	n.a.
tomato *(B&M)*, 8 oz.	3.0	1.0
western style *(Van Camp's)*, 1 cup	3.8	n.a.
Beans, black, boiled, 1/2 cup	.5	.1
Beans, black turtle soup, canned, w/liquid, 4 oz.	.3	.1
Beans, broad:		
boiled, drained, 4 oz.	.6	.2
canned, mature, w/liquid, 1/2 cup	.3	< .1
dried, mature, boiled, 1/2 cup	.3	.1
Beans, chili, canned:		
(Hunt's), 4 oz.	0	0
(S&W), 1/2 cup	1.0	n.a.
caliente style *(Green Giant)*, 1/2 cup	1.0	n.a.
in chili gravy *(Dennison's)*, 7.5 oz.	1.0	n.a.
hot or Mexican style *(Allens)*, 1/2 cup	< 1.0	n.a.
Mexican style *(Van Camp's)*, 1 cup	2.4	n.a.
in sauce *(Hormel)*, 5 oz.	3.0	n.a.
spiced *(Gebhardt)*, 4 oz.	1.1	.1
Beans, cranberry, boiled or canned, 1/2 cup	.4	.1
Beans, fava, canned *(Progresso)*, 1/2 cup	< 1.0	n.a.
Beans, great northern:		
boiled, 1/2 cup	.4	.1
canned, w/liquid, 1/2 cup	.5	.2
canned, w/pork *(Luck's)*, 7.25 oz.	5.0	n.a.
Beans, green:		
fresh, raw, canned, or frozen, 1/2 cup	.1	< .1
fresh, boiled, drained, 1/2 cup	.2	< .1
canned, seasoned, w/liquid, 1/2 cup	.2	.1
canned, w/shelled beans and pork *(Luck's)*, 8 oz.	8.0	n.a.

canned, w/potatoes and mushrooms, in
sauce *(Green Giant Pantry Express),*
1/2 cup . . . . 2.0 < 1.0
frozen, in butter sauce *(Green Giant),*
1/2 cup . . . . 1.0 < 1.0
frozen, in butter sauce *(Green Giant* One
Serving), 5.5 oz. 2.0 1.0

Beans, green, combinations, frozen:
Bavarian, w/spaetzle, in sauce *(Birds Eye
International),* 3.3 oz. . . . . 5.0 n.a.
French, w/toasted almonds *(Birds Eye
Combinations),* 3 oz. . . . . 2.0 n.a.
and mushroom, creamy *(Green Giant
Garden Gourmet),* 1 pkg. 11.0 6.0
mushroom casserole *(Stouffer's),* 4.75 oz. 11.0 n.a.

Beans, hyacinth:
fresh, boiled, drained, 1/2 cup . . . . . . .1 .1
dried, boiled, 1/2 cup . . . . .6 n.a.

Beans, kidney:
red, dark or light, boiled or canned,
1/2 cup . . . . .4 .1
red, canned, baked *(B&M),* 8 oz. . . . . 7.0 n.a.
red, canned, baked *(Friends),* 8 oz. . . . 4.0 2.0
white, canned *(Progresso* cannellini), 8 oz. 1.0 (0)

Beans, lima:
fresh, boiled, drained, or frozen, 1/2 cup .3 .1
canned, w/liquid, 1/2 cup . . . . .4 .1
canned, w/ham *(Dennison's),* 7.5 oz. . . . 7.0 n.a.
canned, w/pork *(Luck's),* 7.5 oz. . . . . . 7.0 n.a.
frozen, in butter sauce *(Green Giant),*
1/2 cup . . . . 2.0 < 1.0
frozen, in butter sauce *(Stokely Singles),*
4 oz. . . . . 2.0 n.a.

Beans, lima, mature:
dry, baby, boiled, 1/2 cup . . . . .3 .1
dry, large, boiled, 1/2 cup . . . . .4 .1
canned, w/liquid, 1/2 cup . . . . .2 < .1
Beans, mung, boiled, 1/2 cup . . . . .4 .1
Beans, mungo, boiled, 1/2 cup . . . . .5 < .1
Beans, navy:
boiled, 1/2 cup . . . . .5 .1

Beans, navy, continued

canned, w/liquid, 1/2 cup	.6	.1
Beans, October, canned, w/pork *(Luck's)*, 7.25 oz.	6.0	n.a.
Beans, pink, boiled, 1/2 cup	.4	.1
Beans, pinto:		
boiled or canned, w/liquid, 1/2 cup	.4	.1
canned, baked style, w/pork *(Luck's)*, 7.5 oz.	6.0	n.a.
canned, baked style, and great northern, w/pork *(Luck's)*, 7.25 oz.	5.0	n.a.
canned, picante style *(Green Giant)*, 1/2 cup	1.0	n.a.
frozen, boiled, drained, 4 oz.	.5	.1
Beans, red, canned:		
(Allens), 1/2 cup	< 1.0	tr.
(Green Giant), 1/2 cup	1.0	tr.
(Van Camp's), 1 cup	.6	tr.
small *(Hunt's)*, 4 oz.	0	0
small, baked style *(B&M)*, 8 oz.	5.0	2.0
Beans, refried, canned, except as noted:		
1/2 cup	1.4	.5
(Bearitos Organic), 1 oz.	.5	n.a.
(Del Monte), 1/2 cup	2.0	n.a.
(Gebhardt), 4 oz.	2.0	n.a.
all varieties *(Rosarita)*, 4 oz.	2.0	n.a.
w/cheese *(Old El Paso)*, 1/4 cup	1.0	1.0
jalapeño *(Gebhardt)*, 4 oz.	2.0	n.a.
plain or w/green chilies *(Old El Paso)*, 1/4 cup	< 1.0	n.a.
w/sausage *(Old El Paso)*, 1/4 cup	8.0	n.a.
spicy *(Bearitos* Organic), 1 oz.	.6	n.a.
spicy *(Del Monte)*, 1/2 cup	2.0	n.a.
spicy *(Old El Paso)*, 1/4 cup	1.0	0
vegetarian *(Old El Paso)*, 1/4 cup	1.0	n.a.
mix*, w/butter *(Fantastic Foods)*, 1/2 cup	8.0	n.a.
Beans, shellie, canned, w/liquid, 1/2 cup	.2	< .1
Beans, wax, see "Beans, green"		
Beans, white:		
boiled, 1/2 cup	.3	.1
boiled, small, 1/2 cup	.6	.1

canned, w/liquid, 1/2 cup	.4	.1
Beans, winged:		
fresh, raw or boiled, drained, 1/2 cup . . .	.2	.1
dried, boiled, 1/2 cup	5.0	.7
leaves or tuber, trimmed, 1 oz.	.3	.1
Beans, yardlong:		
fresh, boiled, drained, sliced, 1/2 cup . . .	.1	< .1
dried, boiled, 1/2 cup	.4	.1
Beans, yellow, dried, boiled, 1/2 cup	1.0	.2
Beans, yellow eye, canned, baked *(B&M)*, 8 oz.	7:0	n.a.
Beans and frankfurter dinner, frozen:		
(Banquet), 10 oz.	25.0	n.a.
(Morton), 10 oz.	13.0	n.a.
(Swanson), 10.5 oz.	19.0	n.a.
Béarnaise sauce:		
(Great Impressions), 2 tbsp.	21.0	n.a.
mix, dry, .9-oz. pkt.	2.2	.3
Beechnut, dried, shelled, 1 oz.	14.2	1.6
Beef [1]**,** choice grade, boneless, 4 oz.:		
brisket, whole, all grades, lean w/fat, braised	35.8	14.0
brisket, whole, all grades, lean only, braised	14.5	5.2
chuck:		
arm pot roast, lean w/fat, braised . . .	29.2	11.5
arm pot roast, lean only, braised	10.5	3.8
blade roast, lean w/fat, braised	31.5	12.6
blade roast, lean only, braised	16.3	6.3
flank, trimmed to 0" fat:		
lean w/fat, braised	18.6	7.8
lean w/fat, broiled	14.2	6.0
lean only, braised	14.7	6.3
lean only, broiled	11.5	4.9
ground:		
extra lean, broiled, medium	18.5	7.3
extra lean, pan-fried, medium	18.6	7.3
lean, broiled, medium	20.9	8.2
lean, pan-fried, medium	21.6	8.5

---

[1] *Retail cut, trimmed to 1/4" fat before cooking, except as noted*

Beef, ground, continued

regular, broiled, medium	23.5	9.2
regular, pan-fried, medium	25.6	1.0
ground, frozen patties, broiled, medium	22.3	8.8
porterhouse steak, lean w/fat, broiled	25.1	10.1
porterhouse steak, lean only, broiled	12.2	4.9
rib, whole (ribs 6–12):		
lean w/fat, broiled	33.5	13.6
lean w/fat, roasted	35.4	14.3
lean only, broiled	15.7	6.4
lean only, roasted	15.9	6.4
rib, large end (ribs 6–9):		
lean w/fat, broiled	34.9	14.2
lean w/fat, roasted	36.2	14.6
lean only, broiled	16.6	6.8
lean only, roasted	16.7	6.7
rib, shortrib, lean w/fat, braised	47.6	20.2
rib, shortrib, lean only, braised	20.6	8.7
rib, small end (ribs 10–12):		
lean w/fat, broiled	31.3	12.7
lean w/fat, roasted	34.3	13.8
lean only, broiled	14.3	5.8
lean only, roasted	14.8	5.9
rib eye, small end (ribs 10–12):		
lean w/fat, broiled	25.2	10.2
lean only, broiled	13.3	5.4
round:		
full cut, lean w/fat, broiled	15.4	5.9
full cut, lean only, broiled	8.3	2.9
bottom, lean w/fat, braised	20.3	7.6
bottom, lean w/fat, roasted	10.2	3.5
bottom, lean only, braised	10.7	3.6
botton, lean only, roasted	9.4	3.2
eye of, lean w/fat, roasted	16.0	6.2
eye of, lean only, roasted	6.5	2.3
tip, lean w/fat, roasted	16.9	6.4
tip, lean only, roasted	8.3	2.9
top, lean w/fat, braised	14.6	5.5
top, lean w/fat, broiled	12.0	4.5
top, lean only, braised	7.4	2.5
top, lean only, broiled	6.7	2.3

shank crosscuts, lean w/fat, simmered . .	16.6	6.5
shank crosscuts, lean only, simmered . . .	7.2	2.6
sirloin, top, lean w/fat, broiled	19.0	7.6
sirloin, top, lean only, broiled	9.1	3.5
T-bone steak, lean w/fat, broiled	24.0	9.7
T-bone steak, lean only, broiled	11.8	4.7
tenderloin:		
lean w/fat, broiled	24.8	9.7
lean w/fat, roasted	29.9	11.8
lean only, broiled	12.7	4.8
lean only, roasted	14.2	5.4
top loin (short loin), lean w/fat, broiled	23.8	9.4
top loin (short loin), lean only, broiled. .	11.5	4.4
Beef, corned:		
(*Eckrich* Slender Sliced), 1 oz.	1.0	n.a.
(*Healthy Deli*), 1 oz.	1.0	n.a.
(*Hillshire Farm*), 1 oz.	.4	n.a.
(*Oscar Mayer*), .6-oz. slice	.3	.2
brisket, cured, cooked, 4 oz.	21.5	7.2
loaf, jellied, 1-oz. slice	1.9	.8
canned, 1 oz.	4.2	1.8
canned (*Libby's*, 12 oz.), 2.4 oz.	9.0	n.a.
Beef, corned, hash, canned:		
(*Dinty Moore*), 2 oz.	8.0	n.a.
(*Libby's*, 15 oz.), 7.5 oz.	27.0	n.a.
(*Mary Kitchen*, 15 oz.), 7.5 oz.	24.0	n.a.
Beef, corned, spread (*Hormel*), 1/2 oz. . . .	3.0	n.a.
Beef, dried, cured, 1 oz.	1.1	.5
Beef, roast, see "Beef" and "Beef luncheon meat"		
Beef, roast, hash:		
canned (*Mary Kitchen*), 7.5 oz.	22.0	n.a.
frozen (*Stouffer's*), 10 oz.	22.0	n.a.
Beef, roast, spread, canned:		
(*Hormel*), 1/2 oz.	2.0	n.a.
(*Underwood* Light), 2 1/8 oz.	6.0	2.0
plain or mesquite smoke (*Underwood*), 2 1/8 oz.	11.0	5.0
"Beef," vegetarian, canned:		
slices (*Worthington* Savory Slices), 2 slices	6.0	n.a.

"Beef," vegetarian, canned, continued

steak *(Worthington Prime Stakes),* 3.25 oz.	10.0	n.a.
steak *(Worthington Vegetable Steaks),* 3.2 oz.	2.0	n.a.
stew *(Worthington* Country Stew), 9.5 oz.	10.0	1.0

"Beef," vegetarian, frozen:

(Worthington Stakelets), 2.5-oz. piece . . .	8.0	1.0
corned, slices *(Worthington),* 4 slices . . .	6.0	1.0
corned, roll *(Worthington),* 2.5 oz.	7.0	1.0
pie *(Worthington),* 8-oz. pie	16.0	n.a.
roll *(Worthington),* 2.5 oz.	6.0	n.a.
roll, smoked *(Worthington),* 2 oz.	6.0	n.a.

Beef dinner, frozen:

(Banquet Extra Helpings), 16 oz.	61.0	n.a.
(Swanson), 11.25 oz.	6.0	n.a.
in barbecue sauce *(Swanson),* 11 oz. . . .	17.0	n.a.
chopped *(Banquet),* 11 oz.	32.0	n.a.
chopped steak *(Swanson Hungry-Man),* 16.75 oz.	37.0	n.a.
Mexicana *(The Budget Gourmet),* 12.8 oz.	23.0	n.a.
patty, charbroiled *(Freezer Queen),* 10 oz.	17.0	n.a.
pepper steak *(Armour Classics Lite),* 11.25 oz.	4.0	n.a.
pepper steak *(Healthy Choice),* 11 oz. . .	6.0	3.0
pepper steak *(Le Menu),* 11.5 oz.	13.0	n.a.
pot roast, see "Pot roast dinner"		
Salisbury steak, see "Salisbury steak dinner"		
short ribs, boneless *(Armour Classics),* 9.75 oz.	16.0	n.a.
sirloin, chopped *(Le Menu),* 12.25 oz. . .	24.0	n.a.
sirloin, chopped *(Swanson),* 10.75 oz. . .	16.0	n.a.
sirloin, roast *(Armour Classics),* 10.45 oz.	4.0	n.a.
sirloin tips:		
(Armour Classics), 10.25 oz.	7.0	n.a.
(Healthy Choice), 11.75 oz.	6.0	3.0
(Le Menu), 11.5 oz.	18.0	n.a.
w/Burgundy sauce *(The Budget Gourmet),* 11 oz.	11.0	n.a.
sliced *(Morton),* 10 oz.	5.0	n.a.

sliced *(Swanson Hungry-Man)*, 15.25 oz.	12.0	n.a.
sliced, gravy and *(Freezer Queen)*, 10 oz.	7.0	n.a.
steak Diane *(Armour Classics Lite)*, 10 oz.	9.0	n.a.
Stroganoff *(Armour Classics Lite)*, 11.25 oz.	6.0	n.a.
Stroganoff *(Le Menu)*, 10 oz.	24.0	n.a.
Swiss steak *(The Budget Gourmet)*, 11.2 oz.	22.0	n.a.
Swiss steak *(Swanson)*, 10 oz.	11.0	n.a.
Beef entrée, canned:		
chow mein *(La Choy Bi-Pack)*, 3/4 cup	1.0	n.a.
pepper Oriental *(La Choy Bi-Pack)*, 3/4 cup	2.0	n.a.
stew *(Dinty Moore, 24 oz.)*, 8 oz.	12.0	n.a.
stew *(Estee)*, 7.5 oz.	11.0	5.0
stew *(Hormel/Dinty Moore Micro-Cup)*, 7.5 oz.	9.0	n.a.
stew *(Libby's, 15 oz.)*, 7.5 oz.	5.0	n.a.
stew *(Nalley's Big Chunk)*, 7.5 oz.	7.0	n.a.
stew *(Nalley's Homestyle)*, 8 oz.	5.0	n.a.
stew *(Wolf Brand)*, 7.5 oz.	7.5	n.a.
Beef entrée, frozen:		
(Banquet Platters), 10 oz.	34.0	n.a.
and broccoli *(La Choy Fresh & Lite)*, 11 oz.	5.0	n.a.
Burgundy *(Le Menu)*, 7.5 oz.	23.0	n.a.
casserole *(Pillsbury Microwave Classic)*, 1 pkg.	25.0	n.a.
champignon *(Tyson Gourmet Selection)*, 10.5 oz.	15.0	n.a.
cheeseburger *(MicroMagic)*, 4.75 oz.	25.0	n.a.
chop suey, w/rice *(Stouffer's)*, 12 oz.	9.0	n.a.
creamed, chipped:		
(Banquet Cookin' Bags), 4 oz.	4.0	n.a.
(Freezer Queen Cook-In-Pouch), 5 oz.	2.0	n.a.
(Myers), 3.5 oz.	8.0	n.a.
(Stouffer's), 5.5 oz.	16.0	n.a.
Dijon, w/pasta *(Right Course)*, 9.5 oz.	9.0	2.0
fiesta, w/corn pasta *(Right Course)*, 87/8 oz.	7.0	2.0

Beef entrée, frozen, continued

hamburger *(MicroMagic)*, 4 oz.	18.0	n.a.
London broil, in mushroom sauce *(Weight Watchers)*, 7.37 oz.	3.0	1.0
Oriental *(The Budget Gourmet Slim Selects)*, 10 oz.	9.0	n.a.
Oriental, w/vegetables and rice *(Lean Cuisine)*, 8 5/8 oz.	7.0	2.0
patty, charbroiled, mushroom gravy and:		
(Banquet Cookin' Bags), 5 oz.	15.0	n.a.
(Banquet Family Entrees), 8 oz.	21.0	n.a.
(Freezer Queen Cook-In-Pouch), 5 oz.	3.0	n.a.
(Freezer Queen Family Suppers), 7 oz.	11.0	n.a.
patty, onion gravy and *(Banquet Family Entrees)*, 8 oz.	21.0	n.a.
patty, onion gravy and *(Freezer Queen Family Suppers)*, 7 oz.	12.0	n.a.
and peppers in sauce, w/rice *(Freezer Queen* Single Serve*)*, 9 oz.	3.0	n.a.
pepper Oriental *(Chun King)*, 13 oz. . . .	3.0	n.a.
pepper steak:		
(Dining Lite), 9 oz.	6.0	n.a.
(Healthy Choice), 9.5 oz.	4.0	2.0
(Tyson Gourmet Selection), 11.25 oz.	11.0	n.a.
green, w/rice *(Stouffer's)*, 10.5 oz. . . .	11.0	n.a.
w/rice *(The Budget Gourmet)*, 10 oz.	9.0	n.a.
w/rice *(La Choy Fresh & Lite)*, 10 oz.	8.0	n.a.
ragout, w/rice pilaf *(Right Course)*, 10 oz.	8.0	2.0
Salisbury steak, see "Salisbury steak entrée"		
short ribs *(Tyson Gourmet Selection)*, 11 oz.	24.0	n.a.
short ribs, in gravy *(Stouffer's)*, 9 oz. . . .	20.0	n.a.
sirloin, in herb sauce *(The Budget Gourmet Slim Selects)*, 10 oz.	12.0	n.a.
sirloin, roast *(The Budget Gourmet)*, 9.5 oz.	14.0	n.a.
sirloin tips:		
Burgundy sauce *(Swanson* Homestyle*)*, 7 oz.	5.0	n.a.

w/mushrooms, in wine sauce *(Weight Watchers)*, 7.5 oz.	7.0	3.0
w/vegetables *(The Budget Gourmet)*, 10 oz.	18.0	n.a.
sliced, barbecue sauce and *(Banquet Cookin' Bags)*, 4 oz.	2.0	n.a.
sliced, gravy and:		
(Banquet Cookin' Bags), 4 oz.	5.0	n.a.
(Banquet Family Entrees), 8 oz.	5.0	n.a.
(Freezer Queen Cook-In-Pouch), 4 oz.	1.0	n.a.
(Freezer Queen Deluxe Family Suppers), 7 oz.	3.0	n.a.
steak, breaded *(Hormel)*, 4 oz.	30.0	n.a.
steak, Ranchero *(Lean Cuisine)*, 9.25 oz.	9.0	3.0
stew *(Banquet Family Entrees)*, 7 oz. . . .	5.0	n.a.
stew *(Freezer Queen Family Suppers)*, 7 oz.	6.0	n.a.
Stroganoff:		
(The Budget Gourmet Slim Selects)*, 8.75 oz.	10.0	n.a.
(Myers), 3.5 oz.	6.0	n.a.
(Weight Watchers), 8.5 oz.	9.0	4.0
w/parsley noodles *(Stouffer's)*, 9.75 oz.	20.0	n.a.
Stroganoff sauce with, and noodles *(Banquet Family Entrees)*, 7 oz.	6.0	n.a.
Szechuan *(Chun King)*, 13 oz.	3.0	n.a.
Szechwan, w/noodles *(Lean Cuisine)*, 9.25 oz.	10.0	3.0
teriyaki:		
(Chun King), 13 oz.	2.0	n.a.
(Dining Lite), 9 oz.	5.0	n.a.
w/rice *(La Choy Fresh & Lite)*, 10 oz.	5.0	n.a.
in sauce *(Stouffer's)*, 9.75 oz.	8.0	n.a.
Beef entrée, packaged, 1 serving:		
pepper steak, Oriental *(Hormel Top Shelf)*	10.0	n.a.
ribs, boneless *(Hormel Top Shelf)*	24.0	n.a.
roast, tender *(Hormel Top Shelf)*	7.0	n.a.
Salisbury steak w/potatoes *(Hormel Top Shelf)*	6.0	n.a.
Stroganoff *(Hormel Top Shelf)*	12.0	n.a.

Beef entrée, packaged, continued

sukiyaki *(Hormel Top Shelf)*	10.0	n.a.
Beef gravy, canned:		
1/4 cup	1.4	.7
(Franco-American), 2 oz.	1.0	n.a.
(Hormel Great Beginnings), 5 oz.	7.0	n.a.
Beef jerky (see also "Sausage sticks"), 1 piece:		
(Frito-Lay's), .21 oz.	1.0	n.a.
(Hormel Lumberjack), 1 oz.	9.0	n.a.
(Slim Jim), .14 oz.	1.0	n.a.
(Slim Jim Giant Jerk), .63 oz.	2.0	n.a.
plain or *Tabasco (Slim Jim Super Jerk)*, .31 oz.	1.0	n.a.
Beef luncheon meat, 1 oz., except as noted:		
(Eckrich Slender Sliced)	1.0	n.a.
loaf	7.4	3.2
loaf, jellied *(Hormel* Perma-Fresh), 2 slices	4.0	n.a.
roast *(Healthy Deli)*	.4	n.a.
roast *(Oscar Mayer* Thin Sliced), .4-oz. slice	.4	.2
roast, cured *(Hillshire Farm* Deli Select)	.5	n.a.
roast, Italian *(Healthy Deli)*	.6	n.a.
sandwich steak *(Steak-Umm)*, 2 oz.	16.0	n.a.
sliced	.9	.4
smoked *(Hillshire Farm* Deli Select)	.5	n.a.
smoked *(Oscar Mayer)*, .5-oz. slice	.3	.1
smoked, cured *(Hormel)*	2.0	n.a.
smoked, cured, dried *(Hormel)*	1.0	n.a.
Beef marinade seasoning mix *(Lawry's)*, 1 pkg.	.2	n.a.
Beef pie, frozen:		
(Banquet), 7 oz.	33.0	n.a.
(Banquet Supreme Microwave), 7 oz.	29.0	n.a.
(Morton), 7 oz.	31.0	n.a.
(Myers), 3.5 oz.	6.0	n.a.
(Stouffer's), 10 oz.	32.0	n.a.
(Swanson Pot Pie), 7 oz.	19.0	n.a.
(Swanson Hungry-Man Pot Pie), 16 oz.	31.0	n.a.

Beef pocket sandwich, frozen:

and broccoli *(Lean Pockets)*, 1 pkg. . . .	8.0	n.a.
'n cheddar *(Hot Pockets)*, 5 oz.	7.0	n.a.

Beef seasoning mix, ground, w/onions

(French's), 1/4 pkg.	0	0

Beef stew, see "Beef entrée"

Beef stew seasoning mix:

(French's), 1/6 pkg.	0	0
(Lawry's), 1 pkg.	.7	n.a.
(McCormick/Schilling), 1/4 pkg.	.3	(0)

Beef Stroganoff seasoning mix *(McCormick*

Schilling), 1/4 pkg.	.3	(0)
Beefalo, meat only, roasted, 4 oz.	¯.2	3.0
Beer, alc. and malt liquor (all brands) . . .	0	0
Beer batter mix *(Golden Dipt)*, 1 oz.	0	0

Beerwurst (see also "Salami, beer"):

beef, 1 oz.	8 3	3.4
pork, 1 oz.	5 3	1.8

Beet:

fresh, raw, whole, 2 medium, 2" diam.	.2	< .1
fresh, boiled, drained, 2 medium	.1	tr.
canned, plain, Harvard, or pickled, 1/2 cup	1	< .1

Beet greens:

raw, 1" pieces, 1/2 cup	‹ 1	tr.
boiled, drained, 1" pieces, 1/2 cup	.1	< .1
Berliner, beef and pork, 1 oz.	4.9	1.7
Berry drink or juice, all varieties, 6 fl. oz.	< .2	(0)

Biscuit, 1 piece, except as noted:

(Wonder)	1.0	n.a.
country *(Awrey's 3")*, 2 oz.	5.0	1.0
round or square *(Awrey's 2")*, 1 oz. . . .	3.0	1.0
sliced, unsliced, or square *(Awrey's)*, 2 oz.	5.0	1.0
refrigerated:		
(Big Country Butter Tastin')	4.0	< 1.0
(Pillsbury Big Premium Heat 'n Eat),		
2 pieces	5.0	3.0
(Roman Meal), 2 pieces	3.8	.9
all varieties *(Big Country)*	4.0	< 1.0
all varieties *(1869 Brand)*	5.0	1.0
plain or buttermilk *(Ballard*		
Ovenready)	0	n.a.

Biscuit, refrigerated, continued

butter or country *(Pillsbury)*	1.0	0
buttermilk *(Hungry Jack* Extra Rich)	1.0	0
buttermilk *(Pillsbury)*	1.0	1.0
buttermilk *(Pillsbury* Heat 'n Eat), 2 pieces	5.0	1.0
buttermilk *(Pillsbury* Tender Layer) . .	1.0	0
buttermilk, flaky *(Hungry Jack)*	4.0	< 1.0
buttermilk, fluffy *(Hungry Jack)*	4.0	1.0
flaky *(Hungry Jack/Hungry Jack Butter Tastin')*	4.0	< 1.0
fluffy *(Pillsbury* Good 'n Buttery) . . .	5.0	1.0
oat bran, honey nut, or white *(Roman Meal)*	4.7	1.2
Biscuit dough, frozen *(Bridgford)*, 2 oz.	6.0	n.a.
Biscuit mix:		
(Bisquick), 1/2 cup	8.0	2.0
(Martha White BixMix), 1 piece*	3.0	n.a.
w/skim milk *(Robin Hood/Gold Medal* Pouch), 1/8 mix*	3.0	1.0
Black bean dinner, canned, Western, w/ garden vegetables *(Health Valley Fast Menu)*, 7.5 oz.	1.0	n.a.
Blackberry:		
fresh or frozen, 1/2 cup	.3	(0)
canned, in water *(Allens)*, 1/2 cup	< 1.0	(0)
canned, in heavy syrup, 1/2 cup	.2	(0)
Blackberry cobbler, frozen:		
(Pet-Ritz), 1/6 pkg. or 4.33 oz.	10.0	n.a.
(Stilwell), 4 oz.	8.0	n.a.
Black-eyed pea (see also "Cowpea"):		
canned, fresh or mature *(Allens)*, 1/2 cup	< 1.0	(0)
canned, mature *(Joan of Arc/Green Giant)*, 1/2 cup	1.0	(0)
canned, mature, w/pork *(Luck's)*, 7.5 oz.	6.0	n.a.
frozen *(Seabrook)*, 3.3 oz.	1.0	(0)
Blintz, see "Cheese blintz"		
Blood sausage, 1 oz.	9.8	3.8
Bloody mary mix, bottled *(Holland House* Smooth N' Spicy)	0	0

Blueberry, 1/2 cup:

fresh	.3	(0)
canned, in heavy syrup	.4	(0)

Blueberry cobbler:

deep dish *(Awrey's),* 1/8 pie	14.0	3.0
frozen *(Pet-Ritz),* 1/6 pkg. or 4.33 oz. . . .	12.0	n.a.

Blueberry turnover, frozen *(Pepperidge Farm),* 1 piece . . . . 19.0   n.a.

Bluefish, meat only, raw, 4 oz. 4.8   1.0

Boar, wild, meat only, roasted, 4 oz. 5.0   1.5

Bockwurst, raw, 1 oz. 7.8   2.9

Bologna:

(Eckrich/Eckrich Smorgas Pac), 1-oz. slice	9.0	n.a.
(Eckrich German Brand), 1-oz. slice . . .	7.0	n.a.
(Eckrich Lite), 1 oz.	6.0	n.a.
(Eckrich Thick Sliced), 1 slice	15.0	n.a.
(Hillshire Farm Large or Ring), 1 oz. . .	8.0	n.a.
(Hormel Coarse Ground, 1 lb.), 2 oz. . .	14.0	n.a.
(Hormel Fine Ground, 1 lb.), 2 oz.	16.0	n.a.
(Hormel Perma-Fresh), 2 slices	16.0	n.a.
(Kahn's Deluxe Club/Giant Deluxe), 1 slice	8.0	n.a.
(Kahn's Giant Thick Deluxe), 1 slice . .	10.0	n.a.
(Kahn's Thick Deluxe), 1 slice	13.0	n.a.
(Kahn's Thin Sliced Deluxe), 1 slice . . .	5.0	n.a.
(Light & Lean), 2 slices	12.0	n.a.
(Light & Lean Thin Sliced), 2 slices . . .	6.0	n.a.
(Oscar Mayer), .53-oz. slice	4.4	1.7
(Oscar Mayer), 1-oz. slice	8.3	3.2
(Oscar Mayer), 1.6-oz. slice	13.3	5.1
(Oscar Mayer Light), 1-oz. slice	5.4	1.8
(Oscar Mayer Light), 1.4-oz. slice	7.9	2.7
(Pilgrim's Pride), 1-oz. slice	4.4	n.a.
w/cheese *(Eckrich),* 1-oz. slice	9.0	n.a.
w/cheese *(Oscar Mayer),* .8-oz. slice . . .	6.8	2.6
beef, 1-oz. slice	8.0	3.3
beef *(Eckrich),* 1-oz. slice	8.0	n.a.
beef *(Eckrich* Thick Sliced), 1.5-oz. slice	12.0	n.a.
beef *(Hebrew National* Original Deli), 1 oz.	3.0	n.a.
beef *(Hormel* Coarse Ground), 2 oz. . . .	14.0	n.a.

Bologna, continued

beef *(Hormel* Perma-Fresh), 2 slices . . .	16.0	n.a.
beef *(Kahn's/Kahn's Giant*/Pounder), 1 slice	8.0	n.a.
beef *(Kahn's* Family Pack), 1 slice	6.0	n.a.
beef *(Oscar Mayer),* .53-oz. slice	4.4	1.9
beef *(Oscar Mayer),* 1-oz. slice	8.2	3.7
beef *(Oscar Mayer),* 1.6-oz. slice	13.3	5.8
beef *(Oscar Mayer* Light), 1-oz. slice . . .	5.3	2.1
beef, garlic *(Oscar Mayer),* 1-oz. slice . .	8.3	3.5
beef, garlic *(Oscar Mayer),* 1.4-oz. slice. .	12.1	5.1
beef, Lebanon, 1 oz.	4.2	1.8
beef, Lebanon *(Oscar Mayer),* .8-oz. slice	2.9	1.4
beef and cheddar *(Kahn's),* 1 slice	8.0	n.a.
beef and pork, 1-oz. slice	8.0	3.0
beef and pork *(Healthy Deli),* 1 oz.	2.0	n.a.
garlic *(Eckrich),* 1-oz. slice	9.0	n.a.
garlic or ham *(Kahn's),* 1 slice	8.0	n.a.
pork, 1-oz. slice	5.6	2.0
turkey, see "Turkey bologna"		
"Bologna," vegetarian, frozen *(Worthington Bolono),* 2 slices or 1.3 oz.	2.0	0
Bolognese sauce:		
canned *(Progresso* Authentic Pasta Sauces),* 1/2 cup	8.0	2.0
refrigerated *(Contadina Fresh),* 7.5 oz. . .	11.0	n.a.
Borage:		
raw, 1" pieces, 1/2 cup	.3	(0)
boiled, drained, 4 oz.	.9	(0)
Bouillon (see also "Soup"):		
all flavors:		
(G. Washington's Seasoning & Broth), 1 pkt.	0	0
(Lite-Line Low Sodium), 1 tsp.	< 1.0	n.a.
(Steero), 1 cube or tsp.	< 1.0	n.a.
(Wyler's), 1 cube or tsp.	< 1.0	n.a.
beef flavor, 1 cube	.1	.1
chicken flavor, 1 cube	.2	.1
Boysenberry:		
fresh, see "Blackberry"		
canned or frozen, 1/2 cup	.2	(0)

Brains:

beef, simmered, 4 oz.	14.2	3.3
lamb, braised, 4 oz.	11.5	2.9
pork, braised, 4 oz.	10.8	2.4
veal, braised, 4 oz.	10.9	n.a.

Bran, see "Wheat bran"

Bratwurst:

(Eckrich), 1 link	30.0	n.a.
(Hillshire Farm Fully Cooked), 2 oz. . . .	16.0	n.a.
(Kahn's), 1 link	17.0	n.a.
fresh, smoked, or spicy *(Hillshire Farm)*, 2 oz.	17.0	n.a.
pork, cooked, 1 oz.	7.3	2.6
pork and beef, 1 oz.	7.9	2.8
smoked *(Eckrich Lite* Bratwurst Links), 1 link	17.0	n.a.

Braunschweiger:

(Hormel), 1 oz.	7.0	n.a.
(JM), 1-oz. slice	6.0	n.a.
(Oscar Mayer German Brand or Tube), 1 oz.	8.7	3.0
(Oscar Mayer Slices), 1-oz. slice	8.7	3.2
(Oscar Mayer Slices), .9-oz. slice	8.0	2.9
pork, 1 oz.	9.1	3.1

Brazil nut, shelled, 1 oz., 6 large or 8 medium 18.8   4.6

Bread, 1 piece or slice, except as noted:

all varieties, except high fiber and light *(Wonder)*	1.0	n.a.
apple walnut *(Arnold)*	1.3	n.a.
(Arnold Bran'nola Original)	1.4	n.a.
barbecue *(Colombo* Brand BBQ Loaf), 2 oz.	1.6	n.a.
bran, whole *(Brownberry* Natural)	1.4	n.a.
bran and oat *(Oatmeal Goodness* Light)	< 1.0	n.a.
(Brownberry Bran'nola)	1.4	n.a.
(Brownberry Health Nut)	2.6	n.a.
cinnamon oatmeal *(Oatmeal Goodness)*	2.0	n.a.
cinnamon raisin *(Arnold)*	1.4	n.a.
cinnamon swirl *(Pepperidge Farm)*	2.0	0
date nut roll *(Dromedary)*, 1/2" slice . . .	2.0	n.a.

Bread, continued
French:

(DiCarlo Parisian)	1.0	n.a.
extra sour *(Colombo* Brand), 2 oz. . .	1.3	n.a.
extra sour, sliced *(Colombo* Brand), 2 oz.	1.6	n.a.
sweet *(Colombo* Brand French Stick), 2 oz.	1.9	n.a.
twin *(Pepperidge Farm* Deli Classic), 1 oz.	1.0	n.a.
style *(Pepperidge Farm* Deli Classic), 2 oz.	2.0	n.a.
garlic *(Colombo* Brand), 2 oz.	10.1	n.a.
grain:		
mixed *(Roman Meal* Round Top) . . .	.8	n.a.
mixed *(Roman Meal* Thin Sliced Sandwich)	.7	n.a.
multi *(Roman Meal* Sun Grain)	1.4	n.a.
nutty *(Arnold/Brownberry Bran'nola)*	1.6	n.a.
seven *(Pepperidge Farm* Hearty Slice)	1.0	n.a.
(Hollywood Dark or Light)	1.0	n.a.
honey bran *(Pepperidge Farm)*	1.0	n.a.
Italian:		
(Arnold Bakery Light)	.5	n.a.
(Arnold Francisco International), 1 oz.	1.1	n.a.
(Brownberry Light)	.5	n.a.
thick sliced *(Arnold* Francisco International)	.8	n.a.
(Monk's Hi-Fibre)	1.0	n.a.
oat *(Arnold/Brownberry Bran'nola* Country)	2.0	n.a.
oat, crunchy *(Pepperidge Farm),* 2 slices	4.0	1.0
oat bran *(Awrey's)*	0	0
oat bran *(Roman Meal* Split-Top)	.9	n.a.
oat bran, honey *(Roman Meal)*	1.2	n.a.
oat bran, honey nut *(Roman Meal)*	1.6	n.a.
oatmeal *(Arnold* Bakery Light)	.6	n.a.
oatmeal *(Pepperidge Farm)*	1.0	n.a.
oatmeal *(Pepperidge Farm* Light Style). .	0	0
oatmeal *(Pepperidge Farm* Very Thin) . .	1.0	n.a.
oatmeal and bran *(Oatmeal Goodness)*. .	2.0	n.a.

oatmeal sunflower seed *(Oatmeal Goodness)*	2.0	n.a.
orange raisin *(Brownberry)*	1.2	n.a.
pita, oat bran *(Sahara)*, 1/2 piece	.3	n.a.
pita, white *(Sahara)*, 1 mini or 1/2 regular	.5	n.a.
pita, whole wheat *(Sahara)*	2.0	n.a.
pumpernickel *(Arnold)*	.9	n.a.
pumpernickel *(Pepperidge Farm* Family)	1.0	0
pumpernickel *(Pepperidge Farm* Party), 4 slices	1.0	0
raisin bran or raisin cinnamon *(Brownberry)*	1.3	n.a.
raisin w/cinnamon *(Monk's)*	2.0	n.a.
raisin w/cinnamon swirl *(Pepperidge Farm)*	2.0	0
raisin walnut *(Brownberry)*	2.7	n.a.
rice bran *(Roman Meal)*	1.5	n.a.
rice bran, golden *(Monk's)*	1.0	n.a.
rice bran, honey nut *(Roman Meal)*	1.6	n.a.
rye:		
(Braun's Old Allegheny)	1.0	n.a.
(Pepperidge Farm Party), 4 slices	1.0	0
all varieties *(Beefsteak)*	1.0	n.a.
caraway *(Brownberry* Natural)	.8	n.a.
Dijon, seeded, seedless *(Pepperidge Farm)*	1.0	0
dill *(Arnold)*	1.0	n.a.
Jewish, seeded *(Levy's)*	.9	n.a.
Jewish, seedless *(Levy's)*	.8	n.a.
seedless *(Brownberry* Natural Thin Sliced)	.6	n.a.
sesame wheat *(Pepperidge Farm)*, 2 slices	3.0	1.0
sourdough *(DiCarlo)*	1.0	n.a.
sourdough French *(Boudin)*, 2 oz. or 2 slices	1.0	n.a.
sunflower and bran *(Monk's)*	1.0	n.a.
Vienna *(Pepperidge Farm* Deli Classic)	1.0	0
Vienna *(Pepperidge Farm* Light Style)	0	0
wheat:		
(Arnold Brick Oven)	1.5	n.a.
(Brownberry Hearth), 1 oz.	1.4	n.a.

Bread, wheat, continued

(Brownberry Natural)	1.3	n.a.
(Country Grain)	1.0	n.a.
(Fresh & Natural)	1.0	n.a.
(Pepperidge Farm, 1½ lb.)	2.0	n.a.
(Pepperidge Farm Family, 2 lb.)	1.0	0
(Pepperidge Farm Light Style/Very Thin)	0	0
(Wonder High Fiber/Light)	0	0
all varieties *(Beefsteak)*	1.0	n.a.
all varieties *(Home Pride)*	1.0	n.a.
apple honey *(Brownberry)*	1.9	n.a.
cracked *(Pepperidge Farm)*	1.0	n.a.
dark *(Arnold Bran'nola)*	1.0	n.a.
hearty *(Arnold/Brownberry Bran'nola)*	1.9	n.a.
honey wheatberry *(Arnold)*	1.2	n.a.
light golden *(Arnold* Bakery)	.5	n.a.
oatmeal *(Oatmeal Goodness)*	2.0	n.a.
oatmeal *(Oatmeal Goodness* Light)	< 1.0	n.a.
soft *(Brownberry)*	1.8	n.a.
sprouted *(Pepperidge Farm)*	2.0	n.a.
whole *(Arnold* Stoneground 100%) . .	.7	n.a.
whole *(Daily)*, 2 oz., approx. 1 piece	0	0
whole *(Monk's* 100% Stone Ground)	1.0	n.a.
whole *(Pepperidge Farm* Thin Sliced)	1.0	n.a.
white:		
(Arnold Brick Oven)	1.2	n.a.
(Arnold Country White)	1.8	n.a.
(Arnold/Brownberry Light Premium)	.5	n.a.
(Brownberry Natural)	1.1	n.a.
(Home Pride Butter Top)	1.0	n.a.
(Monk's), 1 slice, approx. 1 oz.	1.0	n.a.
(Pepperidge Farm Country), 2 slices	2.0	1.0
(Pepperidge Farm Large Family Thin Sliced)	1.0	0
(Pepperidge Farm Very Thin)	0	0
(Wonder High Fiber/Light)	0	0
extra fiber *(Arnold* Brick Oven)	.8	n.a.
Bread, brown and serve *(du Jour Austrian/ French)*, 1 slice	1.0	n.a.

Bread, canned:

brown *(S&W* New England), 2 slices . . .	0	0
brown, plain or raisin *(B&M/Friends),* 1.6 oz.	0	0

Bread, sweet, mix*:

banana *(Pillsbury),* 1/12 loaf	6.0	n.a.
blueberry nut *(Pillsbury),* 1/12 loaf	4.0	n.a.
cherry nut *(Pillsbury),* 1/12 loaf	5.0	n.a.
cornbread:		
(Aunt Jemima Easy), 1 serving	6.3	1.3
(Dromedary), 2″ × 2″ square	3.0	n.a.
(Martha White Cotton Pickin'), 1/4 pan	3.0	n.a.
(Pillsbury/Ballard), 1/8 recipe	3.0	n.a.
(Robin Hood/Gold Medal Pouch), 1/6 mix	5.0	n.a.
yellow *(Martha White* Light Crust), 2 oz.	4.0	n.a.
cranberry *(Pillsbury),* 1/12 loaf	4.0	n.a.
date *(Pillsbury),* 1/12 loaf	3.0	n.a.
date nut *(Dromedary),* 1/12 loaf	8.0	n.a.
gingerbread *(Betty Crocker* Classic), 1/9 mix	7.0	2.0
gingerbread *(Pillsbury),* 3″ square	4.0	n.a.
nut *(Pillsbury),* 1/12 loaf	6.0	n.a.

Bread crumbs:

plain *(Devonsheer),* 1 oz.	1.4	n.a.
plain or Italian *(Progresso),* 2 tbsp.	< 1.0	n.a.
Italian style *(Devonsheer),* 1 oz.	1.3	n.a.

Bread dough:

frozen, honey walnut *(Bridgford),* 1 oz.	.9	n.a.
frozen, white *(Bridgford),* 1 oz.	1.2	n.a.
frozen, white *(Rich's),* 2 slices	1.0	n.a.
refrigerated:		
(Roman Meal), 1-oz. slice	2.8	.9
cornbread twists *(Pillsbury),* 1 twist	4.0	< 1.0
French, crusty *(Pillsbury),* 1″ slice . . .	< 1.0	0
wheat or white *(Pipin' Hot),* 1″ slice	2.0	0

Breadfruit, fresh, raw, peeled and seeded,

1/2 cup	.3	(0)

Breadsticks, 1 piece:

plain or pizza *(Stella D'Oro)*	1.2	n.a.

Breadsticks, continued

onion *(Stella D'Oro)*	1.3	n.a.
sesame *(Stella D'Oro)*	2.2	n.a.
wheat *(Stella D'Oro)*	1.4	n.a.
refrigerated *(Roman Meal)*	3.9	n.a.
refrigerated, soft *(Pillsbury)*	2.0	< 1.0
refrigerated, soft *(Roman Meal)*	3.9	1.2

Breakfast, frozen, see specific listings

Breakfast strips, see "Bacon, substitute"

Broccoli:

fresh, raw, 1 spear, 8.7 oz.	.5	.1
fresh, raw or boiled, drained, chopped, ½ cup	.2	< .1
fresh, boiled, drained, 1 spear, 6.3 oz.	.6	.1
frozen:		
boiled, drained, spears or chopped, ½ cup	.1	< .1
in butter sauce *(Green Giant* One Serving), 4.5 oz.	2.0	< 1.0
in butter sauce, spears *(Birds Eye* Butter Sauce Combinations), 3.3 oz.	2.0	n.a.
in butter sauce, spears *(Green Giant)*, ½ cup	2.0	< 1.0
in cheese sauce *(Birds Eye* Cheese Sauce Combinations), 5 oz.	7.0	n.a.
in cheese sauce, cuts *(Green Giant* One Serving), 5 oz.	3.0	< 1.0
in cheese sauce, cuts *(Stokely Singles)*, 4 oz.	4.0	n.a.
in cheese-flavored sauce *(Green Giant)*, ½ cup	2.0	< 1.0

Broccoli, combinations, frozen:

and carrots, baby, and water chestnuts *(Birds Eye* Farm Fresh), 4 oz.	0	0
and carrots, baby whole, and waterchestnuts *(Stokely Singles)*, 3 oz.	1.0	0
and cauliflower *(Stokely Singles)*, 3 oz.	1.0	0
and cauliflower medley *(Green Giant Valley* Combinations), ½ cup	1.0	(0)
cauliflower and carrots:		
(Birds Eye Farm Fresh), 4 oz.	0	0

no sauce *(Green Giant* One Serving), 4 oz.	0	0
baby *(Stokely Singles)*, 3 oz.	1.0	(0)
in butter sauce *(Birds Eye* Butter Sauce Combinations), 3.3 oz.	2.0	n.a.
in butter sauce *(Green Giant)*, 1/2 cup	1.0	< 1.0
w/cheese sauce *(Birds Eye* Cheese Sauce Combinations), 4.5 oz.	5.0	n.a.
in cheese sauce *(Birds Eye For One)*, 5 oz.	5.0	n.a.
in cheese sauce *(Green Giant* One Serving), 5 oz.	3.0	< 1.0
in cheese-flavored sauce *(Green Giant)*, 1/2 cup	2.0	< 1.0
baby, in cheese sauce *(Stokely Singles)*, 4 oz.	3.0	n.a.
corn and red peppers *(Birds Eye* Farm Fresh), 4 oz.	1.0	(0)
fanfare *(Green Giant Valley Combinations)*, 1/2 cup	2.0	n.a.
green beans, pearl onions, and red peppers *(Birds Eye* Farm Fresh), 4 oz.	0	0
red peppers, bamboo shoots, and straw mushrooms *(Birds Eye* Farm Fresh), 4 oz.	0	0
rotini, in cheese sauce *(Green Giant* One Serving), 5.5 oz.	3.0	< 1.0
Brown gravy, 1/4 cup, except as noted:		
canned, plain or w/onion *(Heinz HomeStyle)*	1.0	n.a.
mix* *(French's)*	1.0	n.a.
mix* *(Lawry's)*, 1 cup	1.4	n.a.
mix* *(McCormick/Schilling)*	.8	n.a.
mix* *(McCormick/Schilling* Lite)	1.0	n.a.
mix* *(Pillsbury)*	0	0
Brownie (see also "Cookie"):		
Dutch chocolate *(Awrey's* Cake), 1/16 cake	20.0	4.0
fudge *(Little Debbie)*, 2-oz. piece	8.0	n.a.
fudge nut *(Awrey's* Sheet Cake), 1.25 oz.	9.0	1.0

Brownie, continued

fudge nut, iced *(Awrey's* Sheet Cake), 2.5 oz.	17.0	3.0
fudge walnut *(Tastykake)*, 3-oz. piece	9.5	n.a.
frozen, chocolate *(Weight Watchers)*, 1.25 oz.	3.0	< 1.0
frozen, chocolate chip, double *(Nestlé* Toll House Ready to Bake), 1.4 oz.	7.0	n.a.
frozen, hot fudge *(Pepperidge Farm* Newport), 1 serving	20.0	10.0
mix,* 1 piece:		
(Duncan Hines Gourmet Truffle)	13.0	n.a.
caramel fudge chunk *(Pillsbury)*, 2″ square	7.0	n.a.
caramel swirl *(Betty Crocker)*	4.0	1.0
chocolate, German *(Betty Crocker)*	7.0	2.0
chocolate, milk *(Duncan Hines)*	7.0	n.a.
chocolate chip or frosted *(Betty Crocker)*	6.0	2.0
frosted *(Betty Crocker MicroRave)*	7.0	2.0
fudge *(Betty Crocker)*	6.0	1.0
fudge *(Betty Crocker* Supreme)	3.0	1.0
fudge *(Betty Crocker MicroRave)*	6.0	2.0
fudge *(Duncan Hines)*	7.0	n.a.
fudge *(Pillsbury* Microwave)	9.0	n.a.
fudge, chewy *(Duncan Hines)*	5.0	n.a.
fudge, deluxe *(Pillsbury)*, 2″ square	6.0	n.a.
fudge, deluxe, walnut *(Pillsbury)*, 2″ square	8.0	n.a.
fudge, double *(Pillsbury)*, 2″ square	6.0	n.a.
fudge, peanut butter *(Duncan Hines)*	8.0	n.a.
fudge, triple, chunky *(Pillsbury)*, 2″ square	7.0	n.a.
rocky road, fudge *(Pillsbury)*, 2″ square	8.0	n.a.
walnut *(Betty Crocker)*	7.0	1.0
walnut *(Betty Crocker MicroRave)*	7.0	2.0
white, Vienna *(Duncan Hines)*	12.0	n.a.
Browning sauce *(Gravymaster)*, 1 tsp.	tr.	(0)
Brussels sprouts:		
fresh, raw, 1/2 cup	.1	< .1
fresh, boiled, drained, 1/2 cup	.4	.1

frozen:

boiled, drained, 1/2 cup	.3	.1
in butter sauce *(Green Giant)*, 1/2 cup	1.0	< 1.0
in butter sauce *(Stokely Singles)*, 4 oz.	1.0	n.a.
w/cauliflower and carrots *(Birds Eye*		
Farm Fresh)*, 4 oz.	0	0
w/cheese sauce, baby *(Birds Eye*		
Cheese Sauce Combinations), 4.5 oz.	7.0	n.a.
Buckwheat, whole grain, 1 cup	5.8	1.3

Buckwheat groats:

dry, roasted, 1 cup	4.4	1.0
cooked, 1 cup	1.2	.3

Bulgur (see also "Tabbouleh mix"):

dry, 1 cup	1.9	.3
cooked, 1 cup	.4	.1

Bun, sweet (see also "Roll, sweet"),
1 piece:
honey:

glazed *(Hostess Breakfast Bake Shop)*	21.0	10.0
glazed *(Tastykake)*	12.9	n.a.
iced *(Hostess Breakfast Bake Shop)*	22.0	10.0
iced *(Tastykake)*	12.4	n.a.
frozen, cinnamon *(Rich's Ever Fresh)* . .	14.6	n.a.
frozen, honey, mini *(Rich's Ever Fresh)*	6.6	n.a.
Burbot, meat only, raw, 4 oz.	.9	.2
Burdock root, boiled, drained, 1/2 cup . . .	.1	(0)

Burger King:
breakfast, 1 serving:

bagel	6.0	1.0
bagel, w/cream cheese	16.0	6.0
bagel sandwich	16.0	5.0
bagel sandwich, w/bacon	20.0	7.0
bagel sandwich, w/ham	17.0	6.0
bagel sandwich, w/sausage	36.0	12.0
biscuit	17.0	3.0
biscuit, w/bacon	20.0	5.0
biscuit, w/bacon and egg	27.0	7.0
biscuit, w/sausage	29.0	8.0
biscuit, w/sausage and egg	36.0	10.0
croissant	10.0	2.0
Croissan'wich	19.0	7.0

Burger King, breakfast, continued

Croissan'wich, w/bacon	24.0	8.0
Croissan'wich, w/ham	21.0	7.0
Croissan'wich, w/sausage	40.0	13.0
Danish, apple cinnamon	13.0	3.0
Danish, cheese	16.0	5.0
Danish, cinnamon raisin	18.0	4.0
French toast sticks	32.0	5.0
muffins, mini, blueberry	14.0	3.0
muffins, mini, lemon poppyseed	18.0	3.0
muffins, mini, raisin oat bran	12.0	2.0
scrambled egg platter	34.0	9.0
scrambled egg platter, w/bacon	39.0	11.0
scrambled egg platter, w/sausage	53.0	15.0
Tater Tenders	12.0	3.0
sandwiches and burgers, 1 serving:		
bacon double cheeseburger	31.0	14.0
bacon double cheeseburger deluxe	39.0	16.0
barbecue bacon double cheeseburger	31.0	14.0
BK Broiler chicken sandwich	18.0	3.0
Burger Buddies	17.0	7.0
cheeseburger	15.0	7.0
cheeseburger deluxe	23.0	8.0
chicken sandwich	40.0	8.0
double cheeseburger	27.0	13.0
hamburger	11.0	4.0
hamburger deluxe	19.0	6.0
mushroom Swiss double cheeseburger	27.0	12.0
Ocean Catch fish fillet sandwich	25.0	4.0
Whopper	36.0	12.0
Whopper, w/cheese	44.0	16.0
Whopper, double	53.0	19.0
Whopper, double, w/cheese	61.0	24.0
tenders, chicken, 6 pieces	13.0	3.0
sauces:		
BK Broiler, .5 oz.	10.0	1.0
Bull's Eye barbecue, .5 oz.	0	0
dipping, all varieties, except ranch, 1 oz.	0	0
dipping, ranch, 1 oz.	18.0	3.0

salad, 1 serving:

chef salad	9.0	4.0
chicken salad, chunky	4.0	1.0
garden salad	5.0	3.0
side salad	0	0

salad dressings *(Newman's Own)*, 1 pkt.:

bleu cheese	32.0	7.0
French	22.0	3.0
Italian, reduced-calorie light	18.0	3.0
olive oil and vinegar	33.0	5.0
ranch	37.0	7.0
Thousand Island	26.0	5.0

side dishes:

french fries, medium	20.0	5.0
onion rings	19.0	5.0

desserts and shakes, 1 serving:

apple pie	14.0	4.0
shake, all flavors	10.0	6.0

"Burger," vegetarian:

canned *(Worthington Vegetarian Burger)*, 1/2 cup	4.0	1.0
frozen *(Morningstar Farms Grillers)*, 1 patty	12.0	2.0
frozen *(Worthington FriPats)*, 2.25-oz. piece	12.0	2.0
mix* *(Love Natural Foods Loveburger)*, 4 oz.	11.0	n.a.
mix *(Worthington Granburger)*, 6 tbsp. mix	1.0	n.a.

Burrito, frozen:

(Hormel Burrito Grande), 5.5 oz.	16.0	n.a.
all varieties, except medium beef and bean *(Old El Paso)*, 1 piece	11.0	n.a.
beef *(Hormel)*, 1 piece	8.0	n.a.
beef and bean *(Patio)*, 5-oz. pkg.	16.0	n.a.
beef and bean *(Patio Britos)*, 3.63 oz.	10.0	n.a.
beef and bean, medium *(Old El Paso)*, 1 piece	13.0	5.0
beef and bean green chili *(Patio)*, 5-oz. pkg.	12.0	n.a.
beef and bean red chili *(Patio)*, 5-oz. pkg.	13.0	n.a.

Burrito, frozen, continued

beef nacho *(Patio Britos)*, 3.63 oz.	13.0	n.a.
cheese *(Hormel)*, 1 piece	5.0	n.a.
cheese, nacho *(Patio Britos)*, 3.63 oz.	10.0	n.a.
chicken, spicy *(Patio Britos)*, 3.63 oz.	10.0	n.a.
chicken and rice *(Hormel)*, 1 piece	4.0	n.a.
chili, green or red *(Patio Britos)*, 3.63 oz.	10.0	n.a.
chili, hot *(Hormel)*, 1 piece	8.0	n.a.
red hot *(Patio)*, 5-oz. pkg.	15.0	n.a.
Burrito dinner, frozen:		
(Patio), 12 oz.	16.0	n.a.
beef and bean *(Old El Paso* Festive),		
11 oz.	9.0	n.a.
Burrito entrée, frozen:		
bean and cheese *(Old El Paso)*, 1 pkg.	13.0	n.a.
beef and bean, hot or medium *(Old El*		
Paso), 1 pkg.	14.0	n.a.
beef and bean, mild *(Old El Paso)*, 1 pkg.	13.0	n.a.
chicken *(Weight Watchers)*, 7.62 oz. . . .	13.0	4.0
Burrito filling mix, beans *(Del Monte)*,		
1/2 cup	1.0	n.a.
Burrito mix* *(Old El Paso* Dinner), 1 piece	13.0	4.0
Burrito seasoning mix:		
(Lawry's), 1 pkg.	1.7	n.a.
(Old El Paso), 1/8 pkg.	0	0
Butter, salted or unsalted:		
regular, 1 stick or 4 oz.	92.0	57.2
regular, 1 tbsp.	11.4	7.1
regular, 1 tsp.	3.8	2.4
regular, 1 pat, 90 per lb.	4.1	2.5
whipped, 1/2 cup	61.3	38.2
whipped, 1 tbsp.	7.6	4.7
whipped, 1 tsp.	2.6	1.6
Butterbean, see "Beans, lima"		
Butterbur, raw, 1/2 cup, or boiled drained,		
4 oz.	< .1	(0)
Butterfish, meat only, raw, 4 oz.	9.1	n.a.
Butternut, dried, shelled, 1 oz.	16.2	.4
Butterscotch baking chips *(Nestlé* Toll		
House Morsels), 1 oz.	8.0	n.a.

food and measure	total fat (gms.)	saturated fat (gms.)
Cabbage, 1/2 cup:		
green, raw, shredded	.1	tr.
green or red, boiled, drained, shredded	.2	< .1
red, raw, shredded	.1	< .1
savoy, raw, shredded	< .1	tr.
savoy, boiled, drained, shredded	.1	tr.
Cabbage, Chinese, 1/2 cup:		
bok-choy, raw, shredded	.1	tr.
bok-choy, boiled, drained, shredded . . .	.1	< .1
pe-tsai, raw or boiled, drained, shredded	.1	< .1

Cabbage, stuffed, entrée, frozen, w/meat, in
   tomato sauce *(Lean Cuisine)*, 10.75 oz.   10.0   2.0
Caimit, ripe, trimmed, 1 oz. 5   n.a.
Cake:
  apple streusel *(Awrey's)*, 2″ × 2″ piece   9.0   1.0
  banana, iced *(Awrey's)*, 2″ × 2″ piece . . .   8.0   2.0
  black forest torte *(Awrey's)*, 1/14 cake   21.0   7.0
  carrot supreme, iced *(Awrey's)*, 2″ × 2″
    piece 12.0   3.0
  chocolate:
    (Awrey's), .8-oz. piece 3.0   1.0
    double, iced *(Awrey's)*, 2″ × 2″ piece   6.0   2.0
    double, two-layer *(Awrey's)*, 1/12 cake   11.0   3.0
    double, three-layer *(Awrey's)*, 1/12 cake   14.0   4.0
    double, torte *(Awrey's)*, 1/14 cake . . .   15.0   4.0
    German, iced *(Awrey's)*, 2″ × 2″ piece   9.0   3.0
    German, three-layer *(Awrey's)*,
      1/12 cake 18.0   6.0
    milk, yellow, two-layer *(Awrey's)*,
      1/12 cake 17.0   5.0
    white iced, two-layer *(Awrey's)*,
      1/12 cake 15.0   5.0
  coconut butter cream *(Awrey's)*, 2″ × 2″
    piece 9.0   3.0
  coconut yellow, three-layer *(Awrey's)*,
    1/12 cake 21.0   7.0
  coffee, caramel nut or long John
    (Awrey's), 1/12 cake 8.0   2.0
  devil's food, iced *(Awrey's)*, 2″ × 2″ piece   8.0   3.0
  lemon, three-layer *(Awrey's)*, 1/12 cake   19.0   5.0
  lemon, yellow, two-layer *(Awrey's)*,
    1/12 cake 17.0   5.0
  Neapolitan, torte *(Awrey's)*, 1/14 cake   22.0   7.0
  orange, frosty, iced *(Awrey's)*, 2″ × 2″
    piece 8.0   2.0
  orange, three-layer *(Awrey's)*, 1/12 cake   17.0   4.0
  peanut butter, torte *(Awrey's)*, 1/14 cake   22.0   5.0
  pistachio, torte *(Awrey's)*, 1/14 cake 22.0   7.0
  pound *(Drake's)*, 1/10 cake, approx. 1.1 oz.   5.0   1.0
  pound, golden *(Awrey's)*, 1/14 loaf 5.0   1.0
  raisin spice, iced *(Awrey's)*, 2″ × 2″ piece   8.0   2.0

raspberry nut *(Awrey's)*, 1/16 cake	16.0	3.0
sponge *(Awrey's)*, 2″ × 2″ piece	3.0	1.0
strawberry supreme, torte *(Awrey's)*, 1/14 cake	12.0	3.0
walnut, torte *(Awrey's)*, 1/14 cake	19.0	4.0
yellow *(Awrey's)*, .9-oz. piece	3.0	1.0
yellow, white iced *(Awrey's)*, 2″ × 2″ piece	9.0	3.0
Cake, frozen:		
banana, single layer, iced *(Sara Lee)*, 1/8 cake	6.0	n.a.
Black Forest, two-layer *(Sara Lee)*, 1/8 cake	8.0	n.a.
Boston cream *(Pepperidge Farm Supreme)*, 1/4 cake	14.0	6.0
Boston cream pie *(Weight Watchers)*, 3 oz.	4.0	1.0
carrot *(Weight Watchers)*, 3 oz.	5.0	< 1.0
carrot, single layer, iced *(Sara Lee)*, 1/8 cake	13.0	n.a.
cheesecake:		
(Weight Watchers), 3.9 oz.	7.0	2.0
brownie *(Weight Watchers)*, 3.5 oz.	5.0	1.0
cherry cream *(Sara Lee Original)*, 1/6 cake	8.0	n.a.
cream *(Sara Lee Original)*, 1/6 cake . .	11.0	n.a.
French *(Sara Lee Classics)*, 1/8 cake . .	16.0	n.a.
strawberry *(Weight Watchers)*, 3.9 oz.	4.0	2.0
strawberry, French *(Sara Lee Classics)*, 1/8 cake	13.0	n.a.
strawberry cream *(Sara Lee Original)*, 1/6 cake	8.0	n.a.
cheesecake, nondairy, all flavors *(Tofutti Better Than Cheesecake)*, 2 oz.	10.0	n.a.
cherries and cream *(Weight Watchers)*, 3 oz.	6.0	1.0
chocolate:		
(Pepperidge Farm supreme), 1/4 cake	16.0	7.0
(Sara Lee Free & Light), 1/8 cake . . .	0	0
(Weight Watchers), 2.5 oz.	5.0	< 1.0
double, three layer *(Sara Lee)*, 1/8 cake	11.0	n.a.

Cake, frozen, chocolate, continued

fudge, double *(Weight Watchers)*, 2.75 oz.	5.0	< 1.0
fudge layer *(Pepperidge Farm)*, 1/10 cake	10.0	3.0
fudge stripe layer *(Pepperidge Farm)*, 1/10 cake	9.0	3.0
German *(Weight Watchers)*, 2.5 oz.	7.0	< 1.0
German layer *(Pepperidge Farm)*, 1/10 cake	10.0	4.0
mousse *(Sara Lee* Classics), 1/8 cake	17.0	n.a.
coconut layer *(Pepperidge Farm)*, 1/10 cake	8.0	3.0
coffee:		
all-butter cheese *(Sara Lee)*, 1/8 cake	11.0	n.a.
all-butter pecan *(Sara Lee)*, 1/8 cake	8.0	n.a.
all-butter streusel *(Sara Lee)*, 1/8 cake	7.0	n.a.
cinnamon streusel *(Weight Watchers)*, 2.25 oz.	7.0	1.0
devil's food layer *(Pepperidge Farm)*, 1/10 cake	9.0	3.0
golden layer *(Pepperidge Farm)*, 1/10 cake	9.0	3.0
lemon coconut *(Pepperidge Farm Supreme)*, 1/4 cake	13.0	6.0
lemon cream *(Pepperidge Farm Supreme)*, 1/12 cake	9.0	3.0
pineapple cream *(Pepperidge Farm Supreme)*, 1/12 cake	7.0	2.0
pound *(Sara Lee Free & Light)*, 1/10 cake	0	0
pound, all butter *(Sara Lee)*, 1/10 cake	7.0	n.a.
strawberry:		
cream *(Pepperidge Farm* Supreme), 1/12 cake	7.0	3.0
shortcake *(Sara Lee)*, 1/8 cake	8.0	n.a.
stripe layer *(Pepperidge Farm)*, 1/12 cake	8.0	3.0
vanilla layer *(Pepperidge Farm)*, 1/10 cake	8.0	3.0
Cake, refrigerated, coffee, all varieties *(Pillsbury)*, 1/8 cake	9.0	2.0

Cake, snack, 1 piece, except as noted:

apple:

bar, baked *(Sunbelt)*, 1.31 oz.	2.0	n.a.
delight *(Little Debbie)*, 1.25 oz.	4.0	n.a.
spice *(Hostess* Light)	1.0	< 1.0
spice *(Little Debbie)*, 2.2 oz.	11.0	n.a.

banana:

(Hostess Suzy Q's)	9.0	n.a.
(Hostess Twinkies)	5.0	2.0
(Tastykake Banana Treat), 1.1 oz.	2.9	n.a.
slices *(Little Debbie)*, 3 oz.	12.0	n.a.
twins *(Little Debbie)*, 2.2 oz.	9.0	n.a.

brownie, see "Brownie"

butterscotch *(Tastykake Krimpets)*, 1 oz.	2.1	n.a.
cherry cordial *(Little Debbie)*, 1.3 oz.	8.0	n.a.

chocolate:

(Hostess Choco Bliss)	9.0	4.0
(Hostess Choco-Diles)	11.0	8.0
(Hostess Ding Dongs)	9.0	6.0
(Hostess Ho Hos)	6.0	4.0
(Hostess Suzy Q's)	10.0	4.0
(Little Debbie), 2.5 oz.	14.0	n.a.
(Little Debbie Choco-Cake), 2.7 oz.	15.0	n.a.
(Little Debbie Choco-Jel), 1.16 oz.	7.0	n.a.
(Tastykake Creamie), 1.5 oz.	6.7	n.a.
(Tastykake Juniors), 3.3 oz.	7.7	n.a.
(Tastykake Kandy Kakes), .7 oz.	4.3	n.a.
(Tastykake Tempty), .8 oz.	2.1	n.a.
cream filled *(Drake's Devil Dog)*	6.0	1.0
cream filled *(Drake's Ring Ding)*	10.0	3.0
fudge crispy *(Little Debbie)*, 2.08 oz.	7.0	n.a.
fudge round *(Little Debbie)*, 2.75 oz.	12.0	n.a.
mint, cream filled *(Drake's Ring Ding)*	11.0	3.0
roll, cream filled *(Drake's Yodel)*	9.0	2.0
roll, Swiss, cream filled *(Drake's)*	8.0	2.0
slices *(Little Debbie)*, 3 oz.	9.0	n.a.
twins *(Little Debbie)*, 2.2 oz.	7.0	n.a.
w/vanilla pudding *(Hostess* Light)	1.0	< 1.0
chocolate chip *(Little Debbie)*, 2.4 oz.	16.0	n.a.
coconut *(Tastykake* Juniors), 3.3 oz.	4.0	n.a.
coconut covered *(Hostess Sno Balls)*	4.0	2.0

Cake, snack, continued

coconut crunch *(Little Debbie)*, 2 oz. . . .	19.0	n.a.
coffee:		
(Drake's Jr.)	6.0	1.0
(Drake's Small), 2 oz.	9.0	2.0
(Tastykake Koffee Kake Juniors),		
2.5 oz.	12.3	n.a.
cinnamon crumb *(Drake's)*, 1.33 oz.	6.0	1.0
cream filled *(Tastykake* Koffee Kake),		
1 oz.	5.6	n.a.
crumb cake *(Hostess)*	5.0	2.0
crumb cake *(Hostess* Light)	1.0	< 1.0
cupcake:		
butter cream, cream filled *(Tastykake)*	3.4	n.a.
chocolate *(Hostess)*	6.0	3.0
chocolate *(Tastykake)*, 1.1 oz.	2.7	n.a.
chocolate, cream filled *(Drake's Yankee*		
Doodles)	4.0	1.0
chocolate, cream filled *(Tastykake)*,		
1.1 oz.	3.6	n.a.
chocolate, creme filled *(Hostess* Light)	2.0	< 1.0
creme *(Tastykake* Kreme Kup), .9 oz.	3.3	n.a.
golden, cream filled *(Drake's Sunny*		
Doodles)	3.0	1.0
orange *(Hostess)*	5.0	1.0
devil's food *(Little Debbie* Devil Cremes),		
2.5 oz.	13.0	n.a.
doughnut, see "Doughnut"		
(Drake's Funny Bones)	8.0	2.0
(Drake's Zoinks)	5.0	1.0
fig *(Little Debbie Figaroos)*, 1.5 oz.	4.0	n.a.
golden cremes *(Little Debbie)*, 2.5 oz.	11.0	n.a.
(Hostess Tiger Tails)	8.0	4.0
(Hostess Twinkies)	5.0	2.0
(Hostess Twinkies Light)	2.0	< 1.0
jelly *(Tastykake Krimpets)*, 1 oz.	.8	n.a.
jelly roll *(Little Debbie)*, 2.2 oz.	9.0	n.a.
lemon stix *(Little Debbie)*, 1.5 oz.	10.0	n.a.
(Little Debbie Caravella), 1.2 oz.	9.0	n.a.
marshmallow supreme *(Little Debbie)*,		
1.25 oz.	5.0	n.a.

mint wafer, chocolate-coated *(Little
   Debbie Mint Sprints)*, 1.33 oz. . . . . . . 10.0   n.a.
peanut butter *(Tastykake Kandy Kakes)*,
   .7 oz. . . . . 5.3   n.a.
peanut butter bar *(Little Debbie)*, 2.5 oz. 18.0   n.a.
peanut butter wafer, chocolate coated
   (Little Debbie Nutty Bar), 2.5 oz. . . . . 23.0   n.a.
peanut butter and jelly sandwich *(Little
   Debbie)*, 1.13 oz. . . . . 6.0   n.a.
pecan twins *(Little Debbie)*, 2 oz. . . . . . 10.0   n.a.
pie, see "Pie, snack"
strawberry *(Twinkies Fruit N Creme)*   3.0   1.0
Swiss roll *(Little Debbie)*, 2.25 oz.   . . . . 12.0   n.a.
vanilla *(Little Debbie)*, 3 oz. . . . . 19.0   n.a.
vanilla *(Tastykake Creamie)*, 1.5 oz. . . . 7.5   n.a.
vanilla, cream filled *(Tastykake Krimpets)*,
   1.1 oz. . . . . 3.6   n.a.
wafer, peanut butter filled *(Little Debbie
   Peanut Butter Naturals)*, 1.25 oz. . . . . 10.0   n.a.
Cake, snack, frozen, 1 piece or serving:
apple crisp *(Sara Lee Lights)* . . . . 2.0   n.a.
Black Forest *(Sara Lee Lights)* . . . . . . 5.0   n.a.
carrot *(Pepperidge Farm Classic)* 16.0   6.0
carrot *(Sara Lee Deluxe)* . . . . 7.0   n.a.
carrot *(Sara Lee Lights)* . . . . 4.0   n.a.
cheesecake:
   classic *(Sara Lee)* . . . . 14.0   n.a.
   French *(Sara Lee Lights)* . . . . 4.0   n.a.
   strawberry *(Pepperidge Farm American
     Collection)* 9.0   5.0
   strawberry, French *(Sara Lee Lights)* 2.0   n.a.
chocolate:
   double or German *(Pepperidge Farm
     Classic)* 13.0   4.0
   double *(Sara Lee Lights)* . . . . 5.0   n.a.
   fudge *(Sara Lee)* . . . . 10.0   n.a.
   mousse *(Pepperidge Farm Dessert
     Lights)* 9.0   3.0
   mousse *(Sara Lee)* . . . . 9.0   n.a.
   mousse *(Sara Lee Lights)* . . . . 8.0   n.a.
coconut *(Pepperidge Farm Classic)* 11.0   4.0

Cake, snack, frozen, continued

coffee, apple cinnamon *(Sara Lee)*	13.0	n.a.
coffee, butter streusel *(Sara Lee)*	12.0	n.a.
coffee, pecan *(Sara Lee)*	16.0	n.a.
doughnut, see "Doughnut"		
lemon cream *(Sara Lee Lights)*	6.0	n.a.
lemon supreme *(Pepperidge Farm* Dessert Lights)	5.0	1.0
pound, all butter *(Sara Lee)*	11.0	n.a.
strawberry shortcake *(Pepperidge Farm* Dessert Lights)	5.0	1.0
vanilla fudge swirl *(Pepperidge Farm* Classic)	11.0	4.0
Cake mix*, 1/12 cake, except as noted:		
angel food *(Duncan Hines)*	0	0
angel food, all flavors *(Betty Crocker),* dry	0	0
apple cinnamon *(Betty Crocker SuperMoist)*	10.0	2.0
apple streusel *(Betty Crocker MicroRave),* 1/6 cake	11.0	3.0
banana *(Pillsbury Plus)*	11.0	n.a.
Black Forest cherry *(Pillsbury Bundt),* 1/16 cake	8.0	n.a.
Black Forest mousse *(Duncan Hines Tiarra)*	13.0	n.a.
Boston cream *(Betty Crocker* Classic), 1/8 cake	6.0	n.a.
Boston cream *(Pillsbury Bundt),* 1/16 cake	10.0	n.a.
butter:		
brickle *(Betty Crocker SuperMoist)*	10.0	2.0
chocolate *(Betty Crocker SuperMoist)*	13.0	7.0
pecan *(Betty Crocker SuperMoist)* . . .	11.0	3.0
recipe *(Pillsbury Plus)*	12.0	n.a.
recipe, golden *(Duncan Hines)*	13.0	n.a.
yellow *(Betty Crocker SuperMoist)* . . .	11.0	6.0
carrot *(Betty Crocker SuperMoist)*	11.0	3.0
carrot *(Dromedary)*	15.0	n.a.
carrot 'n spice *(Pillsbury Plus)*	11.0	n.a.
cheesecake, 1/8 cake:		
plain or lemon *(Jell-O* No Bake)	13.0	n.a.

lite *(Royal No-Bake)*	10.0	n.a.
New York style *(Jell-O* No Bake) . . .	12.0	n.a.
real *(Royal No-Bake)*	9.0	n.a.
cherry chip *(Betty Crocker SuperMoist)*	3.0	1.0
cherries and cream *(Duncan Hines Tiarra)*	11.0	n.a.
chocolate:		
(Pillsbury Microwave), 1/8 cake	13.0	n.a.
dark *(Pillsbury Plus)*	12.0	n.a.
double supreme *(Pillsbury* Microwave), 1/8 cake	19.0	n.a.
fudge *(Betty Crocker SuperMoist)* . . .	12.0	3.0
fudge *(Duncan Hines* Butter Recipe)	13.0	n.a.
fudge *(Pillsbury Bundt Tunnel of Fudge)*, 1/16 cake	12.0	n.a.
fudge *(Pillsbury Bundt Tunnel of Fudge* Microwave), 1/8 cake	17.0	n.a.
fudge, dark Dutch *(Duncan Hines)*	15.0	n.a.
fudge, marble *(Duncan Hines)*	11.0	n.a.
fudge, marble *(Pillsbury Plus)*	12.0	n.a.
fudge, w/vanilla frosting *(Betty Crocker MicroRave)*, 1/6 cake	15.0	4.0
German *(Betty Crocker SuperMoist)*	12.0	3.0
German *(Pillsbury Plus)*	11.0	n.a.
German, w/coconut pecan frosting *(Betty Crocker MicroRave)*, 1/6 cake	18.0	5.0
milk *(Betty Crocker SuperMoist)*	12.0	3.0
mousse *(Duncan Hines Tiarra)*	16.0	n.a.
pudding *(Betty Crocker* Classic), 1/6 cake	5.0	n.a.
Swiss *(Duncan Hines)*	15.0	n.a.
w/chocolate or vanilla frosting *(Pillsbury* Microwave), 1/8 cake . . .	17.0	n.a.
chocolate chip *(Betty Crocker SuperMoist)*	14.0	3.0
chocolate chip *(Pillsbury Plus)*	14.0	n.a.
chocolate chip, chocolate *(Betty Crocker SuperMoist)*	12.0	3.0
chocolate macaroon *(Pillsbury Bundt)*, 1/16 cake	10.0	n.a.
cinnamon *(Streusel Swirl)*, 1/16 cake	11.0	n.a.

Cake mix, continued

cinnamon *(Streusel Swirl* Microwave),
  1/8 cake . . . .   11.0   n.a.
cinnamon pecan *(Betty Crocker*
  MicroRave), 1/6 cake 13.0   3.0
coffee *(Aunt Jemima* Easy), 1 serving . .   4.4   .8
coffee, apple cinnamon *(Pillsbury)*,
  1/8 cake . . . .   7.0   n.a.
devil's food:
  (Betty Crocker SuperMoist) 12.0   3.0
  (Duncan Hines) . . . .   15.0   n.a.
  (Pillsbury Plus) . . . .   14.0   n.a.
  w/chocolate frosting *(Betty Crocker*
    MicroRave), 1/6 cake 17.0   5.0
gingerbread *(Dromedary)*, 2″ × 2″ square   2.0   n.a.
lemon:
  (Betty Crocker SuperMoist) 11.0   3.0
  (Duncan Hines Supreme) . . . .   11.0   n.a.
  (Pillsbury Bundt Tunnel of Lemon),
    1/16 cake . . . .   9.0   n.a.
  (Pillsbury Microwave), 1/8 cake . . . . .   13.0   n.a.
  (Pillsbury Plus) . . . .   11.0   n.a.
  (Streusel Swirl), 1/16 cake . . . .   11.0   n.a.
  chiffon *(Betty Crocker* Classic) . . . . .   5.0   n.a.
  double supreme *(Pillsbury* Microwave),
    1/8 cake . . . .   15.0   n.a.
  w/lemon frosting *(Betty Crocker*
    MicroRave), 1/6 cake 16.0   4.0
  w/lemon frosting *(Pillsbury*
    Microwave), 1/8 cake . . . .   17.0   n.a.
  pudding *(Betty Crocker* Classic),
    1/6 cake . . . .   5.0   n.a.
marble *(Betty Crocker SuperMoist)* 11.0   3.0
pineapple *(Duncan Hines* Supreme) . . .   11.0   n.a.
pineapple cream *(Pillsbury Bundt)*,
  1/16 cake . . . .   9.0   n.a.
pineapple upside-down *(Betty Crocker*
  Classic), 1/9 cake 10.0   4.0
pound *(Dromedary)*, 1/2″ slice . . . .   6.0   n.a.
pound *(Martha White)*, 1/10 cake . . . . . .   4.0   n.a.
pound, golden *(Betty Crocker* Classic) . .   9.0   3.0

rainbow chip *(Betty Crocker SuperMoist)*	11.0	3.0
sour cream chocolate *(Betty Crocker SuperMoist)*	12.0	3.0
sour cream white *(Betty Crocker SuperMoist)*	3.0	1.0
spice *(Betty Crocker SuperMoist)*	11.0	3.0
spice *(Duncan Hines)*	11.0	n.a.
strawberry *(Duncan Hines Supreme)*	11.0	n.a.
strawberry *(Pillsbury Plus)*	11.0	n.a.
vanilla, French *(Duncan Hines)*	11.0	n.a.
vanilla, golden *(Betty Crocker SuperMoist)*	14.0	3.0
vanilla, golden, w/rainbow chip frosting *(Betty Crocker MicroRave)*, 1/6 cake	17.0	5.0
white *(Betty Crocker SuperMoist)*	9.0	2.0
white *(Duncan Hines)*	10.0	n.a.
white *(Pillsbury Plus)*	10.0	n.a.
yellow:		
(Betty Crocker SuperMoist)	11.0	3.0
(Duncan Hines)	11.0	n.a.
(Pillsbury Microwave), 1/8 cake	13.0	n.a.
(Pillsbury Plus)	12.0	n.a.
yellow, w/chocolate frosting:		
(Betty Crocker MicroRave), 1/6 cake	16.0	4.0
(Pillsbury Microwave), 1/8 cake	17.0	n.a.
Candy, 1 oz., except as noted:		
almond, candy-coated *(Brach's Jordan Almonds)*	2.0	n.a.
(Baby Ruth)	6.0	n.a.
bridge mix *(Brach's)*	6.0	n.a.
(Butterfinger)	6.0	n.a.
butterscotch *(Callard & Bowser)*	1.9	n.a.
candy cane *(Spangler)*, 1 piece	< 1.0	0
caramel:		
(Brach's Milk Maid)	2.0	n.a.
(Kraft), 1 piece	1.0	0
(Sugar Babies Regular/Tidbits), 15/8-oz. pkg.	2.0	n.a.
(Sugar Daddy), 13/8-oz. pop	1.0	n.a.
chocolate *(Brach's Milk Maid)*	3.0	n.a.
chocolate coated *(Pom Poms)*	3.0	n.a.

Candy, caramel, continued

chocolate coated, w/cookies *(Twix)*, 2 oz.	7.0	n.a.
milk chocolate coated *(Rolo)*, 8 pieces	12.0	n.a.
w/peanut, chocolate coated *(Oh Henry!)*, 2 oz.	14.0	n.a.
carob milk bar *(Caroby)*, 4 sections	9.0	n.a.
cherry, chocolate coated or cream *(Brach's)*	2.0	n.a.

chocolate:

w/almonds *(Hershey's Golden Almond/ Solitaires)*, 1.6 oz. or 1/2 bar	17.0	n.a.
w/almonds, roasted *(Cadbury)*	9.0	n.a.
bell, in foil *(Brach's)*	8.0	n.a.
candy coated *(M&M's)*, 1.69 oz.	12.0	n.a.
w/caramel *(Caramello)*, 1.6 oz.	11.0	n.a.
cream *(Callard & Bowser)*	3.7	n.a.
dark *(Hershey's Special Dark)*, 1.45 oz.	12.0	n.a.
eggs, in foil *(Brach's)*	8.0	n.a.
w/fruit and nuts *(Cadbury)*	8.0	n.a.
w/krisps and honey *(Cadbury)*	7.0	n.a.
milk *(Brach's Stars)*	8.0	n.a.
milk *(Cadbury Dairy Milk)*	8.0	n.a.
milk *(Hershey's)*, 1.55 oz.	14.0	n.a.
milk *(Hershey's Kisses)*, 9 pieces	13.0	n.a.
milk *(Nabisco Stars)*	8.0	n.a.
milk *(Nestlé)*, 1.45 oz.	13.0	n.a.
milk, w/almonds *(Hershey's)*, 1.45 oz.	14.0	n.a.
milk, w/almonds *(Nestlé)*, 1.45 oz.	14.0	n.a.
milk, creamy *(Hershey's Symphony)*, 1.75 oz.	16.0	n.a.
milk, creamy, w/almonds and toffee chips *(Hershey's Symphony)*, 1.75 oz.	17.0	n.a.
milk, w/crisps *(Krackel)*, 1.55 oz.	13.0	n.a.
milk, w/crisps *(Nestlé Crunch)*, 1.4 oz.	10.0	n.a.
milk, w/crisps and peanuts *(Nestlé 100 Grand)*, 1.5 oz.	8.0	n.a.
milk, w/fruit and nuts *(Chunky)*, 1.4 oz.	12.0	n.a.
milk, w/peanuts *(Brach's Peanut Clusters)*	9.0	n.a.

milk, w/peanuts *(Mr. Goodbar),*
   1.75 oz. . . . .   19.0   n.a.
  w/peanuts, candy coated *(M&M's),*
   1.74 oz. . . . .   13.0   n.a.
  white, w/almonds *(Nestlé Alpine),*
   1.25 oz. . . . .   14.0   n.a.
cinnamon, all varieties *(Brach's)*   0   0
coconut, chocolate coated:
  (Mounds), 1.9-oz. piece . . . .   14.0   n.a.
  (Sunbelt Macaroo), 2 oz. . . . .   16.0   n.a.
  dark or milk chocolate *(Bounty),*
   1.05 oz. . . . .   8.0   n.a.
  w/almonds *(Almond Joy),* 1.76-oz. piece   14.0   n.a.
coconut, Neapolitan *(Brach's)* . . . .   2.0   n.a.
corn, Indian or three color *(Brach's)* . . .   0   0
creme center, chocolate coated, 1 piece:
  (Spangler Opera Creme Chocolate
   Drop) . . . .   2.0   n.a.
  caramel w/nuts *(Spangler* Peanut
   Cluster) . . . .   6.0   n.a.
  cherry, maple, or vanilla creme, w/nuts
   (Spangler Peanut Cluster) . . . .   5.0   n.a.
  mint, dark chocolate coated *(Spangler*
   Bittersweets) . . . .   2.0   n.a.
  fudge w/nuts *(Spangler* Peanut Cluster)   6.0   n.a.
  fudge w/nuts *(Spangler* Pecan Cluster)   7.0   n.a.
eggs, creme *(Cadbury),* 1.37 oz. . . . . . .   8.0   n.a.
eggs, creme, mini *(Cadbury)* . . . .   7.0   n.a.
eggs, creme, chocolate coated:
  cherry *(Brach's)* . . . .   2.0   n.a.
  chocolate buttercream or coconut
   (Brach's) . . . .   3.0   n.a.
  fruit and nut, maple or vanilla
   (Brach's) . . . .   2.0   n.a.
filled, assorted *(Brach's)*   0   0
fruit flavored:
  all flavors *(Brach's* Fruit Bunch)   0   0
  all flavors *(Skittles),* 2.3 oz. . . . . . .   3.0   n.a.
  all flavors, chews *(Bonkers!),* 1 piece. .   0   0
  all flavors, chews *(Rascals),* 1 piece . .   tr.   0
  all flavors, chews *(Starburst),* 2.07 oz. .   5.0   n.a.

Candy, continued

fudge:

(Kraft Fudgies), 1 piece	1.0	0
all varieties, except maple walnut		
(Woodys)	4.0	2.0
maple walnut *(Woodys)*	4.0	1.0
gum, chewing, all varieties, 1 average		
piece	< .1	0
hard, all flavors *(Life Savers)*	0	0
(Heath Bits'O Brickle), 3 oz.	28.0	n.a.
(Heath Soft'n Crunchy Bar), 2 pieces	12.0	n.a.
honey *(Bit-O-Honey)*, 1.7 oz.	4.0	n.a.
(Hot Tamales), 1 piece	tr.	0
jellied and gummed:		
all varieties *(Brach's)*	0	0
eggs *(Rodda)*, 1 piece	tr.	0
juicy *(Callard & Bowser)*	0	0
(Jujyfruits), 1 oz. or 11 pieces	< 1.0	0
licorice:		
(Brach's Red Laces/Twin Twists) . . .	0	0
(Brach's Twists)	1.0	(0)
(Pearson's Licorice Nip)	3.0	n.a.
all varieties *(Y&S Bites/Nibs/Twizzlers)*	1.0	(0)
candy coated *(Good & Fruity)*	.1	(0)
candy coated *(Good & Plenty)*	< .1	(0)
lollipop, all flavors:		
all varieties *(Spangler)*, 1 piece	< 1.0	(0)
except chocolate *(Tootsie Pop)*	.6	.1
chocolate *(Tootsie Pop)*	.6	.2
malted milk balls, chocolate coated		
(Brach's)	5.0	n.a.
(Mars), 1.76-oz. bar	11.0	n.a.
marshmallow (see also specific listings):		
(Campfire), 2 large or 24 mini pieces	0	0
(Funmallows/Kraft Jet-Puffed), 1 piece	0	0
coconut, toasted *(Just Born)*, 1 piece	.6	(0)
cup *(Boyer Mallo Cup*, .5 oz.), 1 piece	5.0	n.a.
(Mike & Ikes), 1 piece	tr.	0
(Milky Way), 2.15-oz. bar	11.0	n.a.
(Milky Way Dark), 1.76-oz. bar	8.0	n.a.

mint:
(Brach's Creme de Menthe)	9.0	n.a.
(Brach's Jots/Pearls)	2.0	n.a.
(Brach's Kentucky/Dessert Mints) . . .	0	0
(Certs Sugar Free), 1 piece	tr.	0
(Mint Meltaway), .33-oz. piece	3.0	n.a.
all flavors *(Breath Savers)*, 1 piece . . .	0	0
butter or party *(Kraft)*, 1 piece	0	0

mint, chocolate coated:
(Junior Mints)	3.0	n.a.
(York Peppermint Pattie), 1.5 oz.	4.0	n.a.
dark chocolate *(After Eight)*, 1 piece	1.0	n.a.
regular, creme, or thin *(Brach's)*	2.0	n.a.
(Munch), 1.42-oz. bar	14.0	n.a.
(Necco Sky Bar), 1.5-oz. bar	7.1	n.a.
nonpareils *(Nestlé Sno-Caps)*	6.0	n.a.

nougat, chocolate coated *(Charleston
Chew!)* . . . . 3.0 n.a.
orange sticks, chocolate coated *(Brach's)* 2.0 n.a.

peanut:
(Brach's Jots)	6.0	n.a.
butter toffee *(Flavor House)*	7.0	n.a.
chocolate coated *(Goobers)*, 1³/₈ oz.	13.0	n.a.
chocolate coated *(Nabisco)*	9.0	n.a.
milk chocolate coated *(Brach's)*	9.0	n.a.
filled *(Brach's)*	1.0	n.a.
French burnt *(Brach's)*	5.0	n.a.
peanut brittle *(Kraft)*	5.0	1.0

peanut butter:
(PB Max), 1.48 oz.	16.0	n.a.
candy coated *(Reese's Pieces)*, 1.85 oz.	11.0	n.a.
chocolate coated, w/cookies *(Twix)*, 1 bar	7.0	n.a.
cup *(Boyer*, .5 oz.), 1 piece	7.5	n.a.
cup, chocolate coated *(Reese's)*, 1.8 oz.	17.0	n.a.
kisses *(Brach's)*	2.0	n.a.
peanut caramel cluster *(Brach's)*	8.0	n.a.
peanut parfait *(Brach's)*	10.0	n.a.
peppermint kisses *(Brach's)*	1.0	n.a.

popcorn, caramel coated, w/peanuts
(Cracker Jack) . . . . 3.0 n.a.

Candy,, continued

raisins, chocolate coated:

(*Brach's*)	5.0	n.a.
(*Nabisco*), 1 oz., approx. 29 pieces . . .	5.0	n.a.
(*Raisinets*), 1³/8 oz.	6.0	n.a.
rock (*Brach's* Cut Rock)	0	0
(*Snickers*), 2.07-oz. bar	14.0	n.a.
sour balls (*Brach's*)	0	0
straws, mint filled (*Brach's*)	1.0	n.a.
taffy, all flavors (*Brach's* Salt Water Taffy)	1.0	n.a.
(*3 Musketeers*), 2.13-oz. bar	8.0	n.a.

toffee:

(*Brach's*)	2.0	n.a.
(*Callard & Bowser*)	6.5	n.a.
(*Skor*), 1.4 oz.	14.0	n.a.
English (*Bits'O Heath*), 3.5 oz.	31.0	n.a.
English (*Heath* Bar), 2 pieces, 1³/16 oz.	11.0	n.a.
(*Tootsie Roll*)	2.5	.6

wafer:

assorted (*Necco*), 2.02-oz. roll	0	0
chocolate (*Necco*), 2.02-oz. roll	.1	0
bar, chocolate coated (*Kit Kat*), 1.63 oz.	13.0	n.a.
Cane syrup, 1 tbsp.	0	0
Cannellini bean, see "Beans, kidney, white"		
Cannelloni, canned, mini (*Chef Boyardee*), 7.5 oz.	7.0	n.a.
Cannelloni entrée, frozen:		
beef and pork, w/mornay sauce (*Lean Cuisine*), 9⁵/8 oz.	10.0	4.0
cheese (*Dining Lite*), 9 oz.	9.0	n.a.
cheese, w/tomato sauce (*Lean Cuisine*), 9¹/8 oz.	10.0	5.0
Florentine (*Celentano*), 12 oz.	8.0	n.a.
Cantaloupe, pulp, cubed, ¹/2 cup	.2	(0)
Capocollo (*Hormel*), 1 oz.	6.0	n.a.
Carambola, trimmed, cubed, ¹/2 cup	.2	(0)
Caramel danish, w/nuts, refrigerated (*Pillsbury*), 1 piece	8.0	2.0
Caraway seed, 1 tsp.	.3	tr.
Cardamom, ground or seed, 1 tsp.	.1	tr.

Cardoon, raw, shredded, 1/2 cup, or boiled,
4 oz. . . . . .1 < .1
Carissa (natal plum), sliced, 1/2 cup 1.0 (0)
Carl's Jr.:
  breakfast, 1 serving:
    bacon, 2 strips, .4 oz. 4.0 3.0
    eggs, scrambled, 2.4 oz. 9.0 4.0
    English muffin, w/margarine, 2 oz. . . . 6.0 2.0
    French toast dips, w/out syrup, 4.7 oz. 25.0 10.0
    hash brown nuggets, 3 oz. 9.0 4.0
    hot cakes, w/margarine, w/out syrup,
    5.5 oz. 12.0 3.0
    sausage, 1 patty, .5 oz. 17.0 4.0
    Sunrise Sandwich, w/bacon, 4.5 oz. . . . 19.0 8.0
    Sunrise Sandwich, w/sausage, 6.1 oz. 32.0 12.0
  sandwiches, 1 serving:
    California Roast Beef'n Swiss, 7.4 oz. 8.0 4.0
    Charbroiler BBQ Chicken Sandwich,
    6.3 oz. 5.0 2.0
    Charbroiler Chicken Club Sandwich,
    8.3 oz. 22.0 2.0
    Country Fried Steak Sandwich, 7.2 oz. 33.0 12.0
    Double Western Bacon Cheeseburger,
    7.5 oz. 53.0 25.0
    Famous Star Hamburger, 8.1 oz. 36.0 13.0
    fish fillet, 7.9 oz. 26.0 11.0
    Happy Star hamburger, 3 oz. 8.0 4.0
    Old Time Star hamburger, 5.9 oz. . . . 17.0 7.0
    Super Star hamburger, 10.6 oz. 50.0 21.0
    Western Bacon Cheeseburger, 7.5 oz. 33.0 15.0
  potatoes, 1 serving:
    bacon and cheese, 14.1 oz. 34.0 12.0
    broccoli and cheese, 14 oz. 17.0 5.0
    cheese, 14.2 oz. 22.0 7.0
    Fiesta, 15.2 oz. 23.0 9.0
    Lite, 9.8 oz. 3.0 0
    sour cream and chive, 10.4 oz. 13.0 5.0
  salad-to-go, 1 serving:
    chef, 10.7 oz. 7.0 3.0
    chicken, 10.9 oz. 8.0 3.0
    garden, 4.1 oz. 2.0 1.0

Carl's Jr., salad-to-go, continued

taco, 14.3 oz.	19.0	6.0
salad dressing, 1 oz.:		
blue cheese	15.0	3.0
French, reduced calorie	2.0	0
house or Thousand Island	11.0	3.0
Italian	13.0	2.0
side dishes, 1 serving:		
french fries, regular, 6 oz.	17.0	11.0
onion rings, 3.2 oz.	15.0	7.0
zucchini, 4.3 oz.	16.0	7.0
soup, 1 serving:		
Boston clam chowder, 6.6 oz.	8.0	3.0
broccoli, cream of, 6.6 oz.	6.0	4.0
chicken noodle, old fashioned, 6.6 oz.	1.0	tr.
Lumber Jack Mix vegetable, 6.6 oz.	3.0	tr.
bakery products, 1 serving:		
blueberry muffin, 3.5 oz.	7.0	1.0
bran muffin, 4 oz.	6.0	0
brownie, fudge, 4.5 oz.	27.0	7.0
chocolate chip cookie, 2.5 oz.	17.0	6.0
cinnamon roll, 4 oz.	16.0	1.0
danish (all varieties), 4 oz.	21.0	1.0
shakes, regular, all flavors, 11.6 oz.	7.0	4.0
Carp, meat only:		
raw, 4 oz.	6.4	1.2
baked, broiled, or microwaved, 4 oz.	8.1	1.6
Carrot:		
fresh, raw, 1 medium, or shredded, 1/2 cup	.1	< .1
fresh or frozen, boiled, sliced, 1/2 cup	.1	< .1
canned, sliced, 1/2 cup	.2	< .1
frozen, baby, w/sweet peas and pearl onions *(Birds Eye* Deluxe), 3.3 oz.	0	0
Carrot chips:		
(Hain), 1 oz.	9.0	n.a.
(Hain No Salt Added), 1 oz.	7.0	n.a.
barbecue *(Hain),* 1 oz.	8.0	n.a.
Carrot juice, canned or bottled, 6 fl. oz.	.3	.1
Casaba, pulp, cubed, 1/2 cup	.1	(0)
Cashew:		
dry roasted, 1 oz.	13.2	2.6

dry roasted, whole and halves, 1 cup . . .	63.5	12.5
honey roasted *(Planters)*, 1 oz.	12.0	2.0
oil roasted, 1 oz.	13.7	2.7
Cashew butter:		
(Hain Raw), 2 tbsp.	15.0	3.0
(Hain Raw Unsalted), 2 tbsp.	19.0	3.0
(Hain Toasted), 2 tbsp.	17.0	3.0
Cassava, fresh, trimmed, 1 oz.	.1	< .1
Catfish, meat only:		
fresh, channel, raw, 4 oz.	4.8	1.1
frozen, fillets *(Delta Pride)*, 4 oz.	4.9	n.a.
frozen, ocean *(Booth)*, 4 oz.	3.0	n.a.
Catjang:		
raw, 1/2 cup	1.7	.5
boiled, 1/2 cup	.6	.2
Catsup, 1 tbsp.	.1	< .1
Cauliflower:		
fresh, raw or boiled, drained, pieces,		
1/2 cup	.1	< .1
frozen:		
boiled, drained, 1" pieces, 1/2 cup . . .	.2	< .1
in cheddar sauce *(The Budget Gourmet*		
Side Dish), 5 oz.	5.0	n.a.
in cheese sauce *(Birds Eye* Cheese		
Sauce Combinations), 5 oz.	7.0	n.a.
in cheese sauce *(Green Giant)*, 5.5 oz. .	2.0	n.a.
in cheese sauce *(Stokely Singles)*, 4 oz.	3.0	n.a.
in cheese-flavor sauce *(Green Giant)*,		
1/2 cup	2.0	n.a.
Cauliflower, combinations, frozen:		
broccoli and carrots, in cheese sauce		
(Freezer Queen Family Side Dishes),		
5 oz.	1.0	n.a.
carrots, baby whole, and snow pea pods		
(Birds Eye Farm Fresh), 4 oz.	0	0
zucchini, carrots, and red peppers *(Birds*		
Eye Farm Fresh), 4 oz.	0	0
Cavatelli, frozen *(Celentano)*, 3.2 oz.	1.0	n.a.
Caviar, granular, black and red:		
1 oz.	5.0	n.a.
1 tbsp.	2.9	n.a.

Celeriac, raw, 1/2 cup, or boiled, drained,
4 oz.   .2   (0)
Celery, raw, 1 stalk, 71/2″ long, or boiled,
drained, diced, 1/2 cup 1   < .1
Celery root juice, bottled *(Biotta),* 6 fl. oz.   .2   (0)
Celery salt *(Tone's),* 1 tsp. 4   < .1
Celery seed, 1 tsp. 5   < .1
Celtus, raw, trimmed, 1 oz. 1   (0)
Cereal, ready-to-eat, 1 oz., except as noted:
  bran (see also "oat bran," below):
    (Bran Buds) . . . . 1.0   n.a.
    (Kellogg's 40%+ Bran Flakes) 0   0
    (Kellogg's Heartwise) . . . . 1.0   n.a.
    (Nabisco 100% Bran) . . . . 2.0   n.a.
    (Post Natural Bran Flakes) 0   0
    (Quaker Crunchy Bran) . . . . 1.3   .4
    apple spice or cinnamon *(Ralston Bran
    News)* 0   0
    regular or extra fiber *(All Bran)* . . . . 1.0   n.a.
    w/fruit and nuts *(Mueslix),* 1.4 oz. . . . 2.0   n.a.
    w/raisins *(Kellogg's* Raisin Bran),
    1.4 oz. 1.0   n.a.
    w/raisins *(Post* Natural Raisin Bran),
    1.4 oz. 1.0   n.a.
    w/raisins *(Total Raisin Bran),* 1.5 oz. 1.0   n.a.
    w/raisins and nuts *(Raisin Nut Bran)* 3.0   n.a.
  corn:
    (Corn Chex) 0   0
    (Country Corn Flakes) . . . . < 1.0   n.a.
    (Honeycomb) 0   0
    (Kellogg's Corn Flakes/Frosted Flakes) 0   0
    (Nutri·Grain) . . . . 1.0   n.a.
    (Post Toasties) 0   0
    (Total Corn Flakes) . . . . 1.0   n.a.
    w/nuts and honey *(Nut & Honey
    Crunch)* . . . . 1.0   n.a.
  granola:
    (C.W. Post Hearty) . . . . 4.0   n.a.
    w/almonds *(Sun Country* 100%
    Natural) . . . . 5.3   .6
    banana almond *(Sunbelt)* . . . . 4.0   n.a.

fruit and nut *(Sunbelt)*	5.0	n.a.
w/raisins *(Sun Country)*	4.8	.5
w/raisins, dates *(Sun Country 100% Natural)*	4.5	.5
mixed grain and natural style:		
(Almond Delight)	2.0	n.a.
(Cap'n Crunch)	1.7	.8
(Cap'n Crunch's Peanut Butter Crunch)	3.0	.9
(Cinnamon Toast Crunch)	3.0	n.a.
(Crispix)	0	0
(Crunchy Nut Oh!s)	4.2	2.4
(Double Chex)	0	0
(Familia Champion/No Added Sugar), 2 oz.	4.0	n.a.
(Familia Crunchy)	2.0	n.a.
(Fiber One)	1.0	n.a.
(Golden Grahams)	1.0	n.a.
(Grape Nuts)	0	0
(Grape Nuts Flakes)	1.0	0
(Heartland)	4.0	0
(Honey Graham Oh!s)	3.2	1.5
(Just Right)	1.0	n.a.
(King Vitaman)	1.0	0
(Nutri·Grain Nuggets)	1.0	n.a.
(Product 19)	0	0
(Quaker 100% Natural)	5.5	3.1
(Special K)	0	0
w/almonds *(Honey Bunches of Oats)*	3.0	n.a.
w/almonds and raisins *(Nutri·Grain)*, 1.4 oz.	2.0	n.a.
apple and cinnamon *(Quaker* 100% Natural)	4.9	2.7
coconut *(Heartland)*	5.0	n.a.
w/dates, raisins, walnuts, and oat clusters *(Fruit & Fibre)*, 1.25 oz.	2.0	n.a.
w/fruit and nuts *(Just Right)*, 1.3 oz.	1.0	n.a.
w/fruit and nuts *(Mueslix* Five Grain), 1.45 oz.	1.0	n.a.
w/fruit, tropical and oat clusters *(Fruit & Fibre)*, 1.25 oz.	3.0	n.a.

Cereal, ready-to-eat, mixed grain and natural style, continued

honey roasted *(Honey Bunches of Oats)*	2.0	n.a.
w/peaches, raisins, almonds, and oat clusters *(Fruit & Fibre)*, 1.25 oz.	2.0	n.a.
w/raisins *(Grape Nuts)*	0	0
w/raisins *(Heartland)*	4.0	n.a.
w/raisins and almonds *(Nutrific)*, 1.5 oz.	2.0	n.a.
raisins and dates *(Quaker 100%)*	5.0	2.6
raisins, dates, and almonds *(Ralston Muesli)*, 1.45 oz.	2.0	n.a.
raisins, w/peaches and pecans or walnuts and cranberries *(Ralston Muesli)*, 1.45 oz.	3.0	n.a.
oat:		
(General Mills Toasted Oat)	5.0	n.a.
(Oat Chex)	1.0	n.a.
(Post Oat Flakes)	1.0	n.a.
(Quaker Oat Squares)	1.6	n.a.
honey nut *(Cheerios)*	1.0	n.a.
plain or apple cinnamon *(Cheerios)*	2.0	n.a.
plain or cinnamon *(Life)*	1.7	n.a.
plain or raisin *(General Mills* Oatmeal Crisp)	2.0	n.a.
oat bran:		
(Common Sense)	1.0	n.a.
(Craklin' Oat Bran)	0	0
w/raisins *(General Mills Raisin Oat Bran)*, 1.5 oz.	2.0	n.a.
w/raisins *(Raisin Oat Bran Options)*, 1.45 oz.	1.0	n.a.
rice *(Kellogg's Frosted/Rice Krispies)*	0	0
rice *(Quaker* Puffed Rice), .5 oz.	.1	0
rice *(Rice Chex)*	0	0
wheat:		
(Clusters)	3.0	n.a.
(Honey Smacks)	1.0	n.a.
(Quaker Puffed Wheat), .5 oz.	.2	0
(Total)	1.0	n.a.
(Wheat Chex)	0	0
(Wheaties)	1.0	n.a.

all varieties *(Nutri·Grain)*	0	0
brown sugar *(Nut & Honey Crunch Biscuits)*	1.0	n.a.
fruit filled *(Kellogg's Squares)*	0	0
honey-sweetened puffs *(Super Golden Crisp)*	0	0
w/raisins *(Crispy Wheats'N Raisins)*	1.0	n.a.
raspberry filled *(Fruit Wheats)*	0	0
shredded *(Frosted Mini-Wheats)*	0	0
shredded *(Nabisco)*, 1 biscuit	< 1.0	n.a.
shredded *(Nabisco Shredded Wheat 'n Bran)*	< 1.0	n.a.
shredded *(Nabisco Spoon Size)*	< 1.0	n.a.
shredded *(Quaker)*, 2 biscuits	.6	n.a.
shredded *(S.W. Graham)*	0	0
Cereal, cooking, uncooked, except as noted:		
bran *(H-O Brand Super Bran)*, 1/3 cup	2.0	0
farina, see "wheat," below		
grain, multi, apple cinnamon *(Roman Meal)*, 1/3 cup dry or 2/3 cup cooked	2.8	n.a.
oat bran:		
(Quaker/Mother's), 1/3 cup dry or 2/3 cup cooked	2.1	.2
(3-Minute Brand Regular or Instant), 1 oz.	2.0	n.a.
(Wholesome 'N Hearty), 1 oz.	2.0	n.a.
apple cinnamon or honey *(Wholesome'N Hearty* Instant), 1 pkt.	2.0	n.a.
oatmeal and oats:		
(H-O Brand Quick/Instant-Box), 1/2 cup	2.0	0
(Instant Quaker), 1 pkt.	2.0	.3
(Quaker Quick/Old Fashioned), 1/3 cup dry or 2/3 cup cooked	2.0	.3
(Quaker Extra), 1 pkt.	2.0	.2
(3-Minute Brand Quick/Old Fashioned), 1 oz.	2.0	n.a.
(Total Instant/Quick), 1 oz. or 1 pkt.	2.0	n.a.
all flavors *(H-O Brand* Instant), 1 pkt.	2.0	0
apple and cinnamon *(Instant Quaker)*, 1 pkt.	1.5	.3

Cereal, cooking, oatmeal and oats, continued

apples and spice *(Quaker Extra)*, 1 pkt.	1.9	.3
cinnamon and spice *(Instant Quaker)*, 1 pkt.	2.1	.4
w/fiber *(H-O Brand* Instant-Box), ⅓ cup	2.0	0
maple brown sugar *(Instant Quaker)*, 1 pkt.	2.1	.4
w/oat bran or raisin *(3-Minute Brand)*, 1 oz.	2.0	n.a.
peaches and cream *(Instant Quaker)*, 1 pkt.	2.2	.9
plain or maple *(Maypo)*, 1 oz.	1.0	n.a.
raisins and cinnamon *(Quaker Extra)*, 1 pkt.	1.9	.3
raisins, dates, and walnut *(Instant Quaker)*, 1 pkt.	3.8	.4
raisins and spice *(Instant Quaker)*, 1 pkt.	2.0	.3
strawberries and cream *(Instant Quaker)*, 1 pkt.	2.0	1.1
w/wheat, dates, raisins, and almonds *(Roman Meal* Premium), 1.3 oz. or ⅓ cup	3.0	n.a.
w/wheat, honey, coconut, and almonds *(Roman Meal* Premium), 1.3 oz. or ⅓ cup	6.0	n.a.
w/wheat, rye, bran, and flax *(Roman Meal)*, 1.2 oz. or ⅓ cup	1.7	n.a.
rye, cream of *(Roman Meal)*, 1.3 oz. or ⅓ cup	< 1.0	n.a.
wheat:		
(Cream of Wheat Instant/Quick), 1 oz.	0	0
(Wheat Hearts), 1 oz. or ¾ cup cooked	1.0	n.a.
(Wheatena), 1 oz.	1.0	n.a.
all flavors *(Mix'n Eat Cream of Wheat)*, 1 pkt.	0	0
farina *(H-O Brand* Instant), 1 pkt.	0	0
farina, cream *(H-O Brand)*, 3 tbsp.	0	0
w/rye, bran, and flax *(Roman Meal)*, 1 oz.	.5	n.a.

whole *(Quaker/Mother's* Hot Natural),		
1/3 cup dry or 2/3 cup cooked	.6	.1
wheat and barley *(Maltex)*, 1 oz.	1.0	n.a.

Cereal beverage, see "Coffee substitute"

Cervelat, see "Summer sausage" and "Thuringer cervelat"

Chard, Swiss, boiled, drained, chopped,		
1/2 cup	.1	(0)
Chayote, raw, 1 medium, 7.2 oz.	.6	(0)
Cheddarwurst:		
(Hillshire Farm Bun Size), 2 oz.	18.0	n.a.
(Hillshire Farm Links), 2 oz.	17.0	n.a.
Cheese, 1 oz., except as noted:		
all varieties, except mozzarella *(Kraft*		
Light Naturals)	5.0	3.0
American, processed:		
1 oz.	8.9	5.6
(Borden Loaf or Slices)	9.0	n.a.
(Dorman's/Dorman's Loaf Low		
Sodium)	9.0	n.a.
(Land O'Lakes)	9.0	6.0
(Kraft Deluxe Loaf or Slices)	9.0	5.0
hot pepper *(Sargento)*	9.0	n.a.
sharp *(Old English* Loaf or Slices) . . .	9.0	5.0
asiago, wheel *(Frigo)*	9.0	n.a.
babybel *(Laughing Cow)*	7.0	n.a.
(Bel Paese Domestic Traditional)	8.0	n.a.
(Bel Paese Imported)	7.4	n.a.
(Bel Paese Lite)	5.0	n.a.
(Bel Paese Medallion Process)	5.9	n.a.
blue:		
1 oz.	8.2	5.3
(Dorman's Danablu 50%)	8.2	5.0
(Dorman's Danablu 60%)	9.7	6.9
(Kraft)	9.0	5.0
castello *(Dorman's* 70%)	12.3	9.0
crumbled, 1 cup not packed	38.8	25.2
saga *(Dorman's* 70%)	12.3	9.0
bonbel *(Laughing Cow)*	8.0	n.a.
bonbino *(Laughing Cow)*	9.0	n.a.
brick *(Dorman's)*	8.0	n.a.

Cheese, continued

brick *(Kraft)*	9.0	5.0
brick *(Land O'Lakes)*	8.0	5.0
Brie *(Dorman's)*	6.6	4.0
Brie *(Sargento)*	8.0	n.a.
Cajun *(Sargento)*	9.0	n.a.
caljack *(Churney)*	8.0	n.a.
Camembert *(Dorman's 45%)*	6.3	3.9
Camembert *(Dorman's 50%)*	7.3	4.4
Camembert *(Sargento)*	7.0	n.a.
cheddar:		
shredded, 1 cup not packed	37.5	23.8
(Alpine Lace Cheddar Flavored)	8.0	5.0
(Darigold)	9.0	5.9
(Dorman's)	9.0	n.a.
(Dorman's Chedda-Delite)	7.0	n.a.
(Kraft)	9.0	5.0
(Land O'Lakes)	9.0	6.0
(Laughing Cow)	9.0	n.a.
(Sargento/Sargento New York)	9.0	n.a.
all varieties *(Weight Watchers* Natural)	5.0	3.0
reduced fat *(Dorman's* Low Sodium)	5.0	3.4
sharp, white *(Cracker Barrel Light)*	5.0	3.0
Vermont *(Churny)*	9.0	5.0
cheddar jack *(Dorman's* Chedda-Jack)	7.0	n.a.
Cheshire	8.7	n.a.
colby:		
(Alpine Lace Colby-Lo)	5.0	4.0
(Dorman's)	9.0	n.a.
(Kraft)	9.0	5.0
(Land O'Lakes)	9.0	6.0
(Weight Watchers Natural)	5.0	2.0
cottage cheese, creamed:		
small curd, 1/2 cup not packed	4.7	3.0
large curd, 1/2 cup not packed	5.1	3.2
(Borden, 4% fat), 1/2 cup	5.0	n.a.
(Darigold 4%), 4 oz.	4.2	3.2
(Friendship California Style 4%),		
1/2 cup	5.0	n.a.
(Knudsen), 4 oz.	5.0	3.0

plain or w/pineapple *(Breakstone's)*, 4 oz.	5.0	3.0
w/peaches *(Crowley* 4% fat), 1/2 cup	3.0	n.a.
w/pineapple *(Crowley* 4% fat), 1/2 cup	4.0	n.a.
w/pineapple *(Friendship* 4%), 1/2 cup	4.0	n.a.
cottage cheese, dry curd:		
1/2 cup not packed	.3	.2
(Breakstone's), 4 oz.	0	0
(Darigold), 4 oz.	1.0	.4
cottage cheese, lowfat:		
2%, 4 oz. or 1/2 cup not packed	2.2	1.4
2% *(Breakstone's/Sealtest)*, 4 oz.	2.0	1.0
2% *(Darigold* Trim), 4 oz.	3.2	2.0
2%, w/fruit, all varieties *(Knudsen)*, 4 oz.	2.0	2.0
1%, 4 oz., approx. 1/2 cup not packed	1.2	.7
1% *(Light n' Lively)*, 4 oz.	2.0	1.0
1%, all varieties *(Friendship)*, 1/2 cup	1.0	n.a.
1%, garden salad *(Light n' Lively)*, 4 oz.	2.0	1.0
1%, w/peach and pineapple *(Light n' Lively)*, 4 oz.	1.0	1.0
pot style, 2% *(Friendship)*, 1/2 cup	2.0	n.a.
cottage cheese, nonfat *(Knudsen)*, 4 oz.	0	0
cream cheese:		
(Darigold)	9.9	6.2
(Dorman's 65%)	8.4	5.1
(Dorman's 70%)	9.9	6.1
(Philadelphia Brand)	10.0	6.0
w/chives or pimiento *(Philadelphia Brand)*	9.0	5.0
cream cheese, soft:		
(Philadelphia Brand)	10.0	5.0
w/chives and onion, herb and garlic, or smoked salmon *(Philadelphia Brand)*	9.0	5.0
w/olives and pimiento, pineapple, or strawberries *(Philadelphia Brand)*	8.0	5.0
cream cheese, whipped:		
plain *(Philadelphia Brand)*	10.0	6.0
all flavors *(Philadelphia Brand)*	8.0	5.0
danbo *(Dorman's* 20%)	2.8	1.7

Cheese, continued

danbo *(Dorman's* 45%)	7.5	4.6
(Dorman's Crema Dania 70%)	12.3	9.0
Edam:		
1 oz.	7.9	5.0
(Dorman's)	8.0	n.a.
(Dorman's 45%)	7.0	4.3
(Kraft)	7.0	4.0
(Land O'Lakes)	8.0	5.0
(Laughing Cow)	8.0	n.a.
farmer *(Friendship)*, 1/2 cup	12.0	n.a.
farmer *(Sargento)*	8.0	n.a.
feta, sheep's milk	6.0	4.2
feta *(Churny* Natural)	6.5	4.2
feta *(Dorman's* 45%)	7.3	n.a.
feta *(Sargento)*	6.0	n.a.
fontina	8.8	5.4
fontina *(Sargento)*	9.0	n.a.
gjetost *(Sargento)*	8.0	n.a.
gjetost, goat's milk	8.4	5.4
Gouda:		
1 oz.	7.8	5.0
(Dorman's)	8.0	n.a.
(Kraft)	9.0	5.0
(Land O'Lakes)	8.0	5.0
(Laughing Cow)	9.0	n.a.
(Sargento)	8.0	n.a.
Gruyère	9.2	5.4
havarti:		
(Casino)	11.0	7.0
(Dorman's 45%)	7.0	4.3
(Dorman's 60%)	10.6	6.5
(Sargento)	11.0	n.a.
Italian style, grated *(Sargento)*	8.0	n.a.
Jarlsberg *(Norseland Jarlsberg)*	7.0	4.2
limburger	7.7	4.8
limburger *(Sargento)*	8.0	n.a.
limburger, natural *(Mohawk Valley* Little Gem)	8.0	5.0
mascarpone *(Galbani* Imported)	13.1	n.a.

Monterey Jack:

(Alpine Lace Monti-Jack-Lo)	5.0	4.0
(Dorman's)	8.0	n.a.
(Land O'Lakes)	9.0	5.0
(Weight Watchers Natural)	5.0	2.0
w/caraway seeds *(Kraft)*	8.0	5.0
plain or w/jalapeño pepper *(Kraft)* . . .	9.0	5.0
reduced fat *(Dorman's* Low Sodium)	5.0	3.1

mozzarella:

(Polly-O Lite)	4.0	n.a.
fresh *(Polly-O Fior di Latte)*	6.0	n.a.
regular or shredded *(Weight Watchers)*	4.0	2.0
whole milk	6.1	3.7
whole milk *(Crowley)*	7.0	n.a.
whole milk *(Polly-O)*	6.0	n.a.
whole milk, low moisture *(Frigo)* . . .	7.0	4.0
part skim	4.5	2.9
part skim *(Polly-O)*	5.0	n.a.
part skim, plain or w/jalapeño *(Kraft)*	5.0	3.0
part skim, low moisture *(Alpine Lace)*	5.0	3.0
part skim, low moisture *(Dorman's* Low Sodium)	5.0	2.6
part skim, low moisture *(Land O'Lakes)*	5.0	3.0
part skim, reduced fat *(Frigo)*	3.0	2.0
part skim, w/jalapeño pepper *(Kraft)*	5.0	3.0
low moisture *(Kraft)*	7.0	4.0
reduced fat *(Dorman's* Low Sodium)	4.0	2.5
reduced fat *(Kraft Light Naturals)* . . .	4.0	3.0

Muenster:

1 oz.	8.5	5.4
(Alpine Lace)	8.0	5.0
(Dorman's)	9.0	n.a.
(Dorman's 50%)	8.2	5.0
(Land O'Lakes)	9.0	5.0
reduced fat *(Dorman's* Low Sodium)	5.0	3.1
red rind *(Sargento)*	9.0	n.a.
Neufchâtel	6.6	4.2
Neufchâtel *(Philadelphia Brand Light)* . .	7.0	4.0

Parmesan:

(Kraft)	7.0	4.0

Cheese, Parmesan, continued

fresh *(Sargento)*	7.0	n.a.
hard	7.3	4.7
grated	8.5	5.4
grated, 1 tbsp.	1.5	1.0
grated *(Kraft)*	9.0	5.0
grated *(Polly-O)*	9.0	n.a.
grated *(Progresso)*, 1 tbsp.	2.0	1.0
grated *(Sargento)*	9.0	n.a.
Reggiano *(Galbani* Imported)	7.1	n.a.
wheel or fresh grated *(Frigo)*	7.0	n.a.
Parmesan and Romano, grated *(Frigo)*	9.0	n.a.
Parmesan and Romano, grated *(Sargento)*	7.0	n.a.
pasta, Italian, grated *(Frigo* Parmazest)	8.0	n.a.
pimiento, processed	8.9	5.6
pimiento, processed *(Kraft* Deluxe)	8.0	5.0
pizza, shredded *(Frigo)*	7.0	n.a.
pizza, shredded, low fat *(Frigo)*	3.0	n.a.
Port du Salut	8.0	4.7
pot cheese *(Sargento)*	.2	n.a.
Primavera *(Bel Paese* Lite)	4.0	n.a.
provolone:		
1 oz.	7.6	4.8
(Alpine Lace Provo-Lo)	5.0	5.0
(Dorman's)	7.0	n.a.
(Kraft)	7.0	4.0
(Land O'Lakes)	8.0	5.0
(Sargento)	8.0	n.a.
queso blanco or queso de papa *(Sargento)*	9.0	n.a.
ricotta:		
(Polly-O Lite), 2 oz.	4.0	n.a.
(Sargento)	3.0	n.a.
(Sargento Lite)	1.0	n.a.
whole milk	3.7	2.4
whole milk, 1/2 cup	16.1	10.3
whole milk *(Crowley)*, 2 oz.	7.0	n.a.
whole milk *(Frigo)*	4.0	n.a.
whole milk *(Polly-O)*, 2 oz.	7.0	n.a.
part skim	2.2	1.4
part skim, 1/2 cup	9.8	6.1
part skim *(Crowley)*, 2 oz.	4.0	n.a.

part skim *(Frigo)*	3.0	n.a.
part skim *(Polly-O)*, 2 oz.	6.0	n.a.
part skim *(Sargento)*	2.0	n.a.
low fat *(Frigo)*	1.0	n.a.
Romano:		
(Kraft Natural)	7.0	4.0
(Sargento)	8.0	n.a.
grated *(Frigo)*	9.0	n.a.
grated *(Kraft)*	9.0	6.0
grated *(Polly-O)*	10.0	n.a.
grated *(Progresso)*, 1 tbsp.	2.0	1.0
wedge *(Frigo)*	8.0	n.a.
Roquefort, sheep's milk	8.7	5.5
slim Jack *(Dorman's)*	7.0	n.a.
smoked *(Sargento* Smokestick)	7.0	n.a.
string *(Frigo)*	5.0	n.a.
string *(Polly-O)*, 1-oz. stick	6.0	n.a.
string, plain or smoked *(Sargento)*	5.0	n.a.
Swiss:		
(Alpine Lace Swiss-Lo)	7.0	4.0
(Casino)	8.0	5.0
(Cracker Barrel Natural Baby Swiss)	9.0	5.0
(Dorman's/Dorman's No Salt Added)	8.0	n.a.
(Dorman's Reduced Fat)	5.0	2.8
(Land O'Lakes)	8.0	5.0
(Sargento/Sargento Finland)	8.0	n.a.
(Weight Watchers Natural)	5.0	3.0
all varieties, except processed *(Kraft)*	8.0	5.0
natural	7.8	5.0
processed	7.1	4.6
processed *(Borden)*	8.0	n.a.
processed *(Kraft* Deluxe)	7.0	4.0
smoked *(Dorman's)*	7.0	n.a.
taco, shredded *(Frigo)*	9.0	n.a.
taco, shredded *(Kraft)*	9.0	5.0
taleggio *(Tal-Fino* Brand Imported)	7.4	n.a.
tilsit, whole milk	7.4	4.8
tybo *(Dorman's* 45%)	7.5	4.7
tybo, red wax *(Sargento)*	7.0	n.a.

Cheese, substitute and imitation, 1 oz.:
  American:

(Golden Image)	6.0	2.0
all varieties (Churny Delicia)	6.0	n.a.
all varieties (Weight Watchers Slices)	2.0	1.0
cheddar, imitation (Frigo)	7.0	1.0
cheddar, sharp (Weight Watchers Slices)	2.0	1.0
cheddar or colby, imitation (Golden Image)	9.0	2.0
cheese food (Cheeztwin)	6.0	n.a.
cheese food (Lite-Line Low Cholesterol)	7.0	n.a.
colby (Dorman's LoChol)	6.0	1.1
colby, longhorn style (Churny Delicia)	6.0	n.a.
cream cheese, imitation, all flavors (Tofutti Better than Cream Cheese) . .	8.0	3.0
creamed cheese (Weight Watchers)	2.0	n.a.
mozzarella, imitation (Frigo)	7.0	1.0
mozzarella, imitation (Sargento)	6.0	n.a.
muenster or Swiss (Dorman's LoChol)	7.0	1.1
Swiss (Weight Watchers)	2.0	1.0

Cheese blintz, frozen (King Kold), 2.5-oz.

piece	1.6	n.a.

Cheese danish, 1 piece:

(Awrey's Round), 4.5 oz.	22.0	5.0
(Awrey's Square), 2.5 oz.	11.0	3.0
miniature (Awrey's), 1.7 oz.	9.0	2.0
frozen (Pepperidge Farm)	14.0	n.a.
frozen (Sara Lee Individual), 1.3 oz. . . .	8.0	n.a.
twist, frozen (Sara Lee), 1/8 pkg.	12.0	n.a.

Cheese dip, blue or nacho (Kraft Premium),

2 tbsp.	4.0	2.0

Cheese food, 1 oz.:

(Nippy)	7.0	4.0
all varieties (Cracker Barrel)	7.0	4.0
all varieties, except sharp (Kraft/Kraft Singles)	7.0	4.0
all varieties (Velveeta)	7.0	4.0
American:		
cold pack	6.9	4.4
processed	7.0	4.4
(Darigold)	6.0	3.8

regular or sharp *(Borden* Singles Slices)	7.0	n.a.
cheddar *(Land O'Lakes* La Chedda) . . .	7.0	4.0
cheddar or port wine, cold pack *(Wispride)*	7.0	n.a.
w/jalapeño pepper *(Land O'Lakes)*	7.0	4.0
onion or pepperoni *(Land O'Lakes)* . . .	7.0	4.0
salami *(Land O'Lakes)*	8.0	5.0
sharp *(Kraft* Singles)	8.0	5.0
Swiss, processed	6.8	n.a.
Cheese nuggets, frozen, mozzarella, breaded *(Banquet Cheese Hot Bites)*, 2.63 oz. . . .	13.0	n.a.
Cheese-nut ball or log, 1 oz.:		
ball, sharp cheddar w/almonds *(Cracker Barrel)*	7.0	3.0
log, all varieties *(Cracker Barrel)*	6.0	3.0
log, all varieties *(Sargento)*	7.0	n.a.
Cheese product, processed, 1 oz.:		
(Kraft Free)	0	0
(Velveeta Light)	4.0	2.0
all varieties, except low sodium *(Lite-Line)*	2.0	n.a.
American flavor:		
(Alpine Lace)	7.0	4.0
(Borden Light)	5.0	n.a.
(Harvest Moon)	4.0	2.0
(Kraft Light)	4.0	3.0
(Lite-Line Reduced Sodium/Sodium Lite)	4.0	n.a.
(Light N' Lively Singles)	4.0	3.0
white *(Kraft Light)*	4.0	2.0
white *(Light N' Lively* Singles)	4.0	2.0
cheddar flavor:		
all varieties *(Spreadery)*	4.0	2.0
sharp *(Kraft Light)*	4.0	2.0
sharp *(Light N' Lively* Singles)	4.0	2.0
cream cheese *(Philadelphia Brand Light)*	5.0	3.0
Mexican, w/jalapeños *(Spreadery)*	4.0	3.0
nacho or port wine *(Spreadery)*	4.0	2.0
Neufchâtel:		
French onion or garlic and herb *(Spreadery)*	6.0	4.0

Cheese product, Neufchâtel, continued

ranch flavor *(Spreadery)*	7.0	4.0
w/strawberries *(Spreadery)*	5.0	3.0
vegetable, garden *(Spreadery)*	6.0	3.0
sandwich slices *(Lunch Wagon)*	7.0	2.0
Swiss flavor *(Kraft Light)*	3.0	2.0
Swiss flavor *(Light N' Lively* Singles)	3.0	2.0
Cheese sauce (see also "Welsh rarebit"):		
aged *(White House)*, 3.5 oz.	18.0	n.a.
cheddar:		
(Lucky Leaf/Musselman's), 4 oz.	18.0	n.a.
aged *(Lucky Leaf/Musselman's)*, 4 oz.	20.0	n.a.
aged, mild *(Lucky Leaf/Musselman's)*,		
4 oz.	18.0	n.a.
aged, sharp *(Lucky Leaf/Musselman's)*,		
4 oz.	17.0	n.a.
four cheese *(Contadina* Fresh), 6 oz. . . .	45.0	n.a.
jalapeño or nacho *(White House)*, 3.5 oz.	16.0	n.a.
nacho *(Kaukauna)*, 1 oz.	6.0	n.a.
nacho *(Lucky Leaf/Musselman's)*, 4 oz.	18.0	n.a.
mix* *(French's)*, 1/4 cup	4.0	n.a.
mix, plain/nacho *(McCormick/Schilling)*,		
1/4 pkg.	1.5	n.a.
Cheese spread, 1 oz., except as noted:		
(Cheez Whiz)	6.0	3.0
(Land O'Lakes Golden Velvet)	6.0	4.0
(Laughing Cow Cheezbits), 1/6 oz.	1.0	n.a.
(Micro Melt)	6.0	n.a.
(Velveeta/Velveeta Slices)	6.0	4.0
all varieties, except American or bacon		
(Kraft)	5.0	3.0
all varieties, except jalapeño *(Squeez-A-*		
Snak)	7.0	4.0
all varieties, except Swiss *(Sargento*		
Cracker Snacks)	9.0	n.a.
American, processed *(Kraft)*	6.0	3.0
w/bacon *(Kraft)*	7.0	4.0
blue *(Roka)*	6.0	4.0
cheddar, sharp *(Weight Watchers* Cup),		
2 tbsp.	3.0	2.0
cream cheese, see "Cheese"		

w/jalapeño pepper *(Squeez-A-Snak)* . . .	6.0	4.0
w/jalapeño pepper or Mexican *(Cheez Whiz)*	6.0	4.0
limburger *(Mohawk Valley)*	6.0	3.0
Mexican or pimiento *(Velveeta)*	6.0	3.0
port wine *(Weight Watchers* Cup), 2 tbsp.	3.0	2.0
sharp *(Old English)*	7.0	4.0
Swiss *(Sargento* Cracker Snacks) . . .	7.0	n.a.
Cheese snack sticks, cheddar *(Flavor Tree)*, 1/4 cup	8.1	n.a.
Cheese sticks, breaded, frozen:		
cheddar *(Farm Rich)*, 3 oz.	21.0	n.a.
hot pepper *(Farm Rich)*, 3 oz.	17.0	n.a.
mozzarella *(Farm Rich)*, 3 oz.	13.0	n.a.
provolone *(Farm Rich)*, 3 oz.	16.0	n.a.
Cheesecake mousse mix *(Weight Watchers)*, 1/2 cup	2.0	n.a.
Cherimoya, fresh, 1 medium, 1.9 lb.	2.2	n.a.
Cherry, 1/2 cup, except as noted:		
fresh, sour, red, w/pits	.2	< .1
fresh, sweet, 10 medium	.7	.1
canned, sour, red, in water or syrup . . .	.1	< .1
canned, sweet, in syrup, or frozen, sweetened	.2	< .1
canned, sweet, in juice	< .1	tr.
frozen, sour, red, unsweetened	.3	.1
Cherry, maraschino, in jars, w/liquid, 1 oz.	.1	0
Cherry cobbler: frozen:		
(Pet-Ritz), 1/6 pkg. or 4.33 oz.	10.0	n.a.
(Stilwell), 4 oz.	6.0	n.a.
Cherry drink or juice (all brands), 6 fl. oz.	< .2	(0)
Cherry turnover:		
frozen *(Pepperidge Farm)*, 1 piece	19.0	n.a.
refrigerated *(Pillsbury)*, 1 piece	8.0	2.0
Chervil, dried, 1 tsp.	< .1	(0)
Chestnut, shelled, 1 oz.:		
Chinese, raw	.3	< .1
Chinese, boiled or steamed	.2	< .1
Chinese, dried	.5	.1
Chinese, roasted	.3	.1
European, raw, unpeeled	.6	.1

Chestnut, shelled, continued

European, raw, peeled, boiled, or steamed	.4	.1
European, dried, peeled	1.1	.2
European, roasted, peeled	.6	.1
Japanese, raw or roasted	.2	< .1
Japanese, boiled or steamed	.1	< .1
Japanese, dried	.4	.1
Chia seeds, dried, 1 oz.	7.5	3.0
Chicken, fresh, 4 oz., except as noted:		
broiler-fryer, roasted:		
meat w/skin	15.4	4.3
meat only	8.4	2.3
skin only, 1 oz.	11.5	3.2
dark meat w/skin	17.9	5.0
dark meat only	11.0	3.0
light meat w/skin	12.3	3.5
light meat only	5.1	1.4
capon, roasted, meat w/skin	13.2	3.7
roaster, roasted:		
meat w/skin	15.2	4.2
meat only	7.5	2.1
meat only, chopped or diced, 1 cup unpacked	9.3	2.5
dark meat only	9.9	2.8
light meat only	4.6	1.2
stewing, stewed:		
meat w/skin	21.4	5.8
meat only	13.5	3.5
meat only, chopped or diced, 1 cup unpacked	16.6	4.3
dark meat only	17.3	4.6
light meat only	9.0	2.2
Chicken, boneless and luncheon meat:		
breast:		
(Mr. Turkey), 1 oz.	1.1	n.a.
hickory smoked *(Louis Rich),* 1-oz. slice	.8	.3
oven roasted *(Louis Rich* Deluxe), 1 oz.	.8	.3

oven roasted *(Louis Rich* Thin Sliced), .4 oz.	.3	.1
oven roasted *(Oscar Mayer)*, 1-oz. slice	.7	.2
roast *(Oscar Mayer* Thin Sliced), .4-oz. slice	.4	.1
smoked *(Eckrich Lite)*, 1 oz.	1.0	n.a.
smoked *(Hillshire Farm* Deli Select), 1 oz.	.2	n.a.
smoked *(Oscar Mayer)*, 1-oz. slice	.2	.1
ham, see "Chicken ham"		
roll *(Pilgrim's Pride)*, 1-oz. slice	1.2	n.a.
roll, light meat, 1-oz. slice	2.1	.6
white meat, oven roasted *(Louis Rich)*, 1 oz.	1.7	.5
Chicken, canned (see also "Chicken entrée, canned"):		
chunk:		
breast or white and dark *(Hormel)*, 6.75 oz.	20.0	n.a.
dark *(Hormel)*, 6.75 oz.	18.0	n.a.
style *(Swanson* Mixin' Chicken), 2.5 oz.	8.0	n.a.
white and dark *(Hormel* No Salt), 6.75 oz.	18.0	n.a.
loaf *(Hormel)*, 2 oz.	10.0	n.a.
white or white and dark *(Swanson)*, 2.5 oz.	4.0	n.a.
"Chicken," vegetarian:		
canned:		
(Worthington FriChik), 2 pieces or 3.2 oz.	13.0	n.a.
sliced, drained *(Worthington)*, 2 slices	8.0	n.a.
diced, drained *(Worthington)*, 1/4 cup	8.0	n.a.
frozen:		
(Worthington Crispy Chik), 3 oz.	19.0	n.a.
diced *(Worthington* Meatless), 1/2 cup	13.0	2.0
nuggets, homestyle *(Morningstar Farms Country Crisps)*, 3 oz.	16.0	n.a.
nuggets, zesty *(Morningstar Farms Country Crisps)*, 3 oz.	19.0	3.0
patty *(Morningstar Farms Country Crisps)*, 2.5-oz. patty	15.0	2.0

"Chicken," vegetarian, frozen, continued

patty *(Worthington Crispy Chik)*, 2.5 oz.	15.0	2.0
pie *(Worthington)*, 8-oz. pie	20.0	3.0
roll *(Worthington Chic-ketts)*, 1/2 cup	7.0	1.0
roll *(Worthington* Meatless Chicken), 2.5 oz.	10.0	1.0
slices *(Worthington* Meatless Chicken), 2 oz.	9.0	1.0
sticks *(Worthington Chik Stiks)*, 1 piece	7.0	1.0
Chicken bologna *(Health Valley)*, 1 slice	8.0	n.a.
Chicken dinner, frozen:		
à la king *(Armour Classics Lite)*, 11.25 oz.	7.0	n.a.
à la king *(Le Menu)*, 10.25 oz.	13.0	n.a.
boneless *(Swanson Hungry-Man)*, 17.75 oz.	28.0	n.a.
breast, glazed *(Le Menu* LightStyle), 10 oz.	3.0	n.a.
breast Marsala *(Armour Classics Lite)*, 10.5 oz.	7.0	n.a.
Burgundy *(Armour Classics Lite)*, 10 oz.	2.0	n.a.
cacciatore *(The Budget Gourmet)*, 11 oz.	13.0	n.a.
casserole *(Pillsbury Microwave Classic)*, 1 pkg.	22.0	n.a.
and cheese, casserole *(Pillsbury Microwave Classic)*, 1 pkg.	29.0	n.a.
Cordon Bleu *(Le Menu)*, 11 oz.	20.0	n.a.
and dumplings *(Banquet)*, 10 oz.	24.0	n.a.
fettuccine *(Armour Classics)*, 11 oz.	9.0	n.a.
fried:		
(Banquet), 10 oz.	22.0	n.a.
(Banquet Extra Helping), 16 oz.	28.0	n.a.
(Stouffer's Dinner Supreme), 10 5/8 oz.	23.0	n.a.
barbecue flavored *(Swanson)*, 10 oz.	22.0	n.a.
dark meat *(Swanson)*, 1 pkg.	28.0	n.a.
dark meat *(Swanson Hungry-Man)*, 1 pkg.	45.0	n.a.
white meat *(Banquet Extra Helping)*, 16 oz.	28.0	n.a.
white meat *(Swanson)*, 1 pkg.	25.0	n.a.

white meat *(Swanson Hungry-Man)*, 1 pkg.	46.0	n.a.
glazed *(Armour Classics)*, 10.75 oz.	16.0	n.a.
herb roasted *(Le Menu* LightStyle), 10 oz.	7.0	n.a.
herb roasted *(Healthy Choice)*, 11 oz.	3.0	1.0
meat loaf, see "Meat loaf dinner"		
mesquite *(Armour Classics)*, 9.5 oz.	16.0	n.a.
mesquite *(Healthy Choice)*, 10.5 oz.	2.0	< 1.0
Mexicana *(The Budget Gourmet)*, 12.8 oz.	15.0	n.a.
and noodles *(Armour Classics)*, 11 oz.	7.0	n.a.
nuggets:		
(Swanson), 8.75 oz.	23.0	n.a.
barbecue sauce *(Banquet Extra Helping)*, 10 oz.	36.0	n.a.
platter *(Freezer Queen)*, 6 oz.	23.0	n.a.
sweet and sour sauce *(Banquet Extra Helping)*, 10 oz.	34.0	n.a.
Oriental *(Armour Classics Lite)*, 10 oz.	1.0	n.a.
Oriental *(Healthy Choice)*, 11.25 oz.	2.0	< 1.0
parmigiana *(Armour Classics)*, 11.5 oz.	19.0	n.a.
parmigiana *(Healthy Choice)*, 11.5 oz.	3.0	2.0
parmigiana *(Le Menu)*, 11.5 oz.	20.0	n.a.
and pasta divan *(Healthy Choice)*, 11.5 oz.	4.0	2.0
pattie platter *(Freezer Queen)*, 7.5 oz.	17.0	n.a.
roast *(The Budget Gourmet)*, 11.2 oz.	7.0	n.a.
sweet and sour *(Armour Classics Lite)*, 11 oz.	2.0	n.a.
sweet and sour *(Healthy Choice)*, 11.5 oz.	2.0	< 1.0
sweet and sour *(Le Menu)*, 11.25 oz.	18.0	n.a.
sweet and sour *(Le Menu* LightStyle), 10 oz.	7.0	n.a.
teriyaki *(The Budget Gourmet)*, 12 oz.	12.0	n.a.
in wine sauce *(Le Menu)*, 10 oz.	7.0	n.a.
w/wine and mushroom sauce *(Armour Classics)*, 10.75 oz.	11.0	n.a.
Chicken entrée, canned:		
à la king *(Swanson)*, 5.25 oz.	12.0	n.a.
chow mein *(La Choy* Bi-Pack), 3/4 cup	3.0	n.a.
and dumplings *(Luck's)*, 7.25 oz.	11.0	n.a.
and dumplings *(Swanson)*, 7.5 oz.	11.0	n.a.
Oriental *(La Choy* Bi-Pack), 3/4 cup	2.0	n.a.

Chicken entrée, canned, continued
stew *(Swanson)*, 7⅝ oz.	7.0	n.a.
Chicken entrée, frozen:		
à la gratin *(Myers)*, 3.5 oz.	7.0	n.a.
à la king:		
(Banquet Cookin' Bags), 4 oz.	5.0	n.a.
(Dining Lite), 9 oz.	7.0	n.a.
(Freezer Queen Cook-In-Pouch), 4 oz.	1.0	n.a.
(Le Menu LightStyle), 8.25 oz.	5.0	1.0
(Myers), 3.5 oz.	9.0	n.a.
(Weight Watchers), 9 oz.	6.0	3.0
w/rice *(Freezer Queen* Single Serve),		
9 oz.	5.0	n.a.
w/rice *(Stouffer's)*, 9.5 oz.	9.0	n.a.
almond, w/rice and vegetables *(La Choy*		
Fresh & Lite), 9.75 oz.	8.0	n.a.
à l'orange *(Healthy Choice)*, 9 oz.	2.0	< 1.0
à l'orange *(Tyson Gourmet Selection)*,		
9.5 oz.	8.0	n.a.
à l'orange, w/almond rice *(Lean Cuisine)*,		
8 oz.	5.0	1.0
au gratin *(The Budget Gourmet* Slim		
Selects), 9.1 oz.	11.0	n.a.
breast, boneless:		
barbecue marinated *(Tyson)*, 3.75 oz.	3.0	n.a.
butter garlic marinated *(Tyson)*,		
3.75 oz.	7.0	n.a.
chunks *(Tyson)*, 3 oz.	17.0	n.a.
fillets *(Pilgrim's Pride)*, 3 oz.	10.2	n.a.
fillets *(Tyson)*, 3 oz.	9.0	n.a.
in herb cream sauce *(Lean Cuisine)*,		
9.5 oz.	10.0	3.0
herb roasted *(Le Menu* LightStyle),		
7.75 oz.	6.0	2.0
Italian marinated *(Tyson)*, 3.75 oz.	2.0	n.a.
lemon pepper marinated *(Tyson)*,		
3.75 oz.	2.0	n.a.
Marsala *(Lean Cuisine)*, 8⅛ oz.	5.0	1.0
Parmesan *(Lean Cuisine)*, 10 oz.	8.0	2.0
tenders *(Banquet* Hot Bites), 2.25 oz.	6.0	n.a.

tenders *(Banquet* Hot Bites Microwave), 4 oz.	10.0	n.a.
tenders *(Pilgrim's Pride)*, 3 oz.	9.5	n.a.
tenders, Southern fried *(Banquet* Hot Bites), 2.25 oz.	7.0	n.a.
tenders, Southern fried *(Tyson)*, 3 oz.	11.0	n.a.
teriyaki marinated *(Tyson)*, 3.75 oz.	2.0	n.a.
and broccoli *(Green Giant* Entrees), 9.5 oz.	15.0	n.a.
cacciatore:		
(Freezer Queen Single Serve), 9 oz.	6.0	n.a.
(Swanson Homestyle Recipe), 11 oz.	8.0	n.a.
w/vermicelli *(Lean Cuisine)*, 10⅞ oz.	7.0	1.0
Cajun style *(Pilgrim's Pride)*, 3 oz.	17.0	n.a.
cashew in sauce, w/rice *(Stouffer's)*, 9.5 oz.	16.0	n.a.
w/cheddar *(Tyson* Chick'n Cheddar), 2.6 oz.	15.0	n.a.
chow mein:		
(Chun King), 13 oz.	6.0	n.a.
(Dining Lite), 9 oz.	2.0	n.a.
(Healthy Choice), 8.5 oz.	3.0	1.0
w/out noodles *(Stouffer's)*, 8 oz.	4.0	n.a.
w/rice *(Lean Cuisine)*, 11.25 oz.	5.0	1.0
chunks:		
(Country Pride), 3 oz.	15.0	n.a.
(Tyson Chick'n Chunks), 2.6 oz.	15.0	n.a.
Southern fried *(Country Pride)*, 3 oz.	20.0	n.a.
Southern fried *(Tyson* Chick'n Chunks), 2.6 oz.	15.0	n.a.
Cordon Bleu *(Swift International)*, 6 oz.	17.0	n.a.
Cordon Bleu *(Weight Watchers)*, 8 oz.	9.0	5.0
creamed *(Myers)*, 3.5 oz.	10.0	n.a.
creamed *(Stouffer's)*, 6.5 oz.	21.0	n.a.
croquettes *(Freezer Queen* Family Suppers), 7 oz.	12.0	n.a.
croquettes *(Myers)*, 3.5 oz.	7.0	n.a.
diced *(Tyson)*, 3 oz.	5.0	n.a.
Dijon *(Le Menu* LightStyle), 8.5 oz.	7.0	2.0
Dijon *(Tyson Gourmet Selection)*, 8.5 oz.	17.0	n.a.
divan *(Stouffer's)*, 8.5 oz.	20.0	n.a.

Chicken entrée, frozen, continued
drumsnackers *(Banquet* Hot Bites),
   2.63 oz. . . . . 15.0   n.a.
drumsnackers *(Banquet* Platters), 7 oz.   19.0   n.a.
drumsters *(Pilgrim's Pride),* 3 oz. . . . . .   12.5   n.a.
and dumplings *(Banquet Family Entrées),*
   7 oz. 14.0   n.a.
and egg noodles, w/broccoli *(The Budget*
   Gourmet), 10 oz. . . . . 26.0   n.a.
empress *(Le Menu* LightStyle), 8.25 oz.   5.0   1.0
enchilada, see "Enchilada entrée"
escalloped, and noodles *(Stouffer's),*
   10 oz. . . . . 25.0   n.a.
fajita, see "Fajita entrée"
w/fettuccine *(The Budget Gourmet),*
   10 oz. . . . . 21.0   n.a.
fiesta *(Healthy Choice),* 8.5 oz. 6.0   1.0
Francais *(Tyson Gourmet Selection),*
   9.5 oz. . . . . 14.0   n.a.
French recipe *(The Budget Gourmet* Slim
   Selects), 10 oz. . . . . 10.0   n.a.
fried:
  (Banquet/Banquet Hot'n Spicy), 6.4 oz.   19.0   n.a.
  (Pilgrim's Pride), 3 oz. . . . . 17.7   n.a.
  (Swanson Homestyle Recipe), 7 oz. . .   21.0   n.a.
  (Swanson 1 lb. Pre-Fried), 3.25 oz. . .   16.0   n.a.
  breast portions *(Banquet),* 5.75 oz. . . .   11.0   n.a.
  breast portions *(Swanson),* 4.5 oz. . . .   20.0   n.a.
  thighs and drumsticks *(Banquet),*
    6.25 oz. . . . . 14.0   n.a.
  white meat *(Banquet* Platter), 9 oz. . .   22.0   n.a.
  glazed *(Dining Lite),* 9 oz. . . . .   4.0   n.a.
  glazed *(Healthy Choice),* 8.5 oz. 3.0   1.0
  glazed, vegetable rice *(Lean Cuisine),*
    8.5 oz. 8.0   1.0
  herb roasted *(Le Menu* LightStyle),
    7.75 oz. . . . . 6.0   n.a.
  hot'n spicy *(Banquet* Snack'n), 3.75 oz.   9.0   n.a.
  Imperial *(Chun King),* 13 oz. . . . . . .   1.0   n.a.
  Imperial *(Weight Watchers),* 9.25 oz.   3.0   1.0

Imperial, w/rice *(La Choy Fresh &*		
Lite), 11 oz.	6.0	n.a.
Italiano *(Right Course)*, 9⅝ oz.	8.0	2.0
Kiev *(Swift International)*, 6 oz.	24.0	n.a.
Kiev *(Tyson Gourmet Selection)*,		
9.25 oz.	33.0	n.a.
Kiev *(Weight Watchers)*, 7 oz.	9.0	3.0
Mandarin *(The Budget Gourmet* Slim		
Selects), 10 oz.	6.0	n.a.
Marsala *(The Budget Gourmet)*, 10 oz.	5.0	n.a.
Marsala *(Tyson Gourmet Selection)*,		
10.5 oz.	13.0	n.a.
mesquite *(Tyson Gourmet Selection)*,		
9.5 oz.	10.0	n.a.
nibbles *(Swanson)*, 3.25 oz.	19.0	n.a.
nibbles *(Swanson* Homestyle Recipe),		
4.25 oz.	20.0	n.a.
and noodles:		
(Dining Lite), 9 oz.	7.0	n.a.
(Myers), 3.5 oz.	8.0	n.a.
homestyle *(Stouffer's)*, 10 oz.	15.0	n.a.
homestyle *(Weight Watchers)*, 9 oz.	7.0	2.0
nuggets:		
(Banquet Chicken Hot Bites), 2.63 oz.	14.0	n.a.
(Banquet Platters), 6.4 oz.	21.0	n.a.
(Country Pride), 3 oz.	16.0	n.a.
(Freezer Queen Deluxe Family		
Suppers), 3 oz.	17.0	n.a.
(Pilgrim's Pride), 3 oz.	12.3	n.a.
(Swanson), 3 oz.	14.0	n.a.
(Tyson Microwave), 3.5 oz.	15.0	n.a.
(Weight Watchers), 5.9 oz.	12.0	4.0
breast, Southern fried, w/barbecue		
sauce *(Banquet* Microwave Hot		
Bites), 4.5 oz.	23.0	n.a.
w/cheddar *(Banquet* Hot Bites),		
2.63 oz.	18.0	n.a.
hot'n spicy *(Banquet* Hot Bites),		
2.63 oz.	19.0	n.a.
hot'n spicy, w/barbecue sauce *(Banquet*		
Microwave Hot Bites), 4.5 oz.	21.0	n.a.

Chicken entrée, frozen, nuggets, continued

Southern fried *(Banquet* Hot Bites), 2.63 oz.	14.0	n.a.
w/sweet and sour sauce *(Banquet* Microwave Hot Bites), 4.5 oz.	21.0	n.a.
Oriental:		
(Lean Cuisine), 9³/₈ oz.	6.0	1.0
(Tyson Gourmet Selection), 10.25 oz.	7.0	n.a.
spicy *(La Choy Fresh & Lite)*, 9.75 oz.	4.0	n.a.
parmigiana *(Celentano)*, 9 oz.	20.0	n.a.
parmigiana *(Tyson Gourmet Selection)*, 11.25 oz.	17.0	n.a.
patties:		
(Banquet Platters), 7.5 oz.	21.0	n.a.
(Country Pride), 3 oz.	16.0	n.a.
(Tyson), 2.6 oz.	15.0	n.a.
(Tyson Thick & Crispy), 2.6 oz.	14.0	n.a.
breast *(Banquet* Chicken Hot Bites), 2.63 oz.	13.0	n.a.
breast, and bun *(Banquet* Microwave Hot Bites), 4-oz. pkg.	14.0	n.a.
breast, Southern fried *(Banquet* Hot Bites), 2.63 oz.	12.0	n.a.
breast, Southern fried *(Country Pride)*, 3 oz.	16.0	n.a.
breast, Southern fried *(Tyson)*, 2.6 oz.	15.0	n.a.
breast, Southern fried, and biscuit *(Banquet* Microwave Hot Bites), 4 oz.	14.0	n.a.
Southern fried *(Weight Watchers)*, 6.5 oz.	16.0	7.0
picatta *(Tyson Gourmet Selection)*, 9 oz.	10.0	n.a.
primavera:		
(Celentano), 11.5 oz.	10.0	n.a.
and vegetable *(Banquet Cookin' Bags)*, 4 oz.	2.0	n.a.
and vegetable *(Banquet Family Entrees)*, 7 oz.	3.0	n.a.
sesame *(Right Course)*, 10 oz.	9.0	2.0
sliced, gravy and *(Freezer Queen Cook-In-Pouch)*, 5 oz.	3.0	n.a.

steaks, chicken fried *(Pilgrim's Pride)*,
  3 oz. 10.4 n.a.
sticks *(Banquet* Chicken Hot Bites),
  2.63 oz. . . . . 15.0 n.a.
sticks *(Country Pride)*, 3 oz. . . . . 15.0 n.a.
sweet and sour:
  (Banquet Cookin' Bags), 4 oz. . . . . . 2.0 n.a.
  (Tyson Gourmet Selection), 11 oz. . . . 15.0 n.a.
  w/rice *(The Budget Gourmet)*, 10 oz. 7.0 n.a.
  w/rice *(Freezer Queen* Single Serve),
    9 oz. . . . . 4.0 n.a.
  w/rice *(La Choy Fresh & Lite)*, 10 oz. 3.0 n.a.
  tenders *(Weight Watchers)*, 10.19 oz. 1.0 < 1.0
tenderloins:
  in barbecue sauce *(Right Course)*,
    8.75 oz. 6.0 1.0
  in peanut sauce *(Right Course)*, 9.25 oz. 10.0 2.0
  tenders *(Tyson* Microwave), 3.5 oz. 11.0 n.a.
thighs and drumsticks *(Swanson)*,
  3.25 oz. . . . . 18.0 n.a.
and vegetables *(Lean Cuisine)*,
  11.75 oz. 7.0 1.0
walnut, crunchy *(Chun King)*, 13 oz. 5.0 n.a.
wings *(Pilgrim's Pride* Wing Zappers),
  3 oz. . . . . 12.8 n.a.
wings all varieties *(Tyson Flyers)*,
  3.5 oz. . . . . 14.0 n.a.
wings Southern fried *(Pilgrim's Pride)*,
  3 oz. . . . . 17.2 n.a.
Chicken entrée, packaged, 1 serving:
  Acapulco *(Hormel Top Shelf)* . . . . . 13.0 n.a.
  breast of, glazed *(Hormel Top Shelf)* 3.0 n.a.
  sweet and sour *(Hormel Top Shelf)* . . . 1.0 n.a.
Chicken entrée, refrigerated, 5 oz.:
  bleu cheese, Italian *(Chicken By George)* 8.0 n.a.
  Cajun *(Chicken By George)* . . . . 9.0 n.a.
  lemon herb, mesquite, or teriyaki
    (Chicken By George) . . . . 4.0 n.a.
  mustard, country, and dill *(Chicken By
    George)* . . . . 7.0 n.a.

Chicken entrée, refrigerated, continued
tomato herb and basil *(Chicken By
George)* . . . . 7.0   n.a.
Chicken entrée mix*, all varieties *(Lipton
Microeasy)*, 1/4 pkg. . . . . 6.0   n.a.
Chicken fat, 1 oz. 19.3   5.7
Chicken frankfurter:
   1 oz. 5.5   1.6
   (Longacre), 1 oz. . . . . 5.0   n.a.
   batter-wrapped *(Tyson* Corn Dogs),
      3.5 oz. . . . . 14.0   n.a.
Chicken giblets:
   broiler-fryer, simmered, 4 oz. 5.4   1.7
   roaster, simmered, 4 oz. 5.9   1.9
Chicken gravy:
   canned:
      1 oz. . . . . 1.6   .4
      (Franco-American), 2 oz. . . . . 4.0   n.a.
      (Heinz HomeStyle), 2 oz. or 1/4 cup   2.0   n.a.
      (Hormel Great Beginnings), 5 oz. . . . 8.0   n.a.
      giblet *(Franco-American)*, 2 oz. . . . . 2.0   n.a.
   mix*:
      (French's Gravy for Chicken), 1/4 cup 1.0   n.a.
      (Lawry's), 1 cup . . . . 2.8   n.a.
      (McCormick/Schilling), 1/4 cup 4   n.a.
      (McCormick/Schilling Lite), 1/4 cup . . 1.0   n.a.
Chicken ham *(Pilgrim's Pride)*, 1-oz. slice 1.8   n.a.
Chicken luncheon meat, see "Chicken,
boneless and luncheon meat"
Chicken pie, frozen:
   (Banquet), 7 oz. . . . . 36.0   n.a.
   (Banquet Supreme Microwave), 7 oz. . . 28.0   n.a.
   (Morton), 7 oz. . . . . 28.0   n.a.
   (Stouffer's), 10 oz. . . . . 33.0   n.a.
   (Swanson Homestyle Recipe), 8 oz. . . . 21.0   n.a.
   (Swanson Pot Pie), 7 oz. . . . . 22.0   n.a.
   (Swanson Hungry-Man), 16 oz. . . . . . 35.0   n.a.
Chicken salad:
   (Longacre), 1 oz. . . . . 5.0   n.a.
   (Longacre Saladfest), 1 oz. . . . . 3.0   n.a.

Chicken sandwich, frozen:

(MicroMagic), 4.5 oz.	16.0	n.a.
barbecue *(Tyson* Microwave), 4 oz. . . .	6.0	n.a.
breast *(Tyson* Microwave), 3.5 oz.	12.0	n.a.
mini *(Tyson* Microwave), 3.5 oz.	5.0	n.a.
pocket *(Lean Pockets* Supreme), 1 pkg.	9.0	n.a.
pocket, 'n cheddar *(Hot Pockets),* 5 oz.	11.0	n.a.
pocket, Oriental *(Lean Pockets),* 1 pkg.	6.0	n.a.
pocket, Parmesan *(Lean Pockets),* 1 pkg.	6.0	n.a.

Chicken sauce mix, 1 pkg.:

cacciatore *(McCormick/Schilling* Sauce Blends)	4.8	n.a.
creole *(McCormick/Schilling* Sauce Blends)	4.8	n.a.
curry *(McCormick/Schilling* Sauce Blends)	5.6	n.a.
Dijon *(McCormick/Schilling* Sauce Blends)	6.3	n.a.
Italian marinade *(McCormick/Schilling* Sauce Blends)	.7	n.a.
mesquite marinade *(McCormick/Schilling* Sauce Blends)	3.0	n.a.
stir fry *(McCormick/Schilling* Sauce Blends)	.2	(0)
sweet & sour *(McCormick/Schilling* Sauce Blends)	.9	n.a.
teriyaki *(McCormick/Schilling* Sauce Blends)	3.6	n.a.

Chicken seasoning and coating mix:

(McCormick/Schilling Bag'n Season), 1 pkg.	1.4	n.a.
all varieties *(Shake'n Bake),* 1/4 pouch	2.0	n.a.
all varieties *(Shake'n Bake Oven Fry),* 1/4 pouch	2.0	n.a.

Chicken spread, canned:

chunky *(Underwood),* 2 1/8 oz.	9.0	3.0
chunky *(Underwood* Light), 2 1/8 oz. . . .	3.0	1.0
smoky flavored *(Underwood),* 2 1/8 oz.	8.0	2.0

Chickpea:

boiled, 1/2 cup	2.1	.2
canned, w/liquid, 1/2 cup	1.4	.1

Chicory, witloof, 5–7″ head or 1/2 cup 1   < .1
Chicory greens, trimmed, chopped, 1/2 cup   .3   .1
Chicory root, 1 medium, 2.6 oz., or 1/2 cup
  pieces 1   < .1
Chili, canned:
  (Gebhardt), 4 oz. . . . .   17.0   n.a.
  (Heinz Chili Con Carne), 7.75 oz. . . . .   21.0   n.a.
  (Old El Paso Chili Con Carne), 1 cup . .   7.0   n.a.
  w/beans:
    4 oz. 6.2   2.7
    (Dennison's, 15 oz.), 7.5 oz. . . . .   15.0   n.a.
    (Dennison's Cook-Off), 7.5 oz. . . . . .   19.0   n.a.
    (Hormel, 15 oz.), 7.5 oz. . . . .   17.0   n.a.
    (Hormel Micro-Cup), 7.5 oz. . . . .   11.0   n.a.
    (Libby's, 15 oz.), 7.5 oz. . . . .   13.0   n.a.
    (Old El Paso), 1 cup . . . .   10.0   n.a.
    (Van Camp's), 1 cup . . . .   23.2   n.a.
    (Wolf Brand), 1 cup . . . .   22.0   n.a.
    chunky *(Dennison's),* 7.5 oz. . . . .   14.0   n.a.
    extra spicy *(Wolf* Brand), 7.5 oz. . . . .   20.6   n.a.
    hot *(Dennison's,* 15 oz.), 7.5 oz. . . . .   16.0   n.a.
    hot *(Gebhardt),* 4 oz. . . . .   14.2   .2
    hot *(Hormel,* 15 oz.), 7.5 oz. . . . .   16.0   n.a.
    hot or hot jalapeño *(Nalley's),* 7.5 oz.   10.0   n.a.
    regular or thick *(Nalley's),* 7.5 oz. . . . .   9.0   n.a.
  w/out beans:
    (Dennison's, 15 oz.), 7.5 oz. . . . .   19.0   n.a.
    (Hormel/Hormel Hot, 15 oz.), 7.5 oz.   28.0   n.a.
    (Hormel), 10.5-oz. can . . . .   41.0   n.a.
    (Libby's), 7.5 oz. . . . .   30.0   n.a.
    (Nalley's Big Chunk), 7.5 oz. . . . . . .   16.0   n.a.
    (Nalley's Real/Texas), 7.5 oz. . . . . . .   11.0   n.a.
    (Van Camp's), 1 cup . . . .   33.5   n.a.
    (Wolf Brand), 1 cup . . . .   26.6   n.a.
    (Wolf Brand Chili-Mac), 7.5 oz. . . . .   19.9   n.a.
    extra spicy *(Wolf* Brand), 7.5 oz. . . . .   24.9   n.a.
  w/chicken, spicy *(Hain),* 7.5 oz. . . . . . .   2.0   n.a.
  w/franks *(Van Camp's Chilee Weenee),*
    1 cup . . . .   15.7   n.a.
  vegetarian:
    (Gebhardt), 4 oz. . . . .   17.1   n.a.

(Worthington), 2/3 cup	10.0	1.0
w/lentils, mild *(Health Valley)*, 4 oz.	3.0	n.a.
spicy *(Hain/Hain* Reduced Sodium), 7.5 oz.	1.0	n.a.
spicy *(Natural Touch)*, 2/3 cup	12.0	1.0
tempeh, spicy *(Hain)*, 7.5 oz.	4.0	n.a.
Chili entrée, frozen:		
con carne *(Swanson* Homestyle Recipe), 8.25 oz.	10.0	n.a.
con carne, w/beans *(Stouffer's)*, 8.75 oz.	10.0	n.a.
vegetarian *(Right Course)*, 9.75 oz.	7.0	1.0
Chili entrée, packaged, con carne suprema *(Hormel Top Shelf)*, 1 serving	12.0	n.a.
Chili mix, dry *(Gebhardt Chili Quik)*, 1.5-oz. pkt.	1.1	.1
Chili pepper, see "Pepper, chili"		
Chili powder, 1 tsp.	.4	n.a.
Chili sauce:		
(Heinz), 1 tbsp.	0	0
green, mild *(El Molino)*, 2 tbsp.	0	0
hot dog *(Gebhardt)*, 2 tbsp.	1.0	n.a.
hot dog *(Wolf* Brand), 1/6 cup	2.3	n.a.
tomato *(Del Monte)*, 1/4 cup	0	0
Chili seasoning:		
(Lawry's Seasoning Blends), 1 pkg. . . .	1.8	n.a.
mix *(McCormick/Schilling)*, 1/4 pkg. . . .	.5	n.a.
mix *(Old El Paso)*, 1/5 pkg.	1.0	n.a.
Chimichanga, frozen:		
beef *(Old El Paso)*, 1 piece	21.0	n.a.
chicken *(Old El Paso)*, 1 piece	20.0	n.a.
Chimichanga dinner, frozen, 11 oz.:		
beef *(Old El Paso* Festive Dinners) . . .	21.0	n.a.
beef and cheese *(Old El Paso* Festive Dinners)	23.0	n.a.
Chimichanga entrée, frozen, 1 pkg.:		
bean and cheese *(Old El Paso)*	19.0	n.a.
beef *(Old El Paso)*	23.0	n.a.
beef and pork *(Old El Paso)*	16.0	n.a.
chicken *(Old El Paso)*	21.0	n.a.
Chives, fresh or freeze-dried, chopped, 1 tbsp.	< .1	tr.

Chocolate, see "Candy"
Chocolate, baking, 1 oz., except as noted:
bars:

semisweet *(Baker's)*	9.0	n.a.
semisweet *(Hershey's* Premium)	8.0	n.a.
semisweet *(Nestlé)*	9.0	n.a.
sweet *(Baker's German's)*	10.0	n.a.
unsweetened *(Baker's)*	15.0	n.a.
unsweetened *(Hershey's)*	16.0	n.a.
unsweetened *(Nestlé)*	14.0	n.a.
white *(Nestlé* Premier), .5 oz.	5.0	n.a.

chips:

milk *(Baker's)*	8.0	n.a.
milk *(Hershey's)*	12.0	n.a.
milk *(Nestlé* Toll House Morsels)	7.0	n.a.
milk or semisweet *(Baker's* Big Chip), 1/4 cup	13.0	n.a.
mint *(Hershey's),* 1.5 oz. or 1/4 cup	12.0	n.a.
mint or semisweet *(Nestlé* Toll House Morsels)	8.0	n.a.
semisweet *(Baker's),* 1/4 cup	11.0	n.a.
semisweet *(Hershey's),* 1/4 cup	12.0	n.a.
vanilla, milk *(Hershey's),* 1/4 cup	14.0	n.a.

chunks:

milk *(Hershey's)*	9.0	n.a.
milk *(Nestlé* Toll House *Treasures)*	9.0	n.a.
semisweet *(Hershey's* Chunks)	8.0	n.a.
semisweet *(Nestlé* Toll House *Treasures)*	8.0	n.a.
white *(Nestlé* Toll House Premier *Treasures)*	10.0	n.a.
premelted, unsweetened *(Nestlé Choco Bake)*	16.0	n.a.

Chocolate flavor drink:

canned *(Frostee),* 8 fl. oz.	8.0	n.a.
canned, all varieties *(Sego),* 10 fl. oz.	1.0	n.a.

mix (see also "Cocoa"):

(Carnation Instant Breakfast), 1 pouch	1.0	.5
(Hershey's), .8 oz. or 3 tsp.	4.0	n.a.
(Nestlé Quik), 3/4 oz. or 21/2 heaping tsp.	1.0	n.a.

(Pillsbury Instant Breakfast), 1 pouch	0	0
malt *(Carnation* Instant Breakfast), 1 pouch	2.0	.7
malt *(Pillsbury* Instant Breakfast), 1 pouch	0	0
Chocolate milk, see "Milk, chocolate"		
Chocolate mousse:		
frozen *(Weight Watchers),* 2.5 oz.	6.0	< 1.0
mix*, plain or fudge *(Jell-O Rich & Luscious),* 1/2 cup	6.0	n.a.
Chocolate syrup (see also "Toppings, dessert"):		
1 fl. oz. or 2 tbsp.	.3	.2
(Hershey's), 1 oz. or 2 tbsp.	1.0	n.a.
(Nestlé Quik), 1.22 oz., approx. 2 tbsp.	1.0	n.a.
Chorizo, beef and pork, 1 oz.	10.9	4.1
Chow mein, see specific entrée listings		
Chow mein, vegetarian, mix*, Mandarin, w/tofu *(Tofu Classics),* 1/2 cup	6.0	n.a.
Chub, see "Cisco, smoked"		
Cilantro, see "Coriander"		
Cinnamon, ground, 1 tsp.	.1	tr.
Cinnamon-raisin danish, 1 piece:		
(Awrey's-square), 3 oz.	12.0	3.0
miniature *(Awrey's),* 1.5 oz.	8.0	2.0
frozen *(Pepperidge Farm)*	11.0	n.a.
frozen *(Sara Lee* Individual), 1.3 oz. . . .	8.0	n.a.
refrigerated, w/icing *(Pillsbury)*	7.0	2.0
Cinnamon-walnut danish *(Awrey's* Round), 2.75 oz.	18.0	3.0
Cisco, meat only:		
raw, 4 oz.	2.2	.5
smoked, 4 oz.	13.5	2.0
Citrus fruit juice drink, all blends (all brands), 6 fl. oz.	< .2	(0)
Clam, meat only:		
fresh, mixed species:		
raw, 4 oz.	1.1	.1
raw, 9 large or 20 small	1.8	.2
boiled, poached, or steamed, 4 oz. . . .	2.2	2.1

Clam, continued
canned:

drained, 1 cup	3.1	.3
(Gorton's), 1/2 can	1.0	n.a.
w/liquid *(Doxsee)*, 6.5 oz.	< 1.0	n.a.

Clam dip:

(Breakstone's/Sealtest), 2 tbsp.	4.0	3.0
(Breakstone's Gourmet Chesapeake), 2 tbsp.	4.0	3.0
(Kraft), 2 tbsp.	4.0	1.0
(Kraft Premium), 2 tbsp.	4.0	2.0

Clam entrée, frozen:

battered, fried *(Mrs. Paul's)*, 2.5 oz.	9.0	n.a.
strips, crunchy *(Gorton's* Microwave), 3.5 oz.	22.0	6.0

Clam juice *(Snow's)*, 3 fl. oz. 0   0

Clam sauce:

canned, red *(Buitoni)*, 5 oz.	6.0	1.0
canned, red *(Ferrara)*, 4 oz.	2.0	0
canned, red *(Progresso)*, 1/2 cup	3.0	n.a.
canned, white *(Ferrara)*, 4 oz.	5.0	1.0
canned, white *(Progresso)*, 1/2 cup	8.0	n.a.
canned, white *(Progresso* Authentic Pasta Sauces), 1/2 cup	9.0	1.0
refrigerated, red *(Contadina Fresh)*, 7.5 oz.	4.0	n.a.
refrigerated, white *(Contadina Fresh)*, 6 oz.	23.0	n.a.

Cloves, ground, 1 tsp. 4   .1

Cocktail sauce (see also "Seafood sauce"):

(Del Monte), 1/4 cup	0	0
(Great Impressions), 1 tbsp.	.1	(0)
(Great Impressions Brandy Glow), 1 tbsp.	6.7	n.a.
(Heinz), 1 tbsp.	.1	(0)
(Sauceworks), 1 tbsp.	0	0

Cocoa, powder:

(Bensdorp), 1 oz.	7.0	n.a.
(Hershey's), 1 oz. or 1/3 cup	4.0	n.a.
(Hershey's European), 1 oz.	3.0	n.a.
(Nestlé), 1.5 oz. or 1/2 cup	6.0	n.a.

Cocoa mix:

powder, 1-oz. pkt. or 3–4 heaping tsp. . . .	1.1	.7
(Carnation 70-Calorie), 1 pkt.	.3	.2
(Hills Bros), 2 tbsp.	1.0	n.a.
(Hills Bros Sugar Free), 3 tsp.	2.0	n.a.
(Swiss Miss Lite), .76-oz. pkt.	.8	.2
(Swiss Miss Sugar Free), .5-oz. pkt.	1.0	.2
all varieties *(Swiss Miss),* 1 oz.	1.0	n.a.
chocolate:		
fudge *(Carnation),* 1-oz. pkt.	1.3	1.1
milk or rich *(Carnation),* 1-oz. pkt. . .	1.1	1.0
rich *(Carnation* Sugar Free), 1 pkt. . .	.4	.2
w/marshmallows *(Carnation),* 1 pkt. . . .	1.0	.9
w/marshmallows, chocolate *(Carnation),*		
1 pkt.	1.2	1.1
mocha *(Carnation* Sugar Free), 1 pkt. . .	.3	.2

Coconut, meat only:

fresh, 1 oz.	9.5	8.4
fresh, shredded or grated, 1 cup	26.8	23.8
dried:		
creamed, 1 oz.	19.6	17.4
unsweetened, 1 oz.	18.3	16.3
sweetened, shredded, 1 oz.	10.1	8.9
toasted, 1 oz.	13.4	11.8
canned, sweetened, flaked, 1 oz.	9.0	8.0
packaged, 1 oz.	9.1	8.1

Coconut cream:

fresh (from grated coconut meat), 1 cup	83.2	73.8
canned, sweetened, 1 cup	52.5	46.5

Cod, meat only:

fresh:		
Atlantic, raw, 4 oz.	.8	.1
Atlantic, baked, broiled, or		
microwaved, 4 oz.	1.0	.2
Atlantic, dried, salted, 1 oz.	.7	.1
Pacific, raw, 4 oz.	.7	.1
canned, w/liquid, 4 oz.	1.0	.2
frozen *(Booth),* 4 oz.	1.0	n.a.
frozen *(Gorton's Fishmarket Fresh),* 5 oz.	1.0	n.a.
frozen *(SeaPak),* 4 oz.	1.0	n.a.
frozen *(Van de Kamp's* Natural), 4 oz. . .	1.0	0

Cod entrée, frozen:

au gratin *(Booth),* 9.5 oz.	11.0	n.a.
au gratin *(Weight Watchers),* 9.25 oz.	6.0	1.0
breaded *(Van de Kamp's* Light), 1 piece	11.0	2.0
Florentine *(Booth),* 9.5 oz.	6.0	n.a.
w/lemon butter sauce and rice *(Booth),* 9.5 oz.	38.0	n.a.
w/mushroom sauce and rice *(Booth),* 9.5 oz.	11.0	n.a.
nuggets *(Frionor Bunch O'Crunch),* 8 pieces	21.0	3.0
oven fried *(Weight Watchers),* 7.08 oz.	7.0	< 1.0
Cod liver oil, all varieties *(Hain),* 1 tbsp.	14.0	n.a.

Coffee:

brewed, 6 fl. oz.	0	0
instant, regular, 1 rounded tsp. powder	tr.	tr.
flavored, prepared, 6 fl. oz.:		
all varieties *(Hills Bros* Café Coffees)	2.0	n.a.
all varieties, except café Français or mocha *(General Foods* International)	2.0	n.a.
café Français or mocha *(General Foods* International)	3.0	n.a.

Coffee liqueur:

53 proof, 1 fl. oz.	.1	< .1
cream, 34 proof, 1 fl. oz.	4.9	3.0
Coffee substitute, cereal grain, dry, 1 tsp.	.1	< .1

Cold cuts, see specific listings

Collards:

fresh, raw, chopped, 1/2 cup	< .1	(0)
fresh, boiled, drained, chopped, 1/2 cup	.1	(0)
canned, chopped *(Allens),* 1/2 cup	< 1.0	(0)
canned, chopped, w/pork *(Luck's),* 7.5 oz.	7.0	n.a.
frozen, boiled, drained, chopped, 1/2 cup	.4	(0)

Cookie, 1 piece, except as noted:

almond *(Stella D'Oro* Breakfast Treats)	3.6	n.a.
almond toast *(Stella D'Oro* Mandel)	1.4	n.a.
amaranth *(Health Valley Amaranth Cookies)*	3.0	n.a.
animal crackers *(FFV),* 1.25-oz. pkg.	6.0	1.0
animal crackers *(Keebler),* 5 pieces	2.0	< 1.0
animal crackers *(Sunshine),* 13 pieces	4.0	1.0

anise *(Stella D'Oro* Anisette Toast Jumbo)	1.0	n.a.
apple bar *(Apple Newtons)*	2.0	< 1.0
apple n' raisin *(Archway)*	3.0	n.a.
apricot-raspberry filled *(Pepperidge Farm)*	2.0	1.0
arrowroot biscuit *(National)*	1.0	< 1.0
brownie chocolate nut *(Pepperidge Farm* Old Fashioned)	3.5	1.0
brownie cream sandwich *(Pepperidge Farm* Capri)	5.0	1.0
butter flavor:		
(Pepperidge Farm Chessmen)	2.0	1.0
chocolate coated *(Keebler* Baby Bear), 3 pieces	2.0	< 1.0
chocolate coated *(Keebler E.L. Fudge)*, 2 pieces	4.0	1.0
caramel patties *(FFV)*, 2 pieces	7.0	n.a.
chocolate *(Stella D'Oro Margherite)*	3.1	n.a.
chocolate fudge mint *(Keebler Grasshopper)*	1.5	.5
chocolate middles *(Nabisco)*	5.0	2.0
chocolate snaps *(Nabisco)*, 4 pieces	2.0	1.0
chocolate wafer *(Nabisco* Famous Wafers), 1/2 oz.	2.0	< 1.0
chocolate chip:		
(Almost Home Real)	3.0	1.0
(Archway)	3.0	n.a.
(Chips Ahoy! Mini), 6 pieces	3.0	1.0
(Chips Ahoy! Pure)	2.0	< 1.0
(Drake's), 2 pieces	6.0	2.0
(Duncan Hines), 2 pieces	5.0	n.a.
(Keebler Chips Deluxe/Soft Batch)	4.0	1.0
(Pepperidge Farm Old Fashioned)	2.5	1.0
candy coated *(Keebler Rainbow Chips Deluxe)*	3.0	1.0
chewy *(Chips Ahoy!)*	3.0	1.0
chocolate *(Drake's)*, 2 pieces	5.0	1.0
chocolate walnut *(Chips Ahoy!* Selections)	6.0	2.0
w/chocolate middle *(Keebler Magic Middles)*	5.0	1.0

Cookie, chocolate chip, continued

chunky *(Chips Ahoy!* Selections)	5.0	2.0
fudge *(Almost Home)*	3.0	< 1.0
milk *(Duncan Hines)*, 2 pieces	5.0	n.a.
mint *(Keebler Soft Batch)*	4.0	1.0
snaps *(Nabisco)*, 3 pieces	2.0	< 1.0
sprinkled *(Chips Ahoy!)*	2.0	< 1.0
striped *(Chips Ahoy!)*	5.0	2.0
toffee *(Pepperidge Farm* Old		
Fashioned)	3.5	1.0
walnut *(Keebler Soft Batch)*	4.0	1.0
chocolate chunk:		
(Chips Ahoy! Selections)	5.0	2.0
(Pepperidge Farm Nantucket)	6.0	2.0
chocolate walnut *(Pepperidge Farm*		
Beacon Hill)	7.0	2.0
milk macadamia *(Pepperidge Farm*		
Sausalito)	7.0	2.0
milk macadamia *(Pepperidge Farm*		
Special Collection)	4.0	1.0
pecan *(Chips Ahoy!* Selections)	6.0	2.0
pecan *(Pepperidge Farm* Chesapeake)	7.0	2.0
pecan *(Pepperidge Farm* Special		
Collection)	4.0	1.0
chocolate sandwich:		
(Keebler Chocolate Creme Sandwich)	4.0	1.0
(Oreo)	2.0	< 1.0
(Oreo Big Stuf)	12.0	4.0
(Oreo Double Stuf)	4.0	1.0
(Pepperidge Farm Brussels)	2.5	1.0
(Pepperidge Farm Lido)	5.0	1.0
(Pepperidge Farm Milano)	3.0	1.0
(Pepperidge Farm Orleans)	4.0	1.0
fudge or white fudge covered *(Oreo)*	6.0	4.0
fudge, fudge or peanut butter creme		
filled *(Keebler E.L. Fudge)*	3.0	< 1.0
mint *(Pepperidge Farm* Brussels)	3.5	1.0
mint or orange *(Pepperidge Farm*		
Milano)	3.5	1.0
chocolate peanut bar *(Ideal)*	5.0	2.0
(Cinnamon Raisin Nut Newtons)	2.0	< 1.0

coconut *(Drake's)*, 2 pieces	5.0	2.0
coconut, chocolate filled *(Pepperidge Farm* Tahiti)	6.0	2.0
coconut macaroon *(Stella D'Oro)*	3.4	n.a.
coffee, chocolate-praline filled *(Pepperidge Farm* Cappuccino)	3.0	1.0
date pecan *(Pepperidge Farm* Kitchen Hearth)	2.5	1.0
devil's food cakes *(Nabisco)*	1.0	< 1.0
egg biscuit, Roman *(Stella D'Oro)*	5.0	n.a.
(FFV Kreem Pilot Bread)	2.0	n.a.
(FFV Royal Dainty), 2 pieces	6.0	n.a.
fig bar *(Fig Newtons)*	1.0	< 1.0
fig bar *(Keebler)*	2.0	< 1.0
fig bar, vanilla *(FFV)*	1.0	< 1.0
fig bar, whole wheat *(FFV)*	2.0	< 1.0
fruit slices *(Stella D'Oro)*	2.2	n.a.
fudge bar, caramel and peanut *(Heyday)*	6.0	2.0
ginger *(Pepperidge Farm* Gingerman), 2 pieces	3.0	0
ginger boys *(FFV)*, 1.25-oz. pkg.	5.0	1.0
gingersnaps *(FFV)*, 5 pieces	4.0	1.0
gingersnaps *(Nabisco* Old Fashioned)	1.0	< 1.0
gingersnaps *(Sunshine)*, 5 pieces	3.0	1.0
graham cracker:		
(Keebler), 4 pieces	2.0	< 1.0
(Nabisco), 2 pieces	1.0	< 1.0
(Sunshine Grahamy Bears), 9 pieces	5.0	1.0
all varieties *(Honey Maid* Graham Bites), 11 pieces	2.0	< 1.0
all varieties *(Nabisco Teddy Grahams)*, 11 pieces	2.0	< 1.0
all varieties *(Teddy Grahams Bearwich's)*, 4 pieces	3.0	< 1.0
chocolate *(Keebler Thin Bits)*, 12 pieces	3.0	< 1.0
chocolate *(Nabisco)*	3.0	2.0
cinnamon *(Honey Maid)*, 2 pieces	1.0	< 1.0
cinnamon *(Keebler* Alpha Grahams), 6 pieces	2.0	< 1.0
cinnamon *(Keebler* Cinnamon Crisp), 4 pieces	2.0	< 1.0

Cookie, graham cracker, continued

cinnamon *(Keebler Thin Bits)*, 12 pieces	3.0	< 1.0
cinnamon *(Sunshine)*, 1 piece	3.0	1.0
fudge covered *(Keebler* Deluxe),		
2 pieces	4.0	1.0
w/fudge *(Nabisco Cookies'N Fudge)*	2.0	1.0
honey *(Honey Maid)*, 2 pieces	1.0	< 1.0
honey *(Keebler* Honey Grahams),		
4 pieces	2.0	< 1.0
honey *(Sunshine)*, 1 piece	2.0	< 1.0
oat bran *(Health Valley)*, 7 pieces . . .	2.0	n.a.
wheat *(Carr's* Home Wheat Graham)	3.3	n.a.
hazelnut *(Pepperidge Farm* Old		
Fashioned)	3.0	1.0
jelly tarts *(FFV)*	2.0	< 1.0
lemon nut crunch *(Pepperidge Farm* Old		
Fashioned)	3.5	1.0
marshmallow chocolate cake *(Mallomars)*	3.0	1.0
marshmallow chocolate cake *(Pinwheels)*	5.0	2.0
marshmallow fudge cake *(Nabisco* Puffs)	4.0	3.0
marshmallow fudge cake *(Nabisco* Twirls)	6.0	4.0
mint sandwich *(Mystic Mint)*	5.0	3.0
molasses *(Nabisco Pantry)*	3.0	< 1.0
molasses crisps *(Pepperidge Farm* Old		
Fashioned)	1.5	0
oat bran, raisin *(Awrey's)*	4.0	1.0
oatmeal:		
(FFV), 5 pieces	4.0	1.0
(Keebler Old Fashion)	3.0	1.0
(Sunshine), 2 pieces	5.0	1.0
chocolate chunk *(Chips Ahoy!*		
Selections)	5.0	2.0
w/chocolate middle *(Keebler Magic*		
Middles)	5.0	1.0
date filled *(Archway)*	2.0	n.a.
iced *(Archway)*	5.0	n.a.
Irish *(Pepperidge Farm* Old Fashioned)	2.5	.5
milk chocolate chunk *(Pepperidge Farm*		
Dakota)	6.0	2.0
raisin *(Almost Home)* . . . . . . : . . .	3.0	< 1.0
raisin *(Duncan Hines)*, 2 pieces	5.0	n.a.

raisin *(Keebler Soft Batch)*	3.0	< 1.0
raisin *(Pepperidge Farm* Old Fashioned)	2.5	1.0
raisin *(Pepperidge Farm* Santa Fe) . . .	4.0	1.0
raisin or raisin bran *(Archway)*	3.0	n.a.
peach-apricot bar, vanilla *(FFV)*	1.0	< 1.0
peach-apricot bar, whole wheat *(FFV)*	2.0	< 1.0
peach-apricot pastry *(Stella D'Oro)*	3.8	n.a.
peanut butter:		
chocolate chip *(Keebler Soft Batch)* . .	5.0	1.0
chocolate filled *(Pepperidge Farm* Nassau)	5.0	1.0
cream filled *(Pitter Patter)*	4.0	< 1.0
milk chocolate chunk *(Pepperidge Farm* Cheyenne)	6.0	2.0
nut *(Keebler Soft Batch)*	4.0	1.0
sandwich *(Nutter Butter)*	3.0	< 1.0
peanut creme patties *(Nutter Butter)*, 2 pieces.	4.0	< 1.0
pecan crunch *(Archway)*	3.0	n.a.
(Pepperidge Farm Venice), 2 pieces . . .	6.0	2.0
praline pecan *(FFV)*	2.0	1.0
raisin *(Stella D'Oro* Golden Bars) . . .	4.3	n.a.
raisin bar, iced *(Keebler)*	4.0	1.0
raisin bran *(Pepperidge Farm* Kitchen Hearth).	2.5	1.0
raspberry bar *(Raspberry Newtons)*	2.0	< 1.0
raspberry filled *(Pepperidge Farm* Chantilly)	2.0	1.0
raspberry filled *(Pepperidge Farm* Linzer)	4.0	1.0
sesame *(Stella D'Oro* Regina)	2.2	n.a.
shortbread:		
(Lorna Doone), 3 pieces	4.0	< 1.0
(Pepperidge Farm Old Fashioned) . . .	4.0	1.0
chocolate center *(Keebler Magic Middles)*.	5.0	1.0
country *(FFV)*	4.0	1.0
fudge striped *(Keebler* Fudge Stripes)	3.0	< 1.0
fudge striped *(Nabisco Cookies'N Fudge)*	3.0	1.0
pecan *(Nabisco)*	5.0	1.0

Cookie, shortbread, continued

pecan *(Pecan Sandies)*	5.0	1.0
pecan *(Pepperidge Farm* Old Fashioned)	5.0	2.0
spice drops *(Stella D'Oro* Pfeffernusse)	.8	n.a.
(Stella D'Oro Angel Bars/Angel Wings)	4.7	n.a.
(Stella D'Oro Love Cookies)	5.2	n.a.
strawberry bar *(Strawberry Newtons)* . .	2.0	< 1.0
strawberry filled *(Pepperidge Farm)* . . .	2.5	1.0
sugar *(Almost Home* Old Fashioned)	3.0	< 1.0
sugar *(Pepperidge Farm* Old Fashioned)	2.5	1.0
tea biscuit *(Social Tea)*	1.0	< 1.0
vanilla:		
(Pepperidge Farm Bordeaux), 2 pieces	3.0	1.0
(Stella D'Oro Margherite)	2.8	n.a.
plain or chocolate laced *(Pepperidge Farm* Pirouettes), 2 pieces	4.0	1.0
chocolate coated *(Pepperidge Farm* Orleans)	3.0	1.0
chocolate nut coated *(Pepperidge Farm* Geneva)	3.0	1.0
creme sandwich *(Cameo)*	3.0	1.0
creme sandwich *(Keebler* French Vanilla)	4.0	< 1.0
creme sandwich *(Nabisco Cookie Break)*	2.0	< 1.0
creme sandwich *(Nabisco Giggles)* . . .	3.0	< 1.0
wafer (see also specific listings):		
brown edged *(Nabisco)*, 1/2 oz.	3.0	< 1.0
fudge covered *(Keebler Fudge Sticks)*	2.5	.5
fudge striped *(Nabisco Cookies'N Fudge)*	4.0	2.0
sugar *(Biscos)*, 4 pieces	3.0	< 1.0
vanilla *(FFV)*, 1 oz. or 8 pieces	5.0	1.0
vanilla *(Nilla* Wafers), 1/2 oz.	2.0	< 1.0
vanilla, golden *(Keebler)*, 4 pieces . . .	3.0	1.0
vanilla cinnamon *(Nilla* Wafers), 1/2 oz.	2.0	< 1.0
waffle cremes *(Biscos)*, 2 pieces	4.0	< 1.0
Cookie, frozen, 2 pieces:		
chocolate chip:		
(Nestlé Toll House Ready To Bake) . .	7.0	n.a.

w/nuts *(Nestlé* Toll House Ready To Bake)	8.0	n.a.
oatmeal raisin *(Nestlé* Toll House Ready To Bake)	5.0	n.a.
Cookie, refrigerated:		
all varieties, except oatmeal raisin *(Pillsbury)*, 1 piece	3.0	< 1.0
oatmeal raisin *(Pillsbury)*, 1 piece	2.0	<1.0
Cookie mix*, 2 pieces:		
chocolate chip *(Betty Crocker Big Batch)*	6.0	n.a.
chocolate chip *(Duncan Hines)*	5.0	n.a.
oatmeal raisin or golden sugar *(Duncan Hines)*	6.0	n.a.
peanut butter *(Duncan Hines)*	7.0	n.a.
Coriander, fresh, raw, 1/4 cup	< .1	(0)
Coriander leaf, dried, 1 tsp.	< .1	(0)
Coriander seed, 1 tsp.	.3	< .1
Corn:		
fresh, boiled, drained, cut, 1/2 cup	1.1	.2
canned, 1/2 cup:		
kernel, drained	.8	.1
kernel, vacuum pack or cream style	.5	.1
almondine *(Green Giant)*	3.0	0
w/beans, carrots, and pasta, in tomato sauce *(Green Giant Pantry Express)*	2.0	0
w/rcd and green peppers, w/liquid . . .	.6	.1
frozen:		
on cob, boiled, drained, 4-oz. ear . . .	.5	.1
kernel, boiled, drained, 1/2 cup	.1	tr.
in butter sauce *(The Budget Gourmet* Side Dish)*, 5.5 oz.	6.0	n.a.
in butter sauce *(Green Giant Niblets One Serving)*, 4.5 oz.	2.0	< 1.0
in butter sauce *(Stokely Singles)*, 4 oz.	1.0	n.a.
in butter sauce, on cob *(Stokely Singles)*, 1 ear	1.0	n.a.
in butter sauce *(Birds Eye* Butter Sauce Combinations)*, 3.3 oz.	2.0	n.a.
in sauce, country style *(The Budget Gourmet* Side Dish)*, 5.75 oz.	5.0	n.a.
Corn, grain, 1 cup	7.9	1.1

Corn bran, crude, 1 cup . . . . .7 .1
Corn cake *(Quaker Grain Cakes)*, 1 piece .2 (0)
Corn chips and similar snacks, 1 oz.:
   (Bachman) . . . . 10.0 n.a.
   (Bugles) . . . . 8.0 n.a.
   (Dipsy Doodles Rippled Corn Chips) 10.0 n.a.
   (Fritos/Fritos Dip Size) . . . . 9.0 n.a.
   (Fritos Crisp'n Thin) . . . . 10.0 n.a.
   (Planters) 10.0 2.0
   (Snyder's) 11.0 2.0
   (Wise Corn Chips or Crunchies) . . . . 10.0 n.a.
   barbecue flavor *(Bachman* BBQ) . . . . . 9.0 n.a.
   barbecue flavor *(Fritos* Bar-B-Q) . . . . . 9.0 n.a.
   cheese:
      (Cheetos Balls/Crunchy/Puffs) . . . . . . 10.0 n.a.
      (Cheez Doodles Baked Corn Puffs) 8.0 n.a.
      (Cheez Doodles Fried Corn Puffs) . . . 10.0 n.a.
      (Jax Baked) . . . . 7.0 n.a.
      (Jax Crunchy) . . . . 11.0 n.a.
      (Planters Cheez Balls/Curls) 11.0 2.0
      (Wise Cheez Waffies) . . . . 8.0 n.a.
      crunchy *(Cheetos* Light) . . . . 6.0 n.a.
      nacho *(Bugles)* . . . . 9.0 n.a.
      nacho *(Wise* Corn Spirals) . . . . 10.0 n.a.
   chili cheese *(Fritos)* . . . . 10.0 n.a.
   ranch *(Fritos Wild'n Mild)* . . . . 9.0 n.a.
   tortilla:
      (Buenitos Tortilla Chips) . . . . 8.0 n.a.
      (Doritos) . . . . 6.0 n.a.
      (Doritos Cool Ranch) . . . . 7.0 n.a.
      (Old El Paso Crispy) . . . . 8.0 n.a.
      (Old El Paso Nachips) . . . . 7.0 n.a.
      all varieties *(Doritos* Light) . . . . 4.0 n.a.
      plain or nacho *(Bachman)* . . . . 6.0 n.a.
      plain or nacho *(Tostitos)* . . . . 8.0 n.a.
      nacho *(Bravos* Rounds) . . . . 8.0 n.a.
      nacho, jalapeño flavor *(Bravos)* . . . . . 7.0 n.a.
      nacho, salsa, or taco flavor *(Doritos)*. . 7.0 n.a.
      ranch *(Eagle)* . . . . 8.0 n.a.
      taco style *(Hain)* . . . . 11.0 n.a.

Corn dog, see "Frankfurter, batter-
wrapped"

Corn fritters, frozen *(Mrs. Paul's),* 2 pieces   9.0   n.a.

Corn grits (see also "Hominy"):

dry:

1 cup . . . .   1.8   .3

1 tbsp.   .1   < .1

white, enriched *(Quaker/Aunt Jemima*
Regular/Quick), 3 tbsp. 2   0

cooked, 1 cup 5   .1

instant, dry, 1 pkt.:

w/imitation bacon bits *(Quaker)* 4   0

w/real cheddar cheese flavor *(Quaker)*   1.0   1.0

w/imitation ham bits *(Quaker)* 3   0

white hominy product *(Quaker)* 1   0

Corn nuggets, frozen *(Stilwell Quickkrisp),*

3 oz. . . . .   8.0   n.a.

Corn salad, raw, 1 oz. or 1/2 cup 1   (0)

Corn soufflé, frozen *(Stouffer's),* 4 oz. . . .   7.0   n.a.

Corn syrup, dark or light *(Karo)*   0   0

Cornish game hen, frozen *(Tyson),* 3.5 oz.   14.0   n.a.

Cornmeal (see also "Polenta mix"):

degermed, 1 cup . . . .   2.3   .3

self-rising:

bolted, 1 cup . . . .   4.2   .6

bolted, w/wheat flour, 1 cup . . . .   4.8   .7

degermed, 1 cup . . . .   2.4   .3

white *(Aunt Jemima),* 3 tbsp. 5   0

white, bolted, *(Aunt Jemima),* 3 tbsp.   .9   (0)

white, enriched *(Quaker/Aunt Jemima),*

3 tbsp.   .5   0

whole grain, 1 cup . . . .   4.4   .6

yellow, enriched *(Quaker/Aunt Jemima),*

3 tbsp.   .5   (0)

Cornmeal mix:

buttermilk, self-rising, white *(Aunt*

Jemima), 3 tbsp. . . . .   1.1   n.a.

white, bolted *(Aunt Jemima),* 3 tbsp. 7   n.a.

yellow, self-rising *(Aunt Jemima),* 3 tbsp.   1.0   n.a.

Cornstarch, 1 tbsp. . . . .   tr.   tr.

Cottonseed kernels, roasted, 1 oz. 10.3   2.7

Cottonseed meal, partially defatted, 1 oz.   1.4   .3
Couscous:
  dry, 1 cup . . . .   1.2   .2
  cooked, 1 cup 3   .1
Cowpea, 1/2 cup, except as noted:
  raw, shelled, or boiled, drained 3   .1
  leafy tips, raw, chopped . . . .   < .1   < .1
  young pods, w/seeds, raw or boiled,
    drained 1   < .1
  canned, see "Black-eyed pea"
  frozen, boiled, drained 6   .1
Cowpea, mature:
  dried, boiled, 1/2 cup 5   .1
  canned, plain, w/liquid, 1/2 cup 7   .2
  canned, w/pork, 1/2 cup . . . .   1.9   .7
Crab, meat only:
  fresh:
    Alaska king, raw, 4 oz. 7   n.a.
    Alaska king, boiled, poached, or
      steamed, 4 oz. . . . .   1.7   .2
    blue, raw, 4 oz. . . . .   1.2   .3
    blue, boiled, poached, or steamed,
      1 cup . . . .   2.4   .3
    Dungeness, raw, 4 oz. . . . .   1.1   .1
    queen, raw, 4 oz. . . . .   1.3   .2
  canned, blue, 1 cup . . . .   1.7   .3
  canned, Dungeness *(S&W),* 3.25 oz. . . .   2.0   n.a.
  frozen, snow *(Wakefield),* 3 oz. . . . . . .   1.0   n.a.
Crab, deviled, breaded, frozen:
  (Mrs. Paul's), 1 cake . . . .   9.0   n.a.
  miniature *(Mrs. Paul's),* 3.5 oz. . . . . . .   12.0   n.a.
"Crab," imitation *(Icicle Brand),* 3.5 oz.   .1   tr.
Crab and shrimp, frozen *(Wakefield),* 3 oz.   1.0   n.a.
Crabapple:
  fresh, w/skin, sliced, 1/2 cup 2   .1
  canned, spiced *(Lucky Leaf/Musselman's),*
    4 oz.   0   0
Cracker:
  animal, see "Cookie"
  bacon flavor *(Keebler* Toasteds), 4 pieces   3.0   < 1.0

bacon flavor thins *(Nabisco)*, 7 pieces or 1/2 oz.	4.0	1.0
w/bacon and cheese *(Handi-Snacks)*, 1 pkg.	9.0	4.0
bran, toasted *(Bran Thins)*, 7 pieces	3.0	< 1.0
butter flavor:		
(Escort), 3 pieces or 1/2 oz.	4.0	< 1.0
(Keebler Club Low Salt), 4 pieces	3.0	< 1.0
(Keebler Toasteds Buttercrisp), 4 pieces	3.0	< 1.0
(Keebler Town House), 4 pieces	4.0	< 1.0
(Pepperidge Farm Flutters), 3/4 oz.	4.0	1.0
(Ritz), 4 pieces or 1/2 oz.	4.0	< 1.0
(Ritz Bits), 22 pieces or 1/2 oz.	4.0	< 1.0
dairy *(Nabisco American Classic)*, 4 pieces	3.0	< 1.0
thins *(Pepperidge Farm* Distinctive), 4 pieces	3.0	1.0
cheese or cheese flavor:		
(Better Cheddars), 10 pieces	4.0	< 1.0
(Cheddar Wedges), 31 pieces or 1/2 oz.	3.0	< 1.0
(Cheese Nips), 13 pieces or 1/2 oz.	3.0	< 1.0
(Cheez-It), 12 pieces	4.0	1.0
(Combos), 1.8 oz.	10.0	n.a.
(Nabisco Swiss Cheese), 7 pieces	3.0	< 1.0
(Pepperidge Farm Goldfish Thins), 4 pieces	2.0	0
(Pepperidge Farm Snack Sticks), 8 pieces	5.0	2.0
(Ritz Bits), 22 pieces or 1/2 oz.	4.0	< 1.0
(Tid Bits), 16 pieces or 1/2 oz.	4.0	1.0
cheddar *(Keebler Town House Jrs.)*, 8 pieces	4.0	< 1.0
cheddar *(Pepperidge Farm* Tiny Goldfish), 1 oz.	4.0	1.0
cheddar or Parmesan *(Pepperidge Farm* Goldfish), 1 oz.	4.0	1.0
cheese sandwich:		
(Handi-Snacks), 1 pkg.	8.0	5.0
(Keebler Town House & Cheddar), 1 piece	4.0	1.0

Cracker, cheese sandwich, continued

and peanut butter *(Handi-Snacks)*, 1 pkg.	14.0	4.0
and peanut butter *(Keebler)*, 2 pieces	3.0	< 1.0
wheat and American cheese *(Keebler)*, 1 piece	4.0	1.0
(Chicken In A Biskit), 7 pieces	5.0	1.0
crispbread (see also specific grains):		
(Kavli Norwegian), 1 thick or 2 thin pieces	.3	n.a.
(Wasa Breakfast/Fiber Plus), 1 piece	1.0	n.a.
(Wasa Extra Crisp), 1 piece	0	0
all varieties *(Finn Crisp)*, 2 pieces	< 1.0	n.a.
(FFV Schooners), 33 pieces, approx. 1/2 oz.	2.0	< 1.0
garlic *(Manischewitz Garlic Tams)*, 10 pieces	8.0	6.0
graham, see "Cookie"		
grain, mixed *(Harvest Crisps* 5 Grain), 6 pieces	2.0	< 1.0
herb, garden *(Pepperidge Farm Flutters)*, 3/4 oz.	4.0	1.0
(Manischewitz Tam Tams), 10 pieces	8.0	6.0
(Manischewitz Tam Tams No Salt), 10 pieces	7.0	5.0
matzo:		
(Manischewitz Daily Unsalted), 1 board	.3	0
(Manischewitz Passover), 1 board	.4	0
American *(Manischewitz)*, 1 board	1.9	n.a.
egg *(Manischewitz* Passover), 1 board	2.0	n.a.
egg n' onion *(Manischewitz)*, 1 board	1.0	.2
miniature *(Manischewitz)*, 10 pieces	< 1.0	n.a.
tea, thin *(Manischewitz* Daily), 1 board	.3	0
whole wheat, w/bran *(Manischewitz)*, 1 board	.6	0
melba toast:		
plain or honey bran *(Devonsheer)*, 1 piece	.4	.1
garlic *(Devonsheer* Rounds), 1/2 oz.	1.2	n.a.
oat *(Harvest Crisps)*, 6 pieces, 1/2 oz.	2.0	< 1.0
onion *(Devonsheer* Rounds), 1/2 oz.	.6	n.a.

pumpernickel *(Old London)*, 1/2 oz. . . .	.6	n.a.
rye or vegetable *(Devonsheer)*, 1 piece	.4	.1
sesame *(Devonsheer)*, 1 piece	.5	.1
wheat, whole *(Devonsheer)*, 1 piece . .	.4	.1
white *(Old London)*, 1/2 oz.	.6	n.a.
whole grain *(Old London)*, 1/2 oz. . . .	.9	n.a.
oat *(Oat Thins)*, 8 pieces	3.0	< 1.0
oat bran *(Oat Bran Krisp)*, 2 triple pieces	3.0	n.a.
onion *(Keebler* Toasteds), 4 pieces	3.0	< 1.0
onion *(Manischewitz Onion Tams)*, 10 pieces	8.0	6.0
onion *(Nabisco American Classic)*, 4 pieces.	3.0	< 1.0
peanut butter:		
(Combos), 1.8 oz.	10.0	n.a.
(Handi-Snacks), 1 pkg.	13.0	2.0
sandwich *(Ritz Bits)*, 6 pieces or 1/2 oz.	4.0	< 1.0
toast and *(Keebler)*, 2 pieces	3.0	< 1.0
(Pepperidge Farm Original Goldfish), 1 oz..	5.0	1.0
pizza flavor *(Pepperidge Farm* Goldfish), 1 oz..	5.0	1.0
poppy, toasted *(Nabisco American Classic)*, 4 pieces or 1/2 oz.	3.0	< 1.0
pretzel *(Pepperidge Farm* Goldfish), 1 oz.	3.0	0
pretzel *(Pepperidge Farm* Snack Sticks), 8 pieces	3.0	0
rice bran *(Health Valley)*, 7 pieces	4.0	n.a.
rye:		
(Keebler Toasteds), 4 pieces	3.0	< 1.0
(Pepperidge Farm Snack Sticks), 8 pieces	6.0	1.0
(Rykrisp), 1/2 oz.	0	0
dark or light *(Ryvita* Crisp Bread), 1 piece	< 1.0	n.a.
golden or hearty *(Wasa* Crispbread), 1 piece	0	0
light *(Wasa* Crispbread Lite), 1 piece	0	0
original *(Finn Crisp* Hi-Fiber), 1 piece	0	0
seasoned *(Rykrisp)*, 1/2 oz.	1.0	n.a.
sesame *(Rykrisp)*, 2 triple pieces	2.0	n.a.

Cracker, continued
saltine:

(Premium Regular/Unsalted tops), 5 pieces	2.0	< 1.0
(Premium Fat Free), 5 pieces	0	0
(Premium Bits), 16 pieces or 1/2 oz.	3.0	< 1.0
(Sunshine Krispy), 5 pieces	1.0	< 1.0
plain or wheat *(Zesta)*, 5 pieces	2.0	< 1.0
wheat, whole *(Premium Plus)*, 5 pieces	2.0	< 1.0

sesame:

(FFV Crisp), 1 piece	2.0	< 1.0
(Keebler Toasteds), 4 pieces or 1/2 oz.	3.0	< 1.0
(Pepperidge Farm Distinctive), 4 pieces	4.0	1.0
(Pepperidge Farm Snack Sticks), 8 pieces	5.0	1.0
(Pepperidge Farm Flutters), 3/4 oz. . . .	5.0	1.0
bread wafer *(Meal Mates)*, 3 pieces	3.0	< 1.0
golden *(Nabisco American Classic)*, 4 pieces	3.0	< 1.0
wafer *(FFV* Crisp), 4 pieces or 1/2 oz.	2.0	< 1.0

sesame w/cheese *(Twigs* Snack Sticks),

5 pieces	4.0	< 1.0

soda or water:

(Carr's Table Water, Bite Size), 2 pieces	1.0	n.a.
(Crown Pilot), 1/2-oz. piece	2.0	< 1.0
(FFV Ocean Crisps), 1 piece	2.0	< 1.0
(North Castles English), 1 piece	0	0
(Pepperidge Farm English Water Biscuits), 4 pieces	1.0	0
(Royal Lunch), 1/2-oz. piece	2.0	< 1.0
(Sailor Boy Pilot), 1 piece	3.0	< 1.0

soup and oyster:

(Dandy), 20 pieces or 1/2 oz.	2.0	< 1.0
(Oysterettes), 18 pieces or 1/2 oz.	1.0	< 1.0
(Sunshine), 16 pieces	1.0	< 1.0

sour cream and chive *(Hain/Hain* No Salt), 1 oz.	6.0	n.a.
sourdough *(Hain)*, 1/2 oz.	3.0	n.a.
sourdough *(Hain* Low Salt), 1 oz.	5.0	n.a.

toast (*Uneeda* Biscuits Unsalted Tops), 3 pieces	2.0	< 1.0
vegetable (*Vegetable Thins*), 7 pieces . .	4.0	< 1.0
water, see "soda or water," above		
(*Waverly/Waverly* Low Salt), 4 pieces . .	3.0	< 1.0
wheat:		
(*FFV* Stoned Wheat Wafer), 4 pieces	2.0	< 1.0
(*Manischewitz Wheat Tams*), 10 pieces	8.0	6.0
(*Sociables*), 6 pieces or 1/2 oz.	3.0	< 1.0
(*Sunshine* Wheats), 8 pieces	4.0	1.0
(*Triscuit/Triscuit Bits*), 1/2 oz.	2.0	< 1.0
(*Wheat Thins*), 8 pieces or 1/2 oz. . . .	3.0	< 1.0
(*Wheatsworth* Stone Ground), 4 pieces	3.0	< 1.0
cracked (*Nabisco American Classic*), 4 pieces	4.0	< 1.0
cracked (*Pepperidge Farm* Distinctive), 3 pieces	4.0	1.0
hearty (*Pepperidge Farm* Distinctive), 4 pieces	5.0	1.0
nutty (*Wheat Thins*), 7 pieces	4.0	< 1.0
toasted (*Pepperidge Farm Flutters*), 3/4 oz.	5.0	1.0
toasted, w/onion (*Pepperidge Farm* Distinctive), 4 pieces	3.0	1.0
whole (*Keebler Wheatables*), 12 pieces	3.0	< 1.0
whole grain (*Keebler Harvest Wheats*), 4 pieces or 1/2 oz.	3.0	< 1.0
wheat'n bran (*Triscuit*), 3 pieces or 1/2 oz.	2.0	< 1.0
zwieback toast (*Nabisco*), 2 pieces or 1/2 oz.	1.0	< 1.0
Cracker crumbs and meal:		
(*Golden Dipt*), 1 oz.	0	0
matzo (*Manischewitz Farfel*), 1 cup	.8	0
matzo meal (*Manischewitz* Daily), 1 cup	1.4	0
Cranberry:		
fresh, whole or chopped, 1/2 cup	.1	(0)
canned, see "Cranberry sauce"		
Cranberry drink, juice, or juice cocktail,		
all blends (all brands), 6 fl. oz.	< .2	(0)
Cranberry-orange relish, canned, 1/2 cup . .	.1	(0)

Cranberry sauce, canned:

sweetened, 1/2 cup	.2	(0)
whole, jellied, or blends *(Ocean Spray)*, 2 oz.	0	0

Crawfish entrée, frozen, étouffé *(Cajun Cookin')*, 12 oz. ... 10.0 — n.a.

Crayfish, mixed species, meat only:

raw, 4 oz.	1.2	.2
boiled or steamed, 4 oz.	1.5	.3

Cream, fluid:

half and half, 1 tbsp.	1.7	1.1
light, coffee or table, 1 tbsp.	2.9	1.8
medium, 25% fat, 1 tbsp.	3.8	2.3
nondairy, see "Cream topping, nondairy"		
sour, see "Cream, sour"		
topping, whipped, see "Toppings, dessert"		
whipping:		
light, 1 cup or 2 cups whipped	73.9	46.2
light, 1 tbsp. or 2 tbsp. whipped	4.6	2.9
heavy, 1 cup or 2 cups whipped	88.1	54.8
heavy, 1 tbsp. or 2 tbsp. whipped	5.6	3.5

Cream, sour, cultured:

1 cup	48.2	30.0
1 tbsp.	2.5	1.6
(Breakstone's/Sealtest), 1 tbsp.	3.0	2.0
(Knudsen Hampshire), 1 oz.	6.0	3.0
(Knudsen Light n' Lively), 1 oz.	3.0	2.0
half and half, 1 tbsp.	1.8	1.1
half and half *(Breakstone's Light Choice)*, 1 tbsp.	2.0	1.0
half and half *(Sealtest Light)*, 1 tbsp.	2.0	1.0
onion, French *(Crowley)*, 1 oz.	5.0	n.a.

Cream, sour, nondairy:

1 oz.	5.5	5.0
1 cup	44.9	40.9
dressing *(Crowley)*, 1 oz.	4.0	n.a.

Cream gravy, canned *(Franco-American)*, 2 oz. ... 2.0 — n.a.

Cream puff, frozen, Bavarian *(Rich's)*, 1 piece ... 8.0 — n.a.

Cream of tartar *(Tone's)*, 1 tsp. 0 0
Cream topping, nondairy:
  frozen, semisolid:
    1 cup 19.0 16.3
    1 tbsp. . . . . 1.0 .9
    (Birds Eye Cool Whip), 1 tbsp. . . . . . 1.0 n.a.
    (Birds Eye Cool Whip Lite), 1 tbsp. . . < 1.0 n.a.
    (Kraft Whipped Topping), 1/4 cup . . . 3.0 3.0
    extra creamy *(Birds Eye Cool Whip*
      Dairy Recipe), 1 tbsp. . . . . 1.0 n.a.
  mix* *(D-Zerta)*, 1 tbsp. 1.0 (0)
  mix* *(Dream Whip)*, 1 tbsp. 0 0
  pressurized, 1 tbsp. . . . . .9 .8
  pressurized *(Rich's Richwhip)*, 1/4 oz. . . 2.0 n.a.
  prewhipped *(Rich's Richwhip)*, 1 tbsp. . . 1.0 n.a.
Creamer, nondairy:
  (Diehl), 1 tsp. . . . . < 1.0 0
  (N-Rich), 1 tsp. . . . . .6 .3
  liquid *(Coffee-mate)*, 1 tbsp. . . . . 1.0 .3
  liquid, frozen *(Rich's Coffee Rich)*, 1/2 oz. 2.0 < 1.0
  liquid, frozen *(Rich's Farm Rich)*, 1/2 oz. 2.0 0
  liquid, frozen *(Rich's Poly Rich)*, 1/2 oz. 1.0 < 1.0
  powdered *(Carnation Coffee-mate)*, 1 tsp. < 1.0 .7
  powdered *(Carnation Coffee-mate Lite)*,
    1 tsp. < 1.0 .3
  powdered *(Cremora)*, 1 tsp. . . . . < 1.0 n.a.
Creole sauce, Cajun *(Enrico's* Light), 4 oz. 2.8 n.a.
Cress, garden:
  raw, 1/2 cup . . . . .2 tr.
  boiled, drained, 1/2 cup . . . . .4 < .1
Cress, water, see "Watercress"
Croaker, Atlantic, meat only, raw, 4 oz. . . 3.6 1.2
Croissant, 1 piece:
  butter *(Awrey's)*, 3 oz. 17.0 8.0
  margarine or wheat *(Awrey's)*, 2.5 oz. . . 14.0 3.0
  frozen, butter *(Sara Lee)*, 1.5 oz. . . . . . 9.0 n.a.
  frozen, butter, petite *(Sara Lee)*, 1 oz. . . 6.0 n.a.
Crouton, 1/2 oz.:
  Caesar salad *(Brownberry)* . . . . 2.6 n.a.
  cheddar cheese *(Brownberry)* . . . . 2.8 n.a.
  cheddar and Romano *(Pepperidge Farm)* 2.0 0

Crouton, continued

cheese and garlic *(Pepperidge Farm)* . . .	3.0	1.0
onion and garlic or seasoned *(Brownberry)*	2.2	n.a.
onion and garlic *(Pepperidge Farm)* . . .	3.0	0
seasoned *(Pepperidge Farm)*	3.0	1.0
sour cream and chive *(Pepperidge Farm)*	3.0	1.0
toasted *(Brownberry)*	1.4	n.a.
Cucumber, w/peel, 1 medium, 8¼″ long × 2⅛″	.4	.1
Cucumber dip, creamy *(Kraft* Premium), 2 tbsp.	4.0	3.0
Cucumber and onion dip *(Breakstone's/ Sealtest)*, 2 tbsp.	4.0	3.0
Cumin seed, 1 tsp.	.5	(0)
Cupcake, see "Cake, snack"		
Currant:		
black, European, trimmed, ½ cup	.2	< .1
red or white, trimmed, ½ cup	.1	< .1
Zante, dried, ½ cup	.2	< .1
Curry powder, 1 tsp.	.3	n.a.
Curry sauce mix, 1.25-oz. pkt.	8.2	1.2
Cusk, meat only, raw, 4 oz.	.8	n.a.
Custard, see "Pudding mix"		
Custard apple, trimmed, 1 oz.	.2	(0)
Cutlet, vegetarian, canned:		
(Worthington), 1½ slices or 3.25 oz. . . .	2.0	n.a.
(Worthington Multigrain), 2 slices or 3.25 oz.	1.0	n.a.
Cuttlefish, mixed species, meat only, raw, 4 oz.	.8	.1

D

food and measure	total fat (gms.)	saturated fat (gms.)
Daikon, see "Radish, Oriental"		
Daiquiri mix, bottled or instant *(Holland House)*	0	0
Dairy Queen/Brazier:		
sandwiches, 1 serving:		
BBQ beef, 4.5 oz.	4.0	1.0
chicken fillet, breaded, 6.7 oz.	20.0	4.0
chicken fillet, breaded, w/cheese, 7.2 oz.	25.0	7.0
chicken fillet, grilled, 6.5 oz.	8.0	2.0
fish fillet, 6 oz.	16.0	3.0

Dairy Queen/Brazier, sandwiches, continued

fish fillet, w/cheese, 6.5 oz.	21.0	6.0
hamburger:		
single, 5 oz.	13.0	6.0
single, w/cheese, 5.5 oz.	18.0	9.0
double, 7 oz.	25.0	12.0
double, w/cheese, 8 oz.	34.0	18.0
DQ Homestyle Ultimate Burger,		
9.7 oz.	47.0	21.0
hot dog:		
3.5 oz.	16.0	6.0
w/cheese, 4 oz.	21.0	9.0
w/chili, 4.5 oz.	19.0	7.0
1/4 lb. *Super Dog,* 7 oz.	38.0	16.0
side dishes and dressings:		
dressing, French, reduced calorie, 2 oz.	5.0	1.0
dressing, Thousand Island, 2 oz.	21.0	3.0
french fries, 3.5 oz.	14.0	3.0
french fries, large, 4.5 oz.	18.0	4.0
onion rings, 3 oz.	12.0	3.0
salad, garden, w/out dressing, 10 oz.	13.0	7.0
salad, side, w/out dressing, 4.8 oz.	0	0
desserts and shakes:		
banana split, 13 oz.	11.0	8.0
Blizzard:		
Heath, small, 10.3 oz.	23.0	11.0
Heath, regular, 14.3 oz.	36.0	17.0
strawberry, small, 9.4 oz.	12.0	8.0
strawberry, regular, 13.5 oz.	16.0	11.0
Breeze:		
Heath, small, 9.6 oz.	12.0	3.0
Heath, regular, 13.4 oz.	21.0	6.0
strawberry, small, 8.7 oz.	< 1.0	< 1.0
strawberry, regular, 12.5 oz.	1.0	< 1.0
Buster Bar, 5.3 oz.	29.0	9.0
Brownie Delight, hot fudge, 10.8 oz.	29.0	14.0
cone:		
chocolate, regular, 5 oz.	7.0	5.0
chocolate, large, 7.5 oz.	11.0	8.0
chocolate dipped, regular, 5.5 oz.	16.0	8.0
vanilla, small, 3 oz.	4.0	3.0

vanilla, regular, 5 oz.	7.0	5.0
vanilla, large, 7.5 oz.	10.0	7.0
Dilly Bar, 3 oz.	13.0	6.0
DQ frozen cake slice, undecorated, 5.8 oz.	18.0	8.0
DQ Sandwich, 2.2 oz.	4.0	2.0
malt, vanilla, regular, 14.7 oz.	14.0	8.0
Mr. Misty, regular, 11.6 oz.	0	0
Nutty Double Fudge, 9.7 oz.	22.0	10.0
Peanut Buster parfait, 10.8 oz.	32.0	10.0
QC Big Scoop, chocolate, 4.5 oz.	14.0	10.0
QC Big Scoop, vanilla, 4.5 oz.	14.0	9.0
shake, chocolate or vanilla, regular, 14 oz.	14.0	8.0
shake, vanilla, large, 16.3 oz.	16.0	10.0
sundae, chocolate, regular, 6.2 oz.	7.0	5.0
Waffle Cone Sundae, strawberry, 6.1 oz.	12.0	5.0
yogurt, cone or cup, regular or large	< 1.0	< 1.0
strawberry sundae, regular, 12.5 oz.	< 1.0	< 1.0
Dandelion greens:		
raw, 1 oz. or 1/2 cup chopped	.2	(0)
boiled, drained, chopped, 1/2 cup	.3	(0)
Danish pastry, see specific listings		
Dasheen, see "Taro"		
Date, pitted:		
(Dole), 1/2 cup	0	0
(Dromedary), 5 whole or 1/2 cup chopped	0	0
diced *(Bordo),* 2 oz.	1.1	n.a.
domestic, natural and dry, 10 average dates or 1/2 cup chopped	.4	n.a.
Date bar mix* *(Betty Crocker* Classic), 1 bar	2.0	1.0
Date nut pastry *(Awrey's),* 1.6-oz. piece	10.0	2.0
Diable sauce *(Escoffier),* 1 tbsp.	0	0
Dill dip, creamy *(Nasoya Vegi-Dip),* 1 oz.	4.0	n.a.
Dill seed, 1 tsp.	.3	< .1
Dill weed, dried, 1 tsp.	< .1	(0)
Dip, see specific listings		
Dock:		
raw, trimmed, chopped, 1/2 cup	.5	(0)
boiled, drained, 4 oz.	.7	(0)

Dolphin fish, meat only, raw, 4 oz. . . . . . .8 .2
Domino's Pizza:
  cheese, 2 slices 10.1 5.5
  deluxe, 2 slices 20.4 9.3
  double cheese/pepperoni, 2 slices 25.3 13.3
  ham, 2 slices 11.0 5.9
  pepperoni, 2 slices 17.5 8.4
  sausage/mushroom, 2 slices 15.8 7.7
  veggie, 2 slices 18.5 10.2
Doughnut, 1 piece:
  (Hostess Breakfast Bake Shop Old
    Fashioned) 9.0 4.0
  (Hostess O's) 10.0 4.0
  plain:
    (Awrey's) 30.0 7.0
    *(Hostess Breakfast Bake Shop Donette
      Gems)* 3.0 2.0
    (Hostess Breakfast Bake Shop Pantry) 11.0 5.0
    (Tastykake Assorted), 1.7 oz. . . . . . . 9.1 n.a.
  chocolate coated *(Tastykake* Choco-
    Dipped) . . . . 9.7 n.a.
  cinnamon:
    *(Hostess Breakfast Bake Shop Donette
      Gems)* 3.0 2.0
    (Hostess Breakfast Bake Shop Pantry) 10.0 5.0
    (Tastykake Assorted), 1.7 oz. . . . . . . 9.3 n.a.
    apple filled *(Hostess Breakfast Bake
      Shop Donette Gems)* 3.0 1.0
  coated, mini *(Tastykake)* . . . . 4.7 n.a.
  crumb *(Hostess Breakfast Bake Shop)* . . 10.0 5.0
  crumb *(Hostess Breakfast Bake Shop
    Donette Gems)* 5.0 2.0
  crunch *(Awrey's)* 34.0 8.0
  frosted:
    (Hostess Breakfast Bake Shop), 1.5 oz. 12.0 7.0
    *(Hostess Breakfast Bake Shop Donette
      Gems)* 5.0 3.0
    (Hostess O's) 14.0 9.0
    strawberry filled *(Hostess Breakfast
      Bake Shop Donette Gems)* 4.0 3.0
  fudge iced *(Tastykake* Premium), 2.5 oz. 21.2 n.a.

glazed *(Hostess Breakfast Bake Shop* Old
    Fashioned) 12.0   5.0
glazed, whirl *(Hostess Breakfast Bake
    Shop)* 7.0   3.0
honey wheat:
    (Hostess Breakfast Bake Shop) 12.0   6.0
    (Tastykake Premium), 2.5 oz. . . . . . . 18.2   n.a.
    mini *(Tastykake)* . . . . 2.9   n.a.
orange glazed *(Tastykake* Premium),
    2.5 oz. . . . . 19.5   n.a.
powdered sugar:
    *(Hostess Breakfast Bake Shop Donette
      Gems)* 3.0   2.0
    (Hostess Breakfast Bake Shop Pantry) 10.0   5.0
    (Tastykake, 12/pkg.) . . . . 5.8   n.a.
    mini *(Tastykake,* 6/pkg.) . . . . 3.1   n.a.
    strawberry filled *(Hostess Breakfast
      Bake Shop Donette Gems)* 3.0   1.0
sugared *(Awrey's)* 35.0   8.0
Doughnut, frozen:
glazed *(Rich's Ever Fresh),* 1.2-oz. piece 7.0   n.a.
jelly *(Rich's Ever Fresh),* 2.17-oz. piece 9.5   n.a.
Drum, freshwater, meat only, raw, 4 oz. . . 5.6   1.3
Duck:
domesticated, roasted, meat w/skin, 4 oz. 32.1   11.0
domesticated, roasted, meat only, 4 oz. 12.7   4.7
wild, raw, meat w/skin, 1 oz. 4.3   1.4
wild, raw, breast meat only, 1 oz. . . . . . 1.2   .4
Duck fat, 1 tbsp. 12.8   4.3
Duck sauce, see "Sweet and sour sauce"
Dulcita, frozen:
apple *(Hormel),* 4 oz. . . . . 10.0   n.a.
cherry *(Hormel),* 4 oz. . . . . 9.0   n.a.
Dutch brand loaf, 1 oz., except as noted:
(Eckrich/Eckrich Smorgas Pac) . . . . . . 6.0   n.a.
(Kahn's), 1 slice . . . . 7.0   n.a.
pork and beef, 4″ × 4″ × 3/32″ slice 5.1   1.8

food and measure	total fat (gms.)	saturated fat (gms.)
Eclair, chocolate, frozen *(Rich's)*, 1 piece	10.0	n.a.
Eel, mixed species, meat only:		
raw, 4 oz.	13.2	2.7
baked, broiled, or microwaved, 4 oz. . . .	17.0	3.4
Egg, chicken:		
raw:		
whole, 1 large egg	5.0	1.6
white from 1 large egg	0	0
yolk, fresh, yolk from 1 large egg . . .	5.0	1.6
frozen, yolk, 1 oz.	7.4	2.3

frozen, yolk, sugared, 1 oz.	7.2	2.2
hard-boiled, chopped, 1 cup	14.4	4.4
poached, 1 large egg	5.0	1.5
dried:		
whole, 1 cup, sifted	35.5	10.7
whole, 1 tbsp.	2.1	.6
white, stabilized, flakes or powder,		
1 oz.	< .1	0
yolk, 1 tbsp.	2.5	.7
Egg, duck, fresh, 1 whole egg, 2.5 oz. . . .	9.6	2.6
Egg, goose, fresh, 1 whole egg, 5.1 oz. . . .	19.1	5.2
Egg, pickled *(Penrose),* 1 egg	5.0	n.a.
Egg, quail, fresh, 1 whole egg, .3 oz.	1.0	.3
Egg, substitute or imitation:		
(Fleischmann's Egg Beaters), 1/4 cup . . .	0	0
(Fleischmann's Egg Beaters Cheez),		
1/2 cup	6.0	n.a.
(Morningstar Farms Scramblers), 1/4 cup	3.0	n.a.
(Tofutti Egg Watchers), 2 oz.	2.0	n.a.
mix*, w/tofu *(Tofu Scrambler),* 1/2 cup . .	5.0	n.a.
Egg, turkey, fresh, 1 whole egg, 2.8 oz. . . .	9.4	2.9
Egg breakfast, frozen (see also "Egg		
breakfast sandwich"):		
omelet, w/cheese sauce and ham		
(Swanson Great Starts), 7 oz.	29.0	n.a.
scrambled:		
and bacon, w/home fries *(Swanson*		
Great Starts), 5.6 oz.	26.0	n.a.
and cheddar, w/fried potatoes *(Aunt*		
Jemima), 5.9 oz.	13.0	n.a.
and ham, w/hash browns *(Downyflake),*		
6.25 oz.	26.0	n.a.
and ham, w/pecan twirl *(Downyflake),*		
6.25 oz.	28.0	n.a.
and hash browns, w/sausage		
(Downyflake), 6.25 oz.	34.0	n.a.
and home fries *(Swanson Great Starts),*		
4.6 oz.	19.0	n.a.
and sausage, w/hash browns *(Aunt*		
Jemima), 5.7 oz.	20.0	n.a.

Egg breakfast, frozen, scrambled, continued

and sausages, w/hash browns *(Swanson Great Starts)*, 6.5 oz.	34.0	n.a.
and sausage, w/pancakes *(Aunt Jemima)*, 5.2 oz.	14.0	n.a.
and sausage, w/pecan twirl *(Downyflake)*, 6.25 oz.	33.0	n.a.

"Egg" breakfast, vegetarian, frozen:

Scramblers, hash brown, and links *(Morningstar Farms* Country Breakfast), 7 oz.	23.0	n.a.
Scramblers, pancakes, and links *(Morningstar Farms* Country Breakfast), 6.8 oz.	19.0	n.a.

Egg breakfast sandwich, frozen:

beefsteak and cheese *(Swanson Great Starts* Breakfast on a Muffin), 4.9 oz.	20.0	n.a.
Canadian bacon and cheese *(Swanson Great Starts* Breakfast on a Biscuit), 5.25 oz.	22.0	n.a.
Canadian bacon and cheese *(Swanson Great Starts* Breakfast on a Muffin), 4.1 oz.	15.0	n.a.
English muffin *(Weight Watchers* Microwave), 4 oz.	8.0	3.0
sausage and cheese *(Swanson Great Starts* Breakfast on a Biscuit), 5.5 oz.	28.0	n.a.

Egg foo young mix* *(La Choy),* 8.8 oz.	7.0	n.a.

Egg roll, frozen:

chicken *(Jeno's* Snacks), 6 rolls	9.0	n.a.
chicken or meat and shrimp *(Chun King),* 3.6 oz.	8.0	n.a.
meat and shrimp *(Jeno's* Snacks), 6 rolls	11.0	n.a.
pork *(Chun King* Restaurant Style), 3 oz.	6.0	n.a.
shrimp *(Chun King),* 3.6 oz.	6.0	n.a.
shrimp and cheese *(Jeno's* Snacks), 6 rolls	8.0	n.a.
vegetarian *(Worthington),* 3-oz. roll	6.0	1.0

Egg roll wrapper *(Nasoya)*	0	0

Eggnog, nonalcoholic:

canned *(Borden),* 6 fl. oz.	9.0	n.a.
chilled, 8 fl. oz.	19.0	11.3

chilled *(Crowley)*, 6 fl. oz.	13.0	n.a.
Eggplant, boiled, drained, cubed, 1/2 cup	.1	< .1
Eggplant appetizer *(Progresso)*, 1/2 can	4.0	n.a.
Eggplant entrée, frozen:		
parmigiana *(Celentano)*, 8 oz.	15.0	n.a.
parmigiana *(Celentano)*, 10 oz.	19.0	n.a.
parmigiana *(Mrs. Paul's)*, 4 oz.	16.0	4.0
rollettes *(Celentano)*, 11 oz.	14.0	n.a.
Elderberry, fresh, 1/2 cup	.4	(0)
Enchilada dinner, frozen:		
beef:		
(Banquet), 12 oz.	15.0	n.a.
(Old El Paso Festive Dinners), 11 oz.	8.0	n.a.
(Patio), 13.25 oz.	24.0	n.a.
(Swanson), 13.75 oz.	21.0	n.a.
(Van de Kamp's Mexican Dinner), 1/2 pkg.	7.0	n.a.
cheese:		
(Banquet), 12 oz.	19.0	n.a.
(Old El Paso Festive Dinners), 11 oz.	31.0	n.a.
(Patio), 12.25 oz.	10.0	n.a.
(Van de Kamp's Mexican Dinner), 1/2 pkg.	9.0	n.a.
chicken *(Old El Paso* Festive Dinners), 11 oz.	18.0	n.a.
Enchilada entrée, frozen:		
beef:		
(Hormel), 1 piece	5.0	n.a.
(Old El Paso), 1 pkg.	13.0	n.a.
(Van de Kamp's Mexican Entrees), 1 pkg.	12.0	n.a.
and bean *(Lean Cuisine* Enchanadas), 9.25 oz.	10.0	2.0
chili gravy and *(Banquet Family Entrees)*, 7 oz.	13.0	n.a.
Ranchero *(Weight Watchers)*, 9.12 oz.	10.0	3.0
shredded *(Van de Kamp's* Mexican Entrees), 1 pkg.	14.0	n.a.
sirloin Ranchero *(The Budget Gourmet Slim Selects)*, 9 oz.	15.0	n.a.

Enchilada entrée, continued
cheese:

(Hormel), 1 piece	6.0	n.a.
(Old El Paso), 1 pkg.	12.0	n.a.
(Stouffer's), 10 1/8 oz.	40.0	n.a.
(Van de Kamp's Mexican Entrees), 1 pkg.	15.0	n.a.
Ranchero *(Van de Kamp's* Mexican Entrees), 1/2 pkg.	12.0	n.a.
Ranchero *(Weight Watchers)*, 8.87 oz.	18.0	5.0

chicken:

(Le Menu LightStyle), 8 oz.	8.0	n.a.
(Lean Cuisine Enchanadas), 9 7/8 oz.	9.0	2.0
(Old El Paso), 1 pkg.	12.0	n.a.
(Stouffer's), 10 oz.	29.0	n.a.
(Van de Kamp's Mexican Entrees), 1 pkg.	11.0	n.a.
w/sour cream sauce *(Old El Paso)*, 1 pkg.	19.0	n.a.
Suiza *(The Budget Gourmet* Slim Selects), 9 oz.	9.0	n.a.
Suiza *(Van de Kamp's* Mexican Entrees), 1 pkg.	10.0	n.a.
Suiza *(Weight Watchers)*, 9 oz.	11.0	2.0

Enchilada mix* *(Old El Paso* Dinner), 1 piece . . . . 8.0 — 3.0

Enchilada sauce:

(Rosarita), 3 oz.	0	0
green *(Old El Paso)*, 2 tbsp.	0	0
hot *(El Molino)*, 2 tbsp.	1.0	n.a.
hot or mild *(Del Monte)*, 1/2 cup	0	0
hot or mild *(Old El Paso)*, 1/4 cup . . .	1.0	n.a.
hot or mild *(Ortega)*, 1 oz.	0	0

Enchilada seasoning mix:

(Lawry's), 1 pkg.	1.2	n.a.
(Old El Paso), 1/18 pkg.	0	0

Endive, chopped, 1/2 cup . . . . .1 < .1
Endive, Belgian, see "Chicory, witloof"
Eppaw, trimmed, 1/2 cup 9 (0)
Escarole, see "Endive"

food and measure	total fat (gms.)	saturated fat (gms.)
Fajita entrée, frozen:		
beef *(Weight Watchers)*, 6.75 oz.	7.0	2.0
chicken *(Weight Watchers)*, 6.75 oz. . . .	5.0	2.0
Fajita entrée, refrigerated, chicken *(Chicken By George)*, 5 oz.	6.0	n.a.
Fajita marinade *(Old El Paso)*, 1/8 jar . . .	0	0
Fajita sauce *(Tio Sancho* Skillet Sauce), 1 oz.	.5	n.a.
Fajita seasoning blend *(Lawry's)*, 1 pkg.	.4	n.a.

Falafel:

1 oz.	5.0	.8
mix* *(Near East)*, 3 patties	15.0	n.a.

Farina, whole grain (see also "Cereal, Cooking"):

dry, 1 cup	.9	.1
cooked, 1 cup	.2	< .1

Fat, see specific listings

Fat, imitation *(Rokeach Neutral Nyafat)*,

1 tbsp.	11.0	n.a.
Fennel, fresh *(Frieda* of California), 1 lb.	.5	n.a.
Fennel seed, 1 tsp.	.3	tr.
Fenugreek seed, 1 tsp.	.2	(0)

Fettuccine entrée, frozen:

Alfredo *(Healthy Choice)*, 8 oz.	7.0	2.0
Alfredo *(Stouffer's)*, 1/2 of 10-oz. pkg.	19.0	n.a.
Alfredo *(Weight Watchers)*, 9 oz.	8.0	3.0
w/broccoli *(Dining Lite)*, 9 oz.	12.0	n.a.
chicken *(Weight Watchers)*, 8.25 oz.	9.0	3.0
w/meat sauce *(The Budget Gourmet)*, 10 oz.	10.0	n.a.
primavera *(Green Giant)*, 1 pkg.	8.0	3.0
primavera *(Green Giant* Microwave Garden Gourmet), 1 pkg.	13.0	n.a.

Fettuccine entrée mix, see "Pasta dishes, mix"

Fig:

fresh, 1 large, 2.3 oz.	.2	< .1
canned, in water or syrup, 1/2 cup	.1	< .1
dried, uncooked, 1/2 cup	1.2	.2

Filbert (hazelnut), shelled:

dried, unblanched, 1 oz.	17.8	1.3
dried, blanched, 1 oz.	19.1	1.4
dry roasted, unblanched, 1 oz.	18.8	1.4
oil roasted, unblanched, 1 oz.	18.1	1.3

Finnan haddie, see "Haddock, meat only, smoked"

Fish, see specific listings

Fish dinner, frozen (see also specific listings):

(Morton), 9.75 oz.	13.0	n.a.
'n' chips *(Swanson)*, 10 oz.	20.0	n.a.

Fish entrée, frozen (see also specific
listings):

(Banquet Platters), 8.75 oz.	22.0	n.a.
battered, portions *(Mrs. Paul's),* 2 pieces	19.0	3.0
battered fillets:		
(Gorton's Crispy Batter), 2 pieces . . .	19.0	8.0
(Gorton's Crispy Batter, Large), 1 piece	21.0	n.a.
(Gorton's Crunchy), 2 pieces	13.0	3.0
(Gorton's Crunchy Microwave), 2 pieces	26.0	12.0
(Gorton's Crunchy Microwave, Large), 1 piece	22.0	10.0
(Gorton's Potato Crisp), 2 pieces	20.0	6.0
(Gorton's Value Pack), 1 piece	11.0	n.a.
(Mrs. Paul's Batter Dipped), 2 pieces	17.0	n.a.
(Mrs. Paul's Crispy Crunchy), 2 pieces	9.0	n.a.
(Mrs. Paul's Crunchy Batter), 2 pieces	14.0	n.a.
(Van de Kamp's), 1 piece	10.0	2.0
breaded, portions *(Mrs. Paul's* Crispy Crunchy), 2 pieces	15.0	2.0
breaded fillets:		
(Gorton's Light Recipe), 1 piece	8.0	3.0
(Mrs. Paul's Crispy Crunchy), 2 pieces	9.0	2.0
(Van de Kamp's), 2 pieces	18.0	3.0
crispy *(Van de Kamp's* Microwave), 1 piece	9.0	2.0
crispy *(Van de Kamp's* Microwave, Large), 1 piece	17.0	3.0
butter sauce, fillets *(Mrs. Paul's),* 1 piece	6.0	n.a.
cakes *(Mrs. Paul's),* 2 pieces	7.0	n.a.
Dijon *(Mrs. Paul's* Light), 8.75 oz.	5.0	2.0
fillet of:		
Divan *(Lean Cuisine),* 12 3/8 oz.	7.0	2.0
Florentine *(Lean Cuisine),* 9 oz.	8.0	2.0
in herb sauce *(Gorton's),* 1 pkg.	8.0	5.0
jardiniere, w/souffléed potatoes *(Lean Cuisine),* 11.25 oz.	10.0	4.0
Florentine *(Mrs. Paul's* Light), 8 oz. . . .	8.0	4.0
'n' fries *(Swanson* Homestyle Recipe), 6.5 oz.	16.0	n.a.
gems, fancy style *(Wakefield),* 4 oz.	1.0	n.a.

Fish entrée, frozen, continued

Mornay *(Mrs. Paul's Light)*, 9 oz.	10.0	4.0
ranch, fillets *(Gorton's Microwave, Large)*, 1 piece	21.0	n.a.
sticks, battered:		
(Gorton's Crispy Batter), 4 pieces	18.0	6.0
(Gorton's Crunchy), 4 pieces	13.0	4.0
(Gorton's Crunchy Microwave), 6 pieces	22.0	7.0
(Gorton's Potato Crisp), 4 pieces	16.0	5.0
(Gorton's Value Pack), 4 pieces	9.0	n.a.
(Mrs. Paul's), 4 pieces	12.0	n.a.
(Mrs. Paul's Crispy Crunchy), 4 pieces	8.0	n.a.
(Van de Kamp's), 4 pieces	9.0	2.0
sticks, breaded:		
(Frionor Bunch O' Crunch), 4 pieces	14.0	2.0
(Mrs. Paul's Crispy Crunchy), 4 pieces	6.0	n.a.
(Van de Kamp's), 4 pieces	12.0	2.0
(Van de Kamp's Value Pack), 4 pieces	10.0	2.0
crispy *(Van de Kamp's Microwave)*, 3 pieces	7.0	1.0
whole wheat *(Booth Microwave)*, 2 oz.	8.0	n.a.
tempura *(Gorton's Light Recipe)*, 1 piece	14.0	4.0
"Fish" entrée, vegetarian, frozen		
(Worthington Fillets), 2 pieces or 3 oz.	9.0	2.0
Fish roe, see "Caviar" and "Roe"		
Fish seasoning and coating mix:		
(Shake'n Bake), 1/4 pouch	1.0	n.a.
all varieties *(Golden Dipt)*	0	0
Fish sticks, see "Fish entrée"		
Flatfish, fresh, meat only:		
raw, 4 oz.	1.3	.3
baked, broiled, or microwaved, 4 oz.	1.7	.4
Flavor enhancer *(Ac'cent)*	0	0
Flounder, fresh, see "Flatfish"		
Flounder entrée, frozen:		
battered *(Mrs. Paul's Crunchy)*, 2 pieces	9.0	n.a.
breaded *(Van de Kamp's Light)*, 1 piece	12.0	2.0
stuffed *(Gorton's Microwave Entrées)*, 1 pkg.	18.0	7.0

Flour:

amaranth *(Arrowhead Mills),* 2 oz.	3.0	n.a.
arrowroot, 1 cup	.1	< .1
barley *(Arrowhead Mills),* 2 oz.	1.0	n.a.
buckwheat, 1 cup	3.7	.8
buckwheat, whole grain *(Arrowhead Mills),* 2 oz.	1.0	n.a.
carob, 1 cup	.7	.1
corn, masa, 1 cup	4.3	.6
corn, whole grain, 1 cup	4.5	.6
cottonseed, partially defatted, 1 cup . . .	5.8	1.5
millet, whole grain *(Arrowhead Mills),* 2 oz.	2.0	n.a.
oat, whole grain *(Arrowhead Mills),* 2 oz.	1.0	n.a.
oat blend *(Gold Medal),* 4 oz. or 1 cup	3.0	n.a.
peanut, defatted, 1 cup	.3	< .1
peanut, low fat, 1 cup	13.1	1.8
pecan, 1 oz.	.4	< .1
potato, 1 cup	1.4	.4
rice, brown, 1 cup	4.4	.9
rice, white, 1 cup	2.2	.6
rye:		
dark, 1 cup	3.4	.4
light, 1 cup	1.4	.1
medium, 1 cup	1.8	.2
stone ground *(Robin Hood),* 4 oz. or 1 cup	2.0	n.a.
whole grain *(Arrowhead Mills),* 2 oz.	1.0	n.a.
and wheat *(Pillsbury's Best* Bohemian), 1 cup	1.0	n.a.
sesame (from sesame seed kernels):		
high fat, 1 oz.	10.5	1.5
partially defatted, 1 oz.	3.4	.5
low fat, 1 oz.	.5	.1
soy:		
full fat, raw, 1 cup, stirred	17.6	2.5
full fat, roasted, 1 cup, stirred	18.6	2.7
low fat, 1 cup, stirred	2.4	.9
defatted, 1 cup, stirred	1.2	.1
sunflower seed, partially defatted, 1 cup	1.3	.1
teff, whole grain *(Arrowhead Mills),* 2 oz.	1.0	n.a.

Flour, continued

triticale, whole grain, 1 cup	2.4	.4
wheat, whole grain, 1 cup	2.2	.4
white, 1 cup:		
all-purpose	1.2	.2
bread	2.3	.3
cake	.9	.1
self-rising	1.2	.2
tortilla mix	11.8	4.6
Forestiera sauce *(Contadina Fresh)*, 7.5 oz.	9.0	n.a.
Frankfurter:		
(Eckrich, 12 oz.), 1 link	10.0	n.a.
(Eckrich, 1 lb.), 1 link	14.0	n.a.
(Eckrich Bunsize/Jumbo), 1 link	17.0	n.a.
(Eckrich Lite), 1 link	10.0	n.a.
(Eckrich Lite Bunsize), 1 link	12.0	n.a.
(Hillshire Farm Bun Size Wieners), 2 oz.	16.0	n.a.
(JM, 10/lb.), 1.6-oz. link	13.0	n.a.
(JM German Brand), 2-oz. link	14.0	n.a.
(JM Jumbo), 2-oz. link	17.0	n.a.
(Kahn's Bun Size Frank or Jumbo), 1 link	17.0	n.a.
(Kahn's Wieners), 1 link	13.0	n.a.
(Oscar Mayer Light Wieners), 2-oz. link	10.8	3.8
(Oscar Mayer Wieners), 1.6-oz. link . . .	13.3	5.0
(Oscar Mayer Wieners), 2-oz. link	16.9	6.4
(Oscar Mayer Bun-Length Wieners),		
2-oz. link	16.9	6.2
(Pilgrim's Pride, 1 lb.), 2-oz. link	8.8	n.a.
bacon and cheddar *(Oscar Mayer* Hot		
Dogs), 1.6-oz. link	12.0	5.0
batter-wrapped, frozen *(Hormel* Corn		
Dogs), 1 piece	12.0	n.a.
batter-wrapped, frozen *(Hormel* Tater		
Dogs), 1 piece	14.0	n.a.
beef:		
1 link, 5″ long by 7/8″, approx. 2 oz. . .	16.8	6.8
(Eckrich, 1 lb.), 1 link	14.0	n.a.
(Eckrich Bunsize/Jumbo), 1 link	17.0	n.a.
(Hebrew National), 1.7-oz. link	14.0	n.a.
(Hillshire Farm Bun Size Wieners),		
2 oz.	16.0	n.a.

(Hormel, 12 oz.), 1 link	10.0	n.a.
(Hormel, 1 lb.), 1 link	13.0	n.a.
(JM, 10/lb.), 1.6-oz. link	13.0	n.a.
(JM Jumbo), 2-oz. link	16.0	n.a.
(Kahn's), 1 link	13.0	n.a.
(Kahn's Bun Size Franks), 1 link	17.0	n.a.
(Kahn's Jumbo), 1 link	18.0	n.a.
(King Kold), 2 oz.	16.3	n.a.
(Oscar Mayer Franks), 1.6-oz. link . . .	13.2	5.6
(Oscar Mayer Franks), 2-oz. link	16.7	7.0
(Oscar Mayer Bun-Length Franks), 2-oz. link	16.8	7.3
(Oscar Mayer Bun Length Franks), 4-oz. link	33.5	14.6
(Oscar Mayer Light Franks), 2-oz. link	11.1	4.6
w/cheddar *(Kahn's* Beef n'Cheddar), 1 link	16.0	n.a.
w/cheddar *(Oscar Mayer* Franks), 1.6-oz. link	12.2	5.1
beef and pork, 1 link, 5" long × 7/8", 2 oz.	16.6	6.1
cheese (cheesefurter or cheese smokie):		
1 link, 1.5 oz., 8 per 12-oz. pkg.	12.5	4.5
(Eckrich), 1 link	16.0	m.q
(Hillshire Farm Bun Size Wieners), 2 oz.	16.0	n.a.
(JM Cheese Franks), 1.6-oz. link	13.0	n.a.
(Kahn's Cheese Wiener), 1 link	13.0	n.a.
(Oscar Mayer Hot Dogs), 1.6-oz. link	12.9	5.3
w/cheese *(JM* German Brand), 2-oz. link	14.0	n.a.
chicken, see "Chicken frankfurter"		
chili *(Hormel* Frank 'n Stuff), 1 link . . .	15.0	n.a.
cocktail *(Oscar Mayer* Little Wieners), 1 link	2.6	1.0
hot *(Hillshire Farm* Hot links), 2 oz. . . .	16.0	n.a.
hot, beef *(Hillshire Farm* Hot Links), 2 oz.	17.0	n.a.
meat *(Hormel,* 1 lb.), 1 link	13.0	n.a.
Mexacali *(Hormel* Mexacali Dogs), 5 oz.	21.0	n.a.
natural casing *(Hillshire Farm* Wieners), 2 oz.	17.0	n.a.

Frankfurter, continued
  smoked, 1 link:
    (Hormel Range Brand Wranglers) . . .   16.0   n.a.
    (Kahn's Big Red Smokey) . . . .   14.0   n.a.
    (Kahn's Bun Size Smokey) . . . .   15.0   n.a.
    beef *(Hormel Wranglers)* . . . .   15.0   n.a.
    beef *(Kahn's* Bun Size Beef Smokey)   17.0   n.a.
    w/cheese *(Hormel Wranglers)* . . . . . .   16.0   n.a.
  turkey, see "Turkey frankfurter"
"Frankfurter," vegetarian:
  canned *(Worthington Veja-Links),* 2 links   10.0   n.a.
  canned *(Worthington Super-Links),*
    1.7-oz. link 7.0   1.0
  frozen *(Worthington Leanies),* 1.4-oz. link   6.0   1.0
  frozen, on stick *(Worthington* Dixie
    Dogs), 2.5-oz. piece . . . .   10.0   n.a.
Frankfurter wrap *(Weiner Wrap),* 1 piece   2.0   n.a.
French toast, frozen, 3 oz., except as noted:
  (Aunt Jemima Original) 4.4   1.0
  (Downyflake), 2 pieces . . . .   12.0   n.a.
  (Downyflake Extra Thick), 1 piece . . . .   9.0   n.a.
  cinnamon *(Weight Watchers* Microwave)   4.0   < 1.0
  cinnamon swirl *(Aunt Jemima)* 4.3   1.0
  sticks, apple cinnamon or original *(Farm
    Rich)* . . . .   15.0   n.a.
  sticks, blueberry *(Farm Rich)* . . . .   14.0   n.a.
French toast breakfast, frozen:
  w/links *(Weight Watchers* Microwave),
    4.5 oz..   11.0   3.0
  w/sausages, plain or cinnamon swirl
    (Swanson Great Starts), 5.5 oz. . . . . .   21.0   n.a.
  sticks, w/syrup *(Aunt Jemima),* 5.2 oz. . .   20.0   n.a.
  Texas style, and sausage *(Downyflake),*
    4.25 oz.   24.0   n.a.
  vegetarian, cinnamon swirl, w/patties
    (Morningstar Farms Country), 6.5 oz.   15.0   n.a.
  wedges, w/sausages *(Aunt Jemima),*
    5.3 oz..   17.0   n.a.
Frosting, ready-to-use, 1/12 can, except as
  noted:

Amaretto almond *(Betty Crocker Creamy Deluxe)*	6.0	2.0
butter pecan *(Betty Crocker Creamy Deluxe)*	7.0	2.0
caramel pecan *(Pillsbury Frosting Supreme)*	8.0	n.a.
cherry *(Betty Crocker Creamy Deluxe)*	6.0	2.0
chocolate:		
(Pillsbury Frost It Hot), 1/8 cake	0	0
all varieties *(Duncan Hines)*	7.0	n.a.
all varieties, except mint *(Pillsbury Frosting Supreme)*	6.0	n.a.
plain or fudge *(Betty Crocker Creamy Deluxe)*	7.0	2.0
fudge *(Pillsbury),* 1/8 cake	5.0	n.a.
fudge *(Pillsbury* Funfetti)	6.0	n.a.
milk *(Betty Crocker Creamy Deluxe)*	6.0	2.0
mint *(Pillsbury Frosting Supreme)*	7.0	n.a.
chocolate chip:		
(Betty Crocker Creamy Deluxe)	7.0	3.0
(Pillsbury Frosting Supreme)	5.0	n.a.
double *(Betty Crocker Creamy Deluxe)*	8.0	3.0
chocolate, candy coated *(Betty Crocker Creamy Deluxe Party)*	7.0	2.0
chocolate coconut almond *(Betty Crocker Creamy Deluxe)*	8.0	3.0
coconut almond *(Pillsbury)*	10.0	n.a.
coconut almond *(Pillsbury Frosting Supreme)*	9.0	n.a.
coconut pecan *(Betty Crocker Creamy Deluxe)*	9.0	3.0
coconut pecan *(Pillsbury)*	7.0	n.a.
coconut pecan *(Pillsbury Frosting Supreme)*	10.0	n.a.
cream cheese *(Betty Crocker Creamy Deluxe)*	6.0	2.0
cream cheese *(Pillsbury Frosting Supreme)*	6.0	n.a.
decorator, all flavors *(Pillsbury),* 1 tbsp.	2.0	n.a.
lemon *(Betty Crocker Creamy Deluxe)*	6.0	2.0
lemon *(Pillsbury Frosting Supreme)*	6.0	n.a.

Frosting, ready-to-use, continued

rainbow chip *(Betty Crocker Creamy Deluxe)*	7.0	3.0
rocky road *(Betty Crocker Creamy Deluxe)*	8.0	2.0
sour cream:		
chocolate *(Betty Crocker Creamy Deluxe)*	7.0	2.0
vanilla *(Pillsbury Frosting Supreme)*	6.0	n.a.
white *(Betty Crocker Creamy Deluxe)*	6.0	2.0
strawberry *(Pillsbury Frosting Supreme)*	6.0	n.a.
vanilla:		
(Betty Crocker Creamy Deluxe)	6.0	2.0
(Duncan Hines)	7.0	n.a.
(Pillsbury), 1/8 cake	5.0	n.a.
(Pillsbury Frosting Supreme)	6.0	n.a.
(Pillsbury Funfetti, pink and white)	6.0	n.a.
white, all varieties *(Pillsbury)*	0	0
Fructose *(Estee)*, 1 tsp.	0	0
Fruit, see specific listings		
Fruit, mixed (see also fruit cocktail):		
canned, in heavy syrup, 1/2 cup	.1	< .1
dried, pitted, 1 oz.	.1	< .1
frozen, sweetened, 1/2 cup	.2	< .1
Fruit bar, frozen, 1 bar:		
all flavors:		
(Dole Fresh Lites/Suntops)	< 1.0	n.a.
(Minute Maid Fruit Juicee)	0	0
except piña colada *(Dole Fruit'n Juice)*	< .1	n.a.
except coconut *(Sunkist)*	0	0
coconut *(Sunkist)*	10.0	n.a.
piña colada *(Dole Fruit'n Juice)*	3.0	n.a.
and cream:		
all plain fruit flavors *(Dole* Fruit & Cream)	1.4	n.a.
chocolate/banana *(Dole* Fruit & Cream)	9.0	n.a.
chocolate/strawberry *(Dole* Fruit & Cream)	8.0	n.a.
strawberry *(Sunkist* Strawberry & Cream)	1.0	n.a.

and yogurt, all flavors *(Dole* Fruit &
  Yogurt) . . . . < 1.0   n.a.
Fruit cocktail, canned (see also fruit,
  mixed):
  in juice, 1/2 cup . . . . < .1   tr.
  in syrup, 1/2 cup 1   < .1
Fruit drink or juice, all blends, 6 fl. oz. . . . < .1   (0)
Fruit and nut mix *(Planters* Fruit'n Nut),
  1 oz. 9.0   2.0
Fruit punch drink or cocktail (all brands),
  6 fl. oz. . . . . < .2   (0)
Fruit snack, all flavors (all brands),
  1 serving . . . . <2.0   n.a.
Fruit spread, all flavors (all brands) 0   0
Fruit syrup, all flavors *(Smucker's)* 0   0
Fudge topping, see "Toppings, dessert"

G

food and measure	total fat (gms.)	saturated fat (gms.)
Garbanzo, see "Chickpea"		
Garden salad, canned:		
(Joan of Arc/Read), 1/2 cup	0	0
marinated *(S&W)*, 1/2 cup	0	0
Garlic:		
trimmed, 1 oz.	.1	< .1
1 clove, 11/4″ × 5/8″ × 3/8″	< .1	tr.
Garlic bread spread *(Lawry's)*, 1/2 tbsp. . .	4.6	n.a.
Garlic dressing and dip, w/tofu *(Life* All Natural), 1 tbsp.	7.1	n.a.

Garlic and herb dip *(Nasoya Vegi-Dip)*,
1 oz. . . . . 2.0   n.a.
Garlic powder:
1 tsp. . . . . < .1   (0)
w/parsley *(Lawry's)*, 1 tsp. 9   n.a.
Garlic salt *(Lawry's)*, 1 tsp. . . . . < .1   (0)
Garlic seasoning:
(McCormick/Schilling Season All), 1/4 tsp.   (0)   (0)
(McCormick/Schilling Parsley Patch),
1 tsp. .5   n.a.
Garlic spread, concentrate *(Lawry's)*,
1 tbsp. 1.6   n.a.
Gefilte fish:
all varieties *(Mother's*, 24 oz.), 1 ball . . .   1.0   n.a.
all varieties *(Rokeach)*, 1 regular ball or
8 hors d'oeuvres . . . . 1.0   n.a.
sweet, w/broth, 1 oz. 5   .1
Gelatin, unflavored *(Knox)*, 1 pkt. 0   0
Gelatin bar, frozen, all flavors *(Jell-O
Gelatin Pops)*, 1 bar 0   0
Gelatin dessert mix*, all flavors (all brands)   0   0
Gelatin drink mix, orange flavor *(Knox)*,
1 pkt. .1   (0)
Ghee, 1 oz. . . . . 28.4   n.a.
Ginger, ground, 1 tsp. 1   < .1
Ginger, pickled, Japanese, 1 oz. . . . . < .1   tr.
Ginger root, fresh, sliced, 1/4 cup 2   < .1
Ginkgo nut:
raw, shelled, or canned, drained, 1 oz. . .   .5   .1
dried, 1 oz. 8   .1
Godfather's Pizza:
original cheese:
mini, 1/4 pie, 2.8 oz. . . . . 4.0   n.a.
small, 1/6 pie, 3.6 oz. . . . . 7.0   n.a.
medium, 1/8 pie, 4 oz. . . . . 8.0   n.a.
large, 1/10 pie, 4.4 oz. . . . . 9.0   n.a.
large, hot slice, 1/8 pie, 5.5 oz. . . . . . 11.0   n.a.
original combo:
mini, 1/4 pie, 3.8 oz. . . . . 7.0   n.a.
small, 1/6 pie, 5.6 oz. . . . . 15.0   n.a.
medium, 1/8 pie, 6.2 oz. . . . . 17.0   n.a.

Godfather's Pizza, original combo, continued

large, 1/10 pie, 6.8 oz.	19.0	n.a.
large, hot slice, 1/8 pie, 8.5 oz.	24.0	n.a.
thin-crust cheese:		
small, 1/6 pie, 2.6 oz.	6.0	n.a.
medium, 1/8 pie, 3 oz.	7.0	n.a.
large, 1/10 pie, 3.4 oz.	7.0	n.a.
thin-crust combo:		
small, 1/6 pie, 4.3 oz.	13.0	n.a.
medium, 1/8 pie, 4.9 oz.	14.0	n.a.
large, 1/10 pie, 5.4 oz.	16.0	n.a.
stuffed pie cheese:		
small, 1/6 pie, 4.4 oz.	11.0	n.a.
medium, 1/8 pie, 4.8 oz.	13.0	n.a.
large, 1/10 pie, 5.2 oz.	16.0	n.a.
stuffed pie combo:		
small, 1/6 pie, 6.3 oz.	20.0	n.a.
medium, 1/8 pie, 7 oz.	23.0	n.a.
large, 1/10 pie, 7.6 oz.	26.0	n.a.
Goose, domesticated, roasted:		
meat w/skin, 4 oz.	24.9	7.8
meat only, 4 oz.	14.4	5.2
Goose fat, 1 tbsp.	12.8	3.5
Gooseberry:		
fresh, raw, 1/2 cup	.4	< .1
canned, in light syrup, 1/2 cup	.3	< .1
Gourd, dishcloth, boiled, drained, 1/2 cup	.3	< .1
Gourd, white-flowered, boiled, drained,		
1/2 cup	< .1	tr.
Gourmet loaf *(Eckrich)*, 1-oz. slice	1.0	n.a.
Governor plum, trimmed, 1 oz.	0	0
Grain, see specific listings		
Granadilla, see "Passion fruit"		
Granola and cereal bar, 1 bar:		
w/almonds, chewy *(Sunbelt)*	6.0	n.a.
caramel nut *(Quaker Granola Dipps)* . .	6.4	2.8
chocolate chip:		
(Quaker Chewy)	4.7	1.5
(Quaker Granola Dipps)	6.3	2.8
chewy *(Sunbelt)*	7.0	n.a.
chocolate coated *(Hershey's)*	8.0	n.a.

fudge dipped, chewy *(Sunbelt)*	11.0.	n.a.
w/chocolate chips, chewy *(Sunbelt)*	9.0	n.a.
chocolate fudge *(Quaker Granola Dipps)*	7.9	n.a.
cinnamon *(Nature Valley)*	5.0	1.0
cocoa creme, chocolate coated *(Hershey's)*	9.0	n.a.
Common Sense, raspberry filled *(Kellogg's Smart Start)*	6.0	n.a
cookies and creme, chocolate coated *(Hershey's)*	8.0	n.a.
corn flakes, mixed berry filled *(Kellogg's Smart Start)*	7.0	n.a.
honey and oats *(Quaker Chewy)*	4.4	1.1
nut and raisin, chunky *(Quaker Chewy)*	5.8	1.3
Nutri·Grain, blueberry or strawberry *(Kellogg's Smart Start)*	8.0	n.a.
oat bran-honey graham *(Nature Valley)*	4.0	< 1.0
oats and honey *(Nature Valley)*	5.0	1.0
oats and honey, chewy *(Sunbelt)*	5.0	n.a.
oats and honey, fudge dipped, chewy *(Sunbelt)*	10.0	n.a.
peanut butter:		
(Nature Valley)	6.0	1.0
(Quaker Chewy)	4.9	1.3
(Quaker Granola Dipps)	9.1	3.1
chocolate chip *(Quaker Chewy)*	5.7	1.5
chocolate chip *(Quaker Granola Dipps)*	10.0	n.a.
chocolate coated *(Hershey's)*	10.0	n.a.
chocolate coated *(Kudos)*	12.0	n.a.
w/peanuts, fudge dipped, chewy *(Sunbelt)*, 1.38 oz.	10.0	n.a.
raisin bran *(Kellogg's Smart Start)*	5.0	n.a.
w/raisins, chewy *(Sunbelt)*	6.0	n.a.
w/raisins, fudge dipped, chewy *(Sunbelt)*	12.0	n.a.
raisin and cinnamon *(Quaker Chewy)* . .	5.0	1.1
Rice Krispies, w/almonds *(Kellogg's Smart Start)*	6.0	n.a.
S'mores *(Quaker Chewy)*	4.4	1.4
Grape:		
fresh, American type (slipskin):		
10 medium, 1.4 oz.	.1	< .1

Grape, continued

peeled and seeded, 1/2 cup	.2	.1
fresh, European type (adherent skin):		
seedless, 10 medium, 5/8" × 7/8"	.3	.1
seedless or seeded, 1/2 cup	.5	.2
canned, Thompson seedless, 1/2 cup . . .	.1	< .1
Grape drink or juice, all blends, 6 fl. oz.	<.3	< .2
Grapefruit:		
fresh, all varieties, 1/2 fruit, 3 3/4"-diam. . .	.1	< .1
fresh or canned, sections, 1/2 cup	.1	< .1
Grapefruit drink or juice, all blends, 6 fl. oz.	<.3	< .1
Gravy, see specific listings		
Green bean, see "Beans, green"		
Green pepper, see "Pepper, green and red, sweet"		
Grenadine *(Rose's)*	0	0
Grits, see "Corn grits" and "Hominy"		
Ground cherry, trimmed, 1/2 cup	.5	tr.
Grouper, mixed species, meat only:		
raw, 4 oz.	1.2	.3
baked, broiled, or microwaved, 4 oz. . . .	1.5	.3
Guacamole, see "Avocado dip"		
Guacamole seasoning:		
blend *(Lawry's)*, 1 pkg.	.4	(0)
mix *(Old El Paso)*, 1/7 pkg.	0	0
Guava:		
common, trimmed, 1/2 cup	.5	.1
strawberry, trimmed, 1/2 cup	.7	.2
Guava fruit drink or juice, all blends	0	0
Guava sauce, cooked, 1/2 cup	.2	< .1
Guinea hen, fresh, raw:		
meat w/skin, 1 oz.	1.8	n.a.
meat only, 1 oz.	.7	n.a.

food and measure	total fat (gms.)	saturated fat (gms.)
Haddock, meat only:		
raw, 4 oz.	.8	.1
baked, broiled, or microwaved, 4 oz. . . .	1.1	.2
smoked, 4 oz.	1.1	.2
Haddock entrée, frozen, fillets:		
battered (*Mrs. Paul's* Crunchy), 2 pieces	5.0	n.a.
battered (*Van de Kamp's*), 2 pieces . . .	15.0	3.0
breaded (*Van de Kamp's*), 2 pieces	16.0	3.0
breaded (*Van de Kamp's* Light), 1 piece	11.0	2.0

Haddock entrée, continued
  in lemon butter *(Gorton's Microwave*
    Entrées), 1 pkg. 21.0   10.0
Hake, see "Whiting"
Halibut, meat only:
  Atlantic and Pacific:
    raw, 4 oz. . . . .   2.6   .4
    baked, broiled, or microwaved, 4 oz.   3.3   .5
  Greenland, raw, 4 oz. 15.7   2.7
Halibut entrée, frozen, battered *(Van de*
  Kamp's), 2 pieces 6.0   1.0
Halvah *(Fantastic Foods)*, 1.5-oz. bar . . . .   10.0   n.a.
Ham, fresh, retail cuts, meat only, roasted:
  whole leg:
    lean w/fat, 4 oz. 23.5   8.5
    lean w/fat, chopped or diced, 1 cup
      unpacked 29.0   10.5
    lean only, roasted, 4 oz. 12.5   4.3
    lean only, chopped or diced, 1 cup
      unpacked 15.4   5.3
  rump half, lean w/fat, 4 oz. 20.2   7.3
  rump half, lean only, 4 oz. 12.1   4.2
  shank half, lean w/fat, 4 oz. 25.1   9.1
  shank half, lean only, 4 oz. 11.9   4.1
Ham, cured, boneless:
  whole:
    lean w/fat, unheated, 1 oz. 5.3   1.9
    lean w/fat, roasted, 4 oz. 19.0   6.8
    lean w/fat, roasted, chopped or diced,
      1 cup unpacked 23.5   8.4
    lean only, unheated, 1 oz. . . . .   1.6   .5
    lean only, roasted, 4 oz. 6.2   2.1
    lean only, roasted, chopped or diced,
      1 cup unpacked 7.7   2.6
  regular (approx. 11% fat):
    unheated, 1-oz. slice 3.0   1.0
    roasted, 4 oz. 10.2   3.5
    roasted, chopped or diced, 1 cup
      unpacked 12.6   4.4
  extra lean (approx. 5% fat):
    unheated, 1-oz. slice . . . .   1.4   .5

roasted, 4 oz.	6.3	2.1
roasted, chopped or diced, 1 cup unpacked	7.7	2.5
center slice, lean w/fat, unheated, 1 oz.	3.7	1.3
country style, lean only, raw, 1 oz.	2.4	.8
slice *(Oscar Mayer* Jubilee), 1 oz.	1.1	.4
steak, unheated, 1 oz.	1.2	.4
steak *(Oscar Mayer* Jubilee), 2-oz. slice	1.9	.7
Ham, canned:		
regular (13% fat), unheated, 1 oz.	3.7	1.2
regular, roasted, 4 oz.	17.2	5.7
extra lean (4% fat), unheated, 1 oz.	1.3	.4
extra lean, roasted, 4 oz.	5.5	1.8
(Black Label), 4 oz.	7.0	n.a.
(EXL), 4 oz.	4.0	n.a.
(Holiday Glaze, 3 lb.), 4 oz.	4.0	n.a.
(Hormel Bone-In), 4 oz.	15.0	n.a.
(Hormel Cure 81), 4 oz.	8.0	n.a.
(Hormel Curemaster), 4 oz.	5.0	n.a.
(JM 95% Fat Free), 2 oz.	2.0	n.a.
(Light & Lean Boneless), 2 oz.	2.0	n.a.
(Oscar Mayer Jubilee), 1 oz.	.9	.4
chopped, 1 oz.	5.3	1.8
chopped *(Hormel,* 12 oz.), 2 oz.	9.0	n.a.
hickory smoked *(Rath Black Hawk),* 2 oz.	2.0	n.a.
roll *(Hormel),* 4 oz.	10.0	n.a.
spiced *(Hormel),* 3 oz.	21.0	n.a.
"Ham," vegetarian, frozen, roll or slices *(Worthington Wham),* 3 slices or 2.4 oz.	7.0	1.0
Ham and asparagus au gratin, frozen *(The Budget Gourmet* Slim Selects), 9 oz.	10.0	n.a.
Ham breakfast taco, refrigerated *(Owens Border Breakfasts),* 2.17 oz.	6.0	n.a.
Ham dinner, frozen:		
(Morton), 10 oz.	4.0	n.a.
steak *(Armour Classics),* 10.75 oz.	7.0	n.a.
steak *(Le Menu),* 10 oz.	11.0	n.a.
Ham entrée, frozen:		
(Banquet Platters), 10 oz.	17.0	n.a.
and asparagus bake *(Stouffer's),* 9.5 oz.	35.0	n.a.

Ham entrée, continued
   scalloped potatoes and *(Swanson*
      Homestyle Recipe), 9 oz. . . . . 13.0   n.a.

Ham luncheon meat:
   (Jones Dairy Farm), 1 slice . . . . 1.1   n.a.
   (Jones Dairy Farm Family Ham), 1 oz. 1.2   n.a.
   (Kahn's Low Salt), 1 slice . . . . 1.0   n.a.
   (Oscar Mayer Breakfast Ham),
      1.5-oz. slice . . . . 1.9   .6
   (Oscar Mayer Jubilee), 1 oz. . . . . 2.4   .8
   (Oscar Mayer Jubilee, 8-oz. slice), 1 oz. 1.1   .4
   (Oscar Mayer Lower Salt), .7-oz. slice . . .7   .3
   (Swift Premium Hostess/Sugar Plum),
      1 oz. . . . . 1.0   n.a.
   all varieties *(Healthy Deli),* 1 oz. . . . . . < 1.0   n.a.
   all varieties, except chopped *(Light &*
      Lean), 2 slices . . . . 2.0   n.a.
   baked *(Oscar Mayer),* .75-oz. slice 5   .1
   boiled *(Oscar Mayer),* .75-oz. slice 7   .1
   boiled *(Oscar Mayer* Thin Sliced),
      .4-oz. slice 4   .1
   Cajun *(Hillshire Farm* Deli Select),
      1 oz. 9   n.a.
   chopped, 1 oz. 4.9   1.6
   chopped *(Eckrich),* 1-oz. slice . . . . . . 2.0   n.a.
   chopped *(Hormel* Perma-Fresh), 2 slices 5.0   n.a.
   chopped *(Kahn's),* 1 slice . . . . 3.0   n.a.
   chopped *(Light & Lean),* 2 slices . . . . . 4.0   n.a.
   chopped *(Oscar Mayer),* 1-oz. slice . . . 2.3   .7
   cooked *(Eckrich Lite),* 1 oz. . . . . 1.0   n.a.
   cooked, sliced *(Kahn's),* 1 slice . . . . . . 1.0   n.a.
   honey *(Hillshire Farm* Deli Select), 1 oz. .9   n.a.
   honey *(Oscar Mayer),* .75-oz. slice 6   .3
   honey *(Oscar Mayer* Thin Sliced),
      .4-oz. slice 4   .2
   loaf *(Eckrich),* 1 oz. slice . . . . 4.0   n.a.
   minced, 1 oz. 5.9   2.0
   pepper, black, cracked *(Oscar Mayer),*
      1 slice .7   .3
   peppered, chopped *(Oscar Mayer),*
      1-oz. slice 3.7   1.3

smoked *(Hillshire Farm* Deli Select),		
1 oz.	.9	n.a.
smoked, cooked *(Oscar Mayer)*, .75-oz.		
slice	.7	.3
smoked, golden *(JM)*, 2 oz.	5.0	n.a.
smoked, golden, and water *(JM)*, 2 oz.	2.0	n.a.
Ham patty:		
1 patty, 2.3 oz. unheated	18.4	6.6
(Swift Premium Brown 'N Serve), 1 patty	13.0	n.a.
canned *(Hormel)*, 1 patty	16.0	n.a.
Ham spread, deviled, canned:		
(Underwood), 2¹/8 oz.	19.0	6.0
(Underwood Light), 2¹/8 oz.	8.0	1.0
smoked *(Underwood)*, 2¹/8 oz.	18.0	6.0
Ham and cheese breakfast sandwich,		
refrigerated *(Owens Border Breakfasts)*,		
2 oz.	6.0	n.a.
Ham and cheese casserole, frozen *(Pillsbury*		
Microwave Classic), 1 pkg.	29.0	n.a.
Ham and cheese loaf:		
1-oz. slice	5.7	2.1
(Eckrich), 1-oz. slice	4.0	n.a.
(Hormel Perma-Fresh), 2 slices	7.0	n.a.
(Kahn's), 1 slice	6.0	n.a.
(Light & Lean), 2 slices	6.0	n.a.
(Oscar Mayer), 1-oz. slice	5.0	2.4
Ham and cheese patty, canned *(Hormel)*,		
1 patty	18.0	n.a.
Ham and cheese pocket sandwich, frozen		
(Hot Pockets), 5 oz.	16.0	n.a.
Hamburger, see "Beef entrée, frozen"		
Hamburger entrée mix*, 1 cup, except as		
noted:		
beef noodle *(Hamburger Helper)*	15.0	n.a.
beef Romanoff *(Hamburger Helper)* . . .	16.0	n.a.
cheeseburger macaroni *(Hamburger*		
Helper)	19.0	n.a.
chili, w/beans *(Hamburger Helper)*,		
1¹/4 cup	17.0	n.a.
chili tomato *(Hamburger Helper)*	14.0	n.a.
hamburger hash *(Hamburger Helper)* . .	15.0	n.a.

Hamburger entrée mix, continued

hamburger stew *(Hamburger Helper)*	14.0	n.a.
Italian, cheesy *(Hamburger Helper)* . . .	17.0	n.a.
Italian, zesty *(Hamburger Helper)*	13.0	n.a.
lasagne *(Hamburger Helper)*	14.0	n.a.
meatloaf *(Hamburger Helper)*	22.0	n.a.
pizza *(Hamburger Helper Pizzabake),* 4.5 oz.	14.0	n.a.
pizza dish *(Hamburger Helper)*	14.0	n.a.
potato au gratin *(Hamburger Helper)*	15.0	n.a.
potato Stroganoff *(Hamburger Helper)*	15.0	n.a.
rice Oriental *(Hamburger Helper)*	14.0	n.a.
sloppy Joe *(Hamburger Helper Sloppy Joe Bake),* 5 oz.	15.0	n.a.
spaghetti *(Hamburger Helper)*	15.0	n.a.
Stroganoff, creamy *(Hamburger Helper)*	20.0	n.a.
taco *(Hamburger Helper Tacobake),* 5.75 oz.	15.0	n.a.
tamale pie *(Hamburger Helper)*	16.0	n.a.

Hardee's, 1 serving:

Big Country Breakfast:

bacon, 7.7 oz.	40.0	10.0
country ham, 9 oz.	38.0	9.0
ham, 8.9 oz.	33.0	7.0
sausage, 9.7 oz.	57.0	16.0

breakfast biscuit:

bacon, 3.3 oz.	21.0	4.0
bacon and egg, 4.4 oz.	24.0	5.0
bacon, egg, and cheese, 4.8 oz.	28.0	8.0
Biscuit 'N' Gravy, 7.8 oz.	24.0	6.0
Canadian Rise 'N' Shine, 5.7 oz.	27.0	8.0
chicken, 5.1 oz.	22.0	4.0
Cinnamon 'N' Raisin, 2.8 oz.	17.0	5.0
country ham, 3.8 oz.	18.0	3.0
country ham and egg, 4.9 oz.	22.0	4.0
ham, 3.7 oz.	16.0	2.0
ham and egg, 4.9 oz.	19.0	4.0
ham, egg, and cheese, 5.3 oz.	23.0	6.0
Rise 'N' Shine, 2.9 oz.	18.0	3.0
sausage, 4.2 oz.	28.0	7.0
sausage and egg, 5.3 oz.	31.0	8.0

steak, 5.2 oz.	29.0	7.0
steak and egg, 6.3 oz.	32.0	8.0
Hash Rounds, 2.8 oz.	14.0	3.0
pancake syrup, 1.5 oz.	< 1.0	< 1.0
pancakes, 3 pieces:		
4.8 oz.	2.0	1.0
w/2 bacon strips, 5.3 oz.	9.0	3.0
w/1 sausage patty, 6.2 oz.	16.0	6.0
sandwiches, 1 serving:		
Big Deluxe burger, 7.6 oz.	30.0	12.0
Big Roast Beef, 4.7 oz.	11.0	5.0
Big Twin, 6.1 oz.	25.0	11.0
cheeseburger, 4.3 oz.	14.0	7.0
cheeseburger, bacon, 7.7 oz.	39.0	16.0
cheeseburger, quarter pound, 6.4 oz.	29.0	14.0
chicken breast sandwich, grilled, 6.8 oz.	9.0	1.0
Chicken Fillet, 6.1 oz.	13.0	2.0
Fisherman's Fillet, 7.3 oz.	24.0	6.0
hamburger, 3.9 oz.	10.0	4.0
hot dog, all beef, 4.2 oz.	17.0	8.0
Hot Ham 'N' Cheese, 5.3 oz.	12.0	5.0
Mushroom 'N' Swiss burger, 6.6 oz.	27.0	13.0
roast beef, regular, 4 oz.	9.0	4.0
Turkey Club, 7.3 oz.	16.0	4.0
salads, side dishes, and special items:		
Chicken Stix, 9 pieces, 5.3 oz.	14.0	3.0
Chicken Stix, 6 pieces, 3.5 oz.	9.0	2.0
Crispy Curls, 3 oz.	16.0	3.0
french fries, big, 5.5 oz.	23.0	5.0
french fries, large, 4 oz.	17.0	3.0
french fries, regular, 2.5 oz.	11.0	2.0
salad, chef, 10.4 oz.	15.0	9.0
salad, chicken 'N' pasta, 14.6 oz.	3.0	1.0
salad, garden, 8.5 oz.	14.0	8.0
salad, side, 4 oz.	< 1.0	< 1.0
dressings, sauces, and condiments:		
barbecue dipping sauce, 1 oz.	< 1.0	< 1.0
barbecue sauce, .5-oz. pkt.	< 1.0	< 1.0
Big Twin sauce, .5 oz.	4.0	< 1.0
blue cheese dressing, 2 oz.	18.0	3.0
French dressing, reduced calorie, 2 oz.	5.0	1.0

Hardee's, dressings, sauces, and condiments, continued

honey sauce, .5 oz.	< 1.0	< 1.0
house dressing, 2 oz.	29.0	4.0
Italian dressing, reduced calorie, 2 oz.	8.0	1.0
sweet mustard dipping sauce, 1 oz.	< 1.0	< 1.0
sweet 'n' sour dipping sauce, 1 oz.	< 1.0	< 1.0
tartar sauce, .7 oz.	9.0	1.0
Thousand Island dressing, 2 oz.	23.0	3.0
desserts and shakes:		
apple turnover, 3.2 oz.	12.0	4.0
Big Cookie, 1.7 oz.	13.0	4.0
Cool Twist cone, all flavors, 4.2 oz.	6.0	4.0
Cool Twist sundae, caramel, 6 oz.	10.0	5.0
Cool Twist sundae, hot fudge, 5.9 oz.	12.0	6.0
Cool Twist sundae, strawberry, 5.9 oz.	8.0	5.0
shake, chocolate or strawberry, 12 oz.	8.0	5.0
shake, vanilla, 12 oz.	9.0	6.0
Hazelnut, see "Filbert"		
Head cheese *(Oscar Mayer)*, 1-oz. slice	4.0	1.4
Heart:		
beef, simmered, 4 oz.	6.4	1.9
chicken, broiler-fryer, simmered, 4 oz.	9.0	2.6
lamb, simmered, 4 oz.	9.0	3.6
pork, braised, 4 oz.	5.7	1.5
turkey, simmered, 4 oz.	6.9	2.0
veal, simmered, 4 oz.	7.7	2.1
Herb gravy mix* *(McCormick/Schilling)*, 1/4 cup	.5	n.a.
Herb seasoning and coating mix, Italian: *(McCormick/Schilling* Bag'n Season)*, 1 pkg.	.2	n.a.
(Shake'n Bake), 1/4 pouch	1.0	n.a.
Herb side dish mix *(Hain* 3-Grain), 1/2 cup	1.0	n.a.
Herb and garlic sauce, w/lemon juice *(Lawry's)*, 1/4 cup	.4	n.a.
Herbs, see specific listings		
Herbs, mixed, seasoning *(Lawry's* Pinch of Herbs), 1 tsp.	.5	n.a.
Herring, meat only:		
fresh, Atlantic:		
raw, 4 oz.	10.3	2.3

baked, broiled, or microwaved, 4 oz.	13.1	3.0
kippered, 4 oz.	14.0	3.2
pickled, 4 oz.	20.4	2.7
fresh, Pacific, raw, 4 oz.	15.7	3.7
canned, see "Sardine"		
Herring, lake, see "Cisco"		
Hickory nut, dried, shelled, 1 oz.	18.3	2.0
Hog plum, seeded, 1 oz.	.6	n.a.
Hollandaise sauce:		
(Great Impressions), 2 tbsp.	21.0	n.a.
mix *(McCormick/Schilling),* 1/4 pkg. . . .	3.8	n.a.
Homestyle gravy mix*:		
(French's), 1/4 cup	1.0	n.a.
(McCormick/Schilling), 1/4 cup	.8	n.a.
(Pillsbury), 1/4 cup	0	0
Hominy, canned:		
w/red and green peppers *(Van Camp's),*		
1 cup	.5	n.a.
white or yellow, 1/2 cup	.7	.1
Honey (all brands)	0	0
Honey butter *(Honey Butter),* 1 tbsp. or		
1/2 oz.	1.0	n.a.
Honey loaf:		
(Eckrich/Echrich Smorgas Pac), 1-oz. slice	1.0	n.a.
(Hormel Perma-Fresh), 2 slices	5.0	n.a.
(Kahn's), 1 slice	2.0	n.a.
(Oscar Mayer), 1-oz. slice	1.0	.4
Honey roll sausage, beef, 1 oz.	3.0	1.2
Honeydew, 7″ × 2″ slice or cubed, 1/2 cup	.1	(0)
Horseradish, prepared:		
(Crowley), 1 oz.	< 1.0	(0)
(Kraft), 1 tbsp.	0	0
cream style *(Kraft),* 1 tbsp.	1.0	0
hot or white *(Gold's),* 1 tsp.	< 1.0	(0)
red *(Gold's),* 1 tsp.	0	0
Horseradish sauce:		
(Great Impressions), 1 tbsp.	7.6	n.a.
(Heinz), 1 tbsp.	7.4	n.a.
(Sauceworks), 1 tbsp.	5.0	1.0
strong *(Life* All Natural), 1/2 tbsp.	< 1.0	(0)

Horseradish tree:

leafy tips, boiled, drained, chopped,
1/2 cup 2   n.a.
pods, raw or boiled, drained, sliced,
1/2 cup 1   n.a.

Hot dog, see "Frankfurter"

Hummus:

1 oz. . . . .   2.4   .4
1/2 cup 10.4   1.6
dip mix *(Fantastic Foods),* 2 oz. or 1/4 cup   6.5   n.a.
mix *(Casbah),* 1 oz. dry . . . .   5.0   n.a.

Hush puppy:

frozen *(SeaPak* Regular), 4 oz. . . . . . .   9.0   n.a.
mix, all varieties *(Golden Dipt),* 1 1/4 oz.   0   0

food and measure	total fat (gms.)	saturated fat (gms.)
Ice, Italian, cherry *(Good Humor)*, 6 fl. oz.	.1	(0)
Ice bar (see also "Fruit bar"), 1 piece:		
all flavors *(Good Humor* Ice Stripes) . .	0	0
all flavors *(Popsicle/Popsicle* Big Stick)	0	0
Ice cream, 1/2 cup, except as noted:		
butter almond *(Breyers)*	10.0	4.0
butter crunch *(Sealtest)*	7.0	4.0
butter pecan:		
(Breyers)	12.0	5.0
(Frusen Glädjé)	21.0	9.0

Ice cream, butter pecan, continued

(Häagen-Dazs)	24.0	9.0
(Lady Borden)	12.0	n.a.
(Sealtest)	9.0	4.0
caramel nut sundae *(Häagen-Dazs)*	21.0	n.a.
cherry vanilla *(Breyers)*	7.0	4.0
chocolate:		
(Breyers)	8.0	5.0
(Darigold Classic)	13.0	n.a.
(Frusen Glädjé)	17.0	9.0
(Häagen-Dazs)	17.0	8.0
(Sealtest)	6.0	4.0
chocolate mint *(Häagen-Dazs)*	20.0	n.a.
deep or fudge, deep *(Häagen-Dazs)* . .	14.0	n.a.
Dutch *(Borden Olde Fashioned Recipe)*	6.0	n.a.
mint *(Breyers)*	10.0	6.0
swirl *(Borden)*	6.0	n.a.
triple stripes *(Sealtest)*	7.0	4.0
chocolate, deep, peanut brittle *(H¨aagen-Dazs)*	19.0	n.a.
chocolate, Swiss, almond *(Frusen Glädj´e)*	19.0	9.0
chocolate chip *(Sealtest)*	8.0	4.0
chocolate chocolate chip *(Frusen Glädj´e)*	18.0	9.0
chocolate chocolate chip *(Häagen-Dazs)*	20.0	10.0
chocolate marshmallow sundae *(Sealtest)*	6.0	4.0
coffee *(Breyers)*	8.0	5.0
coffee *(Häagen-Dazs)*	17.0	8.0
coffee *(Sealtest)*	7.0	4.0
cookies n' cream *(Breyers)*	9.0	5.0
fudge, marble *(Dreyer's)*	8.0	n.a.
fudge royale *(Sealtest)*	7.0	4.0
heavenly hash *(Sealtest)*	7.0	4.0
macadamia brittle *(Häagen-Dazs)*	18.0	n.a.
maple walnut *(Sealtest)*	9.0	3.0
peach *(Breyers)*	6.0	3.0
peanut fudge sundae *(Sealtest)*	7.0	4.0
rocky road *(Dreyer's)*	10.0	n.a.
rum raisin *(Häagen-Dazs)*	17.0	8.0
strawberry:		
(Borden)	6.0	n.a.
(Breyers)	6.0	4.0

(Frusen Glädjé)	15.0	10.0
(Häagen-Dazs)	15.0	8.0
(Sealtest)	5.0	3.0
cream *(Borden Olde Fashioned Recipe)*	5.0	n.a.
vanilla:		
(Borden Olde Fashioned Recipe)	7.0	n.a.
(Breyers)	8.0	5.0
(Darigold Classic*)*	12.0	n.a.
(Eagle Brand Homestyle*)*	9.0	n.a.
(Frusen Glädjé)	17.0	9.0
(Good Humor Cup*)*, 3 fl. oz.	5.1	n.a.
(Häagen-Dazs)	17.0	8.0
honey *(Häagen-Dazs)*	16.0	8.0
regular or French *(Sealtest)*	7.0	4.0
nuggets, dark or milk chocolate coated		
(Carnation Bon Bons), 5 pieces . . .	11.0	n.a.
vanilla fudge *(Häagen-Dazs)*	17.0	n.a.
vanilla fudge twirl *(Breyers)*	8.0	4.0
vanilla Swiss almond *(Frusen Glädj´e)*	19.0	9.0
vanilla Swiss almond *(Häagen-Dazs)* . . .	19.0	n.a.
vanilla-chocolate *(Breyers)*	8.0	5.0
vanilla-chocolate-strawberry:		
(Breyers)	8.0	4.0
(Sealtest/Sealtest Cubic Scoops) . .	6.0	3.0
vanilla-orange *(Sealtest Cubic Scoops)*	4.0	2.0
vanilla-peanut butter swirl *(Häagen-Dazs)*	21.0	8.0
vanilla-raspberry *(Sealtest Cubic Scoops)*	4.0	2.0
Ice cream, substitute and imitation, 1/2 cup,		
except as noted:		
all flavors *(Lite-Lite Tofutti)*	< 1.0	n.a.
all flavors *(Sealtest Free)*	0	0
all flavors *(Simple Pleasures)*, 4 oz.	< 1.0	.3
cappuccino *(Tofutti* Love Drops*)*	12.0	3.0
chocolate *(Tofutti* Love Drops*)*	13.0	5.0
chocolate supreme *(Tofutti)*	13.0	3.0
chocolate chip *(Low, Lite'n Luscious)* . .	2.0	n.a.
Jamoca Swiss almond *(Low, Lite'n*		
Luscious)	2.0	n.a.
pineapple coconut *(Low, Lite'n Luscious)*	1.0	n.a.
strawberry *(Low, Lite'n Luscious)*	1.0	n.a.

Ice cream, substitute and imitation, continued
  vanilla:

(Tofutti)	11.0	1.5
(Tofutti Love Drops)	12.0	3.0
chocolate dipped *(Tofutti O's)*, 1 piece	2.0	n.a.
vanilla almond bark *(Tofutti)*	14.0	4.0
wildberry *(Tofutti)*	12.0	3.0

Ice cream bar, 1 bar:

(Heath), 3 fl. oz.	13.0	n.a.
(Klondike/Klondike Krispy), 5 fl. oz. . . .	19.0	n.a.
(Klondike Lite), 2.5 fl. oz.	10.0	n.a.
all varieties, except vanilla-milk chocolate brittle and crunch bars *(Häagen-Dazs)*	27.0	n.a.
almond, toasted *(Good Humor)*, 3 fl. oz.	11.8	n.a.
assorted *(Good Humor Whammy)*, 1.6 fl. oz.	7.2	n.a.
caramel almond *(Häagen-Dazs* Crunch Bar)	18.0	7.0
chip candy crunch *(Good Humor)*, 3 fl. oz.	17.9	n.a.
chocolate:		
(Klondike), 5 fl. oz.	19.0	n.a.
fudge cake *(Good Humor)*, 6.3 fl. oz.	15.0	n.a.
fudge sundae *(Bakers Fudgetastic)* . . .	15.0	n.a.
fudge sundae, crunchy *(Bakers Fudgetastic)*	14.0	n.a.
milk, w/almonds, milk chocolate coated *(Nestlé* Premium), 3.7 fl. oz.	23.0	n.a.
w/milk chocolate coating *(Nestlé Quik)*, 3 fl. oz.	14.0	n.a.
chocolate eclair *(Good Humor)*, 3 fl. oz.	9.9	n.a.
peanut butter *(Häagen-Dazs* Crunch Bar)	21.0	7.0
strawberry shortcake *(Good Humor)*, 3 fl. oz.	8.2	n.a.
vanilla:		
(Häagen-Dazs Crunch Bar)	16.0	6.0
w/caramel peanut center, milk chocolate coated *(Oh Henry!)*, 3 fl. oz.	20.0	n.a.
chocolate flavor coated *(Good Humor)*, 3 fl. oz.	13.7	n.a.

w/milk chocolate brittle *(Häagen-Dazs)*	25.0	n.a.
w/milk chocolate coating and crisps *(Nestlé Crunch),* 3 fl. oz.	13.0	n.a.
w/white chocolate coating *(Nestlé Alpine* Premium), 3.7 fl. oz.	25.0	n.a.

Ice cream bar, substitute and imitation,
1 bar:

all flavors *(Good Humor* Milky Pop)	0	0
all flavors *(Sealtest Free)*	0	0
all flavors, except orange-vanilla *(Crystal Light Cool N'Creamy)*	2.0	n.a.
chocolate:		
(Weight Watchers Treat Bars)	1.0	0
dip *(Weight Watchers)*	7.0	3.0
fudge *(Good Humor),* 2.5 fl oz.	.6	n.a.
fudge, double *(Weight Watchers)*	1.0	0
mousse *(Weight Watchers)*	< 1.0	0
English toffee crunch *(Weight Watchers)*	8.0	4.0
orange-vanilla *(Crystal Light Cool N'Creamy)*	1.0	n.a.
orange-vanilla *(Weight Watchers* Sugar Free Treat Bars)	< 1.0	0
strawberry finger *(Good Humor),* 2.5 fl. oz.	.1	n.a.
vanilla sandwich *(Weight Watchers)*	3.0	2.0

Ice cream cone and cup:

plain *(Little Debbie* Ice Cream Cup), 1 cup	.1	(0)
filled:		
(Good Humor King Cone), 5.5 fl. oz.	12.0	n.a.
boysenberry *(Good Humor* King Cone), 5 fl. oz.	13.1	n.a.
vanilla-chocolate cup *(Good Humor* Combo), 6 fl. oz.	9.2	n.a.

Ice cream mix*, all flavors *(Salada),* 1 cup | 19.0 | n.a.

Ice cream sandwich, 1 piece:

chocolate chip cookie, chocolate *(Good Humor),* 2.7 fl. oz.	8.3	n.a.
chocolate chip cookie, chocolate *(Good Humor),* 4 fl. oz.	10.5	n.a.
vanilla *(Good Humor),* 3 fl. oz.	5.7	n.a.

Ice cream sandwich, continued

vanilla *(Klondike)*, 5 fl. oz.	9.0	n.a.
Ice cream and sorbet, see "Sorbet"		
Ice milk, 1/2 cup:		
caramel nut *(Light n' Lively)*	4.0	2.0
chocolate:		
(Borden)	2.0	n.a.
(Breyers Light)	4.0	2.0
(Weight Watchers Grand Collection) . .	3.0	2.0
fudge twirl *(Breyers* Light)	4.0	2.0
chocolate chip *(Light n' Lively)*	4.0	3.0
chocolate chip *(Weight Watchers Grand Collection)*	4.0	2.0
chocolate swirl *(Weight Watchers Grand Collection)*	3.0	2.0
coffee *(Light n' Lively)*	3.0	1.0
cookies n' cream *(Light n' Lively)*	3.0	2.0
heavenly hash *(Breyers* Light)	5.0	3.0
heavenly hash *(Light n' Lively)*	4.0	2.0
Neapolitan *(Weight Watchers Grand Collection)*	3.0	1.0
pecan pralines'N creme *(Weight Watchers Grand Collection)*	4.0	3.0
praline almond *(Breyers* Light)	5.0	2.0
strawberry *(Borden)*	2.0	n.a.
strawberry *(Breyers* Light)	3.0	2.0
toffee fudge parfait *(Breyers* Light) . . .	5.0	3.0
vanilla:		
(Borden)	2.0	n.a.
(Breyers Light)	4.0	2.0
(Light n' Lively)	3.0	2.0
(Weight Watchers Grand Collection)	3.0	1.0
vanilla chocolate almond *(Light n' Lively)*	4.0	1.0
vanilla-chocolate-strawberry *(Breyers* Light)	4.0	2.0
vanilla-chocolate-strawberry *(Light n' Lively)*	3.0	2.0
vanilla fudge swirl *(Light n' Lively)* . . .	3.0	2.0
vanilla raspberry parfait *(Breyers* Light)	3.0	2.0
vanilla raspberry swirl *(Light n' Lively)*	3.0	1.0

Ice milk cone *(Gold Bond* Olde Nut
  Sundae), 3 fl. oz. . . . .   8.0   n.a.
Iowa brand loaf *(Hormel* Perma-Fresh),
  2 slices . . . .   6.0   n.a.
Italian sausage:
  hot or mild *(Hillshire Farm* Links), 2 oz.   17.0   n.a.
  pork, cooked, 1 oz. 7.3   2.6
  smoked *(Hillshire Farm* Flavorseal), 2 oz.   18.0   n.a.

food and measure	total fat (gms.)	saturated fat (gms.)
Jack-in-the-Box:		
breakfast, 1 serving:		
Breakfast Jack, 4.4 oz.	13.0	5.2
crescent, Canadian, 4.7 oz.	31.0	9.7
crescent, sausage, 5.5 oz.	43.0	15.5
crescent, supreme, 5.1 oz.	40.0	13.2
hash browns, 2.2 oz.	7.0	3.6
pancake platter, 8.1 oz.	22.0	8.6
scrambled egg platter, 8.8 oz.	40.0	17.1

sandwiches, 1 serving:

bacon cheeseburger, 8.1 oz.	39.0	15.0
beef fajita pita, 6.2 oz.	14.0	5.9
cheeseburger, 4 oz.	14.0	5.7
cheeseburger, double, 5.3 oz.	27.0	12.3
cheeseburger, ultimate, 10 oz.	69.0	26.4
chicken fajita pita, 6.7 oz.	8.0	2.9
chicken fillet, grilled, 7.2 oz.	17.0	4.1
chicken supreme, 8.1 oz.	36.0	14.3
fish supreme, 8 oz.	32.0	13.5
hamburger, 3.4 oz.	11.0	4.1
Jumbo Jack, 7.8 oz.	34.0	11.0
Jumbo Jack, w/cheese, 8.5 oz.	40.0	14.0
Swiss and bacon burger, 6.6 oz.	47.0	20.0

Mexican food:

guacamole, 1 oz.	5.0	n.a.
salsa, 1 oz.	< 1.0	< 1.0
taco, 2.9 oz.	11.0	5.2
taco, super, 4.8 oz.	17.0	8.0

salads, 1 serving:

chef, 14 oz.	18.0	9.4
Mexican chicken, 14.6 oz.	23.0	8.6
side, 4 oz.	3.0	2.0
taco, 14.2 oz.	31.0	13.4

finger foods:

chicken strips, 4 pieces, 4.4 oz.	14.0	6.8
chicken strips, 6 pieces, 6.6 oz.	20.0	10.0
egg rolls, 3 pieces, 6 oz.	19.0	7.2
egg rolls, 5 pieces, 10 oz.	32.0	12.0
shrimp, 10 pieces, 3 oz.	16.0	7.2
shrimp, 15 pieces, 4.4 oz.	24.0	10.8
taquitos, 5 pieces, 5 oz.	16.0	5.6
taquitos, 7 pieces, 7 oz.	22.0	7.9

side dishes, 1 serving:

french fries, small, 2.4 oz.	12.0	5.0
french fries, regular, 3.9 oz.	19.0	7.9
french fries, jumbo, 4.8 oz.	24.0	10.0
onion rings, 3.8 oz.	23.0	11.1

dressings and sauces:

BBQ, seafood cocktail, or sweet and sour sauce, 1 oz.	< 1.0	< 1.0

Jack-in-the-Box, dressings and sauces, continued

bleu cheese dressing, 2.5 oz.	22.0	4.0
buttermilk dressing, 2.5 oz.	36.0	5.8
French dressing, reduced calorie, 2.5 oz.	8.0	1.2
mayo-mustard sauce, .7 oz.	13.0	n.a.
mayo-onion sauce, .7 oz.	15.0	n.a.
Thousand Island dressing, 2.5 oz.	30.0	5.0
desserts and shakes:		
apple turnover, 4.2 oz.	24.0	10.8
cheesecake, 3.5 oz.	17.5	9.0
shake, chocolate or strawberry	7.0	4.3
shake, vanilla	6.0	3.6
Jackfruit, trimmed, 1 oz.	.1	(0)
Jalapeño bean dip:		
(Wise), 2 tbsp.	0	0
medium *(Hain)*, 4 tbsp.	1.0	n.a.
Jalapeño loaf *(Kahn's)*, 1 slice	6.0	n.a.
Jalapeño pepper, see "Pepper, jalapeño"		
Jalapeño pepper dip:		
(Kraft), 2 tbsp.	4.0	2.0
cheddar *(Breakstone's* Gourmet), 2 tbsp.	6.0	3.0
cheese *(Kraft* Premium), 2 tbsp.	4.0	3.0
nacho *(Price's)*, 1 oz.	7.1	n.a.
Jam and jelly, fruit, all varieties	0	0
Java plum, seeded, 1/2 cup	.2	(0)
Jelly and peanut butter *(Bama)*, 2 tbsp.	7.0	n.a.
Jerusalem artichoke, raw, pared, sliced, 1/2 cup	< .1	tr.
Jicama, raw, sliced, 1/2 cup or boiled, drained, 4 oz.	.1	(0)
Jujube:		
raw, seeded, 1 oz.	.1	(0)
dried, 1 oz.	.3	(0)
Jute, potherb, boiled, drained, 1/2 cup	.1	< .1

food and measure	total fat (gms.)	saturated fat (gms.)
Kale, 1/2 cup:		
fresh, raw, chopped	.2	< .1
fresh or frozen, boiled, drained, chopped	.3	< .1
canned, chopped *(Allens)*	< 1.0	n.a.
Scotch, fresh, raw, chopped	.2	< .1
Scotch, fresh, boiled, drained, chopped	.3	< .1
Kanpyo, 1/2 cup	.2	< .1
Kasha, see "Buckwheat groats"		

Kentucky Fried Chicken:
chicken, *Original Recipe:*

breast, center, 4.1 oz.	15.3	3.8
breast, side, 3.2 oz.	16.5	4.2
drumstick, 2 oz.	8.5	2.2
thigh, 3.7 oz.	19.7	5.3
wing, 1.9 oz.	11.7	3.0

chicken, *Extra Tasty Crispy:*

breast, center, 4.8 oz.	19.7	4.8
breast, side, 3.9 oz.	22.3	5.5
drumstick, 2.4 oz.	13.9	3.4
thigh, 4.2 oz.	29.8	7.7
wing, 2.3 oz.	18.6	4.4
chicken, Hot Wings, 6 pieces	24.1	5.3
chicken, *Kentucky Nuggets,* .6-oz. piece	2.9	.7

chicken, *Lite N' Crispy:*

breast, center, 3 oz.	11.9	2.9
breast, side, 2.6 oz.	12.4	3.2
drumstick, 1.7 oz.	7.0	1.7
thigh, 2.8 oz.	16.7	4.3

Kentucky Nuggets sauces:

barbeque or sweet and sour, 1 oz. . . .	.6	.1
honey, .5 oz.	< .1	< .1
mustard, 1 oz.	.9	.1

side dishes:

buttermilk biscuits, 2.3 oz.	11.7	3.2
Chicken Littles sandwich, 1.7 oz.	10.1	2.0
coleslaw, 3.2 oz.	6.6	1.0
Colonel's chicken sandwich, 5.9 oz.	27.3	5.7
corn-on-the-cob, 5 oz.	3.1	.5
french fries, regular, 2.7 oz.	11.9	2.6
mashed potatoes and gravy, 3.5 oz. . .	1.6	.4

Ketchup, see "Catsup"

Kidneys:

beef, simmered, 4 oz.	3.9	1.2
lamb, braised, 4 oz.	4.1	1.4
pork, braised, 4 oz.	5.3	1.7
veal, braised, 4 oz.	6.4	2.0

Kielbasa (see also "Polish sausage"):

(Eckrich Lite Polska), 1 oz.	6.0	n.a.
(Hillshire Farm Bun Size), 2 oz.	16.0	n.a.

(Hillshire Farm Polska Flavorseal Lite), 2 oz.	13.0	n.a.
(Hormel Kolbase), 3 oz.	19.0	n.a.
all varieties, except lite *(Hillshire Farm* Polska), 2 oz.	17.0	n.a.
pork and beef, 1 oz.	7.7	2.8
skinless *(Eckrich* Polska), 1 link	16.0	n.a.
skinless *(Hormel),* 1/2 link	14.0	n.a.
Kiwifruit, 1 large, 3.7 oz.	.4	(0)
Knockwurst:		
(Hillshire Farm Links), 2 oz.	16.0	n.a.
beef *(Hebrew National),* 3-oz. link	25.0	n.a.
pork and beef, 1 oz.	7.8	2.9
Kohlrabi, boiled, drained, sliced, 1/2 cup	.1	< .1
Kumquat, 1 medium, .7 oz.	< .1	(0)

food and measure	total fat (gms.)	saturated fat (gms.)
Lamb, domestic, choice grade, meat only, 4 oz.:		
cubed (leg and shoulder), braised or stewed	10.0	3.6
cubed (leg and shoulder), broiled	8.3	3.0
foreshank, braised or stewed, lean w/fat	15.3	6.4
foreshank, braised or stewed, lean only	6.8	2.4
ground, broiled	22.3	9.2
leg, whole, roasted, lean w/fat	18.7	7.8
leg, whole, roasted, lean only	8.8	3.1

loin:
lean w/fat, broiled	26.2	11.1
lean w/fat, roasted	26.8	11.6
lean only, broiled	11.0	3.9
lean only, roasted	11.1	4.2

rib:
lean w/fat, broiled	33.6	14.4
lean w/fat, roasted	33.8	14.5
lean only, broiled	14.7	5.3
lean only, roasted	15.1	5.4

shoulder, whole:
lean w/fat, braised or stewed	27.8	11.7
lean w/fat, broiled	21.8	9.1
lean w/fat, roasted	22.6	9.6
lean only, braised or stewed	18.0	7.0
lean only, broiled	11.9	4.4
lean only, roasted	12.2	4.6

Lamb, New Zealand, frozen, meat only, 4 oz.:
foreshank, lean w/fat, braised or stewed	18.0	8.9
foreshank, lean only, braised or stewed	6.8	3.0
leg, whole, lean w/fat, roasted	17.6	8.6
leg, whole, lean only, roasted	7.9	3.5
loin, lean w/fat, broiled	27.1	13.6
loin, lean only, broiled	9.3	4.1
rib, lean w/fat, roasted	32.6	16.4
rib, lean only, roasted	11.5	5.0
shoulder, whole, lean w/fat, braised or stewed	28.8	13.9
shoulder, whole, lean only, braised or stewed	17.6	7.7

Lambsquarters, boiled, drained, chopped, 1/2 cup	.6	< .1
Lard, pork, 1 tbsp.	12.8	5.0
Lasagna dinner, frozen *(Banquet Extra Helping)*, 16.5 oz.	23.0	n.a.

Lasagna entrée, canned or packaged:
(Chef Boyardee Microwave), 7.5 oz.	9.0	n.a.
(Nalley's), 7.5 oz.	5.0	n.a.
in garden vegetable sauce *(Chef Boyardee* Microwave), 7.5 oz.	1.0	< 1.0

Lasagna entrée, canned or packaged, continued
Italian style *(Hormel Top Shelf)*,
1 serving . . . . 17.0   n.a.
vegetable *(Hormel Top Shelf)*, 10.6 oz.   8.0   n.a.

Lasagna entrée, frozen:
(Celentano), 8 oz. . . . . 19.0   n.a.
(Celentano), 10 oz. . . . . 24.0   n.a.
(Green Giant Entrées), 12 oz. . . . . . . 20.0   n.a.
(Stouffer's), 10.5 oz. . . . . 13.0   n.a.
(Tyson Gourmet Selection), 11.5 oz. . . . 14.0   n.a.
cheese *(Dining Lite)*, 9 oz. . . . . 6.0   n.a.
cheese, Italian *(Weight Watchers)*, 11 oz. 12.0   4.0
cheese, three *(The Budget Gourmet)*,
10 oz. 17.0   n.a.
fiesta *(Stouffer's)*, 10.25 oz. . . . . 22.0   n.a.
garden *(Weight Watchers)*, 11 oz. 7.0   2.0
meat *(Buitoni* Single Serving), 9 oz. . . . 19.0   12.0
w/meat and sauce *(Lean Cuisine)*,
10.25 oz. 8.0   3.0
w/meat sauce:
(Banquet Family Entrées), 7 oz. . . . . 10.0   n.a.
(The Budget Gourmet Slim Selects),
10 oz. . . . . 10.0   n.a.
(Dining Lite), 9 oz. . . . . 5.0   n.a.
(Healthy Choice), 9 oz. 5.0   2.0
(Le Menu LightStyle), 10 oz. . . . . . . 8.0   n.a.
(Swanson Homestyle Recipe), 10.5 oz. 15.0   n.a.
(Weight Watchers), 11 oz. 10.0   4.0
primavera *(Celentano)*, 11 oz. . . . . 14.0   n.a.
in sauce *(Buitoni* Family Style), 7.3 oz.   13.0   7.0
sausage, Italian *(The Budget Gourmet)*,
10 oz. 20.0   n.a.
seafood *(Mrs. Paul's* Light), 9.5 oz. 8.0   3.0
tuna, w/spinach noodles and vegetables
(Lean Cuisine), 9.75 oz. 10.0   2.0
vegetable *(Stouffer's)*, 10.5 oz. . . . . 24.0   n.a.
vegetable, garden *(Le Menu* LightStyle),
10.5 oz. 8.0   3.0
zucchini *(Lean Cuisine)*, 11 oz. 7.0   2.0
Leek:
fresh, raw, 1 medium, 9.9 oz. 4   .1

fresh, boiled, drained, chopped, 1/2 cup	.1	< .1
freeze-dried, 1 tbsp.	tr.	tr.
Lemon, whole, 1 medium, 2 1/8″ diam.	.3	< .1
Lemon butter dill cooking sauce (*Golden Dipt*), 1 fl. oz.	10.0	1.0
Lemon and dill seasoning mix (*McCormick/ Schilling Bag'n Season*), 1 pkg.	11.0	n.a.
Lemon drink, chilled (*Crowley*)	0	0
Lemon extract (*Virginia Dare*)	0	0
Lemon herb marinade (*Golden Dipt*), 1 fl. oz.	14.0	2.0
Lemon juice:		
fresh, 1/2 cup	0	0
canned or bottled, 1/2 cup	.4	< .1
frozen, single strength, 1 tbsp.	.1	tr.
Lemon peel, raw, 1 tsp.	< .1	tr.
Lemon pepper, seasoning:		
(*Lawry's*), 1 tsp.	.1	(0)
(*McCormick/Schilling* Spice Blends), 1 tsp.	0	0
(*McCormick/Schilling Parsley Patch*), 1 tsp.	.6	(0)
Lemon-lime drink, canned or mix (all brands)	0	0
Lemonade, canned, chilled, frozen, or mix* (all brands), 6 fl. oz.	< .2	< .1
Lentil, boiled, 1/2 cup	.4	.1
Lentil sprouts:		
raw, 1/2 cup	.2	< .1
stir-fried, w/out fat, 4 oz.	.5	.1
Lentil dinner, canned, w/garden vegetables (*Health Valley Fast Menu*), 7.5 oz.	4.0	n.a.
Lentil pilaf mix*, (*Casbah*), 1/2 cup	0	0
Lentil rice loaf, frozen (*Harvest Bake*), 4 oz.	9.0	1.0
Lettuce:		
bibb, Boston, or butterhead, 5″-diam. head	.4	< .1
cos or romaine, untrimmed, 1 lb.	.9	.1
iceberg, 6″-diam. head	1.0	.1
looseleaf, untrimmed, 1 lb.	.9	.1
Lime, 1 medium, 2″ diam.	.1	< .1

Lime juice:

fresh, 1/2 cup	.2	< .1
canned or bottled *(Rose's)*	0	0
reconstituted *(ReaLime)*	0	0
Limeade, frozen* *(Minute Maid)*	0	0
Ling, meat only, raw, 4 oz.	.7	n.a.
Lingcod, meat only, raw, 4 oz.	1.2	.2

Linguine entrée, frozen:

w/clam sauce *(Lean Cuisine)*, 95/8 oz.	7.0	1.0
w/scallops and clams *(The Budget Gourmet Slim Selects)*, 9.5 oz.	11.0	n.a.
w/shrimp *(The Budget Gourmet)*, 10 oz.	15.0	n.a.
w/shrimp *(Healthy Choice)*, 9.5 oz.	2.0	1.0

Linguine entrée, packaged, w/clam sauce *(Hormel Top Shelf)*, 1 serving	18.0	n.a.
Liquor, distilled (bourbon, gin, rum, scotch, vodka, etc.), all proofs	0	0

Little Caesars:

Little Caesars Meals, 1 serving:

cheese pizza, salad	21.0	n.a.
green pepper, onion, mushroom pizza, salad	22.0	n.a.
pizza, cheese, single slice, 2.2 oz.	6.0	n.a.
pizza, pepperoni, green pepper, onion, mushroom, single slice, 2.7 oz.	7.0	n.a.

sandwiches, 1 serving:

ham and cheese	21.0	n.a.
Italian sub	28.0	n.a.
tuna melt	37.0	n.a.
vegetarian	30.0	n.a.

salads, w/low-calorie dressing, 1 serving:

antipasto salad, 12 oz.	9.0	n.a.
Greek salad, 11 oz.	8.0	n.a.
tossed salad, 11 oz.	2.0	n.a.

Liver:

beef, braised, 4 oz.	5.5	2.2
chicken, simmered, 4 oz.	6.2	2.1
chicken, simmered, chopped or diced, 1 cup	7.6	2.6
duck, domesticated, raw, 1 oz.	1.3	.4
goose, domesticated, raw, 1 oz.	1.2	.5

lamb, braised, 4 oz.	10.0	3.9
pork, braised, 4 oz.	5.0	1.6
turkey, simmered, 4 oz.	6.7	2.1
veal (calves), braised, 4 oz.	7.8	2.9
Liver cheese:		
(JM), 1-oz. slice	6.0	n.a.
(Oscar Mayer), 1.34-oz. slice	10.0	3.5
pork, 1 oz.	7.3	2.5
Liver loaf:		
(Hormel Perma-Fresh), 2 slices	13.0	n.a.
(Kahn's), 1 slice	15.0	n.a.
Liver pâté, see "Pâté"		
Liverwurst:		
(Jones Dairy Farm, Chub), 1 oz.	6.3	n.a.
(Jones Dairy Farm Slices), 1 slice	6.6	n.a.
pork, 1 oz.	8.1	3.0
Liverwurst spread, canned:		
(Hormel), 1/2 oz.	3.0	n.a.
(Underwood), 2 1/8 oz.	15.0	n.a.
Lobster, northern, meat only:		
raw, 4 oz.	1.0	n.a.
boiled, poached, or steamed, 4 oz.	.7	.1
Lobster entrée, frozen, Newburg		
(Stouffer's), 6.5 oz.	32.0	n.a.
Lobster sauce, rock *(Progresso)*, 1/2 cup	8.0	1.0
Loganberry, fresh, trimmed, 1 cup	.9	n.a.
Longan:		
fresh, shelled and seeded, 1 oz.	< .1	(0)
dried, 1 oz.	.1	(0)
Loquat, peeled and seeded, 1 oz.	.1	< .1
Lotus root, raw, 1 root, 9 1/2" × 1 7/8" or		
boiled, drained, 4 oz.	.1	< .1
Lotus seed:		
raw, shelled, 1 oz.	.2	< .1
dried, 1 oz., 47 small or 36 large	.6	.1
Lox, see "Salmon, fresh, Chinook, smoked"		
Luncheon meat (see also specific listings):		
(Oscar Mayer), 1-oz. slice	8.5	3.3
loaf, spiced *(JM)*, 1-oz. slice	6.0	n.a.
spiced *(Hormel* Perma-Fresh), 2 slices	9.0	n.a.
spiced *(Kahn's* Luncheon Loaf), 1 slice	7.0	n.a.

Luncheon meat, continued

spiced *(Light & Lean)*, 2 slices	9.0	n.a.
canned, plain or smoke flavor *(Spam)*, 2 oz.	15.0	n.a.
canned, w/cheese chunks *(Spam)*, 2 oz.	16.0	n.a.
canned, deviled *(Spam)*, 1 tbsp.	3.0	n.a.
canned, spiced *(Hormel)*, 3 oz.	26.0	n.a.
Luncheon "meat," vegetarian, canned:		
(Worthington Numete), 1/2″ slice, 2.4 oz.	11.0	2.0
(Worthington Protose), 1/2″ slice, 2.7 oz.	8.0	1.0
Lungs, beef, braised, 4 oz.	4.2	1.4
Lupin:		
raw, 1/2 cup	8.8	1.0
boiled, 1/2 cup	2.4	.3
Lychee:		
raw, shelled and seeded, 1/2 cup	.4	tr.
dried, 1 oz.	.3	(0)

food and measure	total fat (gms.)	saturated fat (gms.)
Macadamia nut, shelled:		
dried, 1 oz.	20.9	3.1
dried, 1 cup	98.8	14.8
oil roasted, 1 oz.	21.7	3.3
Macaroni (see also "Pasta"), cooked:		
elbows or spirals, 1 cup	.9	.1
shells, small, 1 cup	.8	.1
vegetable or tri-color, 4 oz.	.1	< .1
whole wheat, 4 oz.	.6	.1

Macaroni and beef, canned:
(Chef Boyardee Beefaroni Microwave), 7.5 oz.	7.0	1.0
(Nalley's), 7.5 oz.	3.0	.n.a.
elbows, in beef sauce *(Chef Boyardee* Microwave), 7.5 oz.	7.0	n.a.

Macaroni and beef dinner, frozen
(Swanson), 12 oz.	15.0	n.a.

Macaroni and beef entrée, frozen, w/
tomatoes *(Stouffer's),* 1/2 of 11.5-oz. pkg.	7.0	n.a.

Macaroni and cheese, canned:
(Franco-American), 73/8 oz.	6.0	n.a.
(Hormel Micro-Cup), 7.5 oz.	6.0	n.a.
shells and cheddar *(Lipton Hearty Ones),* 11 oz.	7.4	n.a.
shells in tomato sauce *(Chef Boyardee),* 7.5 oz.	1.0	n.a.

Macaroni and cheese, frozen:
(Banquet Casserole), 8 oz.	17.0	n.a.
(Banquet Family Entrees), 8 oz.	13.0	n.a.
(The Budget Gourmet Side Dish), 5.3 oz.	8.0	n.a.
(Freezer Queen Family Side Dish), 4 oz.	2.0	n.a.
(Green Giant One Serving), 5.7 oz.	9.0	4.0
(Myers), 3.5 oz.	9.0	n.a.
(Stouffer's), 1/2 of 12-oz. pkg.	13.0	n.a.
(Stouffer's), 1/4 of 20-oz. pkg.	11.0	n.a.
(Swanson Homestyle Recipe), 10 oz.	19.0	n.a.
pie *(Swanson* Pot Pie), 7 oz.	8.0	n.a.

Macaroni and cheese, mix (see also "Pasta dishes, mix"):
(Golden Grain), 1 serving*	15.0	n.a.
(Kraft/Kraft Family Size Dinner), 3/4 cup*	13.0	3.0
(Kraft Deluxe Dinner), 3/4 cup*	8.0	4.0
cheddar *(Fantastic Foods* Traditional), 1/2 cup*	2.0	n.a.
cheddar *(Golden Grain),* 1.81 oz. dry	2.1	.8
Parmesan and herbs *(Fantastic Foods),* 1/2 cup*	2.0	n.a.
shells:		
(Velveeta), 1/2 cup*	8.0	4.0

w/bacon *(Velveeta* Bits of Bacon),		
1/2 cup*	10.0	5.0
Mexican *(Velveeta* Touch of Mexico),		
1/2 cup*	8.0	4.0
spirals *(Kraft* Dinner), 3/4 cup*	18.0	4.0
Macaroni and cheese dinner, frozen:		
(Banquet), 10 oz.	20.0	n.a.
(Swanson), 12.25 oz.	15.0	n.a.
Macaroni and cheese loaf *(Eckrich),* 1-oz.		
slice	6.0	n.a.
Mace, ground, 1 tsp.	.6	.2
Mackerel, meat only:		
fresh:		
Atlantic, raw, 4 oz.	15.8	3.7
Atlantic, baked, broiled, or		
microwaved, 4 oz.	20.2	4.7
king, raw, 4 oz.	2.3	.4
Pacific or jack, raw, 4 oz.	8.9	2.5
Spanish, raw, 4 oz.	7.1	2.1
Spanish, baked, broiled, or microwaved,		
4 oz.	7.2	2.0
canned, Jack, drained, 1 cup	12.0	3.5
Mai tai mix, bottled or instant *(Holland*		
House).	0	0
Malacca apple, seeded, 1 oz.	< .1	tr.
Malted milk powder:		
natural *(Kraft),* 3 tsp.	2.0	n.a.
chocolate *(Kraft),* 3 tsp.	1.0	n.a.
Mammy apple, peeled and seeded, 1 oz.	.1	n.a.
Mango, sliced, 1/2 cup	.2	.1
Mango nectar *(Libby's)*	0	0
Manhattan mix, bottled *(Holland House)*	0	0
Manicotti dinner, frozen, three cheese *(Le*		
Menu), 11.75 oz.	15.0	n.a.
Manicotti entrée, frozen:		
(Buitoni Single Serving), 9-oz. pkg.	14.0	8.0
(Celentano), 8 oz.	11.0	n.a.
cheese:		
(Le Menu), 8.5 oz.	20.0	n.a.
(Weight Watchers), 9.25 oz.	8.0	4.0

Manicotti entrée, frozen, cheese, continued

w/meat sauce *(The Budget Gourmet)*, 10 oz.	26.0	n.a.
w/sauce *(Celentano)*, 7 oz.	16.0	n.a.
w/sauce *(Celentano)*, 10 oz.	14.0	n.a.
Maple syrup, all varieties	0	0
Margarine, 1 tbsp., except as noted:		
(Country Morning Stick), 1 tsp.	4.0	n.a.
(Country Morning Tub), 1 tsp.	3.0	n.a.
(Country Morning Light Stick or Tub), 1 tsp.	2.0	n.a.
(Diet *Mazola*)	6.0	1.0
(Land O'Lakes Stick or Tub), 1 tsp. . . .	4.0	n.a.
(Mazola)	11.0	2.0
(Nucoa)	11.0	2.0
(Nucoa Heart Beat)	3.0	< 1.0
(Parkay/Parkay Soft)	11.0	2.0
all varieties *(Hain* Safflower)	11.0	2.0
soft:		
(Chiffon Cup)	10.0	1.0
(Chiffon Stick)	11.0	2.0
(Chiffon Unsalted)	10.0	2.0
(Diet *Parkay)*	6.0	1.0
(Nucoa)	10.0	2.0
spread:		
(Kraft "Touch of Butter" Bowl)	6.0	1.0
(Kraft "Touch of Butter" Stick)	10.0	2.0
(Land O'Lakes Tub), 1 tsp.	3.0	n.a.
(Mazola Corn Oil Light)	6.0	1.0
(Parkay 50% Vegetable Oil)	7.0	1.0
w/sweet cream *(Land O'Lakes* Stick), 1 tsp.	4.0	n.a.
w/sweet cream *(Land O'Lakes* Tub), 1 tsp.	3.0	n.a.
squeeze *(Parkay)*	10.0	2.0
whipped *(Chiffon)*	8.0	1.0
whipped *(Miracle* Brand Cup or Stick) . .	7.0	1.0
whipped *(Parkay* Cup or Stick)	7.0	1.0
Margarita mix, all varieties *(Holland House)*	0	0
Marjoram, dried, 1 tsp.	< .1	(0)
Marmalade, fruit (all brands)	0	0

Marshmallow, see "Candy" and "Toppings, dessert"

Mayonnaise, 1 tbsp.:

(Cains)	11.0	2.0
(Hain Canola)	11.0	1.0
(Hain Canola Reduced Calorie/*Hain* Light)	6.0	1.0
(Hain Real/Eggless/Cold Processed)	12.0	2.0
(Hain Safflower)	12.0	1.0
(Hellmann's/Best Foods)	11.0	2.0
(Hellmann's/Best Foods Light)	5.0	1.0
(Kraft Light)	5.0	1.0
(Kraft Real)	12.0	2.0
(Rokeach)	11.0	2.0

Mayonnaise, imitation (see also "Salad dressing"):

(Hellmann's Cholesterol Free), 1 tbsp.	5.0	1.0
(Nucoa Heart Beat), 1 tbsp.	4.0	< 1.0
(Weight Watchers Cholesterol Free), 1 tbsp.	5.0	1.0
soybean *(Featherweight Soyamaise),* 1 tbsp.	11.0	n.a.
sunflower *(Life* All Natural), 1 tbsp.	8.0	n.a.
tofu *(Nasoya Naoynaise),* 1 tbsp.	4.0	n.a.

McDonald's:

apple bran muffin, 3 oz.	0	0
breakfast biscuit, 1 serving:		
w/bacon, egg, and cheese, 5.5 oz.	26.4	8.2
w/biscuit spread, 2.6 oz.	12.7	3.4
w/sausage, 4.3 oz.	29.0	9.3
w/sausage and egg, 6.3 oz.	34.5	11.2
danish:		
apple, 4.1 oz.	17.9	3.5
cinnamon raisin, 3.9 oz.	21.0	4.2
iced cheese, 3.9 oz.	21.8	5.9
raspberry, 4.1 oz.	15.9	3.1
Egg McMuffin, 4.9 oz.	11.2	3.8
eggs, scrambled, 3.5 oz.	9.8	3.3
English muffin, w/butter, 2.1 oz.	4.6	2.4
hash brown potatoes, 1.9 oz.	7.3	3.2
hotcakes, w/butter and syrup, 6.2 oz.	9.2	3.7

McDonald's, continued

sausage, pork, 1.7 oz.	16.3	5.9
Sausage McMuffin, 4.1 oz.	21.9	7.8
Sausage McMuffin, w/egg, 5.9 oz.	26.8	9.5
sandwiches and chicken, 1 serving:		
Big Mac, 7.6 oz.	32.4	10.1
cheeseburger, 4.1 oz.	13.8	5.2
Chicken McNuggets, 4 oz.	16.3	4.1
Filet-O-Fish, 5 oz.	26.1	5.2
hamburger, 3.6 oz.	9.5	3.6
McChicken, 6.7 oz.	28.6	5.4
McD.L.T., 8.3 oz.	36.8	11.5
McLean Deluxe, 7.3 oz.	10.0	4.0
McLean Deluxe (patty only), 3 oz.	7.0	3.0
McLean Deluxe, w/cheese, 7.7 oz.	14.0	5.0
Quarter Pounder, 5.9 oz.	20.7	8.1
Quarter Pounder, w/cheese, 6.8 oz.	29.2	11.2
Chicken McNuggets sauces:		
barbecue, 1 oz.	.5	.1
honey, 1.5 oz.	0	0
hot mustard, 1 oz.	3.6	.5
sweet and sour, 1 oz.	.2	tr.
french fries:		
small, 2.4 oz.	12.0	2.7
medium, 3.4 oz.	17.1	3.9
large, 4.3 oz.	21.6	5.0
salads, 1 serving:		
chef, 10 oz.	13.3	5.9
chunky chicken, 8.8 oz.	3.4	0.9
garden, 7.5 oz.	6.6	2.9
side salad, 4.1 oz.	3.3	1.5
dressings and condiments:		
bacon bits, .1 oz.	1.2	0
bleu cheese dressing, 1/5 pkg.	6.9	1.3
croutons, .4 oz.	2.2	.5
French dressing, reduced calorie, 1/4 pkg.	1.9	.3
peppercorn dressing, 1/5 pkg.	8.7	1.4
Thousand Island dressing, 1/5 pkg.	7.5	1.2
vinaigrette dressing, lite, 1/4 pkg.	.5	.1

desserts and shakes, 1 serving:

apple pie, 2.9 oz.	14.8	4.8
cookies, chocolaty chip, 2.3 oz.	15.6	5.0
cookies, *McDonaldland*, 2.3 oz.	9.2	1.9
shake, lowfat, chocolate	1.7	.8
shake, lowfat, strawberry or vanilla	1.3	.6
yogurt cone, vanilla, 3 oz.	.8	.4
yogurt sundae, hot caramel, 6.1 oz.	2.8	1.5
yogurt sundae, hot fudge, 6 oz.	3.2	2.4
yogurt sundae, strawberry, 6 oz.	1.1	.6

Meat, see specific listings

Meat, potted, canned:

(Hormel Food Product), 1 tbsp.	2.0	n.a.
(Libby's), 1.83 oz.	9.0	n.a.

Meat loaf dinner, frozen:

(Armour Classics), 11.25 oz.	17.0	n.a.
(Banquet), 11 oz.	27.0	n.a.
(Morton), 10 oz.	17.0	n.a.
(Swanson), 10.75 oz.	15.0	n.a.

Meat loaf entrée, frozen:

(Banquet Cookin' Bags), 4 oz.	14.0	n.a.
tomato sauce and *(Freezer Queen Family Suppers)*, 7 oz.	13.0	n.a.

Meat loaf entrée mix*, homestyle *(Lipton Microeasy)*, 1/4 pkg. 22.0 n.a.

"Meat" loaf entrée mix, vegetarian *(Natural Touch* Loaf Mix), 4 oz. 7.0 n.a.

Meat loaf seasoning mix:

(French's), 1/8 pkg.	0	0
(Lawry's Seasoning Blends), 1 pkg.	1.2	n.a.

Meat marinade mix *(French's)*, 1/8 pkg. 0 0

"Meatball," vegetarian, canned

(Worthington Non-Meat Balls), 3 pieces 6.0 n.a.

Meatball dinner, frozen, Swedish *(Armour Classics)*, 11.25 oz. 18.0 n.a.

Meatball entrée, frozen:

Italian style, w/noodles and peppers *(The Budget Gourmet)*, 10 oz. 12.0 n.a.

stew *(Lean Cuisine)*, 10 oz. 10.0 3.0

Swedish:

(Le Menu LightStyle), 8 oz. 8.0 n.a.

Meatball entrée, Swedish, continued

(*Swanson* Homestyle Recipe), 8.5 oz.	20.0	n.a.
in gravy (*Stouffer's*), 11 oz.	26.0	n.a.
w/noodles (*The Budget Gourmet*), 10 oz.	39.0	n.a.
sauce and (*Dining Lite*), 9 oz.	10.0	n.a.
Meatball seasoning mix (*French's*), 1/4 pkg.	0	0
Meatball stew, canned (*Dinty Moore*), 8 oz.	15.0	n.a.
Melon, see specific listings		
Melon balls (cantaloupe/honeydew), frozen, 1/2 cup	.2	tr.
Menudo, canned (*Old El Paso*), 1/2 can	52.0	21.0
Mesquite sauce, w/lime juice (*Lawry's*), 1/4 cup	.4	(0)
Mexican bean dip (*Hain*), 4 tbsp.	1.0	n.a.
Mexican dinner, frozen (see also specific listings):		
(*Swanson Hungry-Man*), 20.25 oz.	41.0	n.a.
fiesta (*Patio*), 12.25 oz.	20.0	n.a.
style (*Banquet*), 12 oz.	18.0	n.a.
style (*Morton*), 10 oz.	10.0	n.a.
style (*Patio*), 13.25 oz.	25.0	n.a.
style, combination (*Banquet*), 12 oz. . . .	17.0	n.a.
style, combination (*Swanson*), 14.25 oz.	18.0	n.a.
Mexican entrée, frozen (*Van de Kamp's*), 1/2 pkg.	10.0	n.a.
Milk, fluid, 8 fl. oz.:		
buttermilk, cultured	2.2	1.3
whole, 3.7% fat, producer	8.9	5.6
whole, 3.3% fat	8.2	5.1
whole, low sodium	8.4	5.3
lowfat 2%	4.7	2.9
lowfat 2%, protein fortified	4.9	3.0
lowfat, 1%	2.6	1.6
lowfat 1%, w/nonfat milk solids	2.4	1.5
lowfat 1%, protein fortified	2.9	1.8
skim	.4	.3
skim, w/nonfat milk solids or protein fortified	.6	.4
Milk, canned:		
condensed, sweetened, 8 fl. oz.	26.6	16.8

evaporated, lowfat *(Carnation)*, 4 fl. oz.	3.0	n.a.
evaporated, skim, 8 fl. oz.	.5	.3
evaporated, whole, 8 fl. oz.	19.1	11.6
evaporated, filled *(Pet/Dairymate)*, 4 fl. oz.	8.0	1.0
evaporated, imitation, filled *(Diehl)*, 4 fl. oz.	8.0	2.0
Milk, chocolate, dairy, 8 fl. oz.:		
8 fl. oz.	8.5	5.3
(Hershey's)	9.0	n.a.
lowfat 2% *(Borden* Dutch Brand)	5.0	n.a.
lowfat 2% *(Darigold)*	5.0	3.1
lowfat 2% *(Hershey's)*	5.0	n.a.
lowfat 1% *(Knudsen)*	3.0	n.a.
Milk, dry:		
buttermilk, sweet cream, 1 tbsp.	.4	.2
whole, 1 cup	34.2	21.4
nonfat, regular, 1 cup	.9	.6
nonfat, instant, 3.2-oz. envelope or 1 1/3 cup	.5	.3
nonfat, instant, calcium reduced, 1 oz.	.1	< .1
Milk, goat's, fluid, whole, 8 fl. oz.	10.1	6.5
Milk, malted:		
chocolate flavor *(Carnation)*, 3 heaping tsp.	.8	.5
original flavor *(Carnation)*, 3 heaping tsp.	1.8	1.0
Milk, sheep's, fluid, whole, 8 fl. oz.	17.2	11.3
Milk beverages, see specific flavors		
Milkfish, meat only, raw, 4 oz.	7.6	n.a.
Milkshake, frozen:		
chocolate *(MicroMagic)*, 11.5 fl. oz.	8.0	n.a.
strawberry *(MicroMagic)*, 11.5 fl. oz.	9.0	n.a.
vanilla *(MicroMagic)*, 11.5 fl. oz.	13.0	n.a.
Millet, cooked, 1 cup	2.4	.4
Miso:		
1 oz.	1.7	.2
1/2 cup	8.4	1.2
w/barley malt (mugi-koji), 1 oz.	1.2	n.a.
w/rice malt (kome-koji), sweet, 1 oz.	.9	n.a.
w/rice malt (kome-koji), dark yellow, 1 oz.	1.6	n.a.

Miso, continued

w/soybean malt (mame-koji), 1 oz.	3.9	n.a.
Molasses, all varieties	0	0
Monkfish, meat only, raw, 4 oz.	1.7	n.a.
Monosodium glutamate *(Tone's)*	0	0
Mortadella, beef and pork, 1 oz.	7.2	2.7
Mostaccioli entrée, frozen, and meat sauce		
(Banquet Family Entrees), 7 oz.	3.0	n.a.
Mothbean, boiled, 1/2 cup	.5	.1
Mother's loaf luncheon meat, pork, 1 oz.	6.3	2.3
Mousse, see specific listings		
Muffin, 1 piece, except as noted:		
apple *(Awrey's),* 2.5 oz.	10.0	2.0
apple streusel *(Awrey's* Grande), 4.2 oz.	13.0	2.0
banana nut *(Awrey's* Grande), 4.2 oz. . .	15.0	3.0
banana walnut or cinnamon apple		
(Hostess Breakfast Bake Shop Mini),		
5 pieces	16.0	2.0
blueberry *(Awrey's),* 2.5 oz.	8.0	1.0
blueberry *(Awrey's* Grande), 4.2 oz. . . .	14.0	2.0
blueberry *(Hostess Breakfast Bake Shop*		
Mini), 5 pieces	13.0	2.0
corn *(Awrey's),* 2.5 oz.	8.0	1.0
cranberry *(Awrey's),* 1.5 oz.	4.0	0
English:		
(Pepperidge Farm)	1.0	0
(Roman Meal Original)	1.8	n.a.
(Thomas')	1.3	n.a.
(Wonder)	1.0	n.a.
all varieties *(Hi Fiber)*	1.0	n.a.
all varieties *(Oatmeal Goodness)*	2.0	n.a.
cinnamon apple *(Pepperidge Farm)* . .	1.0	0
cinnamon chip *(Pepperidge Farm)* . . .	3.0	0
cinnamon raisin *(Pepperidge Farm)* . .	2.0	0
oat bran *(Thomas')*	1.2	n.a.
raisin *(Thomas')*	1.5	n.a.
rye *(Thomas')*	1.0	n.a.
sourdough *(Pepperidge Farm)*	1.0	0
wheat, honey *(Thomas')*	1.1	n.a.
oat bran:		
(Awrey's), 2.75 oz.	7.0	1.0

(Hostess Breakfast Bake Shop)	7.0	1.0
banana nut *(Hostess Breakfast Bake Shop)*	5.0	1.0
pineapple raisin *(Awrey's)*, 2.75 oz.	6.0	1.0
raisin *(Wonder Raisin Rounds)*	2.0	n.a.
raisin bran *(Awrey's)*, 2.5 oz.	7.0	1.0
raisin bran *(Awrey's Grande)*, 4.2 oz.	12.0	2.0
rice bran, raisin *(Health Valley Fancy Fruit Muffins)*	7.0	n.a.
sourdough *(Wonder)*	1.0	n.a.
Muffin, frozen or refrigerated:		
all varieties *(Weight Watchers)*, 2.5 oz.	5.0	1.0
apple oat bran *(Sara Lee)*, 1 piece	6.0	n.a.
apple spice, blueberry, chocolate chunk, or oat bran, frozen *(Sara Lee)*, 1 piece	8.0	n.a.
blueberry *(Sara Lee Free & Light)*, 1 piece	0	0
cheese streusel *(Sara Lee)*, 1 piece	11.0	n.a.
corn, golden, frozen *(Sara Lee)*, 1 piece	13.0	n.a.
English, refrigerated *(Roman Meal)*, 1/2 piece	.5	.1
English, honey nut and oat bran, refrigerated *(Roman Meal)*, 1/2 piece	1.3	.2
raisin bran, frozen *(Sara Lee)*, 2.5 oz.	7.0	n.a.
Muffin mix*, 1 piece:		
apple cinnamon *(Betty Crocker)*, 1/12 pkg.	4.0	1.0
apple cinnamon *(Martha White)*, 1/6 pkg.	3.0	n.a.
apple streusel, Dutch *(Betty Crocker Bake Shop)*, 1/12 pkg.	7.0	n.a.
applesauce or banana *(Robin Hood/Gold Medal Pouch)*, 1/6 pkg.	5.0	n.a.
banana nut *(Betty Crocker)*, 1/12 pkg.	5.0	1.0
blackberry *(Martha White)*, 1/6 pkg.	3.0	n.a.
blueberry:		
(Duncan Hines Bakery Style)	6.0	n.a.
(Martha White), 1/6 pkg.	3.0	n.a.
(Robin Hood/Gold Medal Pouch), 1/6 pkg.	6.0	n.a.
streusel *(Betty Crocker Bake Shop)*, 1/12 pkg.	8.0	n.a.
wild *(Betty Crocker)*, 1/12 pkg.	4.0	1.0

Muffin mix, continued

wild *(Duncan Hines)*	3.0	n.a.
bran *(Martha White)*, 1/6 pkg.	5.0	n.a.
bran and honey *(Duncan Hines)*	4.0	n.a.
bran and honey *(Duncan Hines* Bakery Style)	7.0	n.a.
caramel *(Robin Hood/Gold Medal* Pouch), 1/6 pkg.	5.0	n.a.
carrot nut *(Betty Crocker)*, 1/12 pkg.	5.0	1.0
chocolate chip *(Betty Crocker)*, 1/12 pkg.	6.0	2.0
cinnamon streusel *(Betty Crocker)*, 1/10 pkg.	9.0	2.0
cinnamon swirl *(Duncan Hines* Bakery Style)	7.0	n.a.
corn *(Dromedary)*	4.0	n.a.
corn *(Flako)*	3.3	.6
corn *(Robin Hood/Gold Medal* Pouch), 1/6 pkg.	2.0	n.a.
cranberry orange nut *(Duncan Hines* Bakery Style)	8.0	n.a.
honey bran *(Robin Hood/Gold Medal* Pouch), 1/6 pkg.	6.0	n.a.
oat *(Robin Hood/Gold Medal* Pouch), 1/6 pkg.	5.0	1.0
oat bran:		
(Betty Crocker), 1/8 pkg.	8.0	2.0
apple cinnamon *(Hain)*	3.0	n.a.
banana nut *(Hain)*	4.0	n.a.
raspberry spice *(Hain)*	3.0	n.a.
oatmeal raisin *(Betty Crocker)*, 1/12 pkg.	4.0	1.0
orangeberry *(Martha White)*, 1/6 pkg.	3.0	n.a.
pecan crunch *(Duncan Hines* Bakery Style)	11.0	n.a.
raspberry or strawberry *(Martha White)*, 1/6 pkg.	3.0	n.a.
strawberry crown *(Betty Crocker)*, 1/10 pkg.	5.0	2.0
Mulberry, fresh, 1/2 cup	.3	(0)
Mullet, striped, meat only:		
raw, 4 oz.	4.3	1.3
baked, broiled, or microwaved, 4 oz.	5.5	1.6

Mung bean long rice, dehydrated, 1/2 cup   < .1   tr.
Mushroom:
   fresh, raw, or canned, drained, pieces,
     1/2 cup 2   < .1
   fresh, boiled, drained, pieces, 1/2 cup 4   < .1
   frozen, whole *(Birds Eye* Deluxe), 2.6 oz.   0   0
   frozen, battered *(Stilwell Quick Krisp)*,
     2 oz.   8.0   n.a.
   Japanese honey *(Frieda* of California),
     1 oz.   < .1   (0)
   Oriental straw, canned *(Green Giant)*,
     2 oz.   0   0
   oyster *(Frieda* of California), 1 oz. 1   (0)
   shiitake, fresh, cooked, pieces, 1/2 cup   .2   < .1
   shiitake, dried, 1 oz. 3   .1
Mushroom gravy:
   canned, 1/4 cup . . . .   1.6   .2
   canned *(Franco-American)*, 2 oz. . . . . .   1.0   n.a.
   canned *(Heinz* HomeStyle), 2 oz. or
     1/4 cup . . . .   1.0   n.a.
   mix* *(French's)*, 1/4 cup . . . .   1.0   n.a.
   mix* *(McCormick/Schilling)*, 1/4 cup 5   n.a.
Mushroom and herb dip *(Breakstone's*
   Gourmet), 2 tbsp. 4.0   3.0
Mushroom sauce mix, 1-oz. pkt. . . . . . .   2.7   .4
Mussel, blue, meat only, boiled or steamed,
   4 oz. 5.1   1.0
Mustard, prepared:
   all varieties *(Gulden's)*, 1/4 oz.   0   0
   all varieties *(Kraft)*, 1 tbsp. 1.0   0
   Dijon *(French's)*, 1 tsp. . . . .   1.0   n.a.
   Dijon *(Grey Poupon)*, 1 tbsp. . . . .   1.0   n.a.
   English *(Life* All Natural), 1 tbsp. . . . .   2.0   n.a.
   w/horseradish or Medford *(French's)*,
     1 tbsp. . . . .   1.0   n.a.
   jalapeño *(Great Impressions)*, 2 tsp. 3   n.a.
   w/onion, spicy, or yellow *(French's)*, 1 tsp.   0   0
   yellow *(Heinz)*, 1 tsp. 2   (0)
Mustard greens:
   fresh, raw, trimmed, 1 oz. or 1/2 cup
     chopped 1   tr.

Mustard greens, continued

fresh, boiled, drained, chopped, 1/2 cup	.2	tr.
canned, chopped *(Allens)*, 1/2 cup	< 1.0	n.a.
frozen, boiled, drained, chopped, 1/2 cup	.2	< .1
Mustard powder *(Spice Islands)*, 1 tsp. . . .	.6	n.a.
Mustard seed, yellow, 1 tsp.	1.0	.1
Mustard spinach, raw or boiled, drained, chopped, 1/2 cup	.2	n.a.

food and measure	total fat (gms.)	saturated fat (gms.)
Nacho seasoning *(Lawry's* Seasoning Blends), 1 pkg.	6.8	n.a.
Natto, 1/2 cup	9.7	1.4
Nectarine, whole, 1 medium, 21/2″ diam.	.6	n.a.
New England Brand sausage:		
(Eckrich), 1 oz. or 1 slice	1.0	n.a.
(Light & Lean), 2 slices	6.0	n.a.
(Oscar Mayer), .8-oz. slice	1.3	.6
pork and beef, 1 oz.	2.2	.7

New Zealand spinach:

raw, trimmed, 1 oz. or 1/2 cup chopped	.1	tr.
boiled, drained, chopped, 1/2 cup	.2	< .1

Newberg sauce, w/sherry, canned *(Snow's),*

1/3 cup	8.0	n.a.

Noodle, egg:

plain, dry, 2 oz., or cooked, 1 cup	2.4	.5
spinach, cooked, 1 cup	2.5	.6

Noodle, Chinese:

cellophane or long rice, dehydrated, 2 oz.	< .1	tr.
chow mein, 1 cup	13.8	2.0

Noodle, Japanese:

soba (buckwheat), cooked, 1 cup	.1	< .1
somen (wheat), cooked, 1 cup	.3	< .1
udon (wheat), cooked, 4 oz.	.6	n.a.

Noodle dinner, and chicken, frozen:
(Banquet/Banquet Family Favorites),

10 oz.	15.0	n.a.
(Swanson), 10.5 oz.	8.0	n.a.

Noodle dishes, mix*, 1/2 cup, except as
noted:
Alfredo:

(Lipton Noodles and Sauce)	10.0	n.a.
(Minute Microwave Family Size)	6.0	n.a.
(Minute Microwave Single Size)	5.0	n.a.
(Mueller's Chef's Series)	9.0	n.a.
beef, w/butter *(Lipton* Noodles and		
Sauce)	7.0	n.a.
butter *(Lipton* Noodles and Sauce)	10.0	n.a.
butter and herb *(Lipton* Noodles and		
Sauce)	9.0	n.a.
carbonara Alfredo *(Lipton* Noodles and		
Sauce)	11.0	n.a.
cheese *(Kraft* Dinner), 3/4 cup	17.0	4.0
cheese, w/butter *(Lipton* Noodles and		
Sauce)	8.0	n.a.
chicken:		
(Kraft Dinner), 3/4 cup	9.0	2.0
(Lipton Noodles and Sauce)	8.0	n.a.
(Minute Microwave Family Size)	5.0	n.a.
(Minute Microwave Single Size)	4.0	n.a.

(Mueller's Chef's Series)	8.0	n.a.
broccoli *(Lipton* Noodles and Sauce)	9.0	n.a.
mushroom *(Golden Grain/Noodle Roni)*, 1.2 oz. dry	2.4	.6
fettuccini *(Golden Grain/Noodle Roni)*, 1.5 oz. dry	5.1	1.5
garlic and butter *(Mueller's Chef's Series)*	7.0	n.a.
garlic, creamy *(Golden Grain/Noodle Roni)*, 1.5 oz. dry	4.2	1.5
herb and butter *(Golden Grain/Noodle Roni)*, 1 oz. dry.	2.7	.8
Parmesan:		
(Lipton Noodles and Sauce)	11.0	n.a.
(Minute Microwave Family Size)	6.0	n.a.
(Minute Microwave Single Size)	5.0	n.a.
(Golden Grain/Noodle Roni), 1.2 oz. dry	2.9	.9
Romanoff *(Golden Grain/Noodle Roni)*, 1.5 oz. dry	4.1	1.6
sour cream and chive *(Lipton* Noodles and Sauce).	9.0	n.a.
sour cream and chive *(Mueller's Chef's Series)*	8.0	n.a.
Stroganoff *(Golden Grain/Noodle Roni)*, 2 oz. dry	6.4	2.2
Stroganoff *(Lipton* Noodles and Sauce)	9.0	n.a.
Stroganoff *(Mueller's Chef's Series)*	9.0	n.a.
Noodle entrée, canned:		
w/chicken *(Hormel/Dinty Moore Micro-Cup)*, 7.5 oz.	8.0	n.a.
w/chicken, all varieties *(Nalley's)*, 7³/8 oz.	5.0	n.a.
w/franks *(Van Camp's Noodle Weenee)*, 1 cup	8.5	n.a.
Noodle entrée, frozen:		
w/beef, gravy *(Banquet Family Entrees)*, 8 oz.	7.0	n.a.
and julienne beef, w/sauce *(Banquet Family Entrees)*, 7 oz.	3.0	n.a.
Romanoff *(Stouffer's)*, 1/3 of 12-oz. pkg.	9.0	n.a.
Nutmeg, ground, 1 tsp.	.8	.6
Nuts, see specific listings		

Nuts, mixed, 1 oz.:

dry roasted, w/peanuts	14.6	2.0
oil roasted, w/peanuts	16.0	2.5
oil roasted, w/out peanuts	16.0	2.6

food and measure	total fat (gms.)	saturated fat (gms.)
Oat (see also "Cereal"):		
whole grain, 1 cup	10.8	1.9
rolled or oatmeal, dry, 1 cup	5.1	.9
rolled or oatmeal, cooked, 1 cup	2.4	.4
Oat bran (see also "Cereal"):		
raw, 1 cup	6.6	1.2
cooked, 1 cup	1.9	.4
Oat bran pilaf dinner, canned, w/garden vegetables *(Health Valley Fast Menu),* 7.5 oz.	7.0	n.a.

Oat groats *(Arrowhead Mills)*, 2 oz. . . . . .   4.0   n.a.
Ocean perch, meat only:
  Atlantic, raw, 4 oz. . . . .   1.8   .3
  Atlantic, baked, broiled, or microwaved,
    4 oz.   2.4   .4
Ocean perch entrée, frozen:
  breaded *(Mrs. Paul's* Crispy Crunchy),
    2 pieces 20.0   4.0
  breaded *(Van de Kamp's* Light), 1 piece   14.0   3.0
Octopus, meat only, raw, 4 oz. . . . .   1.8   .3
Oil, 1 tbsp., except as noted:
  almond 13.6   1.1
  apricot kernel *(Hain)* 14.0   1.0
  avocado 14.0   1.6
  butter 12.7   7.9
  canola 14.0   1.0
  cocoa butter 13.6   8.1
  coconut 13.6   11.8
  cod liver, see "Cod liver oil"
  corn 13.6   1.7
  corn, spray *(Mazola* No Stick), 2.5-second
    spray . . . .   1.0   .1
  cottonseed 13.6   3.5
  hazelnut 13.6   1.0
  mustard 14.0   1.6
  nutmeg butter 13.6   12.2
  olive 13.5   1.8
  palm 13.6   6.7
  palm kernel 13.6   11.1
  peanut 13.5   2.3
  poppyseed 13.6   1.8
  rice bran 13.6   2.7
  safflower, linoleic 13.6   1.2
  safflower, oleic . . . .   13.6   .8
  sesame 13.6   1.9
  soybean 13.6   2.0
  soybean and cottonseed, hydrogenated . .   13.6   2.4
  soybean lecithin 13.6   2.1
  sunflower, linoleic 13.6   1.4
  sunflower, hydrogenated 13.6   1.8

vegetable:
(Crisco)	14.0	2.0
(Crisco Puritan)	14.0	1.0
(Hain All Blend)	14.0	2.0
(Wesson)	14.0	2.1
w/garlic (Hain Garlic & Oil)	14.0	3.0
walnut (Hain)	14.0	2.0

Okra:
fresh, raw, or boiled, drained, sliced, 1/2 cup	.1	< .1
fresh, boiled, drained, 8 pods, 3″ × 5/8″	.1	< .1
frozen, boiled, drained, sliced, 1/2 cup	.3	.1

Old-fashioned drink mix, bottled (Holland
House)	0	0

Old-fashioned loaf (Oscar Mayer), 1-oz.
slice	4.0	1.6

Olive:
green:
10 small, select or standard	3.6	n.a.
10 large	4.9	n.a.
10 giant	8.3	n.a.
pitted, 1 oz.	3.6	n.a.

ripe, Manzanillo or Mission varieties, pitted:
all sizes, 1 oz.	3.0	.4
(Lindsay), 10 small	3.5	.6
(Lindsay), 10 medium	4.1	.7
(Lindsay), 10 large	4.8	.8
(Lindsay), 10 extra large	5.9	1.1

ripe, mixed varieties, pitted:
sliced or chopped (Lindsay), 1 oz.	2.7	.5
sliced (Lindsay), 1/2 cup	6.5	1.1

ripe, Sevillano and Ascolano varieties, pitted:
all sizes, 1 oz.	1.9	.3
(Lindsay), 10 jumbo	5.7	1.0
(Lindsay), 10 colossal	7.7	1.3
(Lindsay), 10 super colossal	10.4	1.8
salad (Progresso), 1/2 cup	15.0	2.0

salt-cured, oil-coated, Greek style:
pitted, 1 oz.	10.2	n.a.

Olive, salt-cured, continued

10 medium, approx. .8 oz. w/pits	6.9	n.a.
10 extra large, approx. 1.2 oz. w/pits	9.5	n.a.
Olive appetizer:		
(Progresso), 1/2 cup	21.0	3.0
(Progresso Condite), 1/2 cup	14.0	2.0
Olive loaf:		
(Eckrich), 1-oz. slice	6.0	n.a.
(Hormel Perma-Fresh), 2 slices . . .	7.0	n.a.
(Oscar Mayer), 1-oz. slice	4.3	1.5
pork, 1-oz. slice, 4″ × 4″ × 3/32″	4.7	1.7
Onion, mature:		
fresh, raw or canned, chopped, 1/2 cup . .	.1	< .1
fresh, boiled, drained, chopped, 1/2 cup. .	.2	< .1
canned, cocktail, spiced *(Vlasic)*, 1 oz. . . .	0	0
canned, sweet *(Heinz)*, 1 oz.	0	0
dried, flakes, 1/4 cup	.1	< .1
dried, minced, w/green onion *(Lawry's)*, 1 tsp.	.2	(0)
frozen, whole, or chopped, boiled, drained, 4 oz. or 1/2 cup	.1	< .1
frozen, small, w/cream sauce *(Birds Eye* Combinations), 5 oz.	10.0	n.a.
Onion, green (scallion), w/top, chopped, 1/2 cup	.1	< .1
Onion, Welsh, fresh, trimmed, 1 oz.	.1	< .1
Onion dip:		
all varieties *(Kraft/Kraft* Premium), 2 tbsp.	4.0	2.0
bean *(Hain)*, 4 tbsp.	1.0	n.a.
French *(Breakstone's/Sealtest)*, 2 tbsp.	5.0	3.0
French *(Nasoya Vegi-Dip)*, 1 oz.	3.0	n.a.
toasted *(Breakstone's* Gourmet), 2 tbsp.	5.0	3.0
Onion-flavored snack:		
(Funyuns), 1 oz.	6.0	n.a.
rings *(Wise)*, 1 oz.	5.0	n.a.
Onion gravy mix*:		
(French's), 1/4 cup	1.0	n.a.
(McCormick/Schilling), 1/4 cup	.6	n.a.
Onion powder *(Spice Islands)*, 1 tsp.	< .1	tr.

Onion ring, frozen:
(Ore-Ida Onion Ringers), 2 oz.	7.0	3.0
battered (Stilwell), 3 oz.	16.0	n.a.
battered (Farm Rich Batter Dipt), 4 oz.	13.0	n.a.
crispy (Farm Rich Onion O's), 5 rings	9.0	n.a.
crispy (Mrs. Paul's), 2.5 oz.	12.0	n.a.
Onion ring batter mix (Golden Dipt), 1 oz.	0	0
Onion salt (Tone's), 1 tsp.	tr.	tr.

Orange:
California navel, 1 medium, 2⅞″ diam.	.1	< .1
California Valencia, 1 medium,		
2⅝″ diam.	.4	< .1
Florida, 1 medium, 2¹¹/₁₆″ diam.	.3	< .1
Mandarin, see "Tangerine"		

Orange danish, refrigerated, w/icing
(Pillsbury), 1 piece	7.0	2.0
Orange drink, all blends, 6 fl. oz.	< .1	(0)
Orange extract (Virginia Dare), 1 tsp. . . .	0	0

Orange juice or juice drink, all blends,
6 fl. oz.	<2.0	< .1
Orange sauce, Mandarin (La Choy), 1 tbsp.	tr.	0
Oregano, dried, ground (Tone's), 1 tsp.	.2	< .1
Oriental 5-spice (Tone), 1 tsp.	.3	< .1

Oyster, meat only:
fresh, Eastern:
raw, 4 oz.	2.8	.7
raw, 6 medium, 70 per qt.	2.1	.5
boiled, poached, or steamed, 4 oz. . . .	5.6	1.4
boiled, poached, or steamed, 6 medium	2.1	.5
fresh, Pacific, raw, 4 oz.	2.6	.6
fresh, Pacific, raw, 1 medium, 20 per qt.	1.2	.3
canned (Bumble Bee), 1 cup	5.3	n.a.
canned, Eastern, w/liquid, 1 cup	6.1	1.6
canned, whole (S&W Fancy), 2 oz.	3.0	n.a.

food and measure	total fat (gms.)	saturated fat (gms.)
P&B loaf:		
(JM), 1-oz. slice	5.0	n.a.
(Kahn's), 1 slice	2.0	n.a.
Pancake, frozen:		
(Aunt Jemima Original Microwave),		
3.5 oz.	3.6	n.a.
all varieties *(Downyflake)*, 3 pieces	9.0	n.a.
all varieties *(Pillsbury* Microwave),		
3 pieces	4.0	n.a.

blueberry *(Aunt Jemima* Microwave),		
3.5 oz.	3.7	.7
buttermilk *(Aunt Jemima* Microwave),		
3.5 oz.	3.0	.7
buttermilk *(Aunt Jemima* Lite		
Microwave), 3.5 oz.	3.0	n.a.
buttermilk *(Weight Watchers* Microwave),		
2.5 oz.	3.0	1.0
Pancake batter, frozen:		
(Aunt Jemima Original), 3.6 oz.	2.4	.6
blueberry *(Aunt Jemima),* 3.6 oz.	4.0	.7
buttermilk *(Aunt Jemima),* 3.6 oz.	2.3	.7
Pancake breakfast, frozen:		
w/blueberry or strawberry topping		
(Weight Watchers Microwave), 4.75 oz.	3.0	1.0
w/lite links *(Aunt Jemima* Lite), 6 oz.	10.0	n.a.
w/links *(Weight Watchers* Microwave),		
4 oz.	10.0	4.0
and sausages *(Aunt Jemima),* 6 oz.	16.0	n.a.
and sausages *(Downyflake),* 5.5 oz.	23.0	n.a.
and sausages *(Swanson Great Starts),*		
6 oz.	22.0	n.a.
w/syrup *(Aunt Jemima* Lite), 6 oz.	3.0	n.a.
Pancake and waffle mix*, 3 pieces, 4″ each,		
except as noted:		
(Aunt Jemima Original)	.8	.1
(Aunt Jemima Original Complete)	3.6	.8
(Bisquick Shake'N Pour Complete Waffle		
Mix), 2 pieces	6.0	n.a.
(Hungry Jack Extra Lights)	7.0	n.a.
(Hungry Jack Extra Lights Complete)	2.0	n.a.
(Hungry Jack Panshakes)	6.0	n.a.
(Martha White FlapStax), 1 piece	2.0	n.a.
(Martha White Light Crust), 2 oz. dry	3.0	n.a.
(Robin Hood/Gold Medal Pouch),		
1/8 pouch	2.0	n.a.
all varieties, except oat bran and waffle		
mix *(Bisquick Shake'N Pour)*	5.0	n.a.
blueberry *(Hungry Jack)*	15.0	n.a.
buckwheat *(Aunt Jemima)*	1.6	.2
buttermilk *(Aunt Jemima)*	.7	.1

Pancake and waffle mix, continued

buttermilk *(Aunt Jemima Complete)* . . .	2.8	.7
buttermilk *(Aunt Jemima Lite Complete)*	2.0	n.a.
buttermilk *(Betty Crocker)*	10.0	n.a.
buttermilk *(Hungry Jack)*	11.0	n.a.
buttermilk *(Hungry Jack Complete)* . . .	1.0	n.a.
buttermilk *(Hungry Jack Complete Packets)*	3.0	n.a.
multigrain *(Arrowhead Mills),* 1/2 cup	2.0	n.a.
oat bran *(Bisquick Shake'N Pour)*	4.0	n.a.
whole wheat *(Aunt Jemima)*	1.0	.2
Pancake syrup, all table blends	0	0
Pancreas, braised:		
beef, 4 oz.	19.5	n.a.
lamb, 4 oz.	17.1	7.8
pork, 4 oz.	12.2	n.a.
veal, 4 oz.	16.6	n.a.
Papaya, whole, 1 lb., or 1 medium, 31/2″ × 51/8″	.4	.1
Papaya nectar, canned, 6 fl. oz.	.3	.1
Papaya punch *(Veryfine)*	0	0
Paprika, 1 tsp.	.3	< .1
Parsley:		
fresh, chopped, 1/2 cup	.1	(0)
dried or freeze-dried, 1 tbsp.	< .1	(0)
Parsley seasoning, all purpose *(McCormick/ Schilling Parsley Patch)*	0	0
Parsnip:		
raw or boiled, drained, sliced, 1/2 cup	.2	< .1
boiled, drained, 1 medium, 9″ × 21/4″ diam.	.5	.1
Passion fruit, purple, whole, 1 medium, 1.2 oz.	.1	(0)
Passion fruit juice, fresh:		
purple, 6 fl. oz.	.1	(0)
yellow, 6 fl. oz.	.3	(0)
Passion fruit juice cocktail or drink, all blends	0	0
Pasta, dry, 2 oz., uncooked, except as noted:		
plain, 2 oz. dry or 1 cup cooked	.9	.1

all varieties, except whole-wheat *(Al Dente)*	2.0	n.a.
all varieties *(Antoine's)*	1.0	n.a.
all varieties *(Health Valley)*	1.0	n.a.
corn	1.2	.2
corn, cooked, 1 cup	1.0	.1
corn, wheat-free *(De Boles)*	2.0	n.a.
garlic and parsley, Jerusalem artichoke, or spinach *(De Boles)*	1.0	n.a.
spinach, cooked, 1 cup	.9	.1
spinach, w/egg *(Creamette)*	3.0	n.a.
tomato and basil or tri-color *(De Boles)*	1.0	n.a.
tri-color *(Creamette)*	1.0	0
whole wheat *(Al Dente* Fettuccine)	1.0	n.a.
whole wheat *(De Boles* Natural Gourmet)	< 1.0	n.a.
whole wheat, w/bran *(Misura)*	1.0	n.a.
whole wheat, cooked, 1 cup	.6	.1
Pasta, fresh-refrigerated:		
w/egg, cooked, 4 oz.	1.2	.2
spinach, w/egg, cooked, 4 oz.	1.1	.2
Pasta dinner, see specific listings		
Pasta dishes, canned, 7.5 oz., except as noted:		
in cheese-flavored sauce *(Chef Boyardee* ABC's/123's/Dinosaurs Microwave)	1.0	< 1.0
garden medley *(Lipton Hearty Ones),* 11 oz.	3.8	n.a.
Italiano *(Lipton Hearty Ones),* 11 oz.	1.9	n.a.
w/meatballs *(Chef Boyardee* Dinosaurs Microwave)	9.0	3.0
w/meatballs *(Chef Boyardee* Tic Tac Toes Microwave)	10.0	3.0
w/mini meatballs *(Chef Boyardee* ABC's/ 123's Microwave)	11.0	4.0
rings or twists, in sauce *(Buitoni)*	4.0	1.0
rings or twists w/meatballs, in sauce *(Buitoni)*	7.0	5.0
shells, in meat sauce *(Chef Boyardee* Microwave)	6.0	n.a.
shells, in mushroom sauce *(Chef Boyardee* Microwave)	1.0	< 1.0

Pasta dishes, frozen (see also "Pasta entrée"):

Alfredo, w/broccoli *(The Budget Gourmet Side Dish)*, 5.5 oz.	8.0	n.a.
creamy cheddar, garlic, or primavera *(Green Giant Pasta Accents)*, 1/2 cup	5.0	2.0
Dijon *(Green Giant* Garden Gourmet), 1 pkg.	17.0	9.0
garden herb *(Green Giant Pasta Accents)*, 1/2 cup	3.0	< 1.0
Florentine *(Green Giant* Garden Gourmet), 1 pkg.	9.0	5.0
marinara *(Green Giant* One Serving), 5.5 oz.	5.0	< 1.0
Parmesan, w/sweet peas *(Green Giant* One Serving), 5.5 oz.	5.0	2.0
and vegetables, w/out added ingredients:		
in creamy Stroganoff sauce *(Birds Eye Custom Cuisine)*, 4.6 oz.	5.0	n.a.
w/white cheese sauce *(Birds Eye Custom Cuisine)*, 4.6 oz.	6.0	n.a.

Pasta dishes, mix*, 1/2 cup, except as noted:

(Kraft Light Rancher's Choice Pasta Salad)	7.0	1.0
Alfredo *(McCormick/Schilling Pasta Prima)*	13.0	n.a.
w/bacon *(Kraft Rancher's Choice* Pasta Salad)	16.0	3.0
bacon vinaigrette *(Country Recipe* Pasta Salad)	4.0	n.a.
broccoli, cheddar, w/fusilli *(Lipton* Pasta & Sauce)	9.0	n.a.
broccoli, creamy *(Lipton* Pasta Salad)	10.0	n.a.
broccoli and vegetables *(Kraft* Pasta Salad)	16.0	2.0
buttermilk, country *(Mueller's* Salad Bar)	16.0	n.a.
carbonara Alfredo *(Lipton* Pasta and Sauce)	4.2	n.a.
cheese:		
cheddar *(Minute* Microwave Family Size)	7.0	n.a.

cheddar *(Minute* Microwave Single Size)	6.0	n.a.
cheddar, tangy *(Hain* Pasta & Sauce), 1/4 pkg.	6.0	n.a.
cheddar broccoli *(Kraft* Pasta & Cheese)	8.0	3.0
supreme *(Lipton* Pasta and Sauce) . . .	2.3	n.a.
three, w/vegetables *(Kraft* Pasta & Cheese)	8.0	3.0
chicken broccoli *(Lipton* Pasta and Sauce)	2.0	n.a.
chicken w/herbs *(Kraft* Pasta and Cheese)	7.0	2.0
cucumber, creamy *(Mueller's* Salad Bar)	16.0	n.a.
Dijon, creamy *(Country Recipe* Pasta Salad)	10.0	n.a.
fettuccine Alfredo *(Hain* Pasta & Sauce), 1/4 pkg.	4.0	n.a.
fettuccine Alfredo *(Kraft* Pasta & Cheese).	9.0	3.0
garlic, creamy *(Lipton* Pasta & Sauce)	10.0	n.a.
garlic, creamy *(McCormick/Schilling Pasta Prima),* 1 pkg. dry	5.3	n.a.
herb, Italian *(Hain* Pasta & Sauce), 1/5 pkg.	2.0	n.a.
herb, Italian, w/oil *(Fantastic* Pasta Salad)	9.0	n.a.
herb and garlic *(McCormick/Schilling Pasta Prima)*	12.0	n.a.
herb tomato *(Lipton* Pasta & Sauce) . . .	7.0	n.a.
homestyle *(Kraft* Pasta Salad)	16.0	2.0
homestyle *(Mueller's* Salad Bar)	16.0	n.a.
Italian:		
(Kraft Light Pasta Salad)	3.0	1.0
creamy *(Country Recipe* Pasta Salad)	7.0	n.a.
creamy *(Mueller's* Salad Bar)	22.0	n.a.
robust *(Lipton* Pasta Salad)	8.0	n.a.
zesty *(Mueller's* Salad Bar)	5.0	n.a.
marinara *(McCormick/Schilling Pasta Prima)*	8.0	n.a.
mushroom, creamy *(Lipton* Pasta & Sauce)	9.0	n.a.
mushroom and chicken flavors *(Lipton* Pasta and Sauce)	.8	n.a.

Pasta dishes, mix, continued

Oriental, w/fusilli *(Lipton* Pasta and Sauce)	.7	n.a.
Oriental, spicy *(Fantastic* Pasta Salad)	10.0	n.a.
Parmesan *(Kraft* Pasta & Cheese)	8.0	2.0
Parmesan, creamy *(Hain* Pasta & Sauce), 1/4 pkg.	3.0	n.a.
pasta salad *(McCormick/Schilling Pasta Prima)*	23.0	n.a.
pesto *(McCormick/Schilling Pasta Prima)*	6.0	n.a.
primavera *(Hain* Pasta & Sauce), 1/4 pkg.	4.0	n.a.
primavera, garden *(Kraft* Pasta Salad)	7.0	2.0
ranch *(Country Recipe* Pasta Salad) . . .	5.0	n.a.
seafood, creamy *(McCormick/Schilling Pasta Prima)*, 1 pkg. dry	1.8	n.a.
sour cream w/chives *(Kraft* Pasta & Cheese).	8.0	2.0
Swiss, creamy *(Hain* Pasta & Sauce), 1/5 pkg.	4.0	n.a.
Pasta entrée, frozen (see also "Pasta dishes" and specific listings):		
angel hair *(Weight Watchers)*, 10 oz. . . .	5.0	1.0
baked, and cheese *(Celentano)*, 6 oz. . . .	13.0	n.a.
carbonara *(Stouffer's)*, 9.75 oz.	45.0	n.a.
casino *(Stouffer's)*, 9.25 oz.	10.0	n.a.
Dijon *(Green Giant* Microwave Garden Gourmet), 1 pkg.	20.0	n.a.
Mexicali *(Stouffer's)*, 10-oz. pkg.	31.0	n.a.
Oriental *(Stouffer's)*, 97/8-oz. pkg.	14.0	n.a.
primavera *(Stouffer's)*, 105/8-oz. pkg. . . .	42.0	n.a.
primavera *(Weight Watchers)*, 8.5 oz. . . .	11.0	< 1.0
rigati *(Weight Watchers)*, 10.63 oz.	9.0	2.0
shells, and beef *(The Budget Gourmet)*, 10 oz.	14.0	n.a.
shells, cheese, w/tomato sauce *(Stouffer's)*, 9.25 oz.	15.0	n.a.
shells, stuffed:		
(Buitoni Single Serving), 9 oz.	13.0	7.0
(Celentano), 8 oz.	11.0	n.a.
w/sauce *(Celentano)*, 10 oz.	14.0	n.a.
w/sauce *(Celentano)*, 6.25 oz.	16.0	n.a.

trio *(Tyson Gourmet Selection)*, 11 oz.	17.0	n.a.
Pasta sauce (see also "Tomato sauce" and specific listings):		
(Prego), 4 oz.	5.0	n.a.
(Ragu), 4 oz.	4.0	n.a.
(Ragu Chunky Garden or Italian Style), 4 oz.	3.0	n.a.
(Ragu Homestyle), 4 oz.	2.0	n.a.
(Ragu Thick & Hearty), 4 oz.	3.0	n.a.
all varieties *(Enrico's)*, 4 oz.	1.0	n.a.
all varieties *(Progresso* Spaghetti Sauce), 1/2 cup	5.0	1.0
cheese, three *(Prego)*, 4 oz.	2.0	n.a.
garden combination *(Prego* Extra Chunky), 4 oz.	2.0	n.a.
marinara or meat *(Prego)*, 4 oz.	6.0	n.a.
marinara *(Progresso* Authentic Pasta Sauces), 1/2 cup	6.0	1.5
meat, mushroom, or traditional *(Hunt's)*, 4 oz.	2.0	n.a.
meatless *(Chef Boyardee* Jars), 4 oz.	1.0	n.a.
mushroom or mushroom-tomato *(Prego)*, 4 oz.	5.0	n.a.
mushroom-green pepper or mushroom-onion *(Prego* Extra Chunky), 4 oz.	4.0	n.a.
mushroom-spice *(Prego* Extra Chunky), 4 oz.	3.0	n.a.
onion-garlic *(Prego)*, 4 oz.	4.0	n.a.
primavera, creamy *(Progresso* Authentic Pasta Sauces), 1/2 cup	17.0	10.0
sausage-green pepper *(Prego* Extra Chunky), 4 oz.	8.0	n.a.
Sicilian *(Progresso* Authentic Pasta Sauces), 1/2 cup	2.5	< 1.0
tomato-basil *(Prego)*, 4 oz.	2.0	n.a.
tomato-onion *(Prego* Extra Chunky), 4 oz.	5.0	n.a.
Pasta sauce mix:		
(Lawry's Rich & Thick), 1 pkg.	2.2	n.a.
(McCormick/Schilling Spaghetti Sauce), 1/4 pkg.	.3	n.a.

Pasta sauce mix, continued

all varieties *(French's Pasta Toss)*, 2 tsp.	2.0	n.a.
Italian style or mushroom *(French's)*,		
⁵/8 cup*	4.0	n.a.
w/imported mushrooms *(Lawry's)*, 1 pkg.	1.5	n.a.
Pasta snack chip *(Bachman Pastapazazz)*,		
1 oz.	9.0	n.a.
Pastrami:		
(Healthy Deli Round), 1 oz.	1.1	n.a.
(Hillshire Farm Deli Select), 1 oz.	.4	n.a.
(Oscar Mayer), .6-oz. slice	.3	.2
beef, 1-oz. slice	8.3	3.0
turkey, see "Turkey pastrami"		
Pastry pocket, refrigerated *(Pillsbury)*,		
1 piece	13.0	3.0
Pastry shells, see "Pie crust shell" and		
"Puff pastry"		
Pâté, canned:		
1 oz.	7.9	n.a.
1 tbsp.	3.6	n.a.
(Sells Liver Pâté), 2¹/8 oz.	16.0	n.a.
chicken liver, 1 oz.	3.7	n.a.
chicken liver, 1 tbsp.	1.7	n.a.
goose liver, smoked, 1 oz.	12.4	n.a.
goose liver, smoked, 1 tbsp.	5.7	n.a.
Peach, 1/2 cup, except as noted:		
fresh, 1 medium, 2¹/2″ diam.	.1	tr.
fresh, peeled, sliced, or canned in water	.1	tr.
canned, in extra light or heavy syrup, or		
spiced	.1	< .1
dehydrated, sulfured, uncooked	.6	.1
dried, sulfured, uncooked, 10 halves . . .	1.0	.1
frozen, sliced, sweetened	.2	< .1
Peach butter *(Smucker's)*	0	0
Peach cobbler, frozen:		
(Pet-Ritz), 1/6 pkg. or 4.33 oz.	10.0	n.a.
(Stilwell), 4 oz.	5.0	n.a.
Peach drink *(Hi-C)*, 6 fl. oz.	< .1	(0)
Peach juice, all blends (all brands), 6 fl. oz.	< .1	(0)
Peach nectar, canned, 6 fl. oz.	< .1	< .1

Peach turnover, frozen *(Pepperidge Farm)*,
1 piece . . . . 18.0   n.a.
Peanut, 1 oz.:
all varieties, raw, shelled 13.8   1.9
all varieties, dry roasted 13.9   1.9
all varieties, oil roasted 13.8   1.9
cocktail, oil roasted *(Planters)* 15.0   3.0
honey roasted *(Planters)* 13.0   2.0
oil roasted *(Planters)* 15.0   3.0
redskin, oil roasted *(Planters)* 15.0   5.0
Spanish, dry roasted *(Planters)* 14.0   3.0
Spanish, oil roasted 13.7   2.1
Valencia, oil roasted 14.4   2.2
Virginia, oil roasted 13.6   1.8
Peanut butter, 2 tbsp.:
chunk or creamy *(Jif)* 16.0   3.0
chunk or creamy *(Peter Pan)* 16.0   2.0
chunk or creamy *(Skippy)* 17.0   3.0
chunk or creamy *(Smucker's)* 16.0   1.0
creamy *(Smucker's* No Salt Added
Natural) 17.0   1.0
Peanut butter flavor baking chips *(Reese's)*,
1.5 oz. or 1/4 cup . . . . 13.0   n.a.
Pear, 1/2 cup, except as noted:
fresh, w/skin, sliced 3   < .1
fresh, 1 Bartlett, 2 1/2″ diam. × 3 1/2″ 7   < .1
canned, halves, in juice or extra light
syrup 1   tr.
canned, halves, in heavy or extra heavy
syrup 2   tr.
dried, sulfured, uncooked, halves 6   < .1
Pear nectar, canned, 6 fl. oz. . . . .   < .1   < .1
Peas, blackeye, see "Black-eyed pea" and
"Cowpea"
Peas, cream, canned *(Allens Fresh)*, 1/2 cup < 1.0   n.a.
Peas, crowder:
canned *(Allens Fresh)*, 1/2 cup . . . . < 1.0   n.a.
frozen *(Seabrook)*, 3 oz. . . . . 1.0   n.a.
Peas, edible-podded:
fresh, raw, trimmed, 1/2 cup 1   < .1
fresh, boiled, drained, 1/2 cup 2   < .1

Peas, edible-podded, continued
  frozen:
    boiled, drained, 1/2 cup 3   .1
    Chinese *(Chun King)*   0   0
    snow or sugar snap *(Birds Eye* Deluxe)   0   0
    sugar snap, w/baby carrots and water
      chestnuts *(Birds Eye* Farm Fresh)   0   0
Peas, field, canned, all varieties *(Allens*
  Fresh),* 1/2 cup . . . .   < 1.0   n.a.
Peas, green or sweet, 1/2 cup, except as
  noted:
    fresh, raw, shelled or canned, drained   .3   .1
    fresh or frozen, boiled, drained, w/out
      sauce 2   < .1
    frozen, in butter sauce:
      early *(Green Giant* One Serving),
        4.5 oz. . . . .   2.0   < 1.0
      early *(LeSueur)* . . . .   2.0   < 1.0
      sweet *(Green Giant)* . . . .   2.0   < 1.0
      sweet *(Stokely Singles),* 4 oz. . . . . .   1.0   n.a.
    frozen, w/cream sauce *(Birds Eye*
      Combinations),* 5 oz. . . . .   11.0   n.a.
Peas, green, combinations, frozen:
    and carrots, see "Peas and carrots"
    and cauliflower, in cream sauce *(The*
      Budget Gourmet Side Dish), 5.75 oz.   7.0   n.a.
    LeSueur style *(Green Giant Valley*
      Combination), 1/2 cup . . . .   2.0   n.a.
    mini, w/pea pods and water chestnuts,
      butter sauce *(LeSueur),* 1/2 cup . . . . .   2.0   n.a.
    and onions, see "Peas and onions"
    w/onions and carrots, in butter sauce
      (LeSueur), 1/2 cup . . . .   3.0   n.a.
    and potatoes, w/cream sauce *(Birds Eye*
      Combinations),* 5 oz. . . . .   12.0   n.a.
    and water chestnuts Oriental *(The Budget*
      Gourmet Side Dish), 5 oz. . . . .   3.0   n.a.
Peas, purple hull:
    canned *(Allens* Fresh),* 1/2 cup . . . . < 1.0   (0)
    frozen *(Frosty Acres),* 3.3 oz.   0   0

Peas, sprouted, mature seeds:

raw, 1/2 cup	.4	.1
boiled, drained, 4 oz.	.6	.1

Peas, white acre, canned, fresh *(Allens),*

1/2 cup	< 1.0	(0)

Peas and carrots:

canned, w/liquid, 1/2 cup	.4	.1
frozen, boiled, drained, 1/2 cup	.3	.1

Peas and onions:

canned or frozen, 1/2 cup	.2	< .1
frozen, pearl onions, w/cheese sauce *(Birds Eye* Combinations), 5 oz.	5.0	n.a.

Pecan, shelled:

dried, 1 oz.	19.2	1.5
dried, halves, 1 cup	73.1	5.9
dry roasted, 1 oz.	18.4	1.5
oil roasted, 1 oz.	20.2	1.6

Pepper, ground:

black, 1 tsp.	.1	< .1
chili *(Spice Islands),* 1 tsp.	.3	(0)
red or cayenne, 1 tsp.	.3	.1
white, 1 tsp.	.1	(0)
seasoned *(Lawry's),* 1 tsp.	.1	(0)

Pepper, cherry:

hot *(Progresso),* 1/2 cup	20.0	3.0
hot, pickled *(Progresso),* 1/2 cup	12.0	2.0
mild *(Vlasic),* 1 oz.	0	0

Pepper, chili, hot, green and red:

raw, 1 medium, 1.6 oz.	.1	tr.
raw, chopped, 1/2 cup	.2	< .1
canned, seeded, chopped, 1/2 cup	.1	tr.
canned *(Old El Paso),* 2 tbsp. or 1 whole chili	< 1.0	n.a.

Pepper, green and red, sweet:

fresh, raw, 1 medium, 33/4″ × 3″ diam.	.1	< .1
fresh, raw or boiled, chopped, 1/2 cup	.1	< .1
canned, w/liquid, halves, 1/2 cup	.2	< .1
in jars, roasted *(Progresso),* 1/2 cup	< 1.0	< 1.0
in jars, sweet fried *(Progresso),* 1/2 jar	3.0	< 1.0
freeze-dried, 1/4 cup	.1	tr.
frozen, boiled, drained, chopped, 4 oz.	.2	< .1

Pepper, hot (see also specific listings):

whole or diced *(Ortega)*, 1 oz.	0	0
rings *(Vlasic)*, 1 oz.	0	0

Pepper, jalapeño, canned, chopped, 1/2 cup | .4 | < .1

Pepper, pepperoncini:

(Progresso Tuscan), 1/2 cup	0	0
salad *(Vlasic)*, 1 oz.	0	0

Pepper, piccalilli *(Progresso)*, 1/2 cup | 20.0 | 3.0

Pepper, stuffed, entrée, frozen:

w/beef in tomato sauce *(Stouffer's)*, 7.75 oz.	9.0	n.a.
sweet red *(Celentano)*, 13 oz.	20.0	n.a.

Pepper sauce, hot:

(Gebhardt Louisiana Style), 1/2 tsp.	0	0
(Tabasco), 1/4 tsp.	tr.	(0)

Peppered loaf:

(Eckrich), 1-oz. slice	1.0	n.a.
(Kahn's), 1 slice	2.0	n.a.
(Oscar Mayer), 1-oz. slice	1.5	.8

Pepperoni:

(Hormel Chunk/Leoni Brand), 1 oz.	12.0	n.a.
(Hormel Perma-Fresh), 2 slices	7.0	n.a.
(Hormel/Hormel Rosa/Rosa Grande), 1 oz.	13.0	n.a.
(JM), 8 slices or 1/2 oz.	6.0	n.a.
pork and beef, 1 oz.	12.5	4.6

Pepperoni bits *(Hormel)*, 1 tbsp. | 3.0 | n.a.

Perch (see also "Ocean perch"), meat only:

raw, 4 oz.	1.0	.2
baked, broiled, or microwaved, 4 oz.	1.3	.3

Perch entrée, frozen:

battered *(Van de Kamp's)*, 2 pieces	21.0	4.0
breaded *(Mrs. Paul's* Light), 4.25 oz.	13.0	n.a.

Persimmon:

Japanese, fresh, 1 medium, 2 1/2″ × 3 1/2″	.3	(0)
Japanese, dried, 1 oz.	.2	(0)
native, fresh, 1 medium, 1.1 oz.	.1	(0)

Pesto sauce:

mix *(French's Pasta Toss)*, 2 tsp. dry	1.0	n.a.
refrigerated *(Contadina Fresh)*, 2 1/3 oz.	34.0	n.a.

Pheasant, fresh, raw:

meat w/skin, 1 oz.	2.6	.8
meat only, 1 oz.	1.0	.4
breast, meat only, 1 oz.	.9	.3
leg, meat only, 1 oz.	1.2	.4

Picante sauce (see also "Salsa"):

(Gebhardt), 1 tbsp.	0	0
(Old El Paso), 2 tbsp.	< 1.0	n.a.
(Old El Paso Chunky), 2 tbsp.	0	0
(Pace), 2 tsp.	.1	(0)
(Wise), 2 tbsp.	0	0
mild *(Azteca)*, 1 tbsp.	0	0
mild *(Rosarita Chunky)*, 3.5 oz.	< 1.0	n.a.

Pickle, all varieties (all brands), 1 oz. ..... < .2   < .1

Pickle loaf:

(Eckrich/Eckrich Smorgas Pac), 1-oz. slice	6.0	n.a.
(Hormel Perma-Fresh), 2 slices	7.0	n.a.
(Kahn's), 1 slice	7.0	n.a.
(Light & Lean), 2 slices	6.0	n.a.
beef *(Kahn's Family Pack)*, 1 slice	5.0	n.a.

Pickle and pimiento loaf *(Oscar Mayer)*,

1 oz.	4.1	1.5

Pickling spice *(Tone's)*, 1 tsp. 6   .1

Picnic loaf *(Oscar Mayer)*, 1-oz. slice 4.3   1.6

Pie, frozen, 1 serving:

apple:

(Banquet Family Size), 1/6 pie	11.0	n.a.
(Mrs. Smith's "Pie In Minutes"), 1/8 pie	9.0	2.0
(Pet-Ritz), 1/6 pie	12.0	n.a.
(Sara Lee Homestyle), 1/10 of 9" pie	12.0	n.a.
(Sara Lee Homestyle High), 1/10 of 10" pie	23.0	n.a.
(Weight Watchers), 1/2 pkg.	5.0	1.0
Dutch *(Sara Lee Homestyle)*, 1/10 of 9" pie	12.0	n.a.
streusel *(Sara Lee Free & Light)*, 1/8 pie	2.0	n.a.
banana cream *(Banquet)*, 1/6 pie	10.0	n.a.
banana cream *(Pet-Ritz)*, 1/6 pie	9.0	n.a.
blackberry *(Banquet Family Size)*, 1/6 pie	11.0	n.a.

blueberry:

(Banquet Family Size), 1/6 pie	11.0	n.a.

Pie, frozen, blueberry, continued

(Mrs. Smith's "Pie In Minutes"), 1/8 pie	9.0	2.0
(Pet-Ritz), 1/6 pie	12.0	n.a.
(Sara Lee Homestyle), 1/10 of 9″ pie	12.0	n.a.
cherry:		
(Banquet Family Size), 1/6 pie	11.0	n.a.
(Mrs. Smith's "Pie In Minutes"), 1/8 pie	9.0	2.0
(Pet-Ritz), 1/6 pie	12.0	n.a.
(Sara Lee Homestyle), 1/10 of 9″ pie	13.0	n.a.
streusel *(Sara Lee Free & Light)*,		
1/10 pie	2.0	n.a.
chocolate cream *(Banquet)*, 1/6 pie	10.0	n.a.
chocolate cream *(Pet-Ritz)*, 1/6 pie	8.0	n.a.
chocolate mocha *(Weight Watchers)*,		
1/2 pkg.	5.0	3.0
coconut cream *(Banquet)*, 1/6 pie	11.0	n.a.
coconut cream or egg custard *(Pet-Ritz)*,		
1/6 pie	8.0	n.a.
lemon cream *(Banquet)*, 1/6 pie	9.0	n.a.
lemon cream or mince *(Pet-Ritz)*, 1/6 pie	9.0	n.a.
lemon meringue *(Mrs. Smith's)*, 1/8 pie . .	5.0	n.a.
mince *(Sara Lee* Homestyle), 1/10 of		
9″ pie	13.0	n.a.
mincemeat *(Banquet* Family Size), 1/6 pie	11.0	n.a.
Neapolitan cream *(Pet-Ritz)*, 1/6 pie . . .	10.0	n.a.
peach:		
(Banquet Family Size), 1/6 pie	11.0	n.a.
(Mrs. Smith's "Pie In Minutes"), 1/8 pie	9.0	2.0
(Pet-Ritz), 1/6 pie	12.0	n.a.
(Sara Lee Homestyle), 1/10 of 9″ pie . .	12.0	n.a.
pecan *(Mrs. Smith's "Pie In Minutes")*,		
1/8 pie	13.0	2.0
pecan *(Sara Lee* Homestyle), 1/10 of 9″		
pie	18.0	n.a.
pumpkin:		
(Banquet Family Size), 1/6 pie	8.0	n.a.
(Mrs. Smith's "Pie In Minutes"), 1/8 pie	6.0	2.0
(Sara Lee Homestyle), 1/10 of 9″ pie	10.0	n.a.
custard *(Pet-Ritz)*, 1/6 pie	9.0	n.a.
raspberry *(Sara Lee* Homestyle), 1/10 of 9″		
pie	13.0	n.a.

strawberry cream *(Banquet)*, 1/6 pie	9.0	n.a.
strawberry cream *(Pet-Ritz)*, 1/6 pie	9.0	n.a.
sweet potato *(Pet-Ritz)*, 1/6 pie	7.0	n.a.
Pie, snack, 1 piece:		
apple *(Drake's)*	10.0	2.0
apple *(Tastykake)*, 4 oz.	12.2	n.a.
apple, French *(Tastykake)*, 4.2 oz.	12.5	n.a.
apple, regular or French *(Hostess)*	20.0	9.0
blackberry or blueberry *(Hostess)*	18.0	9.0
blueberry *(Tastykake)*, 4 oz.	11.7	n.a.
blueberry apple *(Drake's)*	10.0	2.0
cherry *(Hostess)*	20.0	9.0
cherry *(Tastykake)*, 4 oz.	12.7	n.a.
cherry apple *(Drake's)*	10.0	2.0
chocolate pudding *(Tastykake)*, 4.2 oz.	16.2	n.a.
coconut creme *(Tastykake)*, 4 oz.	22.3	n.a.
lemon *(Drake's)*	11.0	2.0
lemon *(Hostess)*	20.0	10.0
lemon *(Tastykake)*, 4 oz.	13.2	n.a.
peach *(Hostess)*	19.0	9.0
peach *(Tastykake)*, 4 oz.	12.4	n.a.
pecan *(Little Debbie)*, 3 oz.	3.0	n.a.
pineapple *(Tastykake)*, 4 oz.	12.0	n.a.
pumpkin *(Tastykake)*, 4 oz.	14.2	n.a.
strawberry *(Hostess)*	19.0	9.0
strawberry *(Tastykake)*, 3.7 oz.	11.9	n.a.
vanilla pudding *(Tastykake)*, 4.2 oz.	18.5	n.a.
Pie crust shell, frozen or refrigerated:		
(Mrs. Smith's, 8" or 9"), 1/8 shell	5.0	1.0
(Mrs. Smith's, 95/8"), 1/8 shell	7.0	2.0
(Pet-Ritz), 1/6 shell	7.0	n.a.
(Pet-Ritz, 95/8"), 1/6 shell	11.0	n.a.
(Pillsbury All Ready), 1/8 of 2 crust pie	15.0	n.a.
all vegetable shortening *(Pet-Ritz)*, 1/6 shell	8.0	2.0
deep dish *(Pet-Ritz)*, 1/6 shell	8.0	n.a.
deep dish, all vegetable shortening *(Pet-Ritz)*, 1/6 shell	9.0	2.0
graham cracker *(Pet-Ritz)*, 1/6 shell	6.0	n.a.
Pie crust shell mix:		
(Betty Crocker), 1/16 pkg.	8.0	2.0

Pie crust shell mix, continued

(Flako), 1 serving*	15.0	4.5
Pie crust stick *(Betty Crocker)*, 1/8 stick	8.0	2.0
Pie filling, canned:		
all fruits *(White House)*, 3.5 oz.	1.0	(0)
all fruits, except banana and lemon		
(Comstock/Comstock Lite), 3.5 oz.	0	0
banana *(Comstock)*, 3.5 oz.	2.0	(0)
chocolate or coconut *(Comstock)*, 3.5 oz.	3.0	n.a.
lemon *(Comstock)*, 3.5 oz.	1.0	(0)
mincemeat:		
(Borden None Such), 1/3 cup	1.0	(0)
(Comstock), 3.5 oz.	1.0	(0)
w/brandy *(S&W Old Fashioned)*, 4 oz.	2.3	n.a.
w/brandy and rum *(Borden None		
Such)*, 1/3 cup	2.0	n.a.
condensed *(Borden None Such)*,		
1/4 pkg.	2.0	n.a.
pumpkin *(Comstock)*, 3.5 oz.	0	0
pumpkin *(Stokely)*, 1/2 cup	0	0
pumpkin pie mix *(Libby's)*, 1 cup	.3	0
Pie filling mix, see "Pudding mix"		
Pie mix*, 1/8 pie, except as noted:		
banana cream *(Jell-O No Bake)*	14.0	n.a.
chocolate mint *(Royal No-Bake)*	15.0	n.a.
chocolate mousse *(Jell-O No Bake)* . . .	17.0	n.a.
chocolate mousse *(Royal No-Bake)*	12.0	n.a.
coconut cream *(Jell-O No Bake)*	16.0	n.a.
lemon meringue *(Royal No-Bake)*	11.0	n.a.
pumpkin *(Jell-O No Bake)*	13.0	n.a.
pumpkin *(Libby's)*, 1/6 pie	17.0	5.0
Pigeon pea:		
boiled, drained, 1/2 cup	1.1	.1
dried, boiled, 1/2 cup	.3	.1
Pig's feet, pickled, cured, 1 oz.	4.6	1.6
Pig's knuckles, pickled, *(Penrose)*, 6-oz.		
piece	21.0	n.a.
Pike, meat only:		
Northern, raw, 4 oz.	.8	.1
Northern, baked, broiled, or microwaved,		
4 oz.	1.0	.2

walleye, raw, 4 oz.	1.4	.3
Pilinut-canarytree, dried, shelled, 1 oz. . . .	22.6	8.9
Pimiento, canned or in jars, 2 oz.	.2	< .1
Pimiento spread *(Price's),* 1 oz.	6.0	n.a.
Piña colada mix *(Holland House),* .56 oz.		
dry	3.0	n.a.
Pine nut, dried, shelled:		
pignolia, 1 oz.	14.4	2.2
piñon, 1 oz.	17.3	2.7
Pineapple:		
fresh, sliced, 1 slice, 3½″ diam. × ¾″ . . .	.4	< .1
fresh, diced, ½ cup	.3	< .1
canned or frozen, all varieties, ½ cup	.1	< .1
Pineapple danish, miniature *(Awrey's),*		
1.7 oz.	8.0	2.0
Pineapple juice:		
canned, 6 fl. oz.	.2	< .1
frozen*, 6 fl. oz.	.1	< .1
Pineapple nectar *(Libby's)*	0	0
Pineapple-orange juice *(Minute Maid),*		
6 fl. oz.	.1	(0)
Pineapple-orange-banana juice *(Dole),*		
6 fl. oz.	.1	(0)
Pistachio nut, shelled:		
dried, 1 oz.	13.7	1.7
dried, 1 cup	61.9	7.8
dry roasted *(Planters),* 1 oz.	15.0	2.0
Pitanga, fresh, trimmed, ½ cup	.3	(0)
Pizza, frozen:		
Canadian bacon *(Jeno's* Crisp'n Tasty),		
½ pie	11.0	n.a.
Canadian bacon *(Tombstone),* ¼ pie . .	13.0	5.0
Canadian bacon *(Totino's Party),* ½ pie	10.0	2.0
(Celentano 9-Slice Pizza), 2.7 oz.	4.0	n.a.
(Celentano Thick Crust), 4.3 oz.	11.0	n.a.
(Celeste Suprema), ¼ pie	24.1	7.0
(Celeste Suprema Pizza For One), 1 pie	39.3	12.0
cheese:		
(Celeste), ¼ pie	16.6	7.0
(Celeste Pizza For One), 1 pie	24.5	11.0
(Jeno's Crisp'n Tasty), ½ pie	14.0	n.a.

Pizza, frozen, cheese, continued

(Jeno's 4-Pack), 1 pie	8.0	n.a.
(Pillsbury Microwave), 1/2 pie	10.0	n.a.
(Stouffer's), 1/2 pkg.	15.0	n.a.
(Stouffer's Extra Cheese), 1/2 pkg. . . .	19.0	n.a.
(Tombstone), 1/4 pie	13.0	6.0
(Totino's Microwave), 1 pie	10.0	4.0
(Totino's Party), 1/2 pie	10.0	3.0
(Totino's Party Family Size), 1/3 pie	11.0	4.0
(Weight Watchers), 5.86-oz. pkg.	7.0	3.0
three *(Tombstone* Double Top), 1/4 pie	25.0	13.0
three *(Tombstone* Microwave), 7.7 oz.	27.0	13.0
two *(Tombstone* Thin Crust), 1/4 pie	16.0	7.0
cheese, double, 1/4 pie:		
hamburger *(Tombstone* Double Top)	27.0	12.0
sausage *(Tombstone* Double Top) . . .	25.0	11.0
sausage *(Tombstone* Double Top		
Deluxe)	25.0	11.0
cheese combination, 1/4 pie:		
hamburger *(Tombstone)*	16.0	6.0
hamburger *(Tombstone* Thin Crust)	17.0	7.0
pepperoni *(Tombstone)*	18.0	7.0
pepperoni *(Tombstone* Thin Crust)	19.0	8.0
sausage *(Tombstone)*	14.0	6.0
sausage *(Tombstone* Thin Crust)	18.0	7.0
sausage, mushroom *(Tombstone)*	15.0	6.0
combination:		
(Jeno's 4-Pack), 1 pie	9.0	n.a.
(Pillsbury Microwave), 1/2 pie	15.0	n.a.
(Totino's Microwave), 1 pie	13.0	3.0
(Totino's Party), 1/2 pie	15.0	4.0
(Totino's Party Family Size), 1/3 pie	16.0	4.0
(Weight Watchers Deluxe), 7.15 oz.	10.0	3.0
deluxe *(Celeste),* 1/4 pie	22.1	7.0
deluxe *(Celeste* Pizza For One), 1 pie	31.8	10.0
deluxe *(Stouffer's),* 1/2 of 10-oz. pkg. . . .	19.0	n.a.
golden topping *(Fox Deluxe),* 1/2 pie . . .	11.0	n.a.
golden topping *(John's),* 1/2 pie	11.0	n.a.
hamburger *(Fox Deluxe),* 1/2 pie	12.0	n.a.
hamburger *(Jeno's* Crisp'n Tasty), 1/2 pie	15.0	n.a.
hamburger *(Totino's Party),* 1/2 pie	13.0	3.0

pepperoni:

(Celeste), 1/4 pie	21.3	7.0
(Celeste Pizza For One), 1 pie	29.6	9.0
(Fox Deluxe), 1/2 pie	13.0	n.a.
(Jeno's Crisp'n Tasty), 1/2 pie	15.0	n.a.
(Jeno's 4-Pack), 1 pie	9.0	n.a.
(Pillsbury Microwave), 1/2 pie	15.0	n.a.
(Stouffer's), 1/2 of 8.75-oz. pkg.	18.0	n.a.
(Tombstone Real Deluxe), 1/4 pie	18.0	7.0
(Totino's Microwave), 1 pie	13.0	3.0
(Totino's Party), 1/2 pie	14.0	3.0
(Totino's Party Family Size), 1/3 pie	15.0	4.0
(Weight Watchers), 6.09-oz. pkg.	10.0	3.0
double cheese *(Tombstone Double Top)*, 1/4 pie	31.0	14.0
double cheese *(Tombstone Double Top Deluxe)*, 1/4 pie	30.0	13.0

sausage:

(Celeste), 1/4 pie	21.7	7.0
(Celeste Pizza For One), 1 pie	31.7	10.0
(Fox Deluxe), 1/2 pie	13.0	n.a.
(Jeno's Crisp'n Tasty), 1/2 pie	16.0	n.a.
(Jeno's 4-Pack), 1 pie	9.0	n.a.
(Pillsbury Microwave), 1/2 pie	13.0	n.a.
(Stouffer's), 1/2 of 93/8-oz. pkg.	18.0	n.a.
(Tombstone Deluxe), 1/4 pie	14.0	6.0
(Tombstone Deluxe Microwave), 8.7 oz.	25.0	10.0
(Totino's Microwave), 1 pie	13.0	3.0
(Totino's Party), 1/2 pie	15.0	3.0
(Totino's Party Family Size), 1/3 pie	16.0	4.0
(Weight Watchers), 6.26-oz. pkg.	10.0	2.0
Italian *(Tombstone Microwave)*, 8 oz.	29.0	12.0
smoked *(Tombstone)*, 1/4 pie	14.0	6.0

sausage combination:

(Tombstone), 1/4 pie	16.0	7.0
mushroom *(Celeste Pizza For One)*, 1 pie	32.3	11.0
pepperoni *(Fox Deluxe)*, 1/2 pie	13.0	n.a.
pepperoni *(Jeno's Crisp'n Tasty)*, 1/2 pie	16.0	n.a.
pepperoni *(Stouffer's)*, 1/2 pkg.	21.0	n.a.

Pizza, frozen, sausage combination, continued
    pepperoni *(Tombstone* Double Top),
        1/4 pie 29.0   13.0
    pepperoni *(Tombstone* Microwave),
        8 oz. 29.0   12.0
    (Tombstone Thin Crust Supreme), 1/4 pie 18.0   7.0
    vegetable *(Celeste),* 1/4 pie . . . . 16.0   n.a.
    vegetable *(Celeste* Pizza For One), 1 pie 26.0   n.a.
Pizza, croissant pastry, frozen:
    cheese or deluxe *(Pepperidge Farm),*
        1 pie . . . . 23.0   n.a.
    pepperoni *(Pepperidge Farm),* 1 pie . . . 22.0   n.a.
Pizza, French bread, frozen:
    Canadian-style bacon *(Stouffer's),* 1/2 pkg. 14.0   n.a.
    cheese *(Banquet Zap),* 4.5 oz. . . . . 10.0   n.a.
    cheese *(Lean Cuisine),* 5 1/8-oz. pkg. . . . 10.0   3.0
    cheese *(Lean Cuisine* Extra Cheese),
        5.5 oz. 12.0   4.0
    cheese *(Pillsbury* Microwave), 1 piece 15.0   n.a.
    cheese *(Stouffer's),* 1/2 pkg. . . . . 13.0   n.a.
    cheese *(Stouffer's* Double Cheese),
        1/2 pkg. . . . . 18.0   n.a.
    deluxe *(Banquet Zap),* 4.8 oz. . . . . 13.0   n.a.
    deluxe *(Lean Cuisine),* 6 1/8-oz. pkg. . . . 12.0   3.0
    deluxe *(Stouffer's),* 1/2 pkg. . . . . 21.0   n.a.
    deluxe *(Weight Watchers),* 6.12-oz. pkg. 12.0   3.0
    hamburger *(Stouffer's),* 1/2 pkg. . . . . . 19.0   n.a.
    pepperoni *(Banquet Zap),* 4.5 oz. . . . . . 16.0   n.a.
    pepperoni *(Lean Cuisine),* 5.25-oz. pkg. 12.0   4.0
    pepperoni *(Pillsbury* Microwave), 1 piece 19.0   n.a.
    pepperoni *(Stouffer's),* 1/2 pkg. . . . . . . 20.0   n.a.
    pepperoni *(Weight Watchers),* 5.25-oz.
        pkg. 11.0   3.0
    pepperoni/mushroom *(Stouffer's),* 1/2 pkg. 22.0   n.a.
    sausage *(Lean Cuisine),* 6-oz. pkg. 11.0   3.0
    sausage *(Pillsbury* Microwave), 1 piece 16.0   n.a.
    sausage *(Stouffer's),* 1/2 pkg. . . . . 20.0   n.a.
    sausage/mushroom *(Stouffer's),* 1/2 pkg. 19.0   n.a.
    sausage/pepperoni *(Pillsbury* Microwave),
        1 piece . . . . 21.0   n.a.
    sausage/pepperoni *(Stouffer's),* 1/2 pkg. 23.0   n.a.

vegetable deluxe *(Stouffer's)*, 1/2 pkg.   20.0   n.a.
Pizza crust:
  (Pillsbury All Ready), 1/8 of crust 1.0   0
  mix *(Robin Hood/Gold Medal* Pouch
    Mix), 1/6 pkg. . . . .   1.0   n.a.
Pizza Hut:
  hand-tossed, 2 slices of medium pie:
    cheese, 7.8 oz. 20.0   13.6
    pepperoni, 6.9 oz. 23.0   12.9
    supreme, 8.4 oz. 26.0   13.8
    super supreme, 8.6 oz. 21.0   10.3
  pan pizza, 2 slices of medium pie:
    cheese, 7.2 oz. 18.0   9.0
    pepperoni, 7.4 oz. 22.0   9.2
    supreme, 9 oz. 30.0   13.8
    super supreme, 9.1 oz. 26.0   12.0
  Personal Pan Pizza, pepperoni, 9 oz.   29.0   12.5
  Personal Pan Pizza, supreme, 9.3 oz.   28.0   11.2
  Thin 'n Crispy, 2 slices of medium pie:
    cheese, 5.2 oz. 17.0   10.4
    pepperoni, 5.1 oz. 20.0   10.6
    supreme, 7.1 oz. 22.0   11.0
    super supreme, 7.2 oz. 21.0   10.3
Pizza pocket sandwich, frozen:
  (Lean Pockets Pizza Deluxe), 1 pkg. . . .   9.0   n.a.
  pepperoni *(Hot Pockets),* 5 oz. . . . . . .   17.0   n.a.
  sausage *(Hot Pockets),* 5 oz. . . . .   16.0   n.a.
Pizza roll, frozen, 3 oz. or 6 rolls:
  all varieties, except cheese *(Jeno's)* . .   13.0   n.a.
  cheese *(Jeno's)* . . . .   12.0   n.a.
Pizza sauce:
  (Enrico's Homemade Style), 4 oz. . . . .   1.0   n.a.
  (Ragu Pizza Quick), 3 tbsp. . . . .   2.0   n.a.
  all varieties, except w/pepperoni
    (Contadina), 1/4 cup . . . .   1.0   n.a.
  w/pepperoni *(Contadina),* 1/4 cup . . . . .   2.0   n.a.
Plantain (see also "Banana"):
  raw, 1 medium, 9.7 oz. 7   n.a.
  raw, sliced, 1/2 cup 3   n.a.
  cooked, sliced, 1/2 cup 1   n.a.

Plum:

fresh, pitted, sliced, 1/2 cup	.5	.4
fresh, Japanese or hybrid, 1 plum,		
2 1/8″ diam.	.4	< .1
canned, purple, in water or juice, 1/2 cup	< .1	tr.
canned, purple, in syrup, 1/2 cup	.1	< .1
Plum sauce, tangy *(La Choy)*, 1 oz.	.1	(0)
Poi, 1/2 cup	.2	< .1
Pokeberry shoots, raw or boiled, drained,		
1/2 cup	.3	n.a.
Polenta mix* *(Fantastic Polenta)*, 1/2 cup	2.0	n.a.
Polish sausage (see also "Kielbasa"):		
1 oz.	8.1	2.9
(Hillshire Farm Links), 2 oz.	17.0	n.a.
(Hormel), 2 links	14.0	n.a.
smoked *(Eckrich Lite* Sausage Links),		
1 link	15.0	n.a.
Pollock, meat only:		
Atlantic, raw, 4 oz.	1.1	.2
walleye, raw, 4 oz.	.9	.2
walleye, baked, broiled, or microwaved,		
4 oz.	1.3	.3
Pomegranate, 1 medium, 3 3/8″ × 3 3/4″	.5	n.a.
Pompano, Florida, meat only:		
raw, 4 oz.	10.7	4.0
baked, broiled, or microwaved, 4 oz.	13.8	5.1
Popcorn, popped:		
(Bachman), 1/2 oz.	6.0	n.a.
(Bachman Lite), 1/2 oz.	1.0	n.a.
(Bearitos Organic Traditional), 1 oz. . . .	9.2	n.a.
(Frito-Lay's), 1/2 oz.	3.0	n.a.
(Jiffy Pop Pan Popcorn), 4 cups	6.0	n.a.
(Orville Redenbacher Natural), 3 cups	5.0	1.1
(Orville Redenbacher Natural Salt Free),		
3 cups	6.0	1.3
(Wise Tender Baby White Corn), 1/2 oz.	6.0	n.a.
butter flavor:		
(Jiffy Pop Pan Popcorn), 4 cups	6.0	n.a.
(Orville Redenbacher), 3 cups	5.0	1.0
(Orville Redenbacher Salt Free), 3 cups	5.0	1.2
(Wise), 1/2 oz. or 1 cup	5.0	n.a.

cheese and cheese flavor:

(*Bachman*), 1/2 oz.	6.0	n.a.
(*Bearitos* Organic), 1 oz.	8.0	n.a.
(*Frito-Lay's*), 1/2 oz.	5.0	n.a.

cheese, cheddar (*Orville Redenbacher*),

3 cups	12.0	n.a.

cheese, cheddar, white:

(*Bachman*), 1/2 oz.	4.0	n.a.
(*Cape Cod*), 1/2 oz.	5.0	n.a.
(*Keebler* Deluxe), 1 oz.	10.0	2.0
(*Smartfood*), 1/2 oz.	5.0	n.a.
(*Wise*), 1/2 oz.	5.0	n.a.

honey caramel (*Keebler* Pop Deluxe),

1 oz.	3.0	1.0

microwave, 3 cups, except as noted:

(*Jolly Time* Natural)	10.0	n.a.
(*Orville Redenbacher* Light Natural)	1.0	n.a.
(*Planters* Natural)	9.0	1.0
(*Pop.Secret* Natural)	6.0	2.0
butter flavor (*Jolly Time*)	7.0	n.a.
butter flavor (*Orville Redenbacher* Lite)	2.0	n.a.
butter flavor (*Planters*)	10.0	1.0
butter flavor (*Pop.Secret*)	6.0	1.0

natural or butter flavor (*Jiffy Pop*),

4 cups	7.0	n.a.

natural or butter flavor (*Pop.Secret* Light)

Light)	3.0	< 1.0
natural or butter flavor (*Pops-Rite*)	5.0	n.a.
original or butter flavor (*Pillsbury*)	13.0	n.a.
cheddar cheese flavor (*Jolly Time*)	11.0	n.a.

cheese flavor (*Pop.Secret*), 1/3 pkg.

unpopped	11.0	n.a.
frozen (*Pillsbury* Salt-Free)	7.0	n.a.

frozen, original or butter flavor

(*Pillsbury*)	13.0	n.a.

Popcorn seasoning (*McCormick/Schilling Parsley Patch*), 1 tsp. 1 (0)

Poppy seed, 1 tsp.	1.3	.1

Porgy, see "Scup"

Pork, fresh (see also "Ham"), retail cuts, meat only:

Pork, continued
  loin, whole:

lean w/fat, broiled, 4 oz.	30.9	11.1
lean w/fat, roasted, 4 oz.	27.5	10.0
lean only, broiled, 4 oz.	17.3	6.0
lean only, roasted, 4 oz.	15.8	5.4
loin, blade:		
lean w/fat, broiled, 4 oz.	38.4	14.2
lean w/fat, roasted, 4 oz.	34.5	12.4
lean only, broiled, 4 oz.	24.3	8.4
lean only, roasted, 4 oz.	21.9	7.5
loin, center:		
lean w/fat, broiled, 4 oz.	25.1	9.1
lean w/fat, roasted, 4 oz.	24.7	8.9
lean only, broiled, 4 oz.	11.9	4.1
lean only, roasted, 4 oz.	14.8	5.1
loin, center rib:		
lean w/fat, broiled, 4 oz.	29.9	10.8
lean w/fat, roasted, 4 oz.	26.8	9.7
lean only, broiled, 4 oz.	16.9	5.8
lean only, roasted, 4 oz.	15.6	5.4
loin, sirloin:		
lean w/fat, broiled, 4 oz.	28.6	10.4
lean w/fat, roasted, 4 oz.	23.1	8.4
lean only, broiled, 4 oz.	15.4	5.3
lean only, roasted, 4 oz.	14.9	5.2
loin, top:		
lean w/fat, broiled, 4 oz.	32.5	11.7
lean w/fat, roasted, 4 oz.	28.5	10.3
lean only, broiled, 4 oz.	16.9	5.8
lean only, roasted, 4 oz.	15.6	5.4
shoulder, whole, lean w/fat, roasted, 4 oz.	29.1	10.5
shoulder, whole, lean only, roasted, 4 oz.	17.0	5.9
shoulder, arm (picnic):		
lean w/fat, braised, 4 oz.	29.0	10.5
lean w/fat, roasted, 4 oz.	29.6	10.7
lean only, braised, 4 oz.	13.8	4.8
lean only, roasted, 4 oz.	14.3	4.9
shoulder, Boston blade:		
lean w/fat, braised, 4 oz.	32.5	11.7
lean w/fat, broiled, 4 oz.	32.3	11.6

lean only, braised, 4 oz.	19.9	6.9
lean only, broiled, 4 oz.	20.9	7.2
lean only, roasted, 4 oz.	19.1	6.6
spareribs, lean w/fat, braised, 6.3 oz. (1 lb.		
raw w/bone)	53.6	20.8
tenderloin, lean only, roasted, 4 oz. . . .	5.5	1.9
Pork, boneless, refrigerated:		
chop *(JM* America's Cut), 6-oz. chop	20.0	n.a.
loin, whole or half, center cut *(JM),* 3 oz.	13.0	n.a.
shoulder butt *(JM),* 3 oz.	18.0	n.a.
tenderloin *(JM),* 3 oz.	5.0	n.a.
Pork, canned:		
1 oz.	8.6	3.1
(Hormel), 3 oz.	21.0	n.a.
chopped *(Hormel),* 3 oz.	16.0	n.a.
Pork, cured (see also "Ham"), shoulder:		
arm (picnic), lean w/fat, roasted, 4 oz.	24.2	8.7
arm (picnic), lean only, roasted, 4 oz.	8.0	2.7
blade roll, lean w/fat, unheated, 1 oz.	6.2	2.3
blade roll, lean w/fat, roasted, 4 oz. . . .	26.6	9.5
Pork, ground *(JM),* 3 oz.	14.0	n.a.
Pork backfat, raw, 1 oz.	25.1	9.1
Pork chow mein, canned *(La Choy* Bi-		
Pack), 3/4 cup	3.0	n.a.
Pork dinner, frozen, loin of *(Swanson),*		
10.75 oz. . . . . ,	12.0	n.a.
Pork entrée, frozen or refrigerated:		
barbecued:		
back ribs *(John Morrell Pork Classics),*		
4.75 oz.	17.0	n.a.
chops *(John Morrell Pork Classics),*		
4.5 oz.	9.0	n.a.
loin *(John Morrell Pork Classics),* 3 oz.	6.0	n.a.
spareribs *(John Morrell Pork Classics),*		
4.5 oz.	18.0	n.a.
tenderloin *(John Morrell Pork*		
Classics), 3 oz.	5.0	n.a.
steak, breaded *(Hormel),* 3 oz.	15.0	n.a.
sweet and sour *(Chun King),* 13 oz. . . .	5.0	n.a.
Pork fat, roasted, 1 oz.	17.5	6.4

Pork gravy:

canned *(Franco-American)*, 2 oz.	3.0	n.a.
canned *(Heinz* HomeStyle), 2 oz. or		
1/4 cup	1.0	n.a.
canned *(Hormel Great Beginnings)*, 5 oz.	8.0	n.a.
mix* *(French's)*, 1/4 cup	1.0	n.a.
mix* *(McCormick/Schilling)*, 1/4 cup . . .	.6	n.a.
Pork luncheon meat *(Eckrich* Slender		
Sliced), 1 oz.	2.0	n.a.
Pork rind snack *(Baken-ets)*, 1 oz.	10.0	n.a.
Pork seasoning and coating mix:		
extra crispy *(Shake'n Bake Oven Fry)*,		
1/4 pouch	3.0	n.a.
chop *(McCormick/Schilling* Bag'n		
Season), 1 pkg.	.4	n.a.
plain or barbecue *(Shake'n Bake* Original		
Recipe), 1/8 pouch	1.0	n.a.
Pot roast dinner, Yankee, frozen:		
(Armour Classics), 10 oz.	12.0	n.a.
(The Budget Gourmet), 11 oz.	21.0	n.a.
(Healthy Choice), 11 oz.	4.0	2.0
(Le Menu), 11 oz.	13.0	n.a.
Pot roast entrée, frozen, homestyle *(Right*		
Course), 9.25 oz.	7.0	2.0
Pot roast seasoning mix:		
(Lawry's Seasoning Blends), 1 pkg. . . .	.7	n.a.
(McCormick/Schilling Bag'n Season),		
1 pkg.	.6	n.a.
Potato:		
raw, peeled, diced, or boiled, 1/2 cup . . .	.1	< .1
baked or microwaved in skin, 1 medium,		
43/4″	.2	.1
Potato, canned or packaged:		
plain, 1/2 cup	.2	< .1
au gratin *(Green Giant Pantry Express)*,		
1/2 cup	5.0	2.0
scalloped, and ham *(Hormel Micro-Cup)*,		
7.5 oz.	16.0	n.a.
Potato, frozen (see also "Potato dishes,		
frozen"):		
whole, peeled, boiled, drained, 4 oz. . . .	.1	< .1

french fried, 3 oz., except as noted:

(MicroMagic)	13.0	n.a.
(Ore-Ida Country Style Dinner Fries)	3.0	2.0
(Ore-Ida Crispers!)	15.0	8.0
(Ore-Ida Crispy Crowns)	9.0	4.0
(Ore-Ida Golden Fries)	4.0	2.0
(Ore-Ida Lites*)*	2.0	< 1.0
cottage cut *(Ore-Ida)*	5.0	2.0
crinkle cut *(Ore-Ida Golden Crinkles)*	4.0	2.0
crinkle cut *(Ore-Ida* Lites*)*	2.0	n.a.
crinkle cut *(Ore-Ida* Microwave*)*, 3.5 oz.	8.0	4.0
crinkle cut *(Ore-Ida Pixie Crinkles)*	6.0	3.0
crinkle cut *(Quick'n Crispy)*, 4 oz.	19.0	n.a.
w/onions *(Ore-Ida Crispy Crowns)*	9.0	5.0
plain or crinkle cut *(Heinz* Deep Fries*)*	6.0	3.0
shoestring *(Heinz* Deep Fries*)*	10.0	5.0
shoestring *(Ore-Ida)*	6.0	3.0
shoestring *(Ore-Ida* Lites*)*	4.0	2.0
shoestring *(Quick'n Crispy)*, 4 oz.	20.0	n.a.
skinny *(MicroMagic)*	15.0	n.a.
thin cuts *(Quick'n Crispy)*, 4 oz.	19.0	n.a.
wedges *(Ore-Ida Home Style Potato Wedges)*	3.0	1.0

hash brown:

(Ore-Ida Golden Patties), 2.5 oz.	8.0	4.0
(Ore-Ida Microwave*)*, 2 oz.	8.0	4.0
(Ore-Ida Southern Style), 3 oz.	< 1.0	n.a.
w/butter and onions *(Heinz* Deep Fries*)*, 3 oz.	7.0	4.0
w/cheddar *(Ore-Ida Cheddar Browns)*, 3 oz.	2.0	1.0
shredded *(Ore-Ida)*, 3 oz.	< 1.0	n.a.
O'Brien *(Ore-Ida)*, 3 oz.	< 1.0	n.a.
puffs *(Ore-Ida Tater Tots)*, 3 oz.	7.0	3.0
puffs *(Ore-Ida Tater Tots* Microwave*)*, 4 oz.	9.0	4.0
puffs, bacon or onion *(Ore-Ida Tater Tots)*, 3 oz.	6.0	3.0
sticks *(MicroMagic* Tater Sticks*)*, 4 oz.	22.0	n.a.
wedges *(Quick'n Crispy)*, 4 oz.	13.0	n.a.

Potato, mix*, (see also "Potato dishes, mix"), 1/2 cup, except as noted:

(Betty Crocker Potato Buds)	6.0	n.a.
au gratin *(Betty Crocker)*	5.0	n.a.
au gratin or spicy cheddar *(Idahoan)* . . .	5.0	n.a.
au gratin, tangy *(French's)*	5.0	n.a.
bacon and cheddar *(Betty Crocker* Twice Baked)	11.0	n.a.
butter, herbed *(Betty Crocker* Twice Baked)	13.0	n.a.
cheddar, w/onion *(Betty Crocker* Twice Baked)	11.0	n.a.
cheddar, smoky or w/bacon *(Betty Crocker)*	5.0	n.a.
cheddar and bacon casserole *(French's)*	5.0	n.a.
country style *(Fantastic Foods)*	.3	n.a.
hash brown *(Idahoan* Quick One-Pan)	7.0	n.a.
hash brown, w/onions *(Betty Crocker)*	6.0	n.a.
herb and butter *(Idahoan)*	6.0	n.a.
julienne *(Betty Crocker)*	5.0	n.a.
mashed *(Country Store* Flakes), 1/3 cup flakes	0	0
mashed *(French's Idaho)*	6.0	n.a.
mashed *(French's Idaho* Spuds)	7.0	n.a.
mashed *(Hungry Jack* Flakes)	7.0	n.a.
mashed *(Idahoan)*	7.0	n.a.
mashed *(Idahoan Instamash* Microwave)	1.0	n.a.
scalloped *(Idahoan)*	5.0	n.a.
scalloped, cheese, real *(French's)*	5.0	n.a.
scalloped, plain or cheesy *(Betty Crocker)*	5.0	n.a.
scalloped, creamy Italian *(French's)* . . .	3.0	n.a.
scalloped, crispy top w/onion *(French's)*	5.0	n.a.
scalloped and ham *(Betty Crocker)*	6.0	n.a.
sour cream/chive *(Betty Crocker)*	5.0	n.a.
sour cream/chive *(Betty Crocker* Twice Baked)	11.0	n.a.
sour cream/chive *(French's)*	7.0	n.a.
sour cream/chive *(Idahoan)*	5.0	n.a.
Stroganoff, creamy *(French's)*	4.0	n.a.
western *(Idahoan)*	4.0	n.a.

Potato chips and crisps, 1 oz., except as
   noted:

(Bachman Kettle Cooked)	8.0	n.a.
(Bachman/Bachman Ridge/Ruffled) . . .	10.0	n.a.
(Cape Cod/Cape Cod Waves)	8.0	n.a.
(Cottage Fries No Salt Added)	11.0	n.a.
(Eagle Extra Crunchy/Idaho Russet) . . .	8.0	n.a.
(Lay's)	10.0	n.a.
(Munchos)	9.0	n.a.
(Pringle's)	13.0	n.a.
(Ruffles)	10.0	n.a.
(Ruffles Light)	6.0	n.a.
(Wise Plain or Rippled)	10.0	n.a.
(Wise New York Deli)	11.0	n.a.
(Wise Ridgies/Wise Ridgies Super Crispy)	10.0	n.a.
all varieties *(Eagle* Ridged/Thins)	10.0	n.a.
all varieties *(O'Boisies)*	9.0	2.0
all varieties *(Pringle's* Light)	8.0	n.a.
all varieties *(Pringle's Idaho Rippled)*	12.0	n.a.
au gratin *(King Kold)*	8.0	n.a.
barbecue *(Bachman)*	9.0	n.a.
barbecue *(Eagle* Extra Crunchy/		
Louisiana)	8.0	n.a.
barbecue *(Lay's* Bar-B-Q)	9.0	n.a.
barbecue or cheddar and sour cream		
(Ruffles)	9.0	n.a.
barbecue *(Wise/Wise Ridgies)*	10.0	n.a.
Cajun *(Ruffles Cajun Spice)*	10.0	n.a.
cheese flavor *(Pringle's* Cheez-ums) . . .	13.0	n.a.
dill and sour cream *(Cape Cod)*	8.0	n.a.
hot *(Bachman)*	9.0	n.a.
hot *(Wise)*	11.0	n.a.
mesquite *(Ruffles* Mesquite Grille)	10.0	n.a.
onion-garlic flavor *(Wise)*	10.0	n.a.
ranch *(Ruffles)*	10.0	n.a.
salt and vinegar *(Lay's)*	9.0	n.a.
Saratoga style *(Bachman* Kettle Cooked)	8.0	n.a.
skins, all varieties *(Tato Skins)*	8.0	1.0
sour cream/onion *(Bachman)*	9.0	n.a.
sour cream/onion *(Lay's)*	10.0	n.a.
sour cream/onion *(Pringle's)*	12.0	n.a.

Potato chips and crisps, continued

sour cream/onion *(Ruffles)*	9.0	n.a.
sour cream/onion *(Wise Ridgies)*	11.0	n.a.
vinegar *(Bachman)*	9.0	n.a.

Potato dishes, frozen:

au gratin *(Birds Eye For One)*, 5.5 oz.	13.0	n.a.
au gratin *(Green Giant* One Serving), 5.5 oz.	10.0	4.0
au gratin *(Stouffer's)*, .5 oz.	6.0	n.a.
and broccoli, in cheese sauce *(Green Giant* One Serving), 5.5 oz.	5.0	1.0
cheddared *(The Budget Gourmet* Side Dish), 5.5 oz.	13.0	n.a.
cheddared, and broccoli *(The Budget Gourmet* Side Dish), 5 oz.	4.0	n.a.
nacho *(The Budget Gourmet* Side Dish), 5 oz.	10.0	n.a.
new, in sour cream sauce *(The Budget Gourmet* Side Dish), 5 oz.	6.0	n.a.
scalloped *(Stouffer's)*, .5 oz.	4.0	n.a.
shredded, 'n vegetables, in cheese sauce *(Stokely Singles)*, 4.5 oz.	6.0	n.a.
sliced, 'n bacon, in cheddar cheese sauce *(Stokely Singles)*, 4.5 oz.	5.0	n.a.
stuffed:		
w/cheddar cheese *(Oh Boy!)*, 6 oz.	4.0	n.a.
w/real bacon *(Oh Boy!)*, 6 oz.	3.0	n.a.
w/sour cream & chives *(Oh Boy!)*, 6 oz.	5.0	n.a.
stuffed, baked:		
w/broccoli and cheese *(Weight Watchers)*, 10.5 oz.	8.0	2.0
w/cheese-flavored topping *(Green Giant)*, 5 oz.	6.0	n.a.
w/chicken divan *(Weight Watchers)*, 11 oz.	4.0	2.0
w/ham Lorraine *(Weight Watchers)*, 11 oz.	4.0	2.0
w/homestyle turkey *(Weight Watchers)*, 12 oz.	6.0	3.0
w/sour cream and chives *(Green Giant)*, 5 oz.	10.0	n.a.

three cheese *(The Budget Gourmet* Side Dish), 5.75 oz.	11.0	n.a.
Potato dishes, mix* (see also "Potato, mix"):		
all varieties, except two cheese *(Kraft* Potatoes & Cheese), 1/2 cup	5.0	2.0
broccoli au gratin or cheddar w/ mushrooms *(Betty Crocker* Potato Medleys), 1/2 cup	4.0	n.a.
scalloped, all varieties *(Betty Crocker* Potato Medleys), 1/2 cup	5.0	n.a.
two cheese *(Kraft* Potatoes & Cheese), 1/2 cup	4.0	2.0
Potato pancake mix* *(French's Idaho),* 3 cakes, 3" each	2.0	n.a.
Potato salad, canned:		
German *(Joan of Arc/Read),* 1/2 cup . . .	3.0	n.a.
homestyle *(Joan of Arc/Read),* 1/2 cup	22.0	n.a.
Potato sticks, canned, shoestring *(Allens),* 1 oz.	8.0	n.a.
Poultry seasoning, 1 tsp.	.1	n.a.
Pout, ocean, meat only, raw, 4 oz.	1.0	.4
Praline pecan mousse, frozen *(Weight Watchers),* 2.71 oz.	7.0	1.0
Preserves, fruit, all flavors	0	0
Pretzel, 1 oz., except as noted:		
(A & Eagle)	2.0	n.a.
(Mr. Salty Juniors)	2.0	n.a.
all varieties, except hard *(Bachman)* . . .	2.0	n.a.
all varieties, except rings or twists *(Mr. Salty)*	1.0	n.a.
all varieties, except rods *(Rold Gold)* . . .	1.0	n.a.
beer *(Quinlan)*.	1.4	n.a.
braids *(Keebler* Butter Pretzels)	1.0	< 1.0
cheddar flavor *(Combos),* 1.8 oz.	9.0	n.a.
hard *(Bachman)*.	< 1.0	n.a.
knots *(Keebler* Butter Pretzels)	1.0	< 1.0
logs *(Quinlan)*	.8	n.a.
oat bran *(Quinlan)*	1.5	n.a.
rice bran *(Quinlan* No-Salt)	2.3	n.a.
rings, plain or butter flavor *(Mr. Salty)*	2.0	n.a.

Pretzel, continued

rods *(Rold Gold)*	2.0	n.a.
sticks or thins *(Quinlan/Quinlan* Ultra Thins)	.6	n.a.
thins, tiny *(Quinlan)*	1.5	n.a.
twists *(Mr. Salty),* 5 pieces	2.0	n.a.
Prickly pear, whole, 1 medium, 4.8 oz.	.5	n.a.
Prosciutto, boneless *(Hormel),* 1 oz.	7.0	n.a.
Prune, 1/2 cup:		
canned, in heavy syrup	.2	< .1
dehydrated, uncooked	.5	< .1
dried, uncooked, w/pits	.4	< .1
dried, stewed, unsweetened, w/pits	.2	< .1
Prune juice, canned, (all brands), 6 fl. oz.	.1	< .1
Pudding, ready-to-serve:		
all flavors *(Hunt's Snack Pack* Lite), 4 oz.	2.0	n.a.
all flavors, except chocolate fudge *(Jell-O* Light Pudding Snacks), 4 oz.	2.0	n.a.
all flavors, except tapioca and vanilla *(Jell-O* Pudding Snacks), 4 oz.	6.0	n.a.
all swirl flavors *(Jell-O* Pudding Snacks), 4 oz.	6.0	n.a.
banana *(Del Monte* Pudding Cup), 5 oz.	5.0	n.a.
butterscotch *(Crowley),* 4.5 oz.	3.0	n.a.
butterscotch *(Del Monte* Pudding Cup), 5 oz.	5.0	n.a.
butterscotch *(White House),* 3.5 oz.	3.0	n.a.
chocolate:		
(Del Monte Pudding Cup), 5 oz.	6.0	n.a.
(Hunt's Snack Pack), 4.25 oz.	5.0	n.a.
(Swiss Miss), 4 oz.	6.0	n.a.
fudge *(Del Monte* Pudding Cup), 5 oz.	6.0	n.a.
fudge *(Jell-O* Light Pudding Snacks), 4 oz.	1.0	n.a.
lemon *(White House),* 3.5 oz.	1.0	n.a.
rice *(Crowley),* 4.5 oz.	2.0	n.a.
rice *(White House),* 3.5 oz.	3.0	n.a.
tapioca *(Del Monte* Pudding Cup), 5 oz.	4.0	n.a.
tapioca *(Hunt's Snack Pack),* 4.25 oz.	4.0	1.1
tapioca *(Jell-O* Pudding Snacks), 4 oz.	4.0	n.a.
tapioca *(Swiss Miss),* 4 oz.	4.0	n.a.

tapioca or vanilla *(Swiss Miss* Lite), 4 oz.	2.0	n.a.
vanilla:		
(Del Monte Pudding Cup), 5 oz.	5.0	n.a.
(Hunt's Snack Pack), 4.25 oz.	6.0	1.6
(Jell-O Pudding Snacks), 4 oz.	7.0	n.a.
(Swiss Miss), 4 oz.	6.0	n.a.
Pudding, frozen:		
butterscotch or vanilla *(Rich's)*, 3 oz.	6.0	n.a.
chocolate *(Rich's)*, 3 oz.	7.0	n.a.
Pudding bar, frozen, 1 bar:		
all varieties, except chocolate-peanut butter swirl *(Jell-O Pudding Pops)* . . .	2.0	n.a.
chocolate-peanut butter swirl *(Jell-O Pudding Pops)*	3.0	n.a.
Pudding mix*, 1/2 cup, except as noted:		
banana cream *(Jell-O* Instant/Microwave)	4.0	n.a.
banana cream *(Royal)*	4.0	n.a.
banana cream *(Royal* Instant)	5.0	n.a.
butter almond, toasted *(Royal* Instant)	4.0	n.a.
butter pecan *(Jell-O* Instant)	5.0	n.a.
butterscotch *(Jell-O/Jell-O* Instant/ Microwave)	4.0	n.a.
butterscotch *(Royal)*	4.0	n.a.
butterscotch *(Royal* Instant)	5.0	n.a.
chocolate *(Jell-O/Jell-O* Instant)	4.0	n.a.
chocolate, plain or milk *(Jell-O* Microwave)	5.0	n.a.
chocolate, all varieties *(Royal/Royal* Instant)	4.0	n.a.
chocolate, fudge or milk *(Jell-O)*	4.0	n.a.
chocolate, fudge or milk *(Jell-O* Instant)	5.0	n.a.
coconut, toasted *(Royal* Instant)	4.0	n.a.
coconut cream *(Jell-O* Instant)	6.0	n.a.
custard or flan w/caramel sauce *(Royal)*	5.0	n.a.
custard, egg, golden *(Jell-O Americana)*	5.0	n.a.
flan *(Jell-O)*	4.0	n.a.
lemon *(Jell-O* Instant)	4.0	n.a.
lemon or key lime *(Royal)*	3.0	n.a.
lemon *(Royal* Instant)	5.0	n.a.
pistachio *(Jell-O* Instant)	5.0	n.a.
pistachio nut *(Royal* Instant)	4.0	n.a.

Pudding mix, continued

rennet custard, all flavors *(Junket)*	4.0	n.a.
rice *(Jell-O Americana)*	4.0	n.a.
tapioca, vanilla *(Jell-O Americana)*	4.0	n.a.
tapioca, vanilla *(Royal)*	4.0	n.a.
vanilla, all varieties *(Jell-O/Jell-O* Instant/ Microwave)	4.0	n.a.
vanilla *(Royal)*	4.0	n.a.
vanilla *(Royal* Instant)	5.0	n.a.
Puff pastry, frozen (see also "Pie crust shell"):		
patty shells *(Pepperidge Farm),* 1 shell . .	15.0	n.a.
sheets *(Pepperidge Farm),* 1/4 sheet	17.0	n.a.
shells, mini *(Pepperidge Farm),* 1 shell	4.0	n.a.
Pummelo, 1 medium, 51/2″ diam.	.2	(0)
Pumpkin:		
fresh, raw or boiled, drained, mashed, 1/2 cup	.1	< .1
canned, 1/2 cup	.3	.2
Pumpkin pie spice, 1 tsp.	.2	n.a.
Pumpkin seed:		
roasted, shelled, 1 oz.	12.0	2.2
roasted, shelled, 1 cup	95.6	18.1
dried, shelled, 1 oz.	13.0	2.5
Purslane, boiled, drained, 1/2 cup	.1	(0)

food and measure	total fat (gms.)	saturated fat (gms.)
Quail, fresh, raw:		
meat w/skin, 1 oz.	3.4	1.0
meat only, 1 oz.	1.3	.4
breast, meat only, 1 oz.	.8	.2
Quince, fresh, 1 medium, 5.3 oz.	.1	tr.
Quinoa, 1 cup	9.9	1.0

food and measure	total fat (gms.)	saturated fat (gms.)
Rabbit, meat only:		
domesticated, roasted, 4 oz.	7.2	2.1
domesticated, stewed, 4 oz.	9.5	2.8
wild, stewed, 4 oz.	4.0	1.2
Radish:		
black, trimmed, 1 oz.	< .1	tr.
Oriental, raw, sliced, 1/2 cup	< .1	< .1
Oriental, boiled, drained, sliced, 1/2 cup	.2	.1
Oriental, dried, 1/2 cup	.4	.1
red, 10 medium, 3/4″–1″ diam.	.2	< .1

red, sliced, 1/2 cup	.3	< .1
white icicle, sliced, 1/2 cup	.1	< .1
Radish sprouts, 1/2 cup	.5	.1
Raisin:		
seeded, 1/2 cup packed	.5	.1
seedless, regular or golden, 1/2 cup packed	.4	.1
Raspberry:		
fresh, trimmed, 1/2 cup	.3	< .1
canned, in syrup or frozen, sweetened, 1/2 cup	.2	tr.
frozen, red, in light syrup *(Birds Eye Quick Thaw Pouch),* 5 oz.	1.0	tr.
Raspberry danish:		
(Awrey's Square), 3 oz.	8.0	2.0
fried *(Hostess Breakfast Bake Shop),* 1 piece	20.0	10.0
frozen *(Pepperidge Farm),* 1 piece	9.0	n.a.
twist, frozen *(Sara Lee),* 1/8 pkg.	9.0	n.a.
Raspberry juice or juice cocktail, all blends (all brands), 6 fl. oz.	<.3	(0)
Raspberry mousse mix* *(Weight Watchers),* 1/2 cup	3.0	n.a.
Raspberry turnover, frozen *(Pepperidge Farm),* 1 piece	17.0	n.a.
Ravioli, canned, 7.5 oz.:		
beef *(Chef Boyardee* Microwave)	4.0	2.0
beef *(Estee)*	11.0	4.0
beef *(Nalley's)*	3.0	n.a.
beef, in meat sauce *(Franco-American RavioliO's)*	8.0	n.a.
beef, in tomato sauce *(Hormel Micro-Cup)*	11.0	n.a.
cheese, in meat sauce *(Chef Boyardee* Microwave)	3.0	n.a.
cheese, in sauce *(Buitoni)*	6.0	2.0
meat, in sauce *(Buitoni)*	4.0	1.0
Ravioli, frozen (see also "Ravioli entrée"):		
(Celentano), 6.5 oz.	11.0	n.a.
cheese *(Buitoni),* 1/4 pkg. or 4 oz.	8.0	5.0
mini *(Celentano),* 4 oz.	5.0	n.a.

Ravioli entrée, frozen:

cheese *(The Budget Gourmet* Slim Selects), 10 oz.	7.0	n.a.
cheese, baked *(Weight Watchers),* 9 oz.	9.0	4.0

Red snapper, see "Snapper"

Redfish, see "Ocean perch"

Refried beans, see "Beans, refried"

Relish, all varieties, 1 oz.	<2.0	(0)
Rhubarb, fresh, raw, diced, or frozen, ½ cup	.1	(0)
Rib sauce *(Dip n'Joy* Saucey Rib), 1 oz.	0	0

Rice, cooked, plain:

basmati, white, long grain *(Texmati),* ½ cup	0	0
brown, long grain, 1 cup	1.8	.4
brown, medium grain, 1 cup	1.6	.3
glutinous or sweet, 1 cup	.5	.1
white, long grain, regular, 1 cup	.6	.2
white, long grain, parboiled, 1 cup	.5	.1
white, long grain, precooked or instant, 1 cup	.3	.1
white, medium or short grain, 1 cup	.4	.1
wild, see "Wild rice"		

Rice beverage, chocolate *(Rice Dream),* 6 fl. oz.	2.0	n.a.

Rice bran, crude:

1 oz.	5.9	1.2
1 cup	17.3	3.5

Rice cake, 1 piece, except as noted:

all varieties *(Hain)*	< 1.0	(0)
all varieties *(Lundberg)*	.5	(0)
all varieties, except multigrain *(Quaker)*	.3	.1
plain, apple cinnamon, honey nut, or teriyaki *(Hain* Mini), ½ oz.	< 1.0	(0)
barbecue or ranch *(Hain* Mini), ½ oz.	3.0	n.a.
brown rice *(Konriko* Original Unsalted)	0	0
cheese, plain or nacho *(Hain* Mini), ½ oz.	2.0	n.a.
multigrain *(Quaker)*	.4	.1

Rice dishes, canned (see also specific listings):

fried *(La Choy)*, 3/4 cup	1.0	n.a.
Spanish *(Old El Paso)*, 1/2 cup	1.0	0
Spanish *(Van Camp's)*, 1 cup	2.7	n.a.
Rice dishes, frozen:		
and broccoli, au gratin *(Birds Eye For One)*, 5.75 oz.	6.0	n.a.
and broccoli, in cheese sauce *(Green Giant One Serving)*, 5.5 oz.	6.0	2.0
and broccoli, in flavored cheese sauce *(Green Giant Rice Originals)*, 1/2 cup	4.0	n.a.
Country or French style *(Birds Eye International)*, 3.3 oz.	0	0
fried, w/chicken *(Chun King)*, 8 oz. . . .	4.0	n.a.
fried, w/pork *(Chun King)*, 8 oz.	6.0	n.a.
Italian blend and spinach, in cheese sauce *(Green Giant Rice Originals)*, 1/2 cup	4.0	2.0
medley *(Green Giant Rice Originals)*, 1/2 cup	1.0	< 1.0
Oriental, and vegetables *(The Budget Gourmet Side Dish)*, 5.75 oz.	10.0	n.a.
peas and mushrooms, w/sauce *(Green Giant One Serving)*, 5.5 oz.	2.0	< 1.0
pilaf *(Green Giant Rice Originals)*, 1/2 cup	1.0	< 1.0
pilaf w/green beans *(The Budget Gourmet Side Dish)*, 5.5 oz.	9.0	n.a.
Spanish style *(Birds Eye* International Rice Recipes), 3.3 oz.	0	0
white and wild rice *(Green Giant Rice Originals)*, 1/2 cup	2.0	< 1.0
wild, sherry *(Green Giant* Microwave Garden Gourmet), 1 pkg.	4.0	2.0
Rice dishes, mix*, 1/2 cup, except as noted:		
Alfredo, w/out butter *(Country Inn)* . . .	4.0	n.a.
almondine *(Hain* 3-Grain Side Dish) . . .	5.0	n.a.
asparagus, w/hollandaise sauce *(Lipton Rice and Sauce)*	7.0	n.a.
asparagus au gratin, w/out butter *(Country Inn)*	3.0	n.a.
au gratin herb *(Success)*	0	0
au gratin, herbed, w/out butter *(Country Inn)*	3.0	n.a.

Rice dishes, mix, continued
  beef flavor:

(*Lipton* Rice and Sauce)	3.0	n.a.
(*Minute* Microwave Family Size)	3.0	n.a.
(*Minute* Microwave Single Size)	2.0	n.a.
(*Mahatma*)	0	0
(*Rice-A-Roni*)	4.0	n.a.
(*Success*)	0	0
and mushroom (*Rice-A-Roni*)	3.0	n.a.
and vermicelli (*Make-it-easy*), 1.3 oz. dry	1.0	n.a.
broccoli almondine, w/out butter (*Country Inn*)	2.0	n.a.
broccoli au gratin (*Golden Grain/Rice-A-Roni Savory Classics*)	9.0	n.a.
broccoli au gratin, w/out butter (*Country Inn*)	3.0	n.a.
broccoli stir-fry (*Suzi Wan* Dinner Recipe), 7.5 oz.	15.0	n.a.
brown and wild (*Success*)	0	0
brown and wild, plain or mushroom (*Uncle Ben's*)	1.0	n.a.
Cajun (*Lipton* Rice and Sauce)	3.0	n.a.
cauliflower au gratin:		
(*Golden Grain/Rice-A-Roni Savory Classics*)	7.0	n.a.
w/out butter (*Country Inn*)	3.0	n.a.
cheddar:		
and broccoli (*Minute* Microwave Family Size)	5.0	n.a.
and broccoli (*Minute* Microwave Single Size)	4.0	n.a.
zesty (*Golden Grain/Rice-A-Roni Savory Classics*)	7.0	n.a.
chicken and chicken flavor:		
(*Lipton* Rice and Sauce)	4.0	n.a.
(*Mahatma*)	0	0
(*Minute* Microwave Family Size)	4.0	n.a.
(*Minute* Microwave Single Size)	3.0	n.a.
(*Rice-A-Roni*)	4.0	n.a.
(*Success*)	2.0	n.a.

and broccoli *(Rice-A-Roni)*	3.0	n.a.
and broccoli, w/out butter *(Suzi Wan)*	1.0	n.a.
creamy, mushroom, w/out butter		
(Country Inn)	3.0	n.a.
drumstick *(Minute)*	4.0	n.a.
homestyle, w/out butter *(Country Inn)*	3.0	n.a.
honey lemon *(Suzi Wan* Dinner		
Recipe), 7.5 oz.	11.0	n.a.
and mushroom *(Rice-A-Roni)*	7.0	n.a.
royale or stock, w/out butter *(Country*		
Inn)	1.0	n.a.
and vegetables *(Rice-A-Roni)*	3.0	n.a.
and vegetables, w/out butter *(Suzi*		
Wan)	1.0	n.a.
and vermicelli *(Make-it-easy)*, 1.3 oz.		
dry	1.0	n.a.
Florentine, w/out butter *(Country Inn)*	3.0	n.a.
Florentine chicken *(Golden Grain/Rice-A-*		
Roni Savory Classics)	4.0	n.a.
fried *(Minute)*	5.0	n.a.
fried *(Rice-A-Roni)*	5.0	n.a.
green bean almondine *(Golden Grain/*		
Rice-A-Roni Savory Classics)	11.0	n.a.
green bean almondine casserole, w/out		
butter *(Country Inn)*	2.0	n.a.
herb and butter *(Rice-A-Roni)*	4.0	n.a.
herb and butter *(Lipton* Rice and Sauce)	5.0	n.a.
long grain and wild:		
(Mahatma)	0	0
(Minute)	4.0	n.a.
(Near East)	4.0	n.a.
w/out butter *(Uncle Ben's* Original/Fast		
Cooking)	< 1.0	n.a.
chicken, w/almonds *(Rice-A-Roni)* . . .	4.0	n.a.
chicken stock, w/out butter *(Uncle*		
Ben's)	2.0	n.a.
mushrooms and herbs *(Lipton* Rice and		
Sauce)	3.0	n.a.
original *(Lipton* Rice and Sauce)	3.0	n.a.
original or pilaf *(Rice-A-Roni)*	3.0	n.a.
Mexican *(Old El Paso)*	2.0	n.a.

Rice dishes, mix, continued

mushroom *(Lipton* Rice and Sauce) . . .	3.0	n.a.
mushroom, creamy, w/out butter *(Country Inn)*	3.0	n.a.
Oriental *(Hain* 3-Grain Goodness)	5.0	n.a.
Parmesan, creamy, and herbs *(Golden Grain Rice-A-Roni Savory Classics)*	7.0	n.a.
pilaf:		
(Casbah)	0	0
(Lipton Rice and Sauce)	6.0	n.a.
(Near East)	5.0	n.a.
(Rice-A-Roni)	4.0	n.a.
(Success)	0	0
beef flavored *(Near East)*	5.0	n.a.
brown, w/miso *(Quick Pilaf)*	1.0	n.a.
chicken flavored *(Near East)*	5.0	n.a.
French style *(Minute* Microwave Family Size)	3.0	n.a.
French style *(Minute* Microwave Single Size)	2.0	n.a.
garden *(Golden Grain/Rice-A-Roni Savory Classics)*	4.0	n.a.
lentil *(Near East)*	7.0	n.a.
nutted *(Casbah)*	2.0	n.a.
Spanish, brown *(Quick Pilaf)*	.7	n.a.
vegetable, w/out butter *(Country Inn)*	1.0	n.a.
wheat *(Near East)*	6.0	n.a.
rib roast *(Minute)*	4.0	n.a.
risotto *(Rice-A-Roni)*	6.0	n.a.
risotto, chicken and cheese, w/out butter *(Country Inn)*	2.0	n.a.
Spanish:		
(Lipton Rice and Sauce)	3.0	n.a.
(Mahatma)	0	0
(Near East)	7.0	n.a.
(Rice-A-Roni)	4.0	n.a.
pilaf *(Casbah)*	0	0
Stroganoff *(Rice-A-Roni)*	8.0	n.a.
sweet and sour *(Suzi Wan* Dinner Recipe), 7.5 oz.	5.0	n.a.
sweet and sour, w/out butter *(Suzi Wan)*	1.0	n.a.

teriyaki *(Suzi Wan* Dinner recipe), 7.5 oz.	12.0	n.a.
teriyaki or 3-flavor, w/out butter *(Suzi Wan)*	1.0	n.a.
vegetable medley, w/out butter *(Country Inn)*	1.0	n.a.
w/vegetables:		
broccoli and cheddar *(Lipton* Rice and Sauce)	7.0	n.a.
spring, and cheese *(Golden Grain/Rice-A-Roni Savory Classics)*	7.0	n.a.
yellow *(Rice-A-Roni)*	4.0	n.a.
yellow *(Mahatma/Success)*	0	0
Rice seasoning, Mexican *(Lawry's* Seasoning Blends), 1 pkg.	2.0	n.a.
Rigatoni entrée, canned *(Chef Boyardee* Microwave), 7.5 oz.	6.0	n.a.
Rigatoni entrée, frozen, bake, w/meat sauce and cheese *(Lean Cuisine),* 9.75 oz.	10.0	3.0
Roast, vegetarian, frozen *(Worthington* Dinner Roast), 2 oz.	8.0	1.0
Robert sauce *(Escoffier* Sauce Robert), 1 tbsp.	0	0
Rockfish, Pacific, meat only:		
raw, 4 oz.	1.8	.4
baked, broiled, or microwaved, 4 oz.	2.3	.5
Roe, mixed species:		
1 oz.	1.8	.4
1 tbsp.	1.0	.2
Roll, 1 piece, except as noted:		
assorted *(Brownberry* Hearth)	2.3	n.a.
brown and serve:		
(Pepperidge Farm Hearth)	1.0	0
buttermilk or gem style *(Wonder)*	2.0	n.a.
club *(Pepperidge Farm)*	1.0	0
French *(Pepperidge Farm),* 1/2 piece	1.0	0
French, petite *(du Jour)*	2.0	n.a.
Italian, crusty *(du Jour)*	1.0	n.a.
crescent, butter *(Pepperidge Farm)*	6.0	2.0
dinner:		
(Arnold 24 Dinner Party)	1.2	n.a.
(Pepperidge Farm Old Fashioned)	2.0	1.0

Roll, dinner, continued

(*Pepperidge Farm* Party)	1.0	0
(*Roman Meal*)	1.2	n.a.
(*Wonder*)	1.0	n.a.
all varieties (*Awrey's*)	1.0	0
country (*Pepperidge Farm*)	1.0	0
wheat (*Home Pride*)	1.0	n.a.
white (*Home Pride*)	2.0	n.a.
egg (*Levy's* Old Country Deli), 1 oz.	2.8	n.a.
egg sandwich (*Arnold* Dutch)	3.3	n.a.
finger, poppy seed (*Pepperidge Farm*)	2.0	0
49er, sour (*Colombo* Brand)	.6	n.a.
49er, sweet (*Colombo* Brand)	1.8	n.a.
French style (*Francisco* International)	1.5	n.a.
French style (*Pepperidge Farm*)	1.0	0
French, sourdough (*Pepperidge Farm*)	1.0	0
hamburger:		
(*Arnold*)	2.2	n.a.
(*Pepperidge Farm*)	2.0	1.0
(*Wonder*)	2.0	n.a.
(*Wonder* Light)	1.0	n.a.
hamburger or hot dog (*Roman Meal*		
Original)	1.9	n.a.
hoagie (*Wonder*)	7.0	n.a.
hoagie, soft (*Pepperidge Farm*)	5.0	1.0
hot dog:		
(*Arnold*)	1.8	n.a.
(*Arnold* New England Style)	2.0	n.a.
(*Country Grain*)	1.0	n.a.
(*Pepperidge Farm*)	3.0	1.0
(*Wonder/Wonder* Light)	1.0	n.a.
Dijon (*Pepperidge Farm*)	5.0	1.0
oat bran (*Awrey's*)	2.0	0
kaiser (*Arnold* Francisco)	2.9	n.a.
kaiser (*Brownberry* Hearth)	2.8	n.a.
Luigi (*Colombo* Brand-Twin Pack)	1.6	n.a.
onion (*Levy's* Old Country Deli), 1 oz.	1.9	n.a.
onion, poppy seed (*Pepperidge Farm*)	3.0	1.0
pan (*Wonder*)	1.0	n.a.
Parker House (*Pepperidge Farm*)	1.0	0
sandwich:		

oat bran *(Awrey's)*	2.0	0
potato *(Pepperidge Farm)*	4.0	1.0
salad *(Pepperidge Farm)*	4.0	n.a.
sesame seed *(Pepperidge Farm)*	3.0	1.0
soft *(Pepperidge Farm* Family)	2.0	1.0
steak, sour *(Colombo* Brand)	2.2	n.a.
steak, sweet *(Colombo* Brand)	3.3	n.a.
twist, golden *(Pepperidge Farm)*	5.0	2.0
frozen, Parkerhouse *(Bridgford)*, 1 oz.	1.3	n.a.
refrigerator, butterflake *(Pillsbury)*	5.0	1.0
refrigerator, crescent *(Pillsbury)*	6.0	1.0
mix*, hot *(Dromedary)*, 2 pieces	5.0	n.a.
mix*, hot *(Pillsbury)*, 2 pieces	17.0	n.a.
Roll, sweet (see also "Bun, sweet"), 1 piece:		
cinnamon *(Awrey's* Homestyle)	7.0	1.0
cinnamon *(Hostess Breakfast Bake Shop)*	4.0	2.0
cinnamon swirl *(Awrey's* Grande)	16.0	3.0
orange swirl *(Hostess Breakfast Bake Shop)*	12.0	6.0
pecan *(Hostess Breakfast Bake Shop Spinners)*	10.0	2.0
pecan-caramel swirl *(Hostess Breakfast Bake Shop)*	15.0	7.0
strawberry *(Aunt Fanny's)*, 2 oz.	3.0	.8
frozen:		
apple or cheese *(Weight Watchers)*	4.0	< 1.0
cinnamon, all butter, w/icing *(Sara Lee)*	11.0	n.a.
strawberry *(Weight Watchers)*, 2.25 oz.	5.0	1.0
refrigerator, cinnamon, iced *(Hungry Jack)*	7.0	n.a.
refrigerator, cinnamon, iced *(Pillsbury)*	5.0	1.0
Roman bean, canned *(Progresso)*, 1/2 cup	< 1.0	n.a.
Rose apple, trimmed, 1 oz.	.1	(0)
Roselle, trimmed, 1 oz. or 1/2 cup	.2	(0)
Rosemary, dried, 1 tsp.	.2	(0)
Rotini entrée, frozen:		
cheddar *(Green Giant* Microwave Garden Gourmet), 1 pkg.	10.0	6.0
seafood *(Mrs. Paul's* Light), 9 oz.	6.0	2.0
Roughy, orange, meat only, raw, 4 oz.	7.9	.1

Roy Rogers:
breakfast,1 piece or serving:

crescent sandwich	27.0	n.a.
crescent sandwich, w/bacon	30.0	n.a.
crescent sandwich, w/ham	29.0	n.a.
crescent sandwich, w/sausage	42.0	n.a.
egg and biscuit platter	34.0	n.a.
egg and biscuit platter, w/bacon	39.0	n.a.
egg and biscuit platter, w/ham	36.0	n.a.
egg and biscuit platter, w/sausage	49.0	n.a.
pancake platter, w/syrup and butter:		
regular	13.0	n.a.
and bacon	17.0	n.a.
and ham	15.0	n.a.
and sausage	28.0	n.a.
chicken, fried, 1 serving:		
breast	24.0	n.a.
breast and wing	37.0	n.a.
leg (drumstick)	8.0	n.a.
leg and thigh	28.0	n.a.
nuggets, 6 pieces	18.0	n.a.
thigh	20.0	n.a.
wing	13.0	n.a.
sandwiches, 1 serving:		
bacon cheeseburger	33.0	n.a.
bar burger	31.0	n.a.
cheeseburger	29.0	n.a.
cheeseburger, small	13.0	n.a.
*Express*burger	32.0	n.a.
Express bacon cheeseburger	41.0	n.a.
Express cheeseburger	37.0	n.a.
fish sandwich	24.0	n.a.
hamburger	25.0	n.a.
hamburger, small	9.0	n.a.
roast beef sandwich, regular	11.0	n.a.
roast beef sandwich, w/cheese	15.0	n.a.
roast beef sandwich, large	12.0	n.a.
roast beef sandwich, large, w/cheese	17.0	n.a.
side dishes, 1 serving:		
biscuit	12.0	n.a.
coleslaw	7.0	n.a.

french fries, 4 oz.	16.0	n.a.
french fries, small, 3 oz.	12.0	n.a.
french fries, large, 5.5 oz.	22.0	n.a.
desserts and shakes, 1 serving:		
shake, chocolate or strawberry	10.0	n.a.
shake, vanilla	11.0	n.a.
sundae, caramel	9.0	n.a.
sundae, hot fudge	13.0	n.a.
sundae, strawberry	7.0	n.a.
Rutabaga, 1/2 cup:		
fresh, raw, cubed	.1	< .1
fresh, boiled, drained, cubed or mashed	.2	< .1
canned, diced *(Allens)*	< 1.0	(0)
Rye, whole grain, 1 cup	4.2	.5
Rye cake *(Quaker* Grain Cakes), 1 piece	.3	0

food and measure	total fat (gms.)	saturated fat (gms.)
Sablefish, meat only:		
raw, 4 oz.	17.4	3.6
smoked, 4 oz.	22.8	4.8
Safflower seed kernels, dried, 1 oz.	10.9	1.0
Safflower seed meal, partially defatted, 1 oz.	.7	.1
Saffron, 1 tsp.	< .1	(0)
Sage, ground, 1 tsp.	.1	< .1
Salad dip, egg-free *(Nasoya Vegi-Dip)*, 1 oz.	3.0	n.a.

Salad dressing, 1 tbsp., except as noted:

all varieties:

(*Kraft Free/Kraft Free Catalina*)	0	0
(*Seven Seas Free/Seven Seas Viva Free*)	0	0
except garden tomato (*Hain* Canola Oil)	5.0	n.a.
bacon, creamy (*Kraft* Reduced Calorie)	2.0	0
bacon and tomato (*Kraft*)	7.0	1.0
bacon and tomato (*Kraft* Reduced Calorie)	2.0	1.0
blue cheese:		
(*Roka* Brand)	6.0	1.0
(*Roka* Brand Reduced Calorie)	1.0	1.0
chunky (*Kraft*)	6.0	1.0
chunky (*Kraft* Reduced Calorie)	2.0	1.0
chunky (*Wish-Bone*)	7.9	1.2
chunky (*Wish-Bone* Lite)	3.7	.8
buttermilk:		
(*Hain* Old Fashioned)	7.0	n.a.
(*Hollywood* Old Fashion)	8.0	1.0
(*Seven Seas Buttermilk Recipe*)	8.0	1.0
creamy (*Kraft*)	8.0	1.0
creamy (*Kraft* Reduced Calorie)	3.0	0
Caesar:		
(*Hollywood*)..................	7.0	1.0
(*Lawry's* Classic), 1 oz.	13.5	1.8
(*Wish-Bone*)	8.0	1.2
creamy (*Hain*)	6.0	n.a.
golden (*Kraft*)	7.0	1.0
Chinese vinegar, w/sesame and ginger (*Lawry's* Classic), 1 oz.	15.0	2.1
coleslaw (*Kraft/Miracle Whip*)	6.0	1.0
creamy (*Rancher's Choice*)	10.0	1.0
creamy (*Rancher's Choice* Reduced Calorie)	3.0	0
creamy, egg-free (*Life* All Natural)....	4.0	n.a.
cucumber, creamy (*Kraft*)	8.0	1.0
cucumber, creamy (*Kraft* Reduced Calorie)	2.0	0
cucumber dill (*Hain*)	8.0	n.a.
Dijon vinaigrette (*Hollywood*)	6.0	1.0

Salad dressing, continued

Dijon vinaigrette *(Wish-Bone* Classic)	6.1	.9
Dijon vinaigrette *(Wish-Bone* Lite Classic)	2.8	n.a.
dill, creamy *(Nasoya Vegi-Dressing)* . . .	3.0	n.a.
French:		
(Catalina)	5.0	1.0
(Catalina/Kraft Reduced Calorie) . . .	1.0	0
(Kraft/Kraft Miracle)	6.0	1.0
(Seven Seas French! Light)	3.0	0
(Wish-Bone Deluxe)	5.4	.8
(Wish-Bone Lite)	2.5	n.a.
(Wish-Bone Lite Sweet'n Spicy)	.5	n.a.
(Wish-Bone Sweet'N Spicy)	5.7	.8
creamy *(Hain)*	6.0	n.a.
creamy *(Hollywood)*	7.0	1.0
creamy *(Seven Seas)*	6.0	1.0
garlic *(Wish-Bone)*	5.3	n.a.
red *(Wish-Bone* Lite)	.4	n.a.
style *(Wish-Bone* Lite)	2.5	.1
garlic, creamy *(Kraft)*	5.0	1.0
garlic, creamy *(Wish-Bone)*	8.0	n.a.
garlic, French *(Wish-Bone)*	5.3	n.a.
garlic and sour cream *(Hain)*	7.0	n.a.
herb *(Seven Seas Viva Herbs & Spices! Light)*	3.0	0
herb, savory *(Hain* No Salt Added) . . .	10.0	n.a.
herb and spice *(Seven Seas Viva)*	6.0	1.0
homestyle *(Dorothy Lynch)*	3.8	.5
homestyle *(Dorothy Lynch* Reduced Calorie)	< 1.0	n.a.
honey and sesame *(Hain)*	5.0	n.a.
Italian:		
(Hain Traditional)	8.0	n.a.
(Hain Traditional No Salt Added) . . .	6.0	n.a.
(Hollywood)	9.0	1.0
(Kraft House Italian)	6.0	1.0
(Kraft Presto)	7.0	1.0
(Nasoya Vegi-Dressing)	3.0	n.a.
(Ott's)	9.1	n.a.
(Seven Seas Viva)	5.0	1.0

(Seven Seas Viva Creamy Italian! Light)	4.0	1.0
(Seven Seas Viva Italian! Light)	3.0	0
(Wish-Bone/Wish Bone Robusto) . . .	4.5	.6
(Wish-Bone Lite)	.3	n.a.
blended *(Wish-Bone)*	3.6	.5
w/bleu cheese *(Lawry's* Classic), 1 oz.	2.0	n.a.
cheese *(Hollywood)*	8.0	1.0
w/cheese *(Wish-Bone)*	9.2	1.3
cheese vinaigrette *(Hain)*	6.0	n.a.
creamy *(Hain/Hain* No Salt Added)	8.0	n.a.
creamy *(Hollywood)*	9.0	1.0
creamy *(Seven Seas)*	7.0	1.0
creamy *(Weight Watchers)*	5.0	1.0
creamy *(Wish-Bone)*	5.5	.9
creamy *(Wish-Bone* Lite)	2.0	.4
creamy, w/real sour cream *(Kraft)* . . .	5.0	1.0
creamy or house *(Kraft* Reduced Calorie)	2.0	0
herbal *(Wish-Bone* Classics)	7.3	n.a.
oil free *(Kraft* Reduced Calorie)	0	0
w/Parmesan cheese *(Lawry's* Classic), 1 oz.	15.1	2.1
zesty *(Kraft)*	5.0	1.0
zesty *(Kraft* Reduced Calorie)	2.0	0
mayonnaise type (see also "Mayonnaise"):		
(Kraft Free/Miracle Whip Free)	0	0
(Miracle Whip)	7.0	1.0
(Miracle Whip Light)	4.0	1.0
(Spin Blend)	5.0	1.0
(Spin Blend Cholesterol Free)	4.0	1.0
(Weight Watchers Whipped)	4.0	1.0
oil and vinegar *(Kraft)*	8.0	1.0
olive oil, Italian *(Wish-Bone* Classic) . . .	3.0	.4
olive oil vinaigrette *(Wish-Bone)*	2.3	n.a.
olive oil vinaigrette *(Wish-Bone* Lite)	.9	.1
onion and chive *(Wish-Bone* Lite)	3.3	n.a.
poppyseed rancher's *(Hollywood)*	8.0	1.0
ranch:		
(Seven Seas Buttermilk Recipe Ranch! Light)	5.0	1.0

Salad dressing, ranch, continued

(Seven Seas Viva)	8.0	1.0
(Seven Seas Viva Ranch! Light)	5.0	1.0
(Wish-Bone)	8.3	1.2
(Wish-Bone Lite)	3.5	.7
red wine vinaigrette *(Wish-Bone)*	3.8	.5
red wine vinegar *(Seven Seas Viva Red Wine! Vinegar & Oil Light)*	4.0	1.0
red wine vinegar, w/Cabernet *(Lawry's Classics)*, 1 oz.	13.7	1.0
Russian:		
(Kraft Reduced Calorie)	1.0	0
(Weight Watchers)	5.0	1.0
(Wish-Bone)	2.5	.4
(Wish-Bone Lite)	.6	.1
creamy *(Kraft)*	5.0	1.0
w/pure honey *(Kraft)*	5.0	1.0
San Francisco, w/Romano cheese *(Lawry's* Classic), 1 oz.	14.0	1.9
sesame garlic *(Nasoya Vegi-Dressing)*	3.0	n.a.
sesame seed	6.9	.9
Swiss cheese vinaigrette *(Hain)*	7.0	n.a.
Thousand Island:		
(Hain)	5.0	n.a.
(Hollywood)	6.0	1.0
(Kraft)	5.0	1.0
(Kraft Reduced Calorie)	1.0	0
(Seven Seas Thousand Island! Light)	2.0	0
(Weight Watchers)	5.0	1.0
(Wish-Bone)	5.6	.8
(Wish-Bone Lite)	3.0	.4
creamy *(Seven Seas)*	5.0	1.0
and bacon *(Kraft)*	6.0	1.0
tomato, garden, vinaigrette *(Hain* Canola Oil)	6.0	n.a.
vinaigrette, see specific listings		
vinegar and oil, red wine *(Kraft)*	4.0	1.0
vinegar and oil, red wine *(Seven Seas Viva)*	7.0	1.0
vintage, w/sherry wine *(Lawry's* Classic), 1 oz.	10.5	2.1

white wine, w/Chardonnay *(Lawry's*
Classic), 1 oz. 15.7   2.0
Salad dressing mix*, 1 tbsp.:
   all varieties, except buttermilk and ranch
     (Good Seasons) . . . . 8.0   n.a.
   all varieties, except ranch *(Good Seasons*
     Lite) . . . . 3.0   n.a.
   bleu cheese *(Hain No Oil)* . . . . 1.0   n.a.
   buttermilk *(Good Seasons* Farm Style) 6.0   n.a.
   buttermilk, Caesar, or garlic and cheese
     (Hain No Oil) . . . . < 1.0   n.a.
   French, herb, Italian, or Thousand Island
     (Hain No Oil) 0   0
   Italian *(Good Seasons* No Oil) 0   0
   ranch *(Good Seasons)* . . . . 6.0   n.a.
   ranch *(Good Seasons* Lite) . . . . 2.0   n.a.
Salad nugget (see also "Crouton"):
   garlic'n cheese *(Flavor Tree),* 1/4 cup . . . 12.4   n.a.
   onion *(Flavor Tree),* 1/4 cup . . . . 11.0   n.a.
   sesame *(Flavor Tree* Original Sesame),
     1/4 cup . . . . 10.9   n.a.
Salad seasoning *(McCormick/Schilling* Salad
   Supreme), 1 tsp. 7   n.a.
Salami:
   beef:
     (Hebrew National Original Deli), 1 oz. 7.0   n.a.
     (Hormel Perma-Frcsh), 2 slices . . . . . 5.0   n.a.
     (Kahn's), 1 slice . . . . 6.0   n.a.
     (Kahn's Family Pack), 1 slice . . . . . . 5.0   n.a.
     (Oscar Mayer Machiaeh Brand), 1 slice 5.0   n.a.
     beer *(Oscar Mayer* Salami for Beer),
      1 slice 5.6   2.5
     cooked, 1 oz. 5.7   2.4
     and pork, cooked, 1 oz. 5.7   2.3
   beer *(Eckrich),* 1-oz. slice . . . . 6.0   n.a.
   beer *(Oscar Mayer* Salami for Beer),
     1 slice 4.0   1.7
   cooked *(Kahn's),* 1 slice . . . . 4.0   n.a.
   cotto:
     (Eckrich), 1-oz. slice . . . . 6.0   n.a.
     (Hormel Chub), 1 oz. . . . . 5.0   n.a.

Salami, cotto, continued

(Hormel Perma-Fresh), 2 slices	7.0	n.a.
(JM), 1-oz. slice	6.0	n.a.
(Kahn's Family Pack), 1 slice	3.0	n.a.
(Light & Lean), 2 slices	6.0	n.a.
(Oscar Mayer), .8-oz. slice	4.2	1.9
beef *(Eckrich),* 1.3 oz.	8.0	n.a.
beef *(Oscar Mayer),* .8-oz. slice	3.4	1.6
Genoa:		
(Hormel DiLusso), 1 oz.	8.0	n.a.
(Hormel/Hormel Gran Valore/San		
Remo), 1 oz.	10.0	n.a.
(JM), 1-oz. slice	8.0	n.a.
(Oscar Mayer), .3-oz. slice	2.8	1.2
hard:		
(Hormel/Hormel Sliced), 1 oz.	10.0	n.a.
(Hormel National Brand), 1 oz.	11.0	n.a.
(Hormel Perma-Fresh), 2 slices	7.0	n.a.
(Oscar Mayer), .3-oz. slice	2.8	1.2
pork, 1 oz.	9.6	3.3
pork and beef, 1 oz.	9.7	3.5
piccolo *(Hormel* Stick), 1 oz.	11.0	n.a.
"Salami," vegetarian, frozen:		
roll *(Worthington),* 1.5 oz.	5.0	1.0
slices *(Worthington),* 2 slices or 1.3 oz.	4.0	1.0
Salisbury steak dinner, frozen:		
(Armour Classics), 11.25 oz.	17.0	n.a.
(Armour Classics Lite), 11.5 oz.	2.0	n.a.
(Banquet), 11 oz.	34.0	n.a.
(Banquet Extra Helping), 18 oz.	60.0	n.a.
(Healthy Choice), 11.5 oz.	7.0	3.0
(Le Menu LightStyle), 10 oz.	9.0	n.a.
(Morton), 10 oz.	17.0	n.a.
(Swanson), 10.75 oz.	17.0	n.a.
(Swanson Hungry-Man), 16.5 oz.	41.0	n.a.
mushroom gravy *(Banquet Extra*		
Helping), 18 oz.	58.0	n.a.
parmigiana *(Armour Classics),* 11.5 oz.	21.0	n.a.
sirloin *(The Budget Gourmet),* 11.5 oz.	22.0	n.a.
Salisbury steak entrée, frozen:		
(Dining Lite), 9 oz.	8.0	n.a.

(Lean Cuisine), 9.5 oz.	15.0	5.0
(Swanson Homestyle Recipe), 10 oz.	16.0	n.a.
charbroiled *(Freezer Queen* Single Serve), 9 oz.	22.0	n.a.
gravy and *(Banquet Cookin' Bags)*, 5 oz.	14.0	n.a.
gravy and *(Banquet Family Entrees)*, 8 oz.	22.0	n.a.
gravy and *(Freezer Queen Family Suppers)*, 7 oz.	13.0	n.a.
in gravy *(Stouffer's)*, 9⅞ oz.	14.0	n.a.
Romana *(Weight Watchers)*, 8.75 oz.	7.0	2.0
sirloin *(The Budget Gourmet* Slim Selects), 9 oz.	8.0	n.a.
supreme *(Tyson Gourmet Selection)*, 10 oz.	26.0	n.a.
Salmon, meat only:		
fresh:		
Atlantic, raw, 4 oz.	7.2	1.1
Chinook, raw, 4 oz.	11.8	2.8
Chinook, smoked or lox, 4 oz.	4.9	1.1
chum, raw, 4 oz.	4.3	1.0
coho, raw, 4 oz.	6.7	1.2
coho, boiled, poached, or steamed, 4 oz.	8.6	1.6
pink, raw, 4 oz.	3.9	.6
sockeye, raw, 4 oz.	9.7	1.7
sockeye, baked, broiled, or microwaved, 4 oz.	12.4	2.2
canned:		
chum, drained, 4 oz.	6.2	1.7
chum, keta *(Bumble Bee)*, 1 cup	11.4	n.a.
coho, Alaska *(Deming's)*, 1/2 cup	5.0	n.a.
pink *(Bumble Bee)*, 1 cup	13.0	n.a.
pink, w/liquid, 4 oz.	6.9	1.7
pink, w/liquid *(Del Monte)*, 1/2 cup	7.0	n.a.
pink, Alaska *(Deming's)*, 1/2 cup	6.0	1.0
pink, chunk, in water *(Deming's)*, 3.25 oz.	5.0	n.a.
red, w/liquid *(Del Monte)*, 1/2 cup	9.0	n.a.
red, blueback *(Rubinstein's)*, 1/2 cup	9.0	n.a.
red sockeye:		
drained, 4 oz.	8.3	1.9

Salmon, canned, red sockeye,, continued

(*Bumble Bee*), 1 cup	20.5	n.a.
(*Libby's*), 7.75 oz.	21.0	n.a.
Alaska (*Deming's*), 1/2 cup	9.0	2.0
Alaska, medium (*Deming's*), 1/2 cup	7.0	2.0

Salsa, canned or in jars:

all varieties (*Del Monte*), 1/4 cup	0	0
(*Ortega*), 1 oz.	0	0
(*Old El Paso*), 2 tbsp.	< 1.0	0
(*Hain*), 1/4 cup	0	0
(*Enrico's* Chunky Style), 2 tbsp.	0	0
taco, mild (*Rosarita*), 2 oz.	.1	tr.

Salsify, raw or boiled, drained, sliced,

1/2 cup	.1	(0)
Salsify, black, 1 oz.	tr.	(0)
Salt, regular, kosher, or sea	0	0

Salt, seasoned, 1 tsp.:

(*Lawry's/Lawry's* Hot n' Spicy)	.1	(0)
(*Lawry's* Lite)	< .1	(0)
(*Morton/Morton Nature's Seasons*)	< .1	(0)

Salt, substitute or imitation:

(*Lawry's* Salt-Free 17), 1 tsp.	.2	(0)
(*Morton*), 1 tsp.	0	0
seasoned (*Health Valley Instead of Salt*), 1 tsp.	.5	(0)
seasoned (*Lawry's* Salt-Free), 1 tsp.	< .1	(0)
seasoned (*Morton*), 1 tsp.	< .1	(0)
Salt pork, raw, 1 oz.	22.8	8.3

Sandwich, see specific listings

Sandwich sauce (*Hunt's Manwich*), 2.5 oz.	0	0

Sandwich spread:

(*Oscar Mayer* Chub), 1 oz.	4.7	1.8
meatless (*Hellman's/Best Foods*), 1 tbsp.	5.0	1.0
meatless (*Kraft*), 1 tbsp.	5.0	1.0
Sapodilla, 1 medium, 3″ × 21/2″	1.9	n.a.
Sapote, 1 medium, 11.2 oz.	1.4	n.a.

Sardine, canned:

Atlantic, in oil, drained, 2 oz.	6.5	.9
Atlantic, in oil, 2 medium	2.8	.4
Brisling, in oil (*Underwood*), 3.75 oz.	20.0	n.a.

Norway, in oil, w/liquid *(Empress)*,
3.75 oz. . . . . 42.0   n.a.
Norway, in oil, drained *(Empress)*,
3.75 oz. . . . . 20.0   n.a.
Norwegian brisling *(S&W)*, 1.5 oz. . . . . 10.0   n.a.
Pacific, in tomato sauce, drained, 2 oz.   6.8   1.8
in mustard sauce *(Underwood)*, 3.75 oz.   16.0   n.a.
in sild oil, drained *(Underwood)*, 3 oz.   42.0   n.a.
in soya oil, drained *(Underwood)*, 3 oz.   18.0   n.a.
in *Tabasco* sauce, drained *(Underwood)*,
3 oz. 16.0   n.a.
in tomato sauce *(Del Monte)*, 1/2 cup   12.0   n.a.
kippered *(Brunswick Kippered Snacks)*,
3.5 oz. . . . . 14.0   n.a.
Sauerkraut, canned, plain (all brands),
1/2 cup . . . . < 1.0   (0)
Sausage (see also specific listings):
(Hillshire Farm Country Recipe), 2 oz.   16.0   n.a.
beef *(Jones Dairy Farm* Golden Brown),
1 link . . . . 6.1   n.a.
beef and cheddar *(Hillshire Farm*
Flavorseal), 2 oz. . . . . 15.0   n.a.
brown and serve:
(Hormel), 2 cooked links . . . . 13.0   n.a.
(Jones Dairy Farm Light), 1 link . . .   4.1   n.a.
(Swift Premium Microwave), 1 link   12.0   n.a.
(Swift Premium Original/Country
Recipe), 1 link or patty . . . .   12.0   n.a.
w/bacon or smoke *(Swift Premium)*,
1 link . . . . 11.0   n.a.
beef or maple flavor *(Swift Premium)*,
1 link . . . . 12.0   n.a.
w/ham *(Swift Premium)*, 1 link . . . . . 13.0   n.a.
heat 'n serve *(Eckrich* Lean Supreme),
2 links . . . . 10.0   n.a.
hot or mild, canned *(Hormel)*, 1 patty   13.0   n.a.
minced roll *(Eckrich)*, 1-oz. slice . . . . 7.0   n.a.
pickled, all varieties *(Penrose)*, .5-oz. link   3.0   n.a.
pork:
(Hormel Little Sizzlers), 2 links . . . . . 9.0   n.a.
(Hormel Midget Links), 2 links . . . . . 13.0   n.a.

Sausage, pork, continued

(JM), 1 cooked patty	6.0	n.a.
(JM Tasty Link), 2 cooked links	18.0	n.a.
(Jones Dairy Farm), 1 link	13.7	n.a.
(Jones Dairy Farm), 1 patty	14.4	n.a.
(Jones Dairy Farm Golden Brown)*, 1 patty	14.7	n.a.
(Jones Dairy Farm Golden Brown Light), 1 link	4.2	n.a.
(Jones Dairy Farm Light), 1 link	5.0	n.a.
(Oscar Mayer Little Friers), 1 cooked link	7.5	2.7
fresh, cooked, 1 link (1 oz. raw)	4.1	1.4
fresh, cooked, 1 patty (2 oz. raw)	8.4	2.9
hot *(JM)*, 1 cooked patty	6.0	n.a.
mild *(Jones Dairy Farm* Golden Brown), 1 link	9.8	n.a.
spicy *(Jones Dairy Farm* Golden Brown), 1 link	9.5	n.a.
pork and bacon *(JM* Tasty Link), 2 cooked links	9.0	n.a.
pork and beef, fresh, cooked, .5-oz. link (1 oz. raw)	4.7	1.7
smoked:		
(Eckrich Skinless), 1 link	16.0	n.a.
(Eckrich Lite), 1 link	13.0	n.a.
(Eckrich Lite Sausage Links), 1 link	17.0	n.a.
(Eckrich Lite Smok-Y-Links), 2 links	10.0	n.a.
(Hillshire Farm Bun Size), 2 oz.	16.0	n.a.
(Hillshire Farm Flavorseal), 2 oz.	17.0	n.a.
(Hillshire Farm Links), 2 oz.	18.0	n.a.
(Hillshire Farm Lite), 2 oz.	13.0	n.a.
(Hormel Smokies), 2 links	14.0	n.a.
(Oscar Mayer Little Smokies), 1 link	2.5	.9
(Oscar Mayer Smokie Links), 1 link	11.3	4.2
beef *(Eckrich)*, 1 oz.	9.0	n.a.
beef *(Eckrich Lite* Sausage Links), 1 link	16.0	n.a.
beef *(Eckrich Smok-Y-Links)*, 2 links	14.0	n.a.
beef *(Hillshire Farm* Bun Size), 2 oz.	16.0	n.a.

beef *(Oscar Mayer* Smokies), 1.5-oz. link	11.0	4.7
cheddar *(Eckrich Lite* Sausage Links), 1 link	16.0	n.a.
cheese *(Eckrich Smok-Y-Links),* 2 links	14.0	n.a.
cheese *(Hormel* Smokie Cheezers), 2 links	15.0	n.a.
cheese *(Oscar Mayer* Smokies), 1.5-oz. link	11.2	4.4
ham *(Eckrich Smok-Y-Links),* 2 links	15.0	n.a.
hot *(Eckrich Smok-Y-Links),* 2 links	14.0	n.a.
hot *(Hillshire Farm* Flavorseal), 2 oz.	16.0	n.a.
original or maple flavored *(Eckrich Smok-Y-Links),* 2 links	14.0	n.a.
pork, 1 oz.	9.0	3.2
pork *(Hormel),* 3 oz.	27.0	n.a.
pork and beef, 1 oz.	8.6	3.0
"Sausage," vegetarian:		
canned *(Worthington Saucettes),* 2 links	9.0	1.0
frozen:		
(Morningstar Farms Breakfast Links), 3 links	14.0	2.0
(Morningstar Farms Breakfast Patties), 2 patties	12.0	2.0
(Worthington Prosage), 3 links	14.0	2.0
(Worthington Prosage), 2 patties	14.0	3.0
roll *(Worthington Prosage),* 2.5 oz.	12.0	2.0
Sausage breakfast biscuit, 1 piece:		
frozen *(Swanson Great Starts)*	22.0	n.a.
frozen *(Weight Watchers* Microwave), 3 oz.	11.0	2.0
refrigerated:		
(Owens Border Breakfasts)	14.0	n.a.
egg and cheese *(Owens Border Breakfasts)*	15.0	n.a.
smoked *(Owens Border Breakfasts)*	6.0	n.a.
Sausage breakfast taco, refrigerated *(Owens Border Breakfasts),* 2.17 oz.	12.0	n.a.
Sausage stick (see also "Beef jerky"), 1 stick:		

Sausage stick, continued
smoked:

(*Slim Jim Big Slim*)	7.0	n.a.
(*Slim Jim Giant Slim*)	16.0	n.a.
(*Slim Jim Jumbo Jim*)	12.0	n.a.
(*Slim Jim Super Slim/Super Slim*		
Tabasco)	10.0	n.a.
all varieties (*Slim Jim* Handi-Paks)	4.0	n.a.
nacho (*Slim Jim Super Slim*), .31 oz.	3.0	n.a.
summer sausage, smoked (*Slim Jim*),		
.5 oz.	7.0	n.a.
Savory, ground, 1 tsp.	.1	(0)
Scallion, see "Onion, green"		
Scallop, meat only:		
fresh, raw, 4 oz.	.9	.1
fresh, raw, 2 large or 5 small	.2	< .1
frozen, fried (*Mrs. Paul's*), 3 oz.	7.0	n.a.
Scallop, imitation (from surimi), raw, 4 oz.	.5	n.a.
"Scallop," vegetarian, canned (*Worthington*		
Vegetable Skallops), 1/2 cup	2.0	n.a.
Scallop and shrimp dinner, frozen, Mariner		
(*The Budget Gourmet*), 11.5 oz.	9.0	n.a.
Scrapple (*Jones Dairy Farm*), 1 slice	3.7	n.a.
Scrod, see "Cod, meat only, fresh Atlantic"		
Scrod entrée, frozen, baked (*Gorton's*		
Microwave Entrees), 1 pkg.	18.0	4.0
Scup, meat only, raw, 4 oz.	3.1	n.a.
Sea bass (see also "Bass"), meat only:		
raw, 4 oz.	2.3	.6
baked, broiled, or microwaved, 4 oz. . . .	2.9	.7
Sea trout (see also "Trout"), meat only,		
raw, 4 oz.	4.1	1.1
Seafood, see specific listings		
Seafood dinner, frozen, w/natural herbs		
(*Armour Classics Lite*), 10 oz.	2.0	n.a.
Seafood entrée, frozen:		
casserole (*Pillsbury Microwave Classic*),		
1 pkg.	24.0	n.a.
combination, breaded (*Mrs. Paul's*), 9 oz.	33.0	8.0
Creole, w/rice (*Swanson* Homestyle		
Recipe), 9 oz.	6.0	n.a.

gumbo *(Cajun Cookin')*, 17 oz.	7.0	n.a.
Newberg *(The Budget Gourmet)*, 10 oz.	12.0	n.a.
Newburg *(Healthy Choice)*, 8 oz.	3.0	1.0
Seafood sauce (see also "Cocktail sauce"):		
(Progresso Authentic Pasta Sauces),		
1/2 cup	15.0	9.0
Creole *(Great Impressions)*, 1 tbsp.	.1	n.a.
dipping *(Great Impressions)*, 1 tbsp.	.7	n.a.
dipping, Polynesian *(Great Impressions)*,		
1 tbsp.	< 1.0	n.a.
mixed *(Progresso)*, 1/2 cup	6.0	< 1.0
Seafood-crabmeat salad *(Longacre*		
Saladfest), 1 oz.	3.0	n.a.
Seaweed, 1 oz.:		
agar, raw	tr.	tr.
agar, dried	.1	< .1
kelp, raw	.2	.1
laver or spirulina, raw	.1	< .1
spirulina, dried	2.2	.8
wakame, raw	.2	< .1
Semolina, whole grain, 1 cup	1.8	.3
Sesame butter:		
paste, from whole sesame seeds, 1 tbsp.	8.1	1.1
tahini (see also "Tahini mix"):		
from raw, stone-ground kernels, 1 tbsp.	7.2	1.0
from unroasted kernels, 1 tbsp.	7.9	1.1
from roasted and toasted kernels,		
1 tbsp.	8.1	1.1
Sesame chips *(Flavor Tree)*, 1/4 cup	9.2	n.a.
Sesame meal, partially defatted, 1 oz.	13.6	1.9
Sesame nut mix, dry roasted *(Planters)*,		
1 oz.	12.0	3.0
Sesame paste, see "Sesame butter"		
Sesame seasoning *(McCormick/Schilling*		
Parsley Patch), 1 tsp.	1.0	n.a.
Sesame seed:		
whole, dried, 1 oz.	14.1	2.0
whole, roasted and toasted, 1 oz.	13.6	1.9
kernels, dried, 1 oz.	15.5	2.2
kernels, toasted, 1 oz.	13.6	1.9

Sesame sticks:

(Flavor Tree), 1/4 cup	9.1	n.a.
(Flavor Tree No Salt), 1/4 cup	8.1	n.a.

7-Eleven:

bacon cheeseburger, 6 oz.	28.7	2.3
bagel and cream cheese, 4 oz.	16.1	9.6
Big Bite (2 oz. beef weiner), 3.4 oz.	18.1	7.3
Big Bite, super (4 oz. beef weiner), 5.4 oz.	34.1	14.1
burrito, bean and cheese, 10 oz.	23.1	7.5
burrito, beef and bean:		
5 oz.	11.5	3.8
green chili, 10 oz.	23.1	7.5
red chili, 5 oz.	11.5	3.8
red hot, 5 oz.	11.6	3.8
red hot, 10 oz.	23.2	7.6
red hot, premium, 5.2 oz.	17.1	5.7
burrito, beef, bean, and cheese, 5.2 oz.	20.5	8.1
burrito, beef and potato, 5.2 oz.	18.4	6.3
burrito, chicken and rice, premium, 5 oz.	5.6	1.0
char sandwich, large, 8.4 oz.	47.2	2.3
chicken, breast of, 4.8 oz.	15.7	n.a.
chimichanga, beef, 5 oz.	14.9	n.a.
enchilada, beef and cheese, 6.5 oz.	21.7	10.2
fajitas, 5 oz.	11.4	3.5
fish sandwich, w/cheese, 5.2 oz.	14.5	2.3
sandito, ham and cheese, 5 oz.	16.0	6.9
sandito, pizza, 5 oz.	17.0	5.1
sausage, red hot, large, 9.3 oz.	59.2	20.3
tacos, soft, twin, 5.9 oz.	19.7	7.9
turkey, wedge, 3.4 oz.	5.6	1.6

Shad, American, meat only, raw, 4 oz. . . . 15.6   n.a.

Shallot:

raw, trimmed, 1 oz., or chopped, 1 tbsp.	< .1	tr.
freeze-dried, 1/4 cup	< .1	tr.

Shark, meat only, raw, 4 oz. 5.1   1.0

Sheepshead, meat only:

raw, 4 oz.	2.7	.7
baked, broiled, or microwaved, 4 oz.	1.8	.4

Shells, stuffed, frozen, 3-cheese *(Le Menu*
LightStyle), 10 oz. . . . . 8.0   n.a.

Sherbet:

all flavors, except rainbow *(Sealtest),*		
1/2 cup	1.0	0
orange, 1/2 cup	1.9	1.2
rainbow *(Sealtest),* 1/2 cup	1.0	1.0

Sherbet bar, frozen, 1 bar:

all flavors *(Creamsicle Sugar Free)*	1.0	n.a.
all flavors *(Fudgsicle Fat Free)*	0	0
all flavors, except fudge nut dipped		
(Fudgsicle Sugar Free)	1.0	n.a.
chocolate *(Fudgsicle)*	1.0	n.a.
chocolate, fudge nut dipped *(Fudgsicle*		
Sugar Free)	8.0	n.a.

Shortening, household, 1 cup:

lard and vegetable oil	205.0	82.6
hydrogenated soybean and cottonseed	205.0	51.2
hydrogenated soybean, and palm	205.0	62.7

Shrimp, meat only:

fresh, raw, 4 oz.	2.0	.4
fresh, raw, 1 oz. or 4 large	.5	.1
fresh, boiled, poached, or steamed, 4 oz.	1.2	.3
fresh, boiled, poached, or steamed,		
4 large	.2	.1
canned, drained, 4 oz.	2.2	.4
canned, drained, 1 cup	2.5	.5

Shrimp cocktail *(Sau-Sea),* 4 oz. ... 1.0 n.a.

Shrimp dinner, frozen:

baby bay *(Armour Classics Lite),* 9.75 oz.	6.0	n.a.
Creole *(Armour Classics Lite),* 11.25 oz.	2.0	n.a.
Creole *(Healthy Choice),* 11.25 oz.	1.0	< 1.0
marinara *(Healthy Choice),* 10.5 oz.	1.0	< 1.0

Shrimp entrée, canned, chow mein *(La Choy* Bi-Pack), 3/4 cup ... 1.0 n.a.

Shrimp entrée, frozen (see also "Shrimp"):

'n batter *(SeaPak),* 4 oz.	15.0	n.a.
'n batter, w/crabmeat stuffing *(SeaPak),*		
4 oz.	13.0	n.a.
breaded, fried *(Mrs. Paul's)*, 3 oz.	11.0	n.a.
Cajun style *(Mrs. Paul's Light),* 9 oz.	5.0	1.0
and chicken Cantonese, w/noodles *(Lean Cuisine),* 10 1/8 oz.	9.0	1.0

Shrimp entrée, frozen, continued
   and clams w/linguini *(Mrs. Paul's* Light),

10 oz.	5.0	2.0
Creole *(Cajun Cookin')*, 12 oz.	11.0	n.a.
crisps *(Gorton's* Specialty), 4 oz.	15.0	n.a.
crunchy, whole *(Gorton's* Microwave Specialty), 5 oz.	20.0	3.0
étouffé *(Cajun Cookin')*, 17 oz.	9.0	n.a.
and fettuccine *(The Budget Gourmet)*, 9.5 oz.	20.0	n.a.
fettuccine Alfredo *(Booth)*, 10 oz.	8.0	n.a.
w/garlic butter sauce and vegetable rice *(Booth)*, 10 oz.	25.0	n.a.
jambalaya *(Cajun Cookin')*, 12 oz.	20.0	n.a.
w/lobster sauce *(La Choy Fresh & Lite)*, 10 oz.	6.2	n.a.
New Orleans, w/wild rice *(Booth)*, 10 oz.	5.0	n.a.
Oriental, w/pineapple rice *(Booth)*, 10 oz.	3.0	n.a.
primavera *(Mrs. Paul's* Light), 9.5 oz.	3.0	1.0
primavera *(Right Course)*, 9 5/8 oz.	7.0	1.0
primavera, w/fettuccine *(Booth)*, 10 oz.	3.0	n.a.
scampi *(Gorton's* Microwave Entrees), 1 pkg.	30.0	n.a.
Shrimp salad *(Longacre* Saladfest), 1 oz.	3.0	n.a.

Sloppy Joe seasoning:

(Lawry's Seasoning Blends), 1 pkg.	.4	n.a.
mix *(French's)*, 1/8 pkg.	0	0
mix *(McCormick/Schilling)*, 1/4 pkg.	.1	(0)

Smelt, rainbow, meat only:

raw, 4 oz.	2.7	.5
baked, broiled, or microwaved, 4 oz.	3.5	.7

Snack mix (see also specific listings):

(Eagle), 1 oz.	6.0	n.a.
(Flavor Tree Party Mix), 1/4 cup	11.0	n.a.
(Pepperidge Farm Classic), 1 oz.	8.0	1.0
(Super Snax), 1 oz.	6.5	n.a.
all flavors *(Ralston Chex)*, 1 oz. or 2/3 cup	5.0	n.a.
lightly smoked *(Pepperidge Farm)*, 1 oz.	9.0	1.0
spicy *(Pepperidge Farm)*, 1 oz.	8.0	2.0

Snap bean, see "Beans, green"

Snapper, mixed species, meat only:

raw, 4 oz.	1.5	.3
baked, broiled, or microwaved, 4 oz.	2.0	.1

Snow peas, see "Peas, edible-podded"

Soft drinks, carbonated, all varieties, 6 fl.

oz.	< 1.0	(0)

Sole, fresh, see "Flatfish"

Sole dinner, frozen, au gratin *(Healthy*

Choice), 11 oz.	5.0	3.0

Sole entrée, frozen:

breaded *(Mrs. Paul's* Light), 4.25 oz.	11.0	n.a.
breaded *(Van de Kamp's* Light), 1 piece	12.0	2.0
in lemon butter *(Gorton's Microwave*		
Entrees), 1 pkg.	24.0	11.0
w/lemon butter sauce *(Healthy Choice),*		
8.25 oz.	4.0	2.0
in wine sauce *(Gorton's Microwave*		
Entrees), 1 pkg.	8.0	3.0

Sorbet (see also "Sherbet" and "Ice"):

orange, pineapple, or strawberry *(Dole),*		
4 oz.	.1	(0)
peach *(Dole),* 4 oz.	.6	n.a.
raspberry *(Dole),* 4 oz.	< .1	(0)
raspberry *(Frusen Glädjé),* 1/2 cup	0	0
w/ice cream, all sorbet flavors, except key		
lime *(Häagen-Dazs),* 1/2 cup	8.0	n.a.
w/ice cream, key lime sorbet *(Häagen-*		
Dazs), 1/2 cup	7.0	n.a.

Sorghum, whole grain, 1 cup	6.3	.9

Sorrel, see "Dock"

Soup, canned, ready-to-serve, 9.5 oz., except
as noted:

bean:

(Grandma Brown's), 1 cup	3.4	n.a.
w/bacon and ham *(Campbell's*		
Microwave), 7.5 oz.	5.0	n.a.
black *(Health Valley),* 7.5 oz.	3.0	n.a.
w/ham *(Campbell's* Home Cookin')	4.0	n.a.
w/ham, chowder *(Hormel Micro-Cup*		
Hearty), 1 pkg.	3.0	n.a.

Soup, canned, ready-to-serve, bean, continued

w/ham (*Campbell's* Chunky Old Fashioned), 9⅝ oz.	8.0	n.a.
beef:		
(*Campbell's* Chunky)	4.0	n.a.
(*Progresso*)	5.0	n.a.
hearty (*Progresso*)	4.0	2.0
Stroganoff (*Campbell's* Chunky), 10.75 oz.	16.0	n.a.
w/vegetables and pasta (*Campbell's* Home Cookin')	2.0	n.a.
beef barley (*Progresso*)	4.0	n.a.
beef broth (*College Inn*), 1 cup	0	0
beef broth (*Swanson*), 7.25 oz.	1.0	n.a.
beef broth, seasoned (*Progresso*), 4 oz.	< 1.0	n.a.
beef minestrone (*Progresso*)	5.0	n.a.
beef noodle (*Progresso*)	4.0	n.a.
beef vegetable (*Hormel Micro-Cup* Hearty), 1 pkg.	1.0	n.a.
beef vegetable (*Lipton Hearty Ones*), 11 oz.	3.0	n.a.
beef vegetable (*Progresso*)	3.0	n.a.
berry fruit, three (*Great Impressions*), 6 oz.	.2	n.a.
blueberry fruit (*Great Impressions*), 6 oz.	.3	n.a.
borscht (*Rokeach*), 1 cup	.3	(0)
borscht (*Rokeach Diet*), 1 cup	.2	(0)
borscht, w/beets (*Manischewitz*), 1 cup	0	0
cherry fruit (*Great Impressions*), 6 oz.	.2	n.a.
chickarina (*Progresso*)	5.0	n.a.
chicken:		
(*Campbell's* Chunky Old Fashioned)	4.0	n.a.
(*Progresso* Homestyle)	3.0	n.a.
cream of (*Progresso*)	11.0	n.a.
gumbo, w/sausage (*Campbell's* Home Cookin')	3.0	n.a.
hearty (*Progresso*)	4.0	n.a.
chicken barley (*Progresso*), 9.25 oz. . . .	2.0	n.a.
chicken broth:		
(*Campbell's* Low Sodium), 10.5 oz.	1.0	n.a.
(*College Inn*), 1 cup	3.0	n.a.

(Hain), 8.75 oz.	6.0	n.a.
(Hain No Salt Added), 8.75 oz.	5.0	n.a.
(Progresso), 4 oz.	0	0
(Swanson), 7.25 oz.	2.0	n.a.
(Swanson Natural Goodness), 7.25 oz.	1.0	n.a.
chicken corn chowder *(Campbell's* Chunky)	19.0	n.a.
chicken minestrone *(Campbell's* Home Cookin')*	5.0	n.a.
chicken minestrone *(Progresso)*	3.0	n.a.
chicken mushroom, creamy *(Campbell's* Chunky), 9³/₈ oz.	17.0	n.a.
chicken noodle:		
(Campbell's Chunky)	7.0	n.a.
(Campbell's Home Cookin')	3.0	n.a.
(Campbell's Low Sodium), 10.75 oz.	5.0	n.a.
(Campbell's Microwave), 7.5 oz.	4.0	n.a.
(Hain/Hain No Salt Added)	4.0	n.a.
(Hormel Micro-Cup Hearty Soups), 1 pkg.	3.0	n.a.
(Lipton Hearty Ones Homestyle), 11-oz. pkg.	4.0	n.a.
(Progresso)	4.0	n.a.
chicken nuggets, w/vegetables and noodles *(Campbell's* Chunky)	6.0	n.a.
chicken rice:		
(Campbell's Chunky)	4.0	n.a.
(Campbell's Home Cookin')	5.0	n.a.
(Campbell's Microwave), 7.5 oz.	4.0	n.a.
(Progresso)	3.0	n.a.
chicken vegetable:		
(Progresso)	4.0	n.a.
(Campbell's Chunky)	6.0	n.a.
country *(Campbell's* Home Cookin')	2.0	n.a.
rice *(Hormel Micro-Cup* Hearty Soups), 1 pkg.	3.0	n.a.
chili beef *(Campbell's* Chunky), 9.75 oz.	6.0	n.a.
chili beef *(Campbell's* Microwave), 7.5 oz.	4.0	n.a.
clam chowder:		
Manhattan *(Campbell's* Chunky)	4.0	n.a.
Manhattan *(Progresso)*	2.0	n.a.

Soup, canned, ready-to-serve, clam chowder, continued

New England *(Campbell's* Chunky)	15.0	n.a.
New England *(Hain),* 9.25 oz.	4.0	n.a.
New England *(Hormel Micro-Cup* Hearty), 1 pkg.	5.0	n.a.
New England *(Progresso),* 9.25 oz.	12.0	n.a.
corn chowder *(Progresso),* 9.25 oz. . . .	10.0	n.a.
Creole style *(Campbell's* Chunky)	7.0	n.a.
escarole in chicken broth *(Progresso),* 9.25 oz.	1.0	n.a.
gazpacho, 1 cup	2.2	.3
ham and bean *(Progresso)*	2.0	n.a.
ham and butter bean *(Campbell's* Chunky), 10.75 oz.	10.0	n.a.
lentil:		
(Progresso)	4.0	n.a.
hearty *(Campbell's* Home Cookin')	1.0	n.a.
vegetarian *(Hain/Hain* No Salt Added)	3.0	n.a.
w/ham, 1 cup	2.8	1.1
w/sausage *(Progresso)*	8.0	n.a.
macaroni and bean *(Progresso)*	5.0	n.a.
minestrone:		
(Campbell's Chunky)	4.0	n.a.
(Campbell's Home Cookin' Old World)	3.0	n.a.
(Hain)	2.0	n.a.
(Hain No Salt Added)	4.0	n.a.
(Hormel Micro-Cup Hearty Soups), 1 pkg.	2.0	n.a.
(Lipton Hearty Ones), 11 oz.	3.2	n.a.
(Progresso)	4.0	n.a.
hearty *(Progresso),* 9.25 oz.	2.0	n.a.
zesty *(Progresso)*	8.0	n.a.
mushroom, cream of *(Campbell's* Low Sodium), 10.5 oz.	14.0	n.a.
mushroom, cream of *(Progresso),* 9.25 oz.	10.0	n.a.
mushroom, creamy *(Hain),* 9.25 oz. . . .	4.0	n.a.
mushroom barley *(Hain)*	2.0	n.a.
pea, split:		
(Campbell's Low Sodium), 10.5 oz.	4.0	n.a.
(Grandma Brown's), 1 cup	4.1	n.a.
(Hain/Hain No Salt Added)	1.0	n.a.

green *(Progresso)*	3.0	n.a.
w/ham *(Campbell's* Chunky)	5.0	n.a.
w/ham *(Campbell's* Home Cookin')	1.0	n.a.
w/ham *(Progresso)*	5.0	n.a.
pepper steak *(Campbell's* Chunky)	3.0	n.a.
potato leek *(Health Valley)*, 7.5 oz.	2.0	n.a.
schav *(Gold's)*, 8 oz.	0	0
sirloin burger *(Campbell's* Chunky)	8.0	n.a.
steak and potato *(Campbell's* Chunky)	4.0	n.a.
tomato:		
(Campbell's Low Sodium), 10.5 oz.	6.0	n.a.
(Progresso)	3.0	n.a.
garden *(Campbell's* Home Cookin')	2.0	n.a.
w/tortellini *(Progresso)*, 9.25 oz.	5.0	n.a.
tomato beef, w/rotini *(Progresso)*	6.0	n.a.
tortellini *(Progresso)*	3.0	n.a.
tortellini, creamy *(Progresso)*, 9.25 oz.	16.0	8.5
turkey rice *(Hain)*	3.0	n.a.
turkey rice *(Hain* No Salt Added)	4.0	n.a.
turkey vegetable *(Campbell's* Chunky), 9³/8 oz.	6.0	n.a.
vegetable:		
(Campbell's Chunky)	4.0	n.a.
(Progresso)	2.0	n.a.
country *(Hormel Micro-Cup* Hearty), 1 pkg.	2.0	n.a.
five bean *(Health Valley)*, 7.5 oz.	2.0	n.a.
Mediterranean *(Campbell's* Chunky)	6.0	n.a.
vegetarian *(Hain)*	4.0	n.a.
vegetarian *(Hain* No Salt Added)	5.0	n.a.
vegetable beef:		
(Campbell's Chunky Old Fashioned)	6.0	n.a.
(Campbell's Home Cookin')	2.0	n.a.
(Campbell's Microwave), 7.5 oz.	2.0	n.a.
chunky *(Campbell's* Low Sodium), 10.75 oz.	5.0	n.a.
vegetable broth *(Hain)*	0	0
vegetable broth *(Hain* Low Sodium)	< 1.0	(0)
vegetable chicken *(Hain/Hain* No Salt Added)	4.0	n.a.
vegetable pasta, Italian *(Hain)*	5.0	n.a.

Soup, canned, ready-to-serve, continued
    vegetable pasta, Italian *(Hain* Low
      Sodium) . . . . 6.0   n.a.
Soup, canned, condensed[1], 8 oz., except
  as noted:
asparagus, cream of *(Campbell's)* . . . . . 4.0   n.a.
barley and mushroom *(Rokeach)*, 1 cup   .2   n.a.
bean *(Campbell's* Homestyle) . . . . . . 1.0   n.a.
bean w/bacon *(Campbell's/Campbell's*
    Special Request) . . . . 4.0   n.a.
bean w/frankfurters, 1 cup 7.0   2.1
beef *(Campbell's)* . . . . 2.0   n.a.
beef broth, bouillon, or consommé
    (Campbell's) 0   0
beef noodle *(Campbell's)* . . . . 3.0   n.a.
beef noodle *(Campbell's* Homestyle) . . . 4.0   n.a.
broccoli, cream of *(Campbell's)* . . . . . . 5.0   n.a.
broccoli, cream of, w/milk *(Campbell's)* 7.0   n.a.
celery, cream of *(Campbell's)* . . . . 7.0   n.a.
cheese, cheddar *(Campbell's)* . . . . 6.0   n.a.
cheese, nacho *(Campbell's)* . . . . 8.0   n.a.
cheese, nacho, w/milk *(Campbell's)* . . . 12.0   n.a.
chicken alphabet *(Campbell's)* . . . . . . 3.0   n.a.
chicken barley *(Campbell's)* . . . . 2.0   n.a.
chicken broth *(Campbell's)* . . . . 2.0   n.a.
chicken broth, and noodles *(Campbell's)* 1.0   n.a.
chicken, cream of *(Campbell's/Campbell's*
    Special Request) . . . . 7.0   n.a.
chicken and dumplings *(Campbell's)* . . . 3.0   n.a.
chicken gumbo *(Campbell's)* . . . . 2.0   n.a.
chicken mushroom, creamy *(Campbell's)* 8.0   n.a.
chicken noodle *(Campbell's* Homestyle) 3.0   n.a.
chicken noodle *(Campbell's/Campbell's*
    Special Request) . . . . 2.0   n.a.
chicken rice *(Campbell's)* . . . . 3.0   n.a.
chicken rice *(Campbell's Special Request)* 3.0   n.a.
chicken and stars *(Campbell's)* . . . . . . 2.0   n.a.
chicken vegetable *(Campbell's)* . . . . . . 3.0   n.a.
chili beef *(Campbell's)* . . . . 5.0   n.a.

[1] *Diluted according to label directions, with water, except as noted; where milk is noted, value is for whole milk.*

clam chowder:

Manhattan *(Campbell's)*	2.0	n.a.
Manhattan *(Doxsee),* 7.5 oz.	2.0	n.a.
Manhattan *(Snow's),* 7.5 oz.	2.0	n.a.
New England *(Campbell's)*	3.0	n.a.
New England, w/milk *(Campbell's)*	7.0	n.a.
New England, w/milk *(Gorton's),*		
1/4 can	5.0	n.a.
New England, w/milk *(Snow's),* 7.5 oz.	6.0	n.a.
corn or fish chowder, w/milk *(Snow's),*		
7.5 oz.	6.0	n.a.
minestrone *(Campbell's)*	2.0	n.a.
mushroom, w/beef stock, 1 cup	4.0	1.6
mushroom, beefy *(Campbell's)*	3.0	n.a.
mushroom, cream of *(Campbell's/*		
Campbell's Special Request)	7.0	n.a.
mushroom, golden *(Campbell's)*	3.0	n.a.
noodle, and ground beef *(Campbell's)*	4.0	n.a.
noodle, curly, w/chicken *(Campbell's)*	3.0	n.a.
onion, cream of *(Campbell's)*	5.0	n.a.
onion, cream of, w/milk and water		
(Campbell's)	7.0	n.a.
onion, French *(Campbell's)*	2.0	n.a.
oyster stew *(Campbell's)*	5.0	n.a.
oyster stew, w/milk *(Campbell's)*	9.0	n.a.
pea, green *(Campbell's)*	3.0	n.a.
pea, split, w/egg barley *(Rokeach),* 1 cup	.5	n.a.
pea, split, w/ham and bacon *(Campbell's)*	4.0	n.a.
pepper pot *(Campbell's)*	4.0	n.a.
potato, cream of *(Campbell's)*	3.0	n.a.
potato, cream of, w/water and milk		
(Campbell's)	4.0	n.a.
Scotch broth *(Campbell's)*	3.0	n.a.
seafood chowder, w/milk *(Snow's),* 7.5 oz.	6.0	n.a.
shrimp, cream of *(Campbell's)*	6.0	n.a.
shrimp, cream of, w/milk *(Campbell's)*	10.0	n.a.
tomato:		
(Campbell's/Campbell's Special		
Request)	2.0	n.a.
w/water and milk *(Campbell's/*		
Campbell's Special Request)	4.0	n.a.

Soup, canned, condensed, tomato, continued

beef, w/noodle, 1 cup	4.3	1.6
bisque *(Campbell's)*	3.0	n.a.
cream of *(Campbell's* Homestyle) . . .	3.0	n.a.
cream of, w/milk *(Campbell's* Homestyle)	7.0	n.a.
rice *(Campbell's* Old Fashioned)	2.0	n.a.
zesty *(Campbell's)*	2.0	n.a.
turkey noodle *(Campbell's)*	2.0	n.a.
turkey vegetable *(Campbell's)*	3.0	n.a.
vegetable:		
(Campbell's/Campbell's Homestyle/Old Fashioned)	2.0	n.a.
beef *(Campbell's/Campbell's Special Request)*	2.0	n.a.
w/beef stock *(Campbell's Special Request)*	2.0	n.a.
won ton *(Campbell's)*	1.0	n.a.
Soup, frozen, 6 fl. oz., except as noted:		
asparagus, cream of *(Kettle Ready)*	4.3	1.5
asparagus, cream of *(Myers),* 9.75 oz.	8.0	n.a.
barley and bean *(Tabatchnick),* 7.5 oz.	2.0	n.a.
bean, northern *(Tabatchnick),* 7.5 oz.	2.0	n.a.
bean, savory, w/ham *(Kettle Ready)* . . .	3.6	1.0
beef, hearty, vegetable *(Kettle Ready)*	3.0	.6
black bean, w/ham *(Kettle Ready)*	6.2	1.3
broccoli, cream of *(Kettle Ready)*	7.2	2.6
broccoli, cream of *(Myers),* 9.75 oz.	11.0	n.a.
broccoli, cream of *(Tabatchnick),* 7.5 oz.	4.0	n.a.
cabbage *(Tabatchnick),* 7.5 oz.	2.0	n.a.
cauliflower, cream of *(Kettle Ready)* . . .	7.0	3.1
cheese and broccoli *(Myers),* 9.75 oz.	23.0	n.a.
cheese, cheddar, cream of *(Kettle Ready)*	12.5	6.1
cheese, cheddar and broccoli, cream of *(Kettle Ready)*	11.3	5.2
chicken *(Tabatchnick),* 7.5 oz.	2.0	n.a.
chicken, cream of *(Kettle Ready)*	6.2	2.3
chicken gumbo *(Kettle Ready)*	3.5	.7
chicken noodle *(Kettle Ready)*	3.0	.6
chicken noodle *(Myers),* 9.75 oz.	5.0	n.a.
chili, jalapeño *(Kettle Ready)*	8.0	2.1

chili, traditional *(Kettle Ready)*	6.5	2.0
clam chowder:		
Boston *(Kettle Ready)*	7.3	1.5
Manhattan *(Kettle Ready)*	2.6	.5
New England *(Kettle Ready)*	6.5	2.4
New England *(Myers)*, 9.75 oz.	5.0	n.a.
New England *(Stouffer's)*, 8 oz.	9.0	n.a.
corn and broccoli chowder *(Kettle Ready)*	5.0	1.8
lentil *(Tabatchnick)*, 7.5 oz.	2.0	n.a.
minestrone *(Tabatchnick)*, 7.5 oz.	2.0	n.a.
minestrone, hearty *(Kettle Ready)*	4.4	1.1
mushroom, cream of *(Kettle Ready)* . . .	6.4	2.4
mushroom, cream of *(Tabatchnick)*, 6 oz.	2.0	n.a.
mushroom barley *(Tabatchnick)*, 7.5 oz.	2.0	n.a.
mushroom barley *(Tabatchnick* No Salt),		
7.5 oz.	1.0	n.a.
onion, French *(Kettle Ready)*	2.2	.4
pea *(Tabatchnick* Regular/No Salt),		
7.5 oz.	1.0	n.a.
pea, split, w/ham *(Kettle Ready)*	4.4	1.3
pea, tortellini, in tomato *(Kettle Ready)*	5.4	1.3
seafood bisque *(Myers)*, 9.75 oz.	8.0	n.a.
spinach, cream of *(Myers)*, 9.75 oz.	11.0	n.a.
spinach, cream of *(Stouffer's)*, 8 oz. . . .	15.0	n.a.
spinach, cream of *(Tabatchnick)*, 7.5 oz.	2.0	n.a.
tomato rice *(Tabatchnick)*, 6 oz.	1.0	n.a.
vegetable *(Tabatchnick)*, 7.5 oz.	1.0	n.a.
vegetable *(Tabatchnick* No Salt), 7.5 oz.	2.0	n.a.
vegetable, garden *(Kettle Ready)*	3.0	.5
vegetable beef *(Myers)*, 9.75 oz.	6.0	n.a.
zucchini *(Tabatchnick)*, 6 oz.	2.0	n.a.
Soup mix*, 6 fl. oz., except as noted:		
all varieties:		
(Campbell's Cup-A-Ramen), 8 oz. . . .	10.0	n.a.
(Campbell's Low Fat Cup-A-Ramen),		
8 oz.	2.0	n.a.
(Campbell's Low Fat Ramen Block),		
8 oz.	1.0	n.a.
(Campbell's Ramen), 8 oz.	8.0	n.a.
except chicken noodle *(Campbell's* Cup		
Microwave), 1.35 oz. pkg.	2.0	n.a.

Soup mix, continued

asparagus, cream of, 1 cup	1.7	.3
bean with bacon, 1 cup	2.2	1.0
beef *(Lipton Cup-A-Soup)*	.7	n.a.
beef, hearty, w/noodles *(Lipton)*, 7 fl. oz.	1.4	n.a.
broccoli, creamy *(Lipton Cup-A-Soup)*	2.4	n.a.
broccoli, creamy, w/cheese *(Lipton Cup-A-Soup)*	3.4	n.a.
broccoli, golden *(Lipton Cup-A-Soup Lite)*.	1.2	n.a.
cauliflower, 1 cup	1.7	.3
celery, cream of, 1 cup	1.6	.2
cheddar, w/noodles *(Fantastic Noodles)*, 7 oz.	8.0	n.a.
cheese *(Hain* Savory Soup & Sauce Mix)	16.0	n.a.
cheese and broccoli *(Hain* Soup & Recipe Mix).	22.0	n.a.
chicken or chicken flavor:		
broth *(Lipton Cup-A-Soup)*	.6	n.a.
cream of *(Lipton Cup-A-Soup)*	4.4	n.a.
creamy, w/vegetables *(Lipton Cup-A-Soup)*	3.1	n.a.
creamy, w/white meat *(Campbell's* Cup 2 Minute Soup)	4.0	n.a.
w/corn *(Lipton Cup-A-Soup* Country Style).	5.5	n.a.
Florentine *(Lipton Cup-A-Soup Lite)*	.5	n.a.
hearty *(Lipton Cup-A-Soup* Country Style).	1.1	n.a.
hearty, supreme *(Lipton Cup-A-Soup)*	5.9	n.a.
lemon *(Lipton Cup-A-Soup Lite)* . . .	.4	n.a.
supreme *(Lipton Cup-A-Soup* Country Style).	5.9	n.a.
chicken noodle:		
(Campbell's Cup Microwave), 1.35-oz. pkg.	3.0	n.a.
(Campbell's Quality Soup & Recipe), 1 cup	2.0	n.a.
(Lipton), 1 cup	1.8	n.a.
(Lipton Cup-A-Soup)	1.1	n.a.
(Mrs. Grass Chickeny Rich), 1/4 pkg.	2.0	n.a.

hearty *(Lipton)*, 1 cup	1.3	n.a.
hearty *(Lipton Lots-A-Noodles Cup-A-Soup)*, 7 fl. oz.	1.6	n.a.
hearty, creamy *(Lipton Lots-A-Noodles Cup-A-Soup)*, 7 fl. oz.	8.2	n.a.
w/meat *(Lipton Cup-A-Soup)*	1.0	n.a.
w/white meat *(Campbell's* Cup 2 Minute Soup)	2.0	n.a.
w/white meat, diced *(Lipton)*, 1 cup	1.8	n.a.
w/vegetables, hearty *(Lipton)*, 1 cup	1.6	n.a.
chicken rice *(Lipton Cup-A-Soup)*	.8	n.a.
chicken vegetable *(Lipton Cup-A-Soup)*	.6	n.a.
clam chowder, Manhattan or New England *(Golden Dipt)*, 1/4 pkg.	2.0	1.0
consommé w/gelatin, 1 cup	< .1	tr.
leek, 1 cup	2.1	1.0
lentil *(Hain* Savory Soup Mix)	2.0	n.a.
lobster bisque *(Golden Dipt)*, 1/4 pkg.	1.0	n.a.
minestrone *(Hain* Savory Soup Mix) . . .	1.0	n.a.
minestrone *(Manischewitz)*	< 1.0	n.a.
mushroom:		
(Hain Savory Soup & Recipe)	15.0	n.a.
(Hain Savory Soup & Recipe No Salt)	20.0	n.a.
beef flavor *(Lipton)*, 1 cup	.5	n.a.
cream of *(Lipton Cup-A-Soup)*	3.2	n.a.
noodle:		
(Campbell's Quality Soup & Recipe), 1 cup	2.0	n.a.
(Lipton Cup-A-Soup Ring Noodle)	.7	n.a.
beef *(Cup O'Noodles)*, 1 cup	14.0	n.a.
beef flavor *(Oodles of Noodles/Top Ramen)*, 1 cup	18.0	n.a.
beefy, hearty, w/vegetables *(Lipton)*, 1 cup	.9	n.a.
chicken *(Cup O'Noodles)*, 1 cup	16.0	n.a.
chicken *(Oodles of Noodles/Top Ramen)*, 1 cup	18.0	n.a.
chicken, country *(Cup O'Noodles Hearty)*, 1 cup	14.0	n.a.
w/chicken broth *(Campbell's* Cup 2 Minute Soup)	2.0	n.a.

Soup mix, noodle, continued

w/chicken broth *(Lipton Giggle Noodle),* 1 cup	2.1	n.a.
w/chicken broth *(Lipton Ring-O-Noodle),* 1 cup	2.0	n.a.
hearty *(Campbell's* Quality Soup & Recipe), 8 oz.	1.0	n.a.
hearty, w/vegetables *(Lipton),* 1 cup	1.6	n.a.
Oriental *(Oodles of Noodles/Top Ramen),* 1 cup	18.0	n.a.
pork *(Oodles of Noodles/Top Ramen),* 1 cup	20.0	n.a.
seafood, savory *(Cup O'Noodles Hearty),* 1 cup	15.0	n.a.
shrimp *(Cup O'Noodles),* 1 cup	14.0	n.a.
vegetable, old fashioned *(Cup O'Noodles Hearty),* 1 cup	15.0	n.a.
vegetable beef *(Cup O'Noodles Hearty),* 1 cup	15.0	n.a.
onion:		
(Campbell's Quality Soup & Recipe), 1 cup	0	0
(Hain Savory Soup, Dip & Recipe Mix)	2.0	
(Hain Savory Soup, Dip & Recipe Mix No Salt Added)	1.0	n.a.
(Lipton), 1 cup	.2	n.a.
(Lipton Cup-A-Soup)	.5	n.a.
(Mrs. Grass Soup & Dip Mix), 1/4 pkg.	< 1.0	n.a.
beefy *(Lipton),* 1 cup	1.0	n.a.
creamy *(Lipton Cup-A-Soup)*	3.2	n.a.
golden, w/chicken broth *(Lipton),* 1 cup	1.5	n.a.
mushroom *(Lipton),* 1 cup	.9	n.a.
Oriental *(Lipton Cup-A-Soup Lite)*	1.7	n.a.
oxtail, 1 cup	2.6	1.3
pea:		
green *(Lipton Cup-A-Soup)*	4.2	n.a.
split *(Hain* Savory Soup Mix)	10.0	n.a.
split *(Manischewitz)*	< 1.0	n.a.
Virginia *(Lipton Cup-A-Soup* Country Style)	6.4	n.a.
potato leek *(Hain* Savory Soup Mix)	18.0	n.a.

seafood chowder *(Golden Dipt)*, 1/4 pkg.
dry 2.0   1.0
shrimp bisque *(Golden Dipt)*, 1/4 pkg. dry   1.0   n.a.
tomato *(Hain* Savory Soup & Recipe
Mix) . . . . 14.0   n.a.
tomato *(Lipton Cup-A-Soup)* 9   n.a.
tomato, creamy, and herb *(Lipton Cup-A-
Soup* Lite) 3   n.a.
vegetable:
   (Campbell's Quality Soup & Recipe),
    8 oz.   0   0
   (Hain/Hain No Salt Savory Soup Mix)   1.0   n.a.
   (Lipton), 1 cup 5   n.a.
   (Manischewitz) . . . .   < 1.0   n.a.
   country *(Lipton)*, 1 cup 7   n.a.
   cream of, 1 cup 5.7   1.4
   curry, w/noodles *(Fantastic Noodles)*,
    7 oz.   7.0   n.a.
   garden *(Lipton Lots-A-Noodles Cup-A-
    Soup)*, 7 fl. oz. . . . .   1.5   n.a.
   harvest *(Lipton Cup-A-Soup* Country
    Style) . . . .   1.2   n.a.
   miso, w/noodles *(Fantastic Noodles)*,
    7 oz.   7.0   n.a.
   noodle, w/meatballs *(Lipton Cup-A-
    Soup* Country Style) . . . .   1.6   n.a.
   spring *(Lipton Cup-A-Soup)* 8   n.a.
   tomato, w/noodles *(Fantastic Noodles)*,
    7 oz.   7.0   n.a.
Sour cream sauce mix *(McCormick/
Schilling)*, 1/4 pkg. . . . .   2.8   n.a.
Sour cream and onion snack sticks *(Flavor
Tree)*, 1/4 cup . . . .   8.3   n.a.
Soursop, trimmed, 1/2 cup 3   n.a
Souse loaf *(Kahn's)*, 1 slice . . . .   7.0   n.a.
Soy beverage (see also "Soy milk"):
   (Soy Moo), 8 fl. oz. . . . .   5.0   n.a.
   all flavors *(Westbrae Natural)*, 6 fl. oz.   11.0   n.a.
   all flavors, except vanilla *(Ah Soy)*,
    6 fl. oz. . . . .   3.0   n.a.
   vanilla *(Ah Soy)*, 6 fl. oz. . . . .   5.0   n.a.

Soy meal, defatted, raw, 1 cup . . . . 2.9　.3
Soy milk (see also "Soy beverage"):
  fluid, 8 fl. oz. . . . . 4.6　.5
  powder, prepared *(Soyamel)*, 8 fl. oz. 7.0　1.0
Soy protein:
  concentrate, w/alcohol or acid water
    wash, 1 oz. . . . . .1　.1
  isolate, w/potassium or sodium, 1 oz. . . . 1.0　.1
Soy sauce:
  (Kikkoman/Kikkoman Lite), 1 tbsp. . . . . tr.　(0)
  (La Choy/La Choy Lite), 1 tsp. . . . . . . 0　0
Soybean, green:
  raw, shelled, 1/2 cup . . . . 8.7　.9
  boiled, drained, 1/2 cup . . . . 5.8　.6
Soybean, dried:
  raw, 1/2 cup . . . . 18.5　2.7
  boiled, 1/2 cup . . . . 7.7　1.1
  dry roasted, 1/2 cup . . . . 18.6　2.7
  roasted, 1/2 cup . . . . 21.8　3.2
Soybean, fermented, see "Miso" and
  "Natto"
Soybean kernels, roasted and toasted, 1 cup 25.9　3.4
Spaghetti, see "Pasta"
Spaghetti dinner, and meatballs, frozen:
  (Banquet), 10 oz. . . . . 10.0　n.a.
  (Morton), 10 oz. . . . . 3.0　n.a.
  (Swanson), 12.5 oz. . . . . 17.0　n.a.
Spaghetti dishes, canned:
  in tomato sauce, w/cheese *(Franco-
    American)*, 7³/₈ oz. . . . . 2.0　n.a.
  in tomato and cheese sauce *(Franco-
    American* SpaghettiO's), 7.5 oz. . . . . 2.0　n.a.
  w/franks *(Van Camp's Spaghettee
    Weenee)*, 1 cup . . . . 7.4　n.a.
  w/franks, in tomato sauce *(Franco-
    American* SpaghettiO's), 7³/₈ oz. . . . . 9.0　n.a.
  and meatballs:
    (Buitoni), 7.5 oz. . . . . 8.0　6.0
    (Chef Boyardee Microwave), 7.5 oz. 10.0　n.a.
    (Estee), 7.5 oz. . . . . 14.0　6.0
    (Franco-American), 7³/₈ oz. . . . . 8.0　n.a.

(Franco-American SpaghettiO's),		
7³/₈ oz.	9.0	n.a.
(Nalley's), 7.5 oz.	4.0	n.a.
Spaghetti dishes, mix*:		
w/meat sauce *(Kraft* Dinner), 1 cup	14.0	4.0
mild *(Kraft* American Style Dinner),		
1 cup	7.0	2.0
tangy *(Kraft* Italian Style Dinner), 1 cup	8.0	2.0
Spaghetti entrée, frozen:		
w/beef *(Dining Lite),* 9 oz.	8.0	n.a.
w/beef, mushroom sauce *(Lean Cuisine),*		
11.5 oz.	7.0	2.0
w/beef sauce, mushrooms *(Le Menu*		
LightStyle), 9 oz.	6.0	n.a.
w/Italian-style meatballs *(Swanson*		
Homestyle Recipe), 13 oz.	18.0	n.a.
w/meat sauce:		
(Banquet Casserole), 8 oz.	8.0	n.a.
(Freezer Queen Single), 10 oz.	12.0	n.a.
(Healthy Choice), 10 oz.	6.0	2.0
(Stouffer's), 12⁷/₈ oz.	11.0	n.a.
(Weight Watchers), 10.5 oz.	7.0	3.0
w/meatballs *(Stouffer's),* 12⁵/₈ oz.	15.0	n.a.
Spaghetti entrée, packaged *(Hormel Top*		
Shelf), 1 serving	5.0	n.a.
Spaghetti sauce, see "Pasta sauce"		
Spice loaf:		
(Kahn's Family Pack), 1 slice	6.0	n.a.
beef *(Kahn's* Family Pack), 1 slice	5.0	n.a.
Spinach:		
fresh, raw, trimmed, 10-oz. pkg.	.7	.1
fresh, raw, trimmed, 1 oz. or ¹/₂ cup		
chopped	.1	< .1
fresh or frozen, cooked w/out sauce,		
¹/₂ cup	.2	< .1
canned, w/liquid, ¹/₂ cup	.4	.1
frozen:		
au gratin *(The Budget Gourmet),* 6 oz.	5.0	n.a.
in butter sauce *(Green Giant),* ¹/₂ cup	2.0	< 1.0
creamed *(Birds Eye* Combinations),		
3 oz.	4.0	n.a.

Spinach, frozen, continued

creamed *(Green Giant),* 1/2 cup	3.0	1.0
creamed *(Stouffer's),* 4.5 oz.	14.0	n.a.
Spinach soufflé, frozen *(Stouffer's),* 4 oz.	9.0	n.a.
Spiny lobster, meat only, raw, 4 oz.	1.7	.3
Spleen, braised, 4 oz.:		
beef	4.8	n.a.
lamb	5.4	n.a.
pork	3.6	1.2
veal	3.3	n.a.
Split peas, boiled, 1/2 cup	.4	.1
Spot, meat only, raw, 4 oz.	5.6	1.6
Spring onion, see "Onion, green"		
Squab, fresh, raw:		
meat w/skin, 1 oz.	6.7	2.4
meat only, 1 oz.	2.1	.6
breast, meat only, 1 oz.	1.3	.3
Squash, fresh:		
acorn, baked, cubed, or boiled, mashed,		
1/2 cup	.1	< .1
banana, baked *(Frieda* of California),		
1 oz.	.1	n.a.
butternut, raw, or baked, cubed, 1/2 cup	.1	< .1
crookneck, boiled, drained, sliced, 1/2 cup	.3	.1
hubbard, baked, cubed, 1/2 cup	.6	.1
hubbard, boiled, drained, mashed, 1/2 cup	.4	.1
scallop, boiled, sliced or mashed, 1/2 cup	.2	< .1
spaghetti, baked or boiled, drained,		
1/2 cup	.2	< .1
zucchini, boiled, sliced or mashed, 1/2 cup	.1	< .1
Squash, canned:		
crookneck, drained, sliced, 1/2 cup	.1	< .1
crookneck, yellow, cut *(Allens),* 1/2 cup	< 1.0	(0)
zucchini, in tomato juice, 4 oz. or 1/2 cup	.1	< .1
Squash, frozen:		
butternut, boiled, drained, mashed,		
1/2 cup	.1	< .1
crookneck, boiled, drained, sliced, 1/2 cup	.2	< .1
zucchini, boiled, drained, 4 oz. or 1/2 cup	.1	< .1
zucchini, breaded *(Stilwell Quickkrisp),*		
3.3 oz.	10.0	n.a.

Squid, meat only:

raw, 4 oz.	1.6	.4
dried, 1 oz.	1.2	n.a.

Star fruit, see "Carambola"

Steak sauce:

(A.1.), 1 tbsp.	0	0
(French's), 1 tbsp.	0	0
(Heinz 57), 1 tbsp.	.2	(0)
(Heinz Traditional), 1 tbsp.	0	0
(Lea & Perrins), 1 oz.	< 1.0	(0)
(Life All Natural), 1 tbsp.	tr.	(0)
(Steak Supreme), 1 tbsp.	0	0

Steak seasoning, broiled (McCormick/ Schilling Spice Blends), 1/4 tsp. ...... (0) | (0)

Stir-fry sauce:

(Kikkoman), 1 tsp.	tr.	(0)
(Lawry's), 1/4 cup	3.8	n.a.

Stomach, pork, raw, 1 oz. ... 2.7 | n.a.

Strawberry:

fresh, untrimmed, 1 pint	1.2	.1
fresh, or canned in heavy syrup, 1/2 cup	.3	< .1
frozen, unsweetened, 1/2 cup	.1	tr.
frozen, sweetened, whole or sliced, 1/2 cup	.2	tr.

Strawberry cobbler, frozen (Pet-Ritz), 1/6 pkg. ... 9.0 | n.a.

Strawberry danish:

(Awrey's Round), 2.75 oz.	14.0	3.0
miniature (Awrey's), 1.7 oz.	8.0	2.0

Strawberry flavor milk drink:

canned (Frostee), 8 fl. oz.	7.0	n.a.
canned (Sego Very Strawberry), 10 fl. oz.	5.0	n.a.
mix (Carnation Instant Breakfast), 1 pouch	.2	.1
mix (Nestlé Quik), 3/4 oz.	0	0
mix (Pillsbury Instant Breakfast), 1 pouch	0	0

Strawberry juice drink (Tang Fruit Box) ... 0 | 0

Strawberry nectar (Libby's) ... 0 | 0

Strawberry yogurt dessert, frozen (Sara Lee Free & Light), 1/10 pkg. ... 1.0 | n.a.

Stroganoff sauce mix:

(Lawry's), 1 pkg.	.3	n.a.

Stroganoff sauce mix, continued
(*Natural Touch*), 4 oz.*	3.0	n.a.
Stuffing, 1 oz.:		
all varieties (*Pepperidge Farm*)	1.0	n.a.
apple raisin or chicken (*Pepperidge Farm* Distinctive)	1.0	n.a.
corn (*Brownberry*)	1.6	n.a.
herb (*Brownberry*)	1.3	n.a.
herb, country garden (*Pepperidge Farm* Distinctive)	4.0	n.a.
vegetable, harvest, and almond (*Pepperidge Farm* Distinctive)	3.0	n.a.
wild rice and mushroom (*Pepperidge Farm* Distinctive)	5.0	n.a.
Stuffing, frozen, 1/2 cup:		
all varieties, except cornbread (*Green Giant Stuffing Originals*)	7.0	n.a.
cornbread (*Green Giant Stuffing Originals*)	6.0	n.a.
Stuffing mix*, 1/2 cup, except as noted:		
all flavors (*Stove Top/Stove Top* Flexible Serving)	9.0	n.a.
all flavors, except broccoli and cheese (*Stove Top* Microwave)	7.0	n.a.
broccoli and cheese (*Stove Top* Microwave)	8.0	n.a.
chicken flavor (*Golden Grain*), 1 oz. dry	1.2	.3
chicken or herb (*Betty Crocker*)	9.0	n.a.
cornbread (*Golden Grain*), 1 oz. dry . . .	1.0	.1
herb and butter (*Golden Grain*), 1 oz. dry	1.1	.2
San Francisco style (*Stove Top* Americana)	9.0	n.a.
wild rice (*Golden Grain*), 1 oz. dry	1.1	.2
Sturgeon, meat only:		
raw, 4 oz.	4.6	1.0
baked, broiled, or microwaved, 4 oz. . . .	5.9	1.3
smoked, 4 oz.	5.0	1.2
Sturgeon roe, see "Caviar"		
Succotash:		
fresh, raw, 1 lb.	4.6	.9
fresh or frozen, boiled, drained, 1/2 cup	.8	.1

canned, w/cream-style corn, 1/2 cup	.7	.1
canned, w/whole kernel corn, w/liquid, 1/2 cup	.6	.1
Sucker, white, meat only, raw, 4 oz.	2.6	.5
Suet, beef, raw, 1 oz.	26.7	14.8
Sugar or sugar substitute, all varieties . . .	0	0
Sugar apple (sweetsop), trimmed, 1/2 cup	.4	(0)
Sugar cane juice, 1 oz.	tr.	0
Sugar snap peas, see "Peas, edible-podded"		
Summer sausage (see also "Thuringer cervelat"):		
(Eckrich), 1 oz. slice	7.0	n.a.
(Hillshire Farm), 2 oz.	16.0	n.a.
(Hormel Perma-Fresh), 2 slices	11.0	n.a.
(Hormel Tangy, Chub), 1 oz.	7.0	n.a.
(Hormel Thuringer), 1 oz.	9.0	n.a.
(Lean & Lite), 1 oz.	2.3	n.a.
(Light & Lean), 2 slices	8.0	n.a.
(Oscar Mayer), .8-oz. slice	6.1	2.7
beef *(Hillshire Farm),* 2 oz.	17.0	n.a.
beef *(Hormel* Beefy), 1 oz.	9.0	n.a.
beef *(Oscar Mayer),* .8-oz. slice	6.2	2.7
w/cheese *(Hillshire Farm),* 2 oz.	18.0	n.a.
Sunfish, pumpkinseed, meat only, raw, 4 oz.	.8	.2
Sunflower seed, kernels:		
dried, 1 oz.	14.1	1.5
dry roasted, 1 oz.	14.1	1.5
oil roasted, 1 oz.	16.3	1.7
toasted, 1 oz.	16.1	1.7
Sunflower seed butter, 1 tbsp.	7.6	.8
Surimi (from Alaska walleye pollock), 4 oz.	1.0	n.a.
Swamp cabbage, raw or boiled, chopped, 1/2 cup	.1	(0)
Swedish meatballs, see "Meatball entrée"		
Sweet potato:		
fresh, baked in skin, 1 medium, or 1/2 cup mashed	.1	< .1
fresh, boiled, pared, mashed, 1/2 cup . . .	.5	.1
canned, in syrup, drained, or vacuum pack, mashed, 1/2 cup	.3	.1

Sweet potato, continued

canned, candied *(Joan of Arc/Princella/ Royal Prince)*, 1/2 cup	0	0
frozen, baked, cubed, 1/2 cup	.1	< .1
frozen, candied *(Mrs. Paul's/Mrs. Paul's Sweets'n Apples)*, 4 oz.	0	0
Sweet potato leaf, raw or steamed, 1/2 cup	.1	< .1
Sweet and sour sauce:		
(Kikkoman), 1 tbsp.	0	0
(Lawry's), 1/4 cup	7.5	n.a.
(Sauceworks), 1 tbsp.	0	0
all varieties *(Great Impressions)*, 2 tbsp.	0	0
duck sauce *(La Choy)*, 1 tbsp.	tr.	0
Sweetbreads, see "Pancreas" and "Thymus"		
Swordfish, meat only:		
raw, 4 oz.	4.5	1.2
baked, broiled, or microwaved, 4 oz. . . .	5.8	1.6
Syrup, see specific listings		
Szechwan sauce, hot and spicy *(La Choy)*, 1 oz.	.2	0

food and measure	total fat (gms.)	saturated fat (gms.)
Tabbouleh mix:		
w/oil and tomatoes *(Fantastic Foods)*, ½ cup*	10.0	n.a.
(Near East), ½ cup*	9.0	n.a.
salad *(Casbah)*, 1 oz. dry	1.0	n.a.
Taco Bell:		
burrito:		
bean, red sauce, 7.3 oz.	14.0	4.0
beef, red sauce, 7.3 oz.	21.0	8.0
chicken, 6 oz.	12.0	4.0

Taco Bell, burrito, continued

combination, red sauce, 7 oz.	16.0	5.0
Supreme, red sauce, 9 oz.	22.0	8.0
cinnamon twists, 1.2 oz.	8.0	3.0
Enchirito, red sauce, 7.5 oz.	20.0	9.0
Mexican pizza, 7.9 oz.	37.0	11.0
Meximelt, 3.7 oz.	15.0	8.0
Meximelt, chicken, 3.8 oz.	15.0	7.0
nachos, 3.7 oz.	18.0	6.0
nachos, *BellGrande,* 10.1 oz.	35.0	12.0
nachos, *Supreme,* 5.1 oz.	27.0	5.0
pintos 'n cheese, red sauce, 4.5 oz.	9.0	4.0
taco:		
2.75 oz.	11.0	5.0
BellGrande, 5.7 oz.	23.0	11.0
chicken, 3 oz.	9.0	3.0
chicken, soft, 3.8 oz.	10.0	4.0
soft, 3.25 oz.	12.0	5.0
steak, soft, 3.5 oz.	11.0	5.0
Supreme, 3.25 oz.	15.0	8.0
Supreme, soft, 4.4 oz.	16.0	8.0
taco salad, 21 oz.	61.0	19.0
taco salad, w/out shell, 18.3 oz.	31.0	14.0
tostada, red sauce, 5.5 oz.	11.0	4.0
tostada, chicken, red sauce, 5.8 oz.	15.0	7.0
Taco dip:		
(Wise), 2 tbsp.	0	0
and sauce *(Hain),* 4 tbsp.	1.0	n.a.
Taco mix:		
(Old El Paso), 1 taco*	3.0	n.a.
vegetarian *(Natural Touch),* 2 tbsp.	2.0	n.a.
Taco salad seasoning *(Lawry's* Seasoning		
Blends), 1 pkg.	.9	n.a.
Taco salad shell, flour *(Azteca),* 1 piece	12.0	n.a.
Taco sauce (see also "Salsa"):		
(Lawry's Chunky), 1/4 cup	.4	(0)
(Lawry's Sauce'n Seasoner), 1/4 cup . . .	.6	(0)
all varieties:		
(Del Monte), 1/4 cup	0	0
(Heinz), 1 tbsp.	0	0
(Old El Paso), 2 tbsp.	< 1.0	(0)

(Ortega), 1 oz.	0	0
Taco seasoning mix:		
(Lawry's Seasoning Blends), 1 pkg.	1.1	n.a.
(Old El Paso), 1/12 pkg.	< 1.0	n.a.
(Tio Sancho), 1.51 oz.	1.7	n.a.
meat *(Ortega)*, 1 oz.*	4.0	2.0
Taco shell, 1 piece, except as noted:		
(Gebhardt)	2.0	n.a.
(Lawry's)	2.1	n.a.
(Lawry's Super)	3.6	n.a.
(Old El Paso)	3.0	n.a.
(Old El Paso Super Size)	6.0	n.a.
(Ortega)	2.0	n.a.
(Rosarita)	2.0	n.a.
(Tio Sancho)	3.1	n.a.
(Tio Sancho Super)	4.7	n.a.
corn *(Azteca)*	3.0	n.a.
miniature *(Old El Paso)*, 3 pieces	4.0	n.a.
Taco starter *(Del Monte)*, 8 oz.	1.0	n.a.
Tahini, see "Sesame butter"		
Tahini mix *(Casbah)*, 1 oz. dry	5.0	n.a.
Tamale, canned, except as noted:		
(Old El Paso), 2 pieces	12.0	n.a.
(Wolf Brand), scant cup, 7.5 oz.	24.5	n.a.
beef *(Gebhardt)*, 4 oz.	17.0	n.a.
beef *(Hormel/Hormel* Hot'N Spicy), 2 pieces	10.0	n.a.
w/sauce *(Van Camp's)*, 1 cup	16.2	n.a.
frozen, beef *(Hormel)*, 1 piece	7.0	n.a.
Tamale dinner, frozen *(Patio)*, 13 oz.	21.0	n.a.
Tamarind, 1/2 cup	.4	.2
Tangerine:		
fresh, 1 medium, 2 3/8" diam.	.2	< .1
canned, in juice, 1/2 cup	< .1	tr.
canned, in light syrup, 1/2 cup	.1	< .1
Tangerine juice:		
fresh or canned, sweetened, 6 fl. oz.	.4	< .1
frozen*, sweetened, 6 fl. oz.	.2	< .1
Tapioca, pearl, dry, 1 cup	< .1	(0)
Taro, raw or cooked, sliced, 1/2 cup	.1	< .1
Taro, Tahitian, cooked, sliced, 1/2 cup	.5	.1

Taro chips, 1/2 cup . . . . 3.1 .9
Tarragon, ground, 1 tsp. . . . . .1 n.a.
Tartar sauce, 1 tbsp.:
   (Golden Dipt) 7.0 1.0
   (Golden Dipt Lite) 4.0 1.0
   (Heinz) . . . . 7.2 n.a.
   (Hellmann's/Best Foods) 8.0 1.0
   (Sauceworks) 5.0 1.0
   lemon and herb flavor *(Sauceworks)* . . . 8.0 1.0
Tea, plain, flavored, or herbal, brewed,
   6 fl. oz. . . . . < .1 (0)
Tempeh, 1/2 cup . . . . 6.4 .9
Tempura batter mix *(Golden Dipt),* 1 oz. 0 0
Teriyaki sauce:
   (Kikkoman/Kikkoman Baste & Glaze),
     1 tbsp. . . . . tr. (0)
   (La Choy Sauce and Marinade), 1 oz. 0 0
   (La Choy Thick and Rich), 1 oz. . . . . .1 < .1
   barbecue marinade *(Lawry's),* 1/4 cup 2.3 n.a.
   ginger marinade *(Golden Dipt),* 1 fl. oz. 7.0 1.0
   w/pineapple juice *(Lawry's),* 1/4 cup 4 (0)
Thuringer cervelat (see also "Summer
   sausage"):
   (Hillshire Farm), 2 oz. . . . . 15.0 n.a.
   (Hormel Old Smokehouse/Hormel
     Viking), 1 oz. . . . . 8.0 n.a.
   (Hormel Old Smokehouse Chub/Sliced),
     1 oz. . . . . 9.0 n.a.
   beef *(JM* Thuringer), 1-oz. slice . . . . . 7.0 n.a.
   beef and pork, 1 oz. 8.5 3.4
Thyme, ground, 1 tsp. . . . . .1 < .1
Thymus:
   beef, braised, 4 oz. . . . . 28.3 n.a.
   veal, braised, 4 oz. . . . . 4.9 n.a.
Tilefish, meat only:
   raw, 4 oz. . . . . 2.6 .5
   baked, broiled, or microwaved, 4 oz. . . . 5.3 1.0
Toaster muffins and pastries, 1 piece:
   all varieties, except cherry *(Toaster*
     Strudel Breakfast Pastries) . . . . 8.0 n.a.

apple, Dutch, frosted *(Kellogg's Pop-Tarts)*	6.0	n.a.
apple cinnamon or strawberry *(Pepperidge Farm* Croissant Toaster Tarts)	7.0	2.0
banana nut *(Thomas' Toast-r-Cakes)*	4.4	n.a.
blueberry *(Thomas' Toast-r-Cakes)*	3.3	n.a.
blueberry, plain or frosted *(Kellogg's Pop-Tarts)*	6.0	n.a.
bran *(Thomas' Toast-r-Cakes)*	2.9	n.a.
brown sugar cinnamon *(Kellogg's Pop-Tarts)*	8.0	n.a.
brown sugar cinnamon, frosted *(Kellogg's Pop-Tarts)*	7.0	n.a.
cheese *(Pepperidge Farm* Croissant Toaster Tarts)	10.0	3.0
cherry *(Kellogg's Pop-Tarts)*	6.0	n.a.
cherry *(Toaster Strudel* Breakfast Pastries)	9.0	n.a.
cherry, chocolate fudge, or chocolate vanilla creme, frosted *(Kellogg's Pop-Tarts)*	5.0	n.a.
corn *(Thomas' Toast-r-Cakes)*	4.0	n.a.
grape, raspberry, or strawberry, frosted *(Kellogg's Pop-Tarts)*	5.0	n.a.
oat bran, w/raisins *(Awrey's* Toastums)	5.0	1.0
strawberry *(Kellogg's Pop-Tarts)*	6.0	n.a.
Tofu:		
raw, 1/2 cup	5.9	.9
raw, firm, 1/2 cup	11.0	1.6
dried-frozen (koyadofu), 1 oz.	8.6	1.2
flavored, all flavors *(Nasoya),* 5 oz.	8.0	n.a.
grilled (yakidofu), 1 oz.	1.7	n.a.
okara, 1 oz.	.5	.1
salted and fermented (fuyu), 1 oz.	2.3	.3
Tofu dishes, mix*, shells 'n curry, w/tofu *(Tofu Classics),* 1/2 cup	3.0	n.a.
Tofu entrée, frozen:		
enchilada, vegetable, w/sauce *(Legume* Mexican), 11 oz.	8.0	3.0
lasagna, w/sauce *(Legume* Classic), 8 oz.	8.0	1.3

Tofu entrée, frozen, continued

lasagna, vegetable, w/sauce *(Legume)*, 12 oz.	8.0	1.7
manicotti, w/sauce *(Legume* Classic), 8 oz.	11.0	1.9
manicotti, w/spinach and sauce *(Legume* Florentine), 11 oz.	7.0	1.0
shells, stuffed, w/vegetables and sauce *(Legume* Provencale), 11 oz.	12.0	1.9
Tofu patty, frozen:		
garden *(Natural Touch)*, 2.5-oz. patty	4.0	1.0
okara *(Natural Touch Okara)*, 2.25-oz. patty	10.0	1.0
Tofu spread, canned:		
green chili or herb and spice *(Natural Touch Tofu Topper)*, 2 tbsp.	4.0	n.a.
Mexican *(Natural Touch Tofu Topper)*, 2 tbsp.	5.0	n.a.
Tomato:		
fresh, raw, green, 1 medium, 2³/5″ diam.	.3	< .1
fresh, raw, ripe, 1 medium, 2³/5″ diam.	.4	.1
fresh, raw, ripe, chopped, 1/2 cup	.3	<.1
fresh, boiled, ripe, 1/2 cup	.5	.1
canned, all varieties (all brands), 1/2 cup	< 1.0	<.1
Tomato, pickled, kosher *(Claussen)*, 1 oz.	< 1.0	(0)
Tomato juice, 6 fl. oz.	.1	<.1
Tomato paste, canned, 1/2 cup	1.2	.2
Tomato sauce (see also "Pasta sauce"):		
(Health Valley), 1 cup	.5	(0)
(S&W), 1/2 cup	0	0
(Stokely), 1/2 cup	0	0
all varieties *(Contadina)*, 1/2 cup	< 1.0	(0)
all varieties *(Del Monte)*, 1 cup	1.0	(0)
all varieties *(Hunt's)*, 4 oz.	0	0
Tomato-beef cocktail *(Beefamato)*, 6 fl. oz.	0	0
Tomato-chile cocktail *(Snap-E-Tom)*, 6 fl. oz.	0	0
Tomato-clam juice cocktail *(Clamato)*, 6 fl. oz.	0	0
Tongue:		
beef, simmered, 4 oz.	23.5	10.1
lamb, braised, 4 oz.	23.0	8.9

pork, braised, 4 oz.	21.1	7.3
pork, cured, canned *(Hormel,* 8 lb.), 3 oz.	13.0	n.a.
veal, braised, 4 oz.	11.5	n.a.
Toppings, dessert, 2 tbsp., except as noted:		
butterscotch *(Kraft)*	2.0	0
butterscotch or caramel *(Smucker's)* . . .	0	0
butterscotch-caramel *(Smucker's* Special		
Recipe)	3.0	n.a.
caramel or chocolate *(Kraft),* 1 tbsp. . . .	0	0
caramel or chocolate fudge, hot		
(Smucker's)	4.0	n.a.
chocolate *(Smucker's Magic Shell)*	15.0	n.a.
chocolate, dark *(Smucker's* Special		
Recipe).	1.0	n.a.
chocolate syrup *(Smucker's)*	2.0	n.a.
chocolate fudge:		
(Hershey's)	4.0	n.a.
(Smucker's)	1.0	n.a.
(Smucker's Magic Shell)	15.0	n.a.
hot *(Kraft)*	4.0	2.0
hot *(Smucker's* Special Recipe)	5.0	n.a.
Swiss milk *(Smucker's)*	1.0	n.a.
chocolate, milk, w/almonds *(Nestlé*		
Candytops), 1.25 oz.	18.0	n.a.
chocolate, milk, w/crisps *(Nestlé Crunch*		
Candytops), 1.25 oz.	17.0	n.a.
chocolate, white, w/almonds *(Nestlé*		
Candytops), 1.25 oz.	19.0	n.a.
chocolate nut *(Smucker's Magic Shell)*	16.0	n.a.
marshmallow *(Marshmallow Fluff),*		
1 heaping tsp.	0	0
marshmallow creme *(Kraft),* 1 oz.	0	0
nut *(Planters),* 1 oz.	16.0	2.0
peanut butter-caramel *(Smucker's)*	2.0	n.a.
pecans or walnuts, in syrup *(Smucker's)*	1.0	n.a.
pineapple or strawberry *(Kraft)*	0	0
pineapple or strawberry *(Smucker's)* . . .	0	0
whipped:		
(Kraft), 1/4 cup	3.0	3.0
(Pet Whip)	2.0	n.a.
frozen *(Kraft* Real Cream), 1/4 cup	2.0	2.0

Toppings, dessert, whipped, continued

frozen *(La Creme)*	2.0	n.a.
pressurized, 1 tbsp.	.7	.4

Tortellini, frozen (see also "Tortellini dishes"):

meatless *(Tofutti)*, 2 oz.	2.0	n.a.
nondairy, regular or spinach *(Tofutti)*, 2 oz.	4.0	n.a.

Tortellini, refrigerated, 4.5 oz.:

egg or spinach, cheese or meat *(Contadina Fresh)*	6.0	n.a.
egg or spinach, chicken and prosciutto *(Contadina Fresh)*	7.0	n.a.

Tortellini dinner, frozen:

cheese *(Le Menu* LightStyle), 10 oz.	6.0	n.a.
w/meat *(Dinner Classics Lite)*, 10 oz.	10.0	n.a.

Tortellini dishes, frozen (see also "Tortellini entrée"):

cheese:

(The Budget Gourmet Side Dish), 5.5 oz.	9.0	n.a.
marinara *(Green Giant* One Serving), 5.5 oz.	9.0	3.0
in tomato sauce *(Birds Eye For One)*, 5.5 oz.	5.0	n.a.
Provencale *(Green Giant* Microwave Garden Gourmet), 1 pkg.	6.0	2.0

Tortellini dishes, packaged:

cheese, w/shrimp and seafood *(Hormel Top Shelf)*, 10 oz.	8.0	n.a.
in marinara sauce *(Hormel Top Shelf)*, 10 oz.	3.0	n.a.

Tortellini entrée, frozen:

beef, w/marinara sauce *(Stouffer's)*, 10 oz.	12.0	n.a.

cheese:

(Weight Watchers), 9 oz.	6.0	1.0
in Alfredo sauce *(Stouffer's)*, 8⅞ oz.	40.0	n.a.
w/meat sauce *(Le Menu* LightStyle), 8 oz.	8.0	1.0
w/tomato sauce *(Stouffer's)*, 9⅝ oz.	16.0	n.a.
w/vinaigrette *(Stouffer's)*, 6⅞ oz.	27.0	n.a.

veal, in Alfredo sauce *(Stouffer's)*, 8 5/8 oz.	30.0	n.a.
Tortilla, 1 piece:		
corn *(Azteca)*	0	0
corn *(Old El Paso)*	1.0	n.a.
flour *(Azteca)*, 9" diam.	3.0	n.a.
flour *(Azteca)*, 7" diam.	2.0	n.a.
flour *(Old El Paso)*	3.0	n.a.
Tortilla chips, see "Corn chips and similar snacks"		
Tortilla entrée, frozen *(Stouffer's* Grande), 9 5/8 oz.	33.0	n.a.
Tostaco shell *(Old El Paso)*, 1 piece	5.0	n.a.
Tostada shell:		
(Lawry's), 1 piece	3.5	n.a.
(Old El Paso), 1 piece	3.0	n.a.
(Ortega), 1 piece	2.0	n.a.
(Tio Sancho), 1 piece	3.2	n.a.
Tripe, beef, raw, 1 oz.	1.1	.6
Triticale, whole grain, 1 cup	4.0	.7
Trout (see also "Sea trout"), meat only:		
mixed species, raw, 4 oz.	7.5	1.3
rainbow, raw, 4 oz.	3.8	.7
rainbow, baked, broiled, or microwaved, 4 oz.	4.9	.9
Tuna, fresh, meat only:		
bluefin, raw, 4 oz.	5.6	1.4
bluefin, baked, broiled, or microwaved, 4 oz.	7.1	1.8
skipjack, raw, 4 oz.	1.1	.4
yellowfin, raw, 4 oz.	1.1	.3
Tuna, canned, 2 oz.:		
in oil:		
chunk light or white *(Bumble Bee)*	12.0	3.0
chunk or solid light *(Star-Kist)*	13.0	1.0
chunk or solid white *(Star-Kist)*	10.0	1.0
solid, Albacore *(Bumble Bee)*	8.0	2.0
in water, chunk light *(Bumble Bee)*	1.0	.5
in water, chunk or solid light *(Star-Kist)*	< 1.0	.2
in water, chunk or solid white *(Bumble Bee)*	2.0	1.0
in distilled water, chunk white *(Star-Kist)*	1.0	.2

Tuna, canned, continued
  in spring water, solid, Albacore *(Star-*
    Kist) . . . .   1.0   .2
"Tuna," vegetarian, frozen *(Worthington*
    Tuno), 2 oz. 7.0   1.0
Tuna entrée, frozen:
  noodle casserole *(Stouffer's)*, 10 oz. . . .   13.0   n.a.
  pie *(Banquet)*, 7 oz. . . . .   33.0   n.a.
Tuna entrée mix*, w/water-packed tuna:
  au gratin or buttery rice *(Tuna Helper)*,
    6 oz. . . . .   11.0   n.a.
  fettuccine Alfredo *(Tuna Helper)*, 7 oz.   13.0   n.a.
  mushroom, creamy *(Tuna Helper)*, 7 oz.   6.0   n.a.
  noodle, cheesy *(Tuna Helper)*, 7.75 oz.   9.0   n.a.
  noodle, creamy *(Tuna Helper)*, 8 oz. . . .   14.0   n.a.
  pot pie *(Tuna Helper)*, 5.1 oz. . . . .   27.0   n.a.
  salad *(Tuna Helper)*, 5.5 oz. . . . .   27.0   n.a.
  tetrazzini *(Tuna Helper)*, 6 oz. . . . .   8.0   n.a.
Tuna salad *(Longacre/Longacre Saladfest)*,
  1 oz.   4.0   n.a.
Turbot, meat only:
  domestic, see "Halibut, Greenland"
  European, raw, 4 oz. . . . .   3.3   n.a.
Turkey, fresh, roasted, 4 oz., except as
  noted:
  fryer-roaster:
    meat w/skin 6.5   1.9
    meat only 3.0   1.0
    meat only, chopped or diced, 1 cup
      unpacked 3.7   1.2
    skin only, 1 oz. 6.6   1.7
    dark meat w/skin 8.0   2.4
    dark meat only 4.9   1.6
    light meat w/skin 5.2   1.4
    light meat only . . . .   1.3   .4
    back, meat w/skin 11.6   3.4
    back, meat only 6.4   2.1
    breast, meat w/skin 3.6   1.0
    breast, meat only 8   .3
    leg, meat w/skin 6.1   1.9
    leg, meat only 4.3   1.4

wing, meat w/skin	11.2	3.1
wing, meat only	3.9	1.2
young hen:		
meat w/skin	12.3	3.6
meat only	6.2	2.1
meat only, chopped or diced, 1 cup		
unpacked	7.7	2.5
skin only, 1 oz.	12.6	3.3
dark meat w/skin	14.5	4.4
dark meat only	8.8	3.0
light meat w/skin	10.7	3.0
light meat only	4.2	1.3
back, meat w/skin	17.7	5.1
breast, meat w/skin	8.9	2.6
leg, meat w/skin	11.9	3.7
wing, meat w/skin	15.3	4.2
young tom:		
meat w/skin	10.3	3.0
meat only	5.3	1.7
meat only, chopped or diced, 1 cup		
unpacked	6.6	2.2
skin only, 1 oz.	10.6	2.8
dark meat w/skin	12.3	3.7
dark meat only	7.9	2.7
light meat w/skin	8.7	2.4
light meat only	3.3	1.1
back, meat w/skin	15.5	4.5
breast, meat w/skin	8.4	2.4
leg, meat w/skin	10.9	3.4
wing, meat w/skin	13.0	3.5
Turkey, boneless and luncheon meat,		
cooked 1 oz., except as noted:		
bologna, see "Turkey bologna"		
breast:		
1 oz.	.4	.1
(Butterball Deli No Salt Added)	2.0	n.a.
*(Butterball Slice 'n Serve/*Cold Cuts) . .	1.0	n.a.
(Healthy Deli Gourmet)	.6	n.a.
(Hormel Perma-Fresh), 2 slices	2.0	n.a.
(Light & Lean), 2 slices	2.0	n.a.
(Longacre Catering/Gourmet/Premium)	1.0	n.a.

Turkey, boneless and luncheon meat, breast, continued

(*Longacre* Gourmet Low Salt/Salt Watchers)	< 1.0	n.a.
(*Mr. Turkey*)	.7	n.a.
barbecue (*Butterball Slice'n Serve*)	2.0	n.a.
honey (*Healthy Deli*)	.5	n.a.
honey roasted (*Louis Rich*)	.8	.3
lean lite, plain or smoked (*Longacre* Deli)	1.0	n.a.
lean lite, skinless (*Longacre* Deli)	< 1.0	n.a.
oven cooked (*Healthy Deli*)	.2	n.a.
oven roasted (*Eckrich Lite*)	1.0	n.a.
oven roasted (*Hillshire Farm* Deli Select)	.2	n.a.
oven roasted (*Louis Rich*)	.8	.3
oven roasted (*Louis Rich* Thin Sliced), .4 oz.	.3	.1
oven roasted (*Oscar Mayer*), 1 slice	.5	.1
roast (*Louis Rich*)	1.0	n.a.
roast (*Oscar Mayer* Thin Sliced), .4-oz. slice	.2	.1
skinless (*Longacre* Catering/Gourmet/ Premium)	< 1.0	n.a.
sliced (*Louis Rich*)	1.0	n.a.
sliced or smoked (*Longacre*)	1.0	n.a.
smoked (*Butterball* Cold Cuts)	1.0	n.a.
smoked (*Eckrich Lite*)	< 1.0	n.a.
smoked (*Healthy Deli/Healthy Deli* Gourmet)	.5	n.a.
smoked (*Hillshire Farm* Deli Select)	.2	n.a.
smoked (*Hormel* Perma-Fresh), 2 slices	2.0	n.a.
smoked (*Louis Rich*), .7-oz. slice	.3	.1
smoked (*Louis Rich* Thin Sliced), .4 oz.	.1	tr.
smoked (*Mr. Turkey*)	.7	n.a.
smoked (*Oscar Mayer*), .75-oz. slice	.2	.1
smoked, hickory (*Butterball Slice'n Serve*)	1.0	n.a.
smoked, sliced (*Longacre*)	< 1.0	n.a.
breast and white (*Longacre Deli Chef*)	1.0	n.a.
breast and white, browned, roasted (*Longacre Deli Chef*)	2.0	n.a.

diced, white and dark meat, seasoned	1.7	.5
ham, see "Turkey ham"		
luncheon loaf (*Louis Rich*)	2.8	.8
luncheon loaf, spiced (*Mr. Turkey*)	3.6	n.a.
pastrami, see "Turkey pastrami"		
roll, light meat	2.1	.6
roll, light and dark meat	2.0	.6
salami, see "Turkey salami"		
sausage, see "Turkey sausage"		
smoked (*Butterball* Cold Cuts)	1.0	n.a.
smoked (*Butterball Turkey Variety Pak*)		
.75 oz.	1.0	n.a.
smoked (*Louis Rich*)	1.0	.4
summer sausage, see "Turkey summer		
sausage"		
Turkey, canned:		
chunk (*Hormel*), 6.75 oz.	10.0	n.a.
white (*Swanson*), 2.5 oz.	1.0	n.a.
Turkey, frozen and refrigerated:		
breast, cooked:		
(*Land O'Lakes*), 3 oz.	1.0	< 1.0
(*Longacre* Cook-N-Bag), 1 oz.	< 1.0	n.a.
(*Louis Rich*), 1 oz.	1.5	.6
all varieties (*Mr. Turkey*), 1 oz.	1.0	n.a.
barbecued (*Louis Rich*), 1 oz.	.9	.3
hen (*Louis Rich*), 1 oz.	2.0	.4
hickory smoked (*Louis Rich*), 1 oz.	1.0	.3
honey roasted or roast (*Louis Rich*),		
1 oz.	.8	.3
oven roasted (*Louis Rich*), 1 oz.	.9	.2
slices or steaks (*Louis Rich*), 1 oz. . . .	.5	.1
smoked (*Louis Rich*), 1 oz.	1.0	.4
tenderloins (*Louis Rich*), 1 oz.	.5	.2
cutlets, raw (*Norbest Tasti-Lean*), 4 oz.	<2.0	n.a.
dark meat, skinless, roasted (*Swift		
Butterball*), 3.5 oz.	10.0	n.a.
drumsticks (*Land O'Lakes*), 3 oz.	5.0	2.0
drumsticks (*Louis Rich*), 1 oz. cooked	2.6	.9
w/gravy, raw (*Norbest*), 4 oz.	2.7	n.a.
ground, see "Turkey, ground"		
hindquarter roast (*Land O'Lakes*), 3 oz.	8.0	3.0

Turkey, frozen and refrigerated, continued

thigh *(Land O'Lakes)*, 3 oz.	10.0	4.0
thigh *(Louis Rich)*, 1 oz. cooked	3.7	1.0
white meat, skinless, roasted *(Swift Butterball)*, 3.5 oz.	4.0	n.a.
white and dark meat w/skin, roasted *(Swift Butterball)*, 3.5 oz.	10.0	n.a.
whole, cooked, w/out giblets *(Louis Rich)*, 1 oz.	2.3	.7
wings:		
(Land O'Lakes), 3 oz.	5.0	2.0
(Louis Rich), 1 oz. cooked	2.7	.8
(Louis Rich Drumettes), 1 oz. cooked	2.2	.7
portions *(Louis Rich)*, 1 oz. cooked	2.9	.7
young *(Land O'Lakes)*, 3 oz.	7.0	2.0
young, butter basted *(Land O'Lakes)*, 3 oz.	8.0	3.0
young, self-basting *(Land O'Lakes)*, 3 oz.	5.0	2.0
Turkey, ground:		
cooked, 4 oz.	15.6	4.3
(Longacre), 1 oz.	4.0	n.a.
(Louis Rich), 1 oz. cooked	3.6	1.1
(Louis Rich 90% Lean), 1 oz. cooked	2.1	.7
(Mr. Turkey), 1 oz.	4.0	n.a.
w/natural flavoring *(Louis Rich)*, 1 oz. cooked	2.2	.7
"Turkey," vegetarian:		
canned *(Worthington* Turkee Slices), 2 slices	9.0	n.a.
canned, drained *(Worthington 209)*, 2 slices	8.0	n.a.
frozen, smoked, roll or slices *(Worthington)*, 4 slices or 2.7 oz.	12.0	n.a.
Turkey bacon, see "Bacon, substitute"		
Turkey bologna, 1 oz., except as noted:		
(Butterball Deli/Slice 'n Serve/Cold Cuts)	6.0	n.a.
(Butterball Turkey Variety Pak), .75 oz.	4.0	n.a.
(Louis Rich)	5.0	1.5
mild *(Louis Rich)*	4.5	1.5
sliced *(Longacre)*	5.0	n.a.

Turkey dinner, frozen:

(Banquet), 10.5 oz.	20.0	n.a.
(Banquet Extra Helping), 19 oz.	42.0	n.a.
(Morton), 10 oz.	6.0	n.a.
(Swanson), 11.5 oz.	11.0	n.a.
(Swanson Hungry-Man), 17 oz.	18.0	n.a.
breast:		
(Healthy Choice), 10.5 oz.	5.0	2.0
Dijon *(The Budget Gourmet)*, 11.2 oz.	12.0	n.a.
sliced *(The Budget Gourmet)*, 11.1 oz.	9.0	n.a.
sliced, mushroom sauce *(Lean Cuisine)*, 8 oz.	7.0	2.0
sliced, w/mushroom gravy *(Le Menu)*, 10.5 oz.	7.0	n.a.
Divan *(Le Menu* LightStyle), 10 oz.	7.0	n.a.
w/dressing and gravy *(Armour Classics)*, 11.5 oz.	12.0	n.a.
sliced *(Le Menu* LightStyle), 10 oz.	5.0	n.a.

Turkey entrée, frozen:

(Tyson Gourmet Selection), 11.5 oz.	11.0	n.a.
à la king, w/rice *(The Budget Gourmet)*, 10 oz.	18.0	n.a.
breast, stuffed *(Weight Watchers)*, 8.5 oz.	10.0	4.0
casserole *(Pillsbury Microwave Classic)*, 1 pkg.	25.0	n.a.
casserole *(Stouffer's)*, 9.75 oz.	17.0	n.a.
croquettes, breaded, gravy and *(Freezer Queen Family Suppers)*, 7 oz.	13.0	n.a.
Dijon *(Lean Cuisine)*, 9.5 oz.	10.0	3.0
w/dressing and potatoes *(Swanson Homestyle Recipe)*, 9 oz.	11.0	n.a.
glazed *(The Budget Gourmet* Slim Selects), 9 oz.	5.0	n.a.
glazed *(Le Menu* LightStyle), 8.25 oz.	6.0	n.a.
and gravy, w/dressing *(Freezer Queen Deluxe Family Suppers)*, 7 oz.	5.0	n.a.
sliced, gravy and:		
(Banquet Cookin' Bags), 5 oz.	6.0	n.a.
(Banquet Family Entrees), 8 oz.	8.0	n.a.
(Freezer Queen Family Suppers), 7 oz.	5.0	n.a.

Turkey entrée, frozen, continued
  sliced, mild curry sauce, w/rice pilaf

(Right Course), 8.75 oz.	8.0	2.0
tetrazzini *(Stouffer's)*, 10 oz.	20.0	n.a.
traditional *(Le Menu* LightStyle), 8 oz.	5.0	1.0
Turkey fat, 1 tbsp.	12.8	3.8
Turkey frankfurter:		
1 oz.	5.0	n.a.
(Butterball), 1 link	11.0	n.a.
(Longacre), 1 oz.	6.0	n.a.
(Louis Rich), 1.6-oz. link	8.2	2.7
(Louis Rich Bun Length), 2-oz. link	10.4	3.4
(Mr. Turkey, 10/lb.), 1.6-oz. link	8.9	n.a.
cheese *(Louis Rich)*, 1.6-oz. link	8.9	2.9
cheese *(Mr. Turkey)*, 1.6-oz. link	9.1	n.a.
Turkey giblets, simmered, 4 oz.	5.8	1.7
Turkey gizzard, simmered, 4 oz.	4.4	1.3
Turkey gravy:		
canned *(Franco-American)*, 2 oz.	2.0	n.a.
canned *(Heinz* HomeStyle), 2 oz. or 1/4 cup	1.0	n.a.
canned *(Hormel Great Beginnings)*, 5 oz.	8.0	n.a.
mix* *(Lawry's)*, 1 cup	4.1	n.a.
mix* *(McCormick/Schilling)*, 1/4 cup	.5	n.a.
Turkey ham, 1 oz., except as noted:		
(Butterball Cold Cuts)	1.0	n.a.
(Butterball Slice 'n Serve)	2.0	n.a.
(Louis Rich Chunk, Water Added)	1.4	.4
(Louis Rich Round)	1.2	.5
(Louis Rich Square), .75-oz. slice	.7	.3
(Louis Rich Thin Sliced), .4-oz. slice	.4	.1
breakfast or buffet style, smoked *(Mr. Turkey)*	1.3	n.a.
chopped *(Louis Rich)*	2.8	.7
chopped *(Mr. Turkey)*	1.6	n.a.
chunk or lean lite *(Longacre)*	2.0	n.a.
cured thigh meat, 1 oz.	1.4	.5
honey cured:		
(Butterball Cold Cuts)	1.0	n.a.
(Butterball Slice 'n Serve)	2.0	n.a.
(Louis Rich), .75-oz. slice	.7	.2

chopped *(Butterball* Cold Cuts)	1.0	n.a.
sliced *(Butterball* Deli Thin)	1.0	n.a.
sliced *(Longacre)*	1.0	n.a.
smoked *(Mr. Turkey)*	1.0	n.a.
smoked *(Mr. Turkey* Chub)	1.3	n.a.
Turkey and ham *(Healthy Deli*		
Doubledecker), 1 oz.	.9	n.a.
Turkey ham salad *(Longacre/Longacre*		
Saladfest), 1 oz.	4.0	n.a.
Turkey kielbasa (see also "Turkey		
sausage"):		
(Louis Rich Polska), 1 oz.	2.2	.7
(Mr. Turkey Polska), 1 oz.	4.4	n.a.
Turkey luncheon meat, see "Turkey,		
boneless and luncheon meat"		
Turkey nugget, cooked *(Louis Rich),* .7-oz.		
piece	3.9	.8
Turkey pastrami, 1 oz., except as noted:		
2 slices or 2 oz.	3.5	1.0
*(Butterball Slice 'n Serve/*Cold Cuts) . . .	1.0	n.a.
(Louis Rich Round)	1.1	.4
(Louis Rich Square),* .8-oz. slice	.7	.1
(Louis Rich Thin Sliced),* .4-oz. slice . . .	.4	.2
(Mr. Turkey)	.9	n.a.
sliced *(Longacre)*	1.0	n.a.
Turkey patty, cooked *(Louis Rich),* 2.8-oz.		
patty	12.3	2.4
Turkey pie, frozen:		
(Banquet), 7 oz.	31.0	n.a.
(Banquet Supreme Microwave), 7 oz.	27.0	n.a.
(Morton), 7 oz.	28.0	n.a.
(Stouffer's), 10 oz.	36.0	n.a.
(Swanson Pot Pie), 7 oz.	21.0	n.a.
(Swanson Hungry-Man), 16 oz.	36.0	n.a.
Turkey pocket sandwich, frozen, w/ham and		
cheese *(Hot Pockets),* 5 oz.	11.0	n.a.
Turkey salad *(Longacre/Longacre*		
Saladfest), 1 oz.	5.0	n.a.
Turkey salami, 1 oz., except as noted:		
*(Butterball Deli/Slice 'n Serve/*Cold Cuts)	4.0	n.a.
(Butterball Turkey Variety Pak), ³/₄ oz.	3.0	n.a.

Turkey salami, continued

(*Louis Rich*)	4.0	1.1
cotto (*Mr. Turkey*)	2.9	n.a.
sliced (*Longacre*)	4.0	n.a.
Turkey sausage (see also "Turkey kielbasa"):		
(*Butterball*), 1 oz.	4.0	n.a.
breakfast (*Louis Rich*), 1 cooked link	2.7	1.5
breakfast (*Mr. Turkey*), 1 oz.	4.3	n.a.
breakfast, ground, cooked (*Louis Rich*), 1 oz.	3.5	1.5
smoked (*Louis Rich*), 1 oz.	2.4	.6
smoked (*Mr. Turkey*), 1 oz.	3.4	n.a.
smoked, w/cheese (*Louis Rich*), 1 oz.	2.8	.8
Turkey spread, chunky (*Underwood* Light), 2 1/8 oz.	2.0	< 1.0
Turkey sticks, cooked (*Louis Rich*), 1 stick	5.0	1.0
Turkey summer sausage (*Louis Rich*), 1-oz. slice	3.9	1.2
Turmeric, ground, 1 tsp.	.2	n.a.
Turnip:		
fresh, boiled, drained, cubed or mashed, 1/2 cup	.1	tr.
canned, diced (*Allens*), 1/2 cup	< 1.0	(0)
frozen, boiled, drained, 4 oz.	.3	<.1
Turnip greens:		
fresh, raw, trimmed, 1 oz. or 1/2 cup chopped	.1	<.1
fresh, boiled, drained, chopped, 1/2 cup	.2	<.1
canned, w/liquid, or frozen, boiled, 1/2 cup	.4	.1
frozen, w/turnips, boiled, drained, 4 oz.	.2	<.1
Turnover, see specific listings		

food and measure	total fat (gms.)	saturated fat (gms.)
Vanilla extract, pure *(Virginia Dare)*	0	0
Vanilla flavor drink:		
canned *(Sego* Very Vanilla), 10 fl. oz.	5.0	n.a.
mix *(Carnation* Instant Breakfast), 1 pouch	.2	.1
mix *(Pillsbury* Instant Breakfast), 1 pouch	0	0
Veal, retail trim, meat only, 4 oz.:		
cubed (leg and shoulder), lean only, braised	4.9	1.5
ground, broiled	8.6	3.4

Veal, continued

leg (top round):

lean w/fat, braised	7.2	2.9
lean w/fat, roasted	5.3	2.1
lean only, braised	5.8	2.2
lean only, roasted	3.8	1.4

loin:

lean w/fat, braised	19.5	7.6
lean w/fat, roasted	14.0	6.0
lean only, braised	10.4	2.9
lean only, roasted	7.9	2.9

rib:

lean w/fat, braised	14.2	5.6
lean w/fat, roasted	15.8	6.1
lean only, braised	8.9	2.9
lean only, roasted	8.4	2.4

shoulder:

whole, lean w/fat, braised	11.5	4.3
whole, lean w/fat, roasted	9.5	3.9
whole, lean only, braised	6.9	1.9
whole, lean only, roasted	7.5	2.8
arm, lean w/fat, braised	11.6	4.5
arm, lean w/fat, roasted	9.4	4.0
arm, lean only, braised	6.0	1.7
arm, lean only, roasted	6.6	2.6
blade, lean w/fat, braised	11.4	4.1
blade, lean w/fat, roasted	9.8	3.9
blade, lean only, braised	7.3	2.1
blade, lean only, roasted	7.8	2.9

sirloin:

lean w/fat, braised	14.9	5.9
lean w/fat, roasted	11.9	5.1
lean only, braised	7.4	2.1
lean only, roasted	7.1	2.7

Veal dinner, frozen:

marsala *(Le Menu* LightStyle), 10 oz.	3.0	n.a.

parmigiana:

(Armour Classics), 11.25 oz.	22.0	n.a.
(Morton), 10 oz.	8.0	n.a.
(Swanson), 12.25 oz.	20.0	n.a.
(Swanson Hungry-Man), 18.25 oz.	26.0	n.a.

breaded *(Freezer Queen)*, 5 oz. . . . . . 12.0   n.a.
platter *(Freezer Queen)*, 10 oz. . . . . . 20.0   n.a.

Veal entrée, frozen:
parmigiana:
   (Banquet Cookin' Bags), 4 oz. . . . . . 11.0   n.a.
   (Banquet Family Entrees), 8 oz. . . . . 18.0   n.a.
   (Freezer Queen Deluxe Family
     Suppers), 7 oz. . . . . 15.0   n.a.
   (Swanson Homestyle Recipe), 10 oz. 13.0   n.a.
   (Weight Watchers), 8.44 oz. 6.0   3.0
primavera *(Lean Cuisine)*, 9 1/8 oz. . . . . 9.0   n.a.
steak *(Hormel)*, 4 oz. . . . . 4.0   n.a.
steak, breaded *(Hormel)*, 4 oz. . . . . . . 13.0   n.a.

Vegetable entrée, canned:
chow mein, meatless *(La Choy)*, 3/4 cup   .4   n.a.
stew *(Dinty Moore)*, 8 oz. . . . . 8.0   n.a.

Vegetable entrée, frozen, and pasta mornay,
w/ham *(Lean Cuisine)*, 9 3/8 oz. 11.0   3.0

Vegetable juice:
(Veryfine 100%), 6 fl. oz. 0   0
all varieties *("V-8")*, 6 fl. oz. 0   0
all varieties *(Smucker's)*, 8 fl. oz. . . . . . <.1   (0)

Vegetable sticks, breaded, frozen:
(Farm Rich), 4 oz. . . . . 10.0   n.a.
(Stilwell Quickkrisp), 3 oz. . . . . 8.0   n.a.

Vegetables, see specific listings

Vegetables, mixed:
canned or frozen, plain (all brands),
   1/2 cup . . . . < 1.0   <.1
frozen, prepared w/out added ingredients:
chow mein, Oriental sauce *(Birds Eye*
   Custom Cuisine), 4.6 oz. . . . . 2.0   n.a.
chow mein style, seasoned sauce *(Birds*
   Eye International), 3.3 oz. . . . . 4.0   n.a.
Italian or Japanese style, seasoned
   sauce *(Birds Eye* International),
   3.3 oz. 5.0   n.a.
New England style, seasoned sauce
   (Birds Eye International), 3.3 oz. 7.0   n.a.
Oriental style, Oriental sauce for beef
   (Birds Eye Custom Cuisine), 4.6 oz. 4.0   n.a.

Vegetables, mixed, frozen, continued

Oriental style, seasoned sauce *(Birds Eye* International), 3.3 oz.	4.0	n.a.
pasta primavera or San Francisco, seasoned sauce *(Birds Eye* International), 3.3 oz.	5.0	n.a.
in butter sauce *(Green Giant)*, 1/2 cup	2.0	< 1.0
w/herb sauce for chicken or shrimp *(Birds Eye Custom Cuisine)*, 4.6 oz.	5.0	n.a.
w/mushroom sauce, for beef *(Birds Eye Custom Cuisine)*, 4.6 oz.	2.0	n.a.
w/mustard sauce, Dijon, for chicken or fish *(Birds Eye Custom Cuisine)*, 4.6 oz.	3.0	n.a.
w/tomato basil sauce for chicken *(Birds Eye Custom Cuisine)*, 4.6 oz.	3.0	n.a.
'n rice, in teriyaki sauce *(Stokely Singles)*, 4 oz.	0	0
'n rotini, in cheddar cheese sauce *(Stokely Singles)*, 4 oz.	3.0	n.a.
'n shells, in Italian style sauce *(Stokely Singles)*, 4 oz.	15.0	n.a.
stew *(Ore-Ida)*, 3 oz.	< 1.0	(0)
w/wild rice, in white wine sauce for chicken *(Birds Eye Custom Cuisine)*, 4.6 oz.	0	0
Vegetarian entrée, frozen *(Natural Touch Dinner Entrée)*, 3-oz. patty	14.0	2.0
Vegetarian foods, see specific listings		
Venison, meat only, roasted, 4 oz.	3.6	1.4
Vienna sausage, canned:		
in barbecue sauce *(Libby's)*, 21/2 oz.	15.0	n.a.
in beef broth *(Libby's,* 9 oz.), 31/2 links	14.0	n.a.
in beef broth *(Libby's,* 5 oz.), 31/2 links	15.0	n.a.
beef and pork, 1 oz.	7.1	2.6
no broth *(Hormel)*, 4 links	18.0	n.a.
Vine spinach, raw, 1 lb.	1.4	n.a.
Vinegar, all varieties, 2 tbsp. or 1 fl. oz.	0	0

food and measure	total fat (gms.)	saturated fat (gms.)
Waffle, frozen, 1 piece, except as noted:		
(*Aunt Jemima* Original)	5.6	1.4
(*Downyflake*)	1.5	.5
(*Downyflake* Hot-N-Buttery)	3.0	n.a.
(*Downyflake* Jumbo)	2.0	.5
(*Roman Meal*)	7.0	n.a.
all varieties, except oat bran (*Eggo/Eggo Common Sense/Nutri·Grain*)	5.0	n.a.
apple cinnamon (*Aunt Jemima*)	5.6	1.3

Waffle, frozen, continued

Belgian *(Weight Watchers* Microwave),
1.5 oz..   4.0   2.0
blueberry *(Aunt Jemima)* 5.2   1.3
blueberry *(Downyflake)* . . . .   2.0   n.a.
buttermilk *(Aunt Jemima)* 5.8   1.4
buttermilk *(Downyflake)* . . . .   2.5   n.a.
multigrain *(Downyflake)* . . . .   7.0   n.a.
oat bran *(Downyflake)*. . . . .   6.5   n.a.
oat bran *(Eggo Common Sense)* . . . . .   4.0   n.a.
oat bran or whole grain wheat *(Aunt
Jemima)* . . . .   2.8   n.a.
rice bran *(Downyflake)* . . . .   5.5   n.a.
Waffle mix, see "Pancake and waffle mix"
Walnut, dried, shelled:
black, 1 oz.. . . . .   16.1   1.0
black, chopped, 1 cup 70.7   4.5
English or Persian, 1 oz. or 14 halves   17.6   1.6
English or Persian, pieces or chips, 1 cup   74.2   6.7
English or Persian, halves, 1 cup 61.9   5.6
Wasabi, powder, 1/4 oz.. . . . .   <.1   0
Wasabi snack chips *(Eden),* 1 oz. . . . . . .   4.0   n.a.
Waterchestnut, Chinese:
raw, sliced, 1/2 cup 1   (0)
canned, 4 medium, or sliced, 1/2 cup . . .   <.1   (0)
Watercress, fresh, chopped, 1/2 cup . . . .   <.1   tr.
Watermelon:
1/16 of 10″-diam. melon, 1″ thick slice   2.0   (0)
diced, 1/2 cup 3   (0)
Watermelon seed, dried, kernels, 1 oz. . . .   13.5   2.8
Wax bean, see "Beans, green"
Welsh rarebit (see also "Cheese sauce"):
canned *(Snow's),* 1/2 cup . . . .   11.0   n.a.
frozen *(Stouffer's),* 10 oz. . . . .   30.0   n.a.
Wendy's:
sandwiches, 1 serving:
Big Classic, 9.2 oz.. . . . .   33.0   5.6
cheeseburger, bacon, Jr., 5.5 oz. 25.0   5.2
cheeseburger, Jr. or Kid's Meal 13.0   3.0
chicken club, 7.2 oz.. . . . .   25.0   4.8
chicken sandwich, 6.9 oz.. . . . .   19.0   2.6

chicken sandwich, grilled, 6.2 oz.	13.0	3.2
fish fillet sandwich, 6 oz.	25.0	4.7
hamburger, Jr. or Kid's Meal	9.0	3.0
hamburger, 1/4 lb.	12.0	5.0
hamburger, single, plain, 4.4 oz.	15.0	5.5
hamburger, single, w/everything, 7.4 oz.	21.0	5.5
steak sandwich, country fried, 5.1 oz.	25.0	5.7
Swiss Deluxe, Jr., 5.8 oz.	18.0	3.0
chicken fillet, grilled, 2.5 oz.	3.0	.6
chicken nuggets, crispy, 6 pieces	20.0	4.5
chicken nuggets sauces:		
barbeque or sweet and sour, 1 oz.	< 1.0	tr.
honey, .5 oz.	< 1.0	tr.
sweet mustard, 1 oz.	1.0	< 1.0
chili, regular, 9 oz.	7.0	2.6
baked potato, hot stuffed, 1 serving:		
plain, 8.8 oz.	< 1.0	tr.
bacon and cheese, 12.8 oz.	18.0	5.1
broccoli and cheese, 12.3 oz.	16.0	2.9
cheese, 11.2 oz.	15.0	4.0
chili and cheese, 14.2 oz.	18.0	4.0
sour cream and chives, 11.4 oz.	23.0	9.3
salads and side dishes, 1 serving:		
chef salad, 9.1 oz.	5.0	1.2
french fries, small, 3.2 oz.	12.0	2.5
garden salad, 8.1 oz.	2.0	0
taco salad, 17.3 oz.	23.0	< 1.0
salad dressing, 1 tbsp.:		
bacon and tomato, reduced calorie	4.0	.6
blue cheese	10.0	1.9
celery seed or French	6.0	.9
French, sweet red	6.0	.8
Hidden Valley Ranch	6.0	1.0
Italian, golden	4.0	.5
Italian, reduced calorie	2.0	.3
Italian Caesar	9.0	1.4
Thousand Island	7.0	1.1
dessert, 1 serving:		
chocolate chip cookie, 2.25 oz.	13.0	4.2
frosty, dairy, small, 8.6 oz.	10.0	5.0
pudding, butterscotch, 1/4 cup	4.0	1.8

Wendy's, dessert, continued

pudding, chocolate, 1/4 cup	4.0	1.7
Western dinner, frozen:		
(*Banquet*), 11 oz.	41.0	n.a.
(*Morton*), 10 oz.	14.0	n.a.
style (*Swanson*), 11.5 oz.	19.0	n.a.
Wheat, whole grain:		
durum, 1 cup	4.7	.9
hard red spring, 1 cup	3.7	.6
hard red winter, 1 cup	3.0	.5
soft red winter, 1 cup	2.6	.5
hard white, 1 cup	3.3	.5
soft white, 1 cup	3.3	.6
Wheat bran:		
crude, 1 cup	2.6	.4
toasted (*Kretschmer*), 1 oz. or 1/3 cup	2.3	.2
unprocessed (*Quaker*), 2 tbsp., 1/4 oz.	.2	0
Wheat cake (*Quaker* Grain Cakes), 1 piece	.3	.1
Wheat germ:		
(*Kretschmer*), 1 oz. or 1/4 cup	3.4	.5
crude, 1 cup	11.2	1.9
honey crunch (*Kretschmer*), 1 oz. or		
1/4 cup	2.8	.4
toasted, 1 oz. or 1/4 cup	3.0	.5
Wheat pilaf mix* (*Casbah*), 1/2 cup	0	0
Wheat sprouts, 1 cup	1.4	.2
Whelk, meat only, raw, 4 oz.	.5	<.1
Whey:		
acid, fluid, 1 cup	.2	.1
sweet, fluid, 1 cup	.9	.6
Whitefish, mixed species, meat only:		
raw, 4 oz.	7.5	1.0
smoked, 4 oz.	1.1	.3
Whiting, meat only:		
fresh, raw, 4 oz.	1.5	.3
fresh, baked, broiled, or microwaved,		
4 oz.	1.9	.4
frozen, all varieties (*Booth*), 4 oz.	1.0	n.a.
Wild rice, cooked, 1 cup	.6	.1
Wine, table or dessert, all varieties	0	0

Wine, cooking:
    all varieties *(Regina)*, 1/4 cup . . . .   < 1.0   (0)
    all varieties *(Holland House)*, 1 fl. oz.   0   0
Wolf fish, Atlantic, meat only, raw, 4 oz.   2.7   .4
Wonton skin *(Nasoya)*, 1 piece   0   0
Worcestershire sauce:
    (Heinz)   0   0
    (Life All Natural), 1/4 fl. oz. or 1/2 tbsp.   < 1.0   (0)
    all varieties *(Lea & Perrins)*, 1 tsp. . . . .   < 1.0   (0)
    regular or smoky *(French's)*   0   0

$$\boxed{\text{Y}}$$

food and measure	total fat (gms.)	saturated fat (gms.)
Yam:		
fresh, raw, baked, or boiled, 1/2 cup . . .	.1	<.1
canned or frozen, see "Sweet potato"		
Yam, mountain, Hawaiian, raw or steamed,		
1/2 cup	.1	<.1
Yam bean tuber, see "Jicama"		
Yeast *(Fleischmann's* Active Dry/		
RapidRise)	0	0
Yellowtail, meat only, raw, 4 oz.	5.9	n.a.

Yogurt, 8 oz., except as noted:

plain:

whole milk	7.4	4.8
lowfat	3.5	2.3
skim milk	.4	.3
(Breyers Lowfat)	3.0	2.0
(Colombo)	8.0	n.a.
(Crowley), 1 cup	8.0	n.a.
(Crowley Lowfat), 1 cup	2.0	n.a.
(Dannon Lowfat)	4.0	n.a.
(Dannon Nonfat)	0	0
(Knudsen)	9.0	5.0
(Knudsen Lowfat)	5.0	1.0

all flavors:

(Colombo Fruit on the Bottom)	6.0	n.a.
(Colombo Nonfat Fruit on the Bottom)	< 1.0	n.a.
(Colombo Nonfat Lite Minipack), 4.4 oz.	0	0
(Crowley Nonfat), 1 cup	< 1.0	0
(Crowley Sundae/Swiss Style), 1 cup	2.0	n.a.
(Dannon Extra Smooth), 4.4 oz.	2.0	n.a.
(Dannon Fruit-on-the-Bottom)	3.0	n.a.
(Friendship Lowfat), 1 cup	3.0	n.a.
(Knudsen Lowfat)	4.0	2.0
(Knudsen Cal 70), 6 oz.	0	0
(Light n' Lively Free), 4.4 oz.	0	0
(Light n' Lively 100)	0	0
(New Country Lowfat/Supreme), 6 oz.	2.0	n.a.
(Ripple 70), 6 oz.	0	0
(Yoplait), 6 oz.	3.0	n.a.
(Yoplait Fat Free/Light), 6 oz.	0	0
(Yoplait Custard Style), 6 oz.	4.0	n.a.
except coffee, lemon, and vanilla *(Dannon* Fresh Flavors)	4.0	n.a.
except strawberry *(Light n' Lively)*	2.0	1.0
except tropical fruit *(Yoplait Breakfast Yogurt)*, 6 oz.	3.0	1.0

all fruit flavors, except black cherry

(Breyers Lowfat)	2.0	1.0

berries, mixed or fruit, orchard *(Dannon* Hearty Nuts & Raisins)

	3.0	n.a.

Yogurt, continued

cherry, black *(Breyers* Lowfat)	3.0	1.0
coffee, lowfat	2.8	1.8
coffee *(Dannon* Fresh Flavors)	3.0	n.a.
fruit, tropical *(Yoplait Breakfast Yogurt),* 6 oz.	4.0	2.0
lemon or vanilla *(Dannon* Fresh Flavors)	3.0	n.a.
strawberry *(Light n' Lively)*	2.0	2.0
strawberry or French vanilla *(Colombo)*	7.0	n.a.
vanilla:		
lowfat	2.8	1.8
(Crowley Lowfat), 1 cup	2.0	n.a.
(Dannon Hearty Nuts & Raisins) . . .	5.0	n.a.
bean *(Breyers* Lowfat)	3.0	2.0
Yogurt, frozen, 3 fl. oz., except as noted:		
all flavors *(Breyers),* 4 fl. oz.	1.0	n.a.
all flavors *(Sealtest Free),* 4 fl. oz.	0	0
caramel pecan chunk *(Colombo* Gourmet)	3.0	n.a.
cheesecake, wild raspberry *(Colombo* Gourmet)	2.0	n.a.
cherry *(Crowley)*	1.0	n.a.
chocolate *(Crowley)*	2.0	n.a.
chocolate *(Häagen-Dazs)*	3.0	2.0
chocolate almond *(Elan),* 4 fl. oz.	7.0	n.a.
chocolate chunk, Bavarian *(Colombo* Gourmet)	4.0	n.a.
Heath bar crunch *(Colombo* Gourmet)	5.0	n.a.
mocha Swiss almond *(Colombo* Gourmet)	5.0	n.a.
peach *(Häagen-Dazs)*	3.0	1.5
peach, raspberry, or strawberry *(Crowley)*	1.0	n.a.
peanut butter cup *(Colombo* Gourmet)	7.0	n.a.
strawberry *(Häagen-Dazs)*	3.0	1.6
strawberry passion *(Colombo* Gourmet)	2.0	n.a.
vanilla *(Crowley)*	2.0	n.a.
vanilla *(Häagen-Dazs)*	3.0	1.7
vanilla almond crunch *(Häagen-Dazs)*	5.0	1.5
vanilla dream *(Colombo* Gourmet)	2.0	n.a.
Yogurt, frozen, soft-serve, all flavors:		
(Bresler's Gourmet), 1 oz.	.5	n.a.
(Bresler's Lite), 1 oz.	0	0

(Dannon), 4 fl. oz.	2.0	n.a.
(Dannon Nonfat), 4 fl. oz.	0	0
Yogurt drink, all flavors *(Dan'up)*, 8 oz.	4.0	n.a.
Yokan, 1 oz.	<.1	(0)

$$\boxed{Z}$$

food and measure	total fat (gms.)	saturated fat (gms.)
Ziti, frozen, in marinara sauce *(The Budget Gourmet* Side Dish), 6.25 oz.	9.0	n.a.
Zucchini, see "Squash"		
Zucchini appetizer, Italian style *(Progresso),* 1/2 cup	2.0	< 1.0
Zucchini combinations, frozen, w/carrots, pearl onions, and mushrooms *(Birds Eye* Farm Fresh), 4 oz.	0	0